メガトーキョー
megatokyo
IR
①

DEC 10

publisher
MIKE RICHARDSON

editor
TIM ERVIN-GORE

designer
DARIN FABRICK

MEGATOKYO™ VOL. 1

Published by Dark Horse Books,
a division of Dark Horse Comics, Inc.
10956 SE Main St.
Milwaukie, OR 97222

First edition: March 2004
ISBN: 1-59307-163-9

3 5 7 9 10 8 6 4 2

Printed in Canada

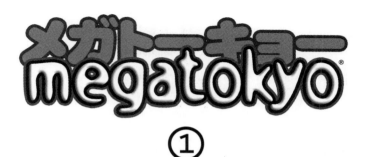

メガトーキョー
megatokyo®

①

SQU33K! SQEEK! SQU34K! SQEEK! SQU33K! SQEEK! SQU34K! SQEEK! SQU33K! SQEEK! SQU34K! SQEEK! SQU33K! SQEEK! SQU34K!

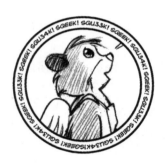

story & art
FRED GALLAGHER

story & co-creator
RODNEY CASTON

"shirt guy dom" comics by
DOMINIC NGUYEN

www.megatokyo.com

™
dark horse books™

This book is dedicated to:

Megatokyo readers and fans, old and new.
Friends, Family and the MT Crew -- past and present.

A special thanks to Young "Merle" Wang and
Christi "Natsuki" Heiskell. Without their help crunching
graphic files, this particular volume would have never been
finished on time. Thank you so much!

And to Sarah, who's job only gets harder as time goes on. :-)

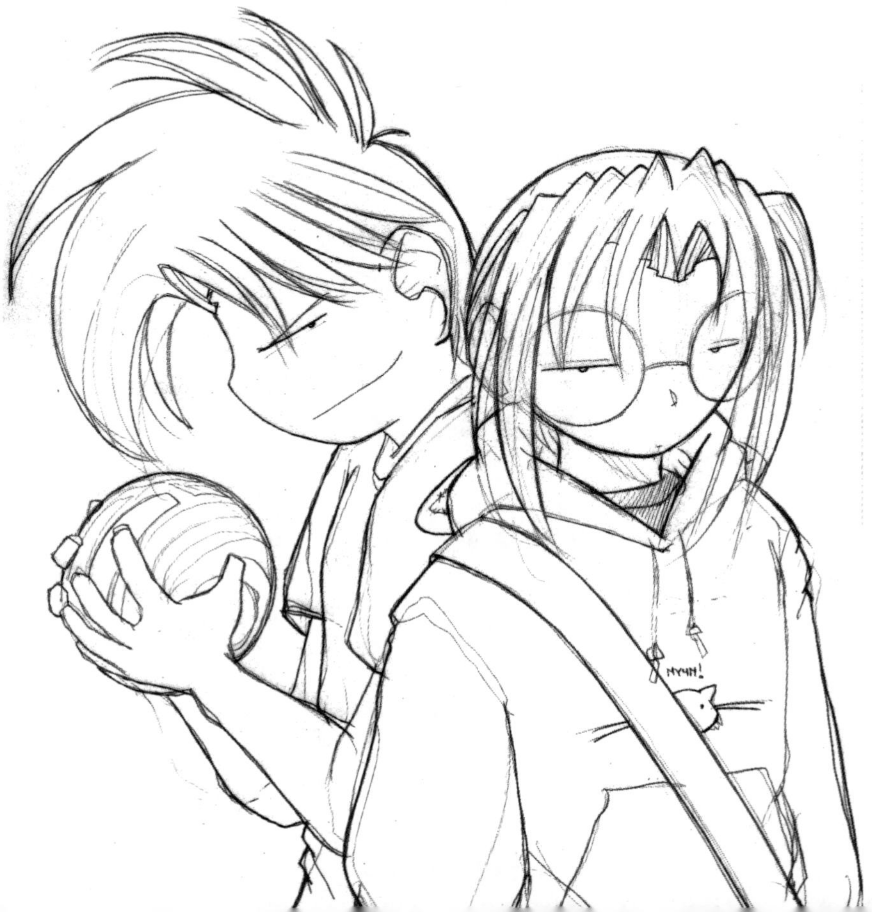

MT_vol_1_fr33talk.txt

A side effect of starting Megatokyo was that I started investigating webcomics. I was surprised by the variety, depth, subtlety, and complexity that many of them offered. It all started me thinking. I contemplated the thought that maybe we could pull off a comic where each page stood on it's own, but when strung together could read as a cohesive, complicated story.

So with that in mind, I stopped trying to ink things (yes, the first two comics were inked, but I suck at inking), I redrew them in pencil and re-designed the website. The next day, Penny Arcade linked us, and I've been madly trying to keep pace with things since.

A lot has happened since the first volume of this book came out. The number of people who read Megatokyo has grown (either that or the same people are just downloading more). I've changed publishers. I've switched to being a Mac user. Chapter 4 finally came to an end. Sarah and I got married.

With this volume comes a significant increase in print quality (not that these early drawings benefit from it -- some of them make me want to feed my hands into a meat grinder in penance), more pages, a new cover design, bigger trim size ... lots of good stuff. If you already own the first version of this book and have purchased this one as well, I hope you find the upgrade worth it.

Megatokyo is a free webcomic that doesn't require subscriptions or fees to access - every comic in this book is available free to read online. In fact, you can pick up where this book leaves off by heading over to *www.megatokyo.com* and starting with comic number 134 (that's where Chapter 1 starts).

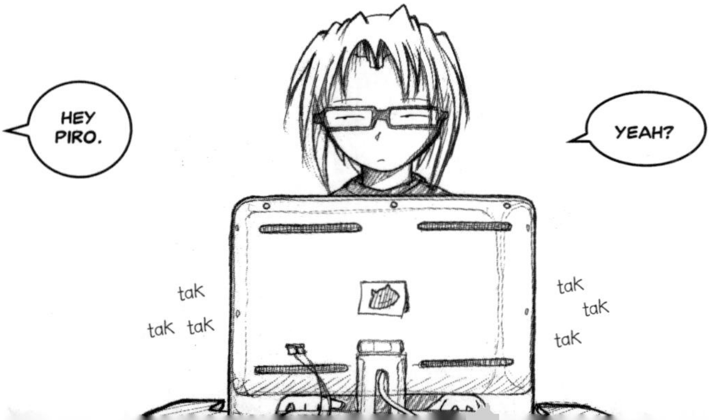
HEY PIRO.
YEAH?
tak
tak tak
tak
tak
tak

MT_vol_1_fr33talk.txt

So why publish print versions?

It may sound odd, but I really feel a lot more comfortable with the fact that you can read and experience Megatokyo without having to pay for it. What it means is that you, as the reader, decide if you want to buy a book, a T-shirt, or the Boo and Belphegor salt and pepper set. It's one less bit of entertainment in your life that isn't metered.

Megatokyo exists and thrives purely because of the people who have made reading the comic part of their routine. It's you people who waste copious amounts of time in the forums, you who can't stop hitting "refresh" when it's almost time for a new comic to be posted. It's people who dress up like Megatokyo characters and go to anime conventions, or plaster printouts of MT strips in the hallways at school. It's the readers who want to make webcomics and are inspired by MT,Casual readers who just like to visit the site every once and a while. You are the folks who buy books like this not because you have to be a MT fan, but because you want to.

I kinda like that, and I wouldn't have it any other way.

Thank you for your support. It's appreciated more than you know.

Piro

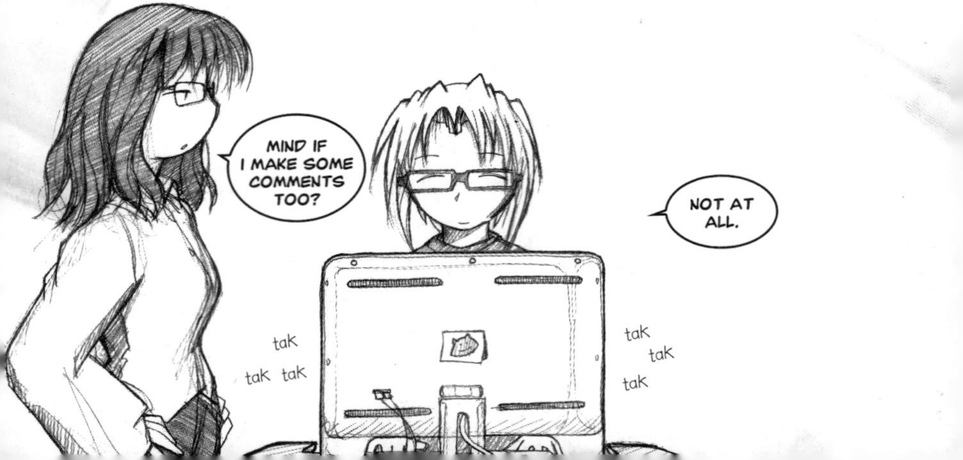
MIND IF I MAKE SOME COMMENTS TOO?
NOT AT ALL.
tak
tak tak
tak
tak
tak

Seraphim_fr33talk.txt

When Megatokyo started I didn't know what to expect, but I sure didn't expect what it has evolved into over the past 3 years. It has become an all-encompassing creature with a website, books, conventions, and fans.

In the beginning I barely knew what anime, manga, and webcomics were and I wasn't a fan. At first Fred wasn't even going to tell me he had yet another web/drawing project on the "side" -- a project that ended up taking 24 plus hours a week in addition to his full time job. It wasn't long before I found out about it. When he took over the dining room for his studio space without warning me I knew something was afoot.

I never thought it would grow like it has over the years. I believe in Fred and love his art, but he had his Fredart site for years and most of the time my origami page had higher traffic. I couldn't help it if there are more origami people who are even more fanatical than anime fans. I didn't really believe that his little MT website would amount to much. That is the only reason I suggested the Seraphim character and agreed to "rant" on the site. No one was going to see it anyway and I would certainly never meet anyone who read it. Life has a way of kicking you in the head and then laughing at you.

We've had many discussions about the Seraphim character over the years. Fred's first character designs had her with bug wings. Bug wings? What kind of angel has bug wings? You know I had something to say about that. I won that discussion even though she is more difficult to draw now. I also have to constantly argue for longer skirts but I always lose those discussions to the artist. She may be a fashion conscious angel but she doesn't wear micro minis.

Megatokyo has added a lot of excitement and way too much drama to our lives. We've always had fun and we hope you have too.

Seraphim

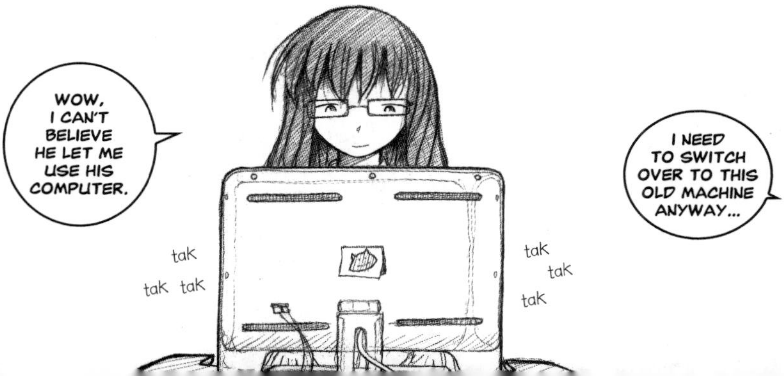
WOW, I CAN'T BELIEVE HE LET ME USE HIS COMPUTER.
tak
tak tak
tak
tak
tak
I NEED TO SWITCH OVER TO THIS OLD MACHINE ANYWAY...

ONE OF THE PROBLEMS WITH WEBCOMICS IS THAT THE FREEDOM YOU HAVE WITH SIZE AND FORMAT IS BOTH A BLESSING AND A CURSE. FREE FROM THE RESTRICTIONS PRINT MEDIA CAN PUT ON YOU, YOU CAN DO JUST ABOUT ANYTHING YOU WANT, AS LONG AS IT WORKS WITH A WEB BROWSER AND DOESN'T MELT DOWN YOUR SERVER.

THERE IS SOMETHING COSMICALLY AMUSING ABOUT THE PROBLEMS I'VE FACED GETTING MATERIAL READY FOR THIS BOOK. THE FIRST HUNDRED OR SO COMICS WERE DONE IN A FOUR PANEL FORMAT, BUT THEN I HAD THE BRIGHT IDEA TO CHANGE TO A RECTANGULAR MANGA STYLE FORMAT. ONLINE THIS WORKS FINE. FOR THE BOOK, IT LEAVES A BIG BLANK SPACE AT THE BOTTOM OF THE PAGE THAT I NEED TO DECIDE HOW TO FILL.

WEBCOMICS ARE DIFFERENT FROM PRINT COMICS BECAUSE THEY ARE BY NATURE A MORE DYNAMIC MEDIUM. EVERY MEGATOKYO COMIC WAS ACCOMPANIED BY VARIOUS "RANTS" AND COMMENTARY BY MYSELF AND LARGO. SOME OF THESE MAKE FOR GOOD READING, OTHERS COULD USE TO BE ACCIDENTALLY DELETED. GIVEN THE SIZE OF MOST OF MY "RANTS" IN PARTICULAR, INCLUDING THEM WOULD DOUBLE THE SIZE OF THIS BOOK -- AND BE A SERIOUS WASTE OF PAPER.

SINCE I'M TOO LAZY TO DRAW NEW MATERIAL AND I CAN PRATTLE ON AIMLESSLY WITH EASE, I'LL USE THIS BLANK SPACE FOR COMMENTS AND OBSERVATIONS.

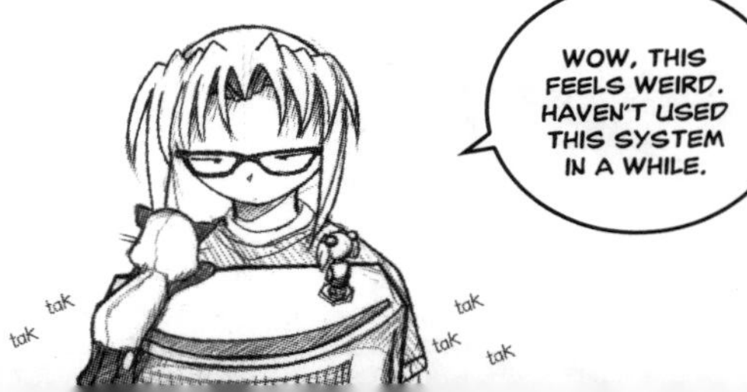
WOW, THIS FEELS WEIRD. HAVEN'T USED THIS SYSTEM IN A WHILE.
tak tak
tak
tak
tak tak

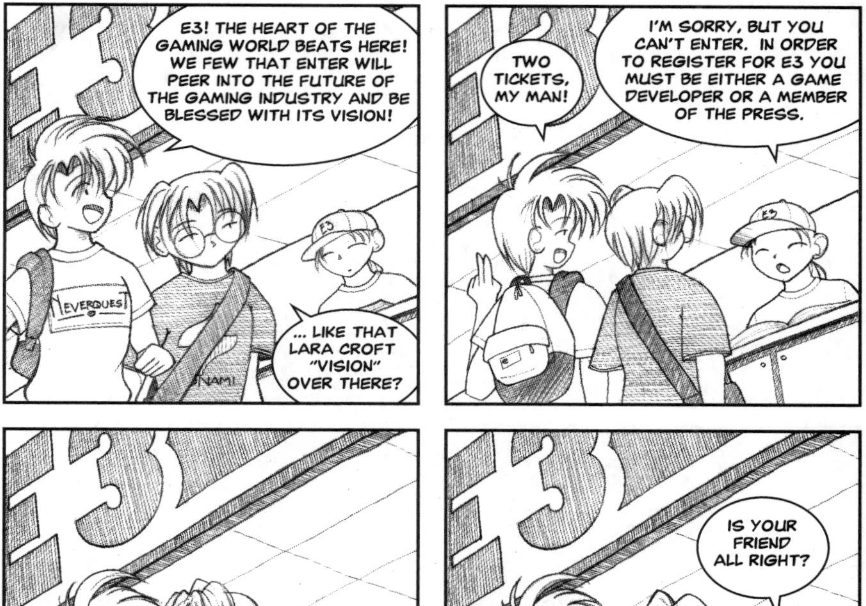
E3! THE HEART OF THE GAMING WORLD BEATS HERE! WE FEW THAT ENTER WILL PEER INTO THE FUTURE OF THE GAMING INDUSTRY AND BE BLESSED WITH ITS VISION!
... LIKE THAT LARA CROFT "VISION" OVER THERE?
TWO TICKETS, MY MAN!
I'M SORRY, BUT YOU CAN'T ENTER. IN ORDER TO REGISTER FOR E3 YOU MUST BE EITHER A GAME DEVELOPER OR A MEMBER OF THE PRESS.
IS YOUR FRIEND ALL RIGHT?
NO. HE'S JUST IN SHOCK. CAN YOU ASK MS. CROFT OVER THERE IF SHE'D HELP ME SNAP HIM OUT OF IT?

THIS IS THE FIRST MEGATOKYO COMIC WE EVER DID. IT WAS DONE ALMOST TWO MONTHS BEFORE MEGATOKYO OFFICIALLY LAUNCHED. ORIGINALLY, I WAS GOING TO INK EVERYTHING, BUT CAME TO MY SENSES WHEN I REALIZED HOW LONG THAT WOULD TAKE.

I NEVER INTENDED TO DO MORE THAN ONE OR TWO COMICS. I DID THIS ONE MAINLY TO GET LARGO TO SHUT UP AND LEAVE ME ALONE. HE SEEMED CONVINCED THAT WE SHOULD DO A WEBCOMIC.

THINGS LIKE STORY, ORGANIZATION, OR WHAT WE WERE GOING TO DO NEXT WERE NOT CONSIDERED VERY IMPORTANT AT THE TIME.

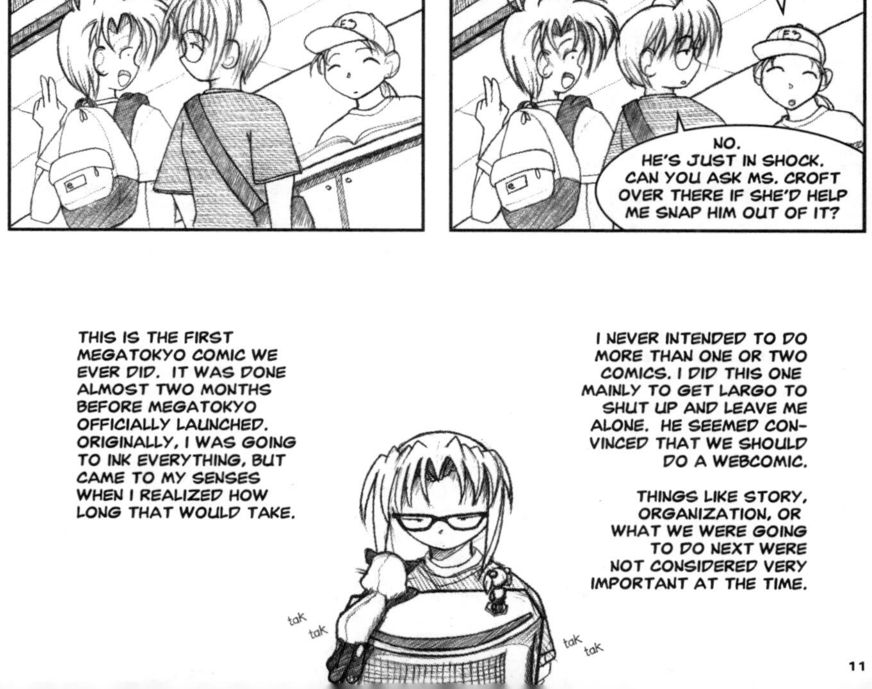
tak
tak
tak
tak

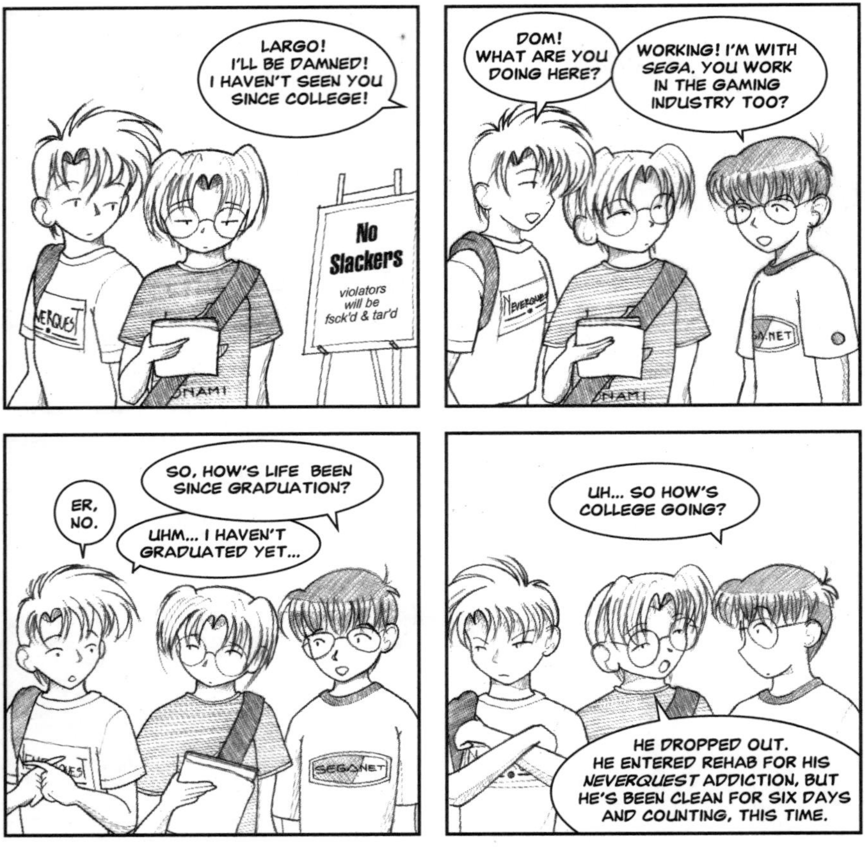
LARGO! I'LL BE DAMNED! I HAVEN'T SEEN YOU SINCE COLLEGE!
No Slackers
violators will be fsck'd & tar'd
DOM! WHAT ARE YOU DOING HERE?
WORKING! I'M WITH *SEGA*. YOU WORK IN THE GAMING INDUSTRY TOO?
ER, NO.
SO, HOW'S LIFE BEEN SINCE GRADUATION?
UHM... I HAVEN'T GRADUATED YET...
UH... SO HOW'S COLLEGE GOING?
HE DROPPED OUT. HE ENTERED REHAB FOR HIS *NEVERQUEST* ADDICTION, BUT HE'S BEEN CLEAN FOR SIX DAYS AND COUNTING, THIS TIME.

THE ONLY PERSON WHO DIDN'T LAUGH AT US WHEN LARGO ASKED FOR OPINIONS ON SCRIPTS WAS DOM.

WE FIGURED THAT IF WE PUT DOM IN THE STRIP, WE COULD CONTROL HIM BETTER. DOM ACTUALLY TURNED OUT TO BE VERY USEFUL WHEN IT CAME TO CAUSING OUR READERS PAIN.

WE LIKE DOM. IT'S WHY WE KEEP HIM AROUND.

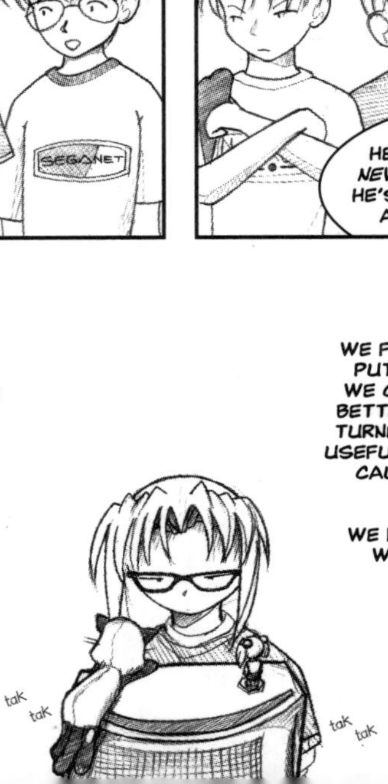
tak tak
tak tak

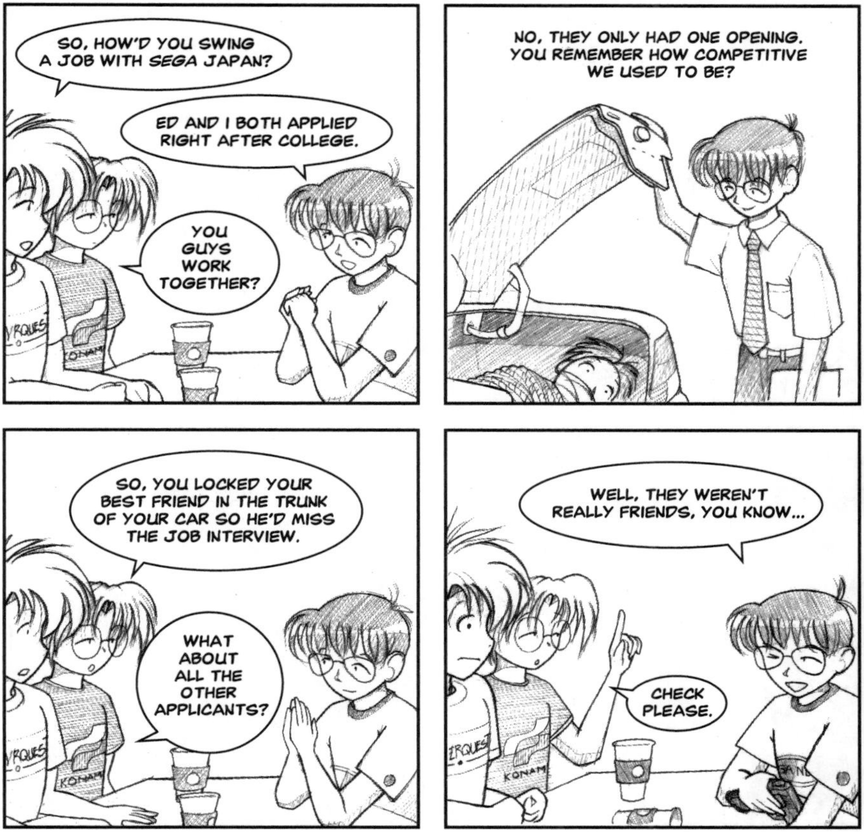
SO, HOW'D YOU SWING A JOB WITH *SEGA JAPAN*?
ED AND I BOTH APPLIED RIGHT AFTER COLLEGE.
YOU GUYS WORK TOGETHER?
NO, THEY ONLY HAD ONE OPENING. YOU REMEMBER HOW COMPETITIVE WE USED TO BE?
SO, YOU LOCKED YOUR BEST FRIEND IN THE TRUNK OF YOUR CAR SO HE'D MISS THE JOB INTERVIEW.
WHAT ABOUT ALL THE OTHER APPLICANTS?
WELL, THEY WEREN'T REALLY FRIENDS, YOU KNOW...
CHECK PLEASE.

ODDLY ENOUGH, DOM AND ED HAVE THIS KIND OF RELATIONSHIP IN REAL LIFE.

I FIGURED THAT IT WOULD BE FUN TO USE DOM AND ED TO PLAY ON THE JAPANESE STEREOTYPE THAT ALL AMERICANS ARE WELL-ARMED AND WILLING TO WHIP OUT GUNS AT THE SLIGHTEST PROVOCATION.

THAT'S A *SIG SAUER* 9MM DOM IS PACKING–JUST SO YOU KNOW.

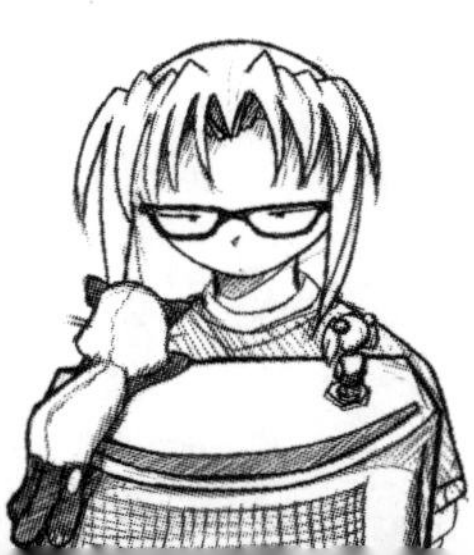

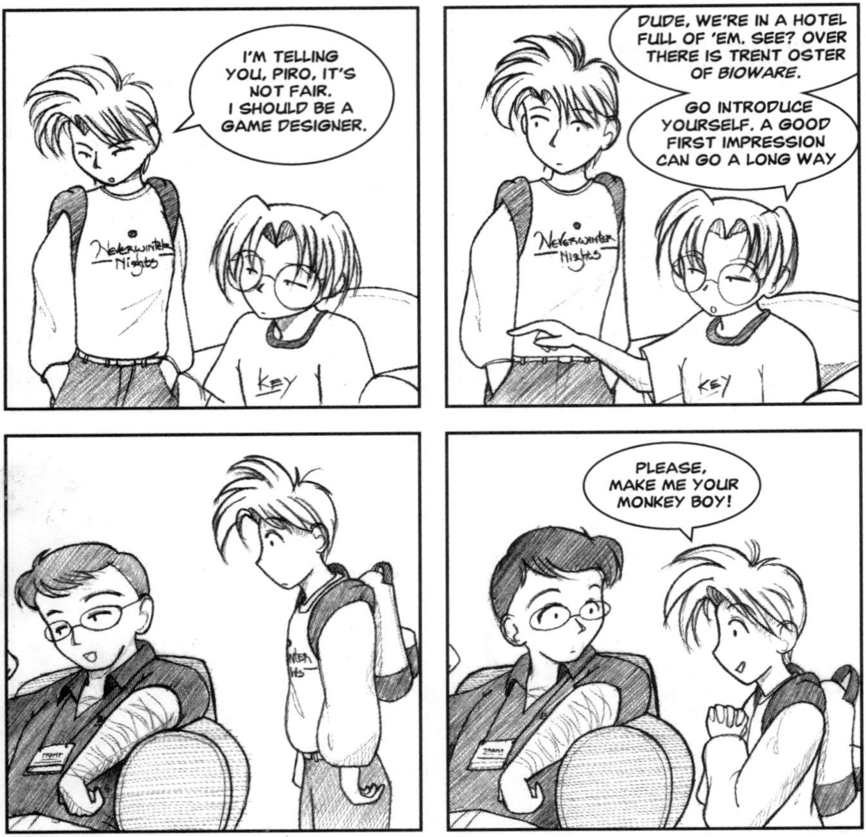
I'M TELLING YOU, PIRO, IT'S NOT FAIR. I SHOULD BE A GAME DESIGNER.
DUDE, WE'RE IN A HOTEL FULL OF 'EM. SEE? OVER THERE IS TRENT OSTER OF *BIOWARE*.
GO INTRODUCE YOURSELF. A GOOD FIRST IMPRESSION CAN GO A LONG WAY
PLEASE, MAKE ME YOUR MONKEY BOY!

LARGO'S OBSESSION WITH *BIOWARE* AND THE GAMES THEY MAKE BORDERS ON THE OBSESSIVE.
NO, IT *IS* OBSESSIVE.

I THINK THAT'S PART OF WHY LARGO IS NOT ALLOWED TO ENTER CANADA ANYMORE.

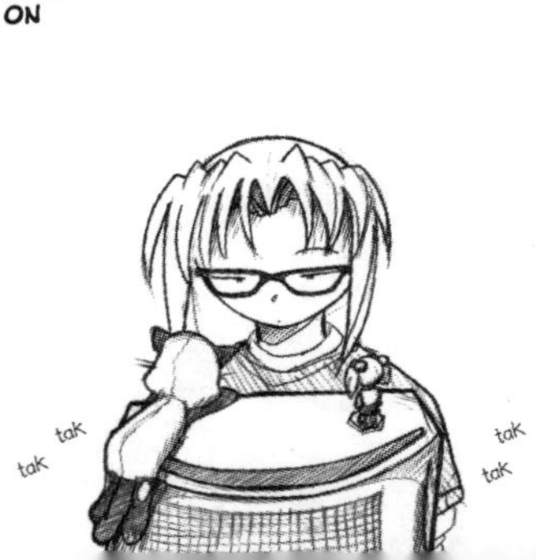
tak
tak
tak
tak

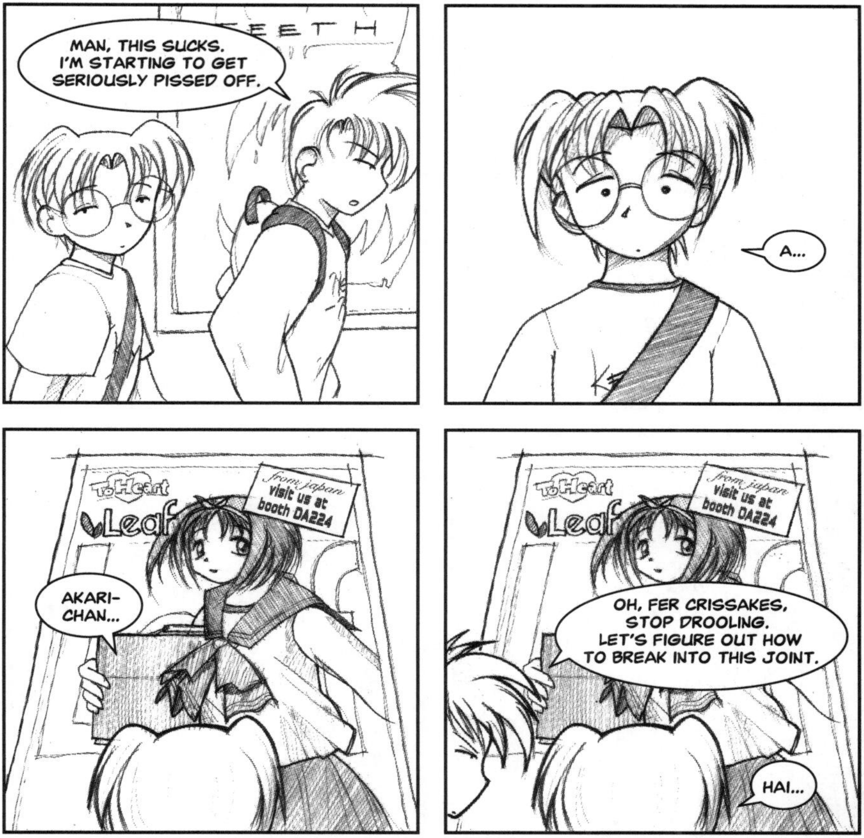
MAN, THIS SUCKS. I'M STARTING TO GET SERIOUSLY PISSED OFF.
A...
To Heart
Leaf
from japan visit us at booth DA224
AKARI-CHAN...
To Heart
Leaf
from japan visit us at booth DA224
OH, FER CRISSAKES, STOP DROOLING. LET'S FIGURE OUT HOW TO BREAK INTO THIS JOINT.
HAI...

IDENTIFYING PIRO'S "OBSESSIONS" WAS A BIT HARDER. MOST READERS CAN UNDERSTAND LARGO'S NEED FOR RPG'S, FIRST PERSON SHOOTERS, AND OTHER THINGS.

EXPLAINING THE TYPES OF GAMES I LIKE WAS HARDER, SINCE VERY FEW ARE AVAILABLE IN ENGLISH.

LARGO AND I DIDN'T WANT THE HUMOR IN MEGATOKYO TO RELY TOO HEAVILY ON WHAT MIGHT BE CONSIDERED "OBSCURE KNOWLEDGE." THE TRICK IS TO PROVIDE HUMOR ON SEVERAL LEVELS SO THAT EVEN IF YOU DON'T GET ALL OF THE REFERENCES, IT'S STILL FUNNY.

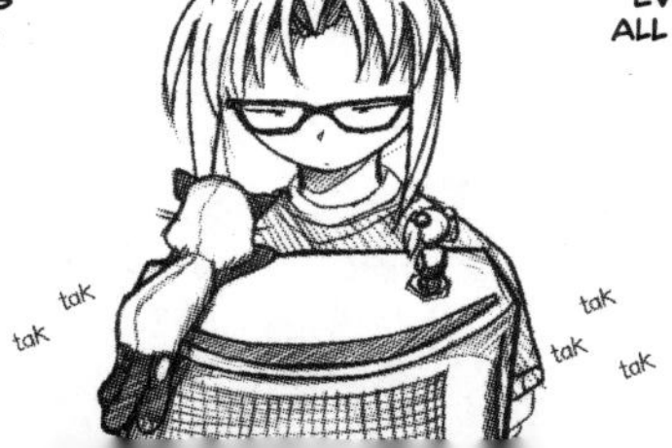
tak
tak
tak
tak
tak

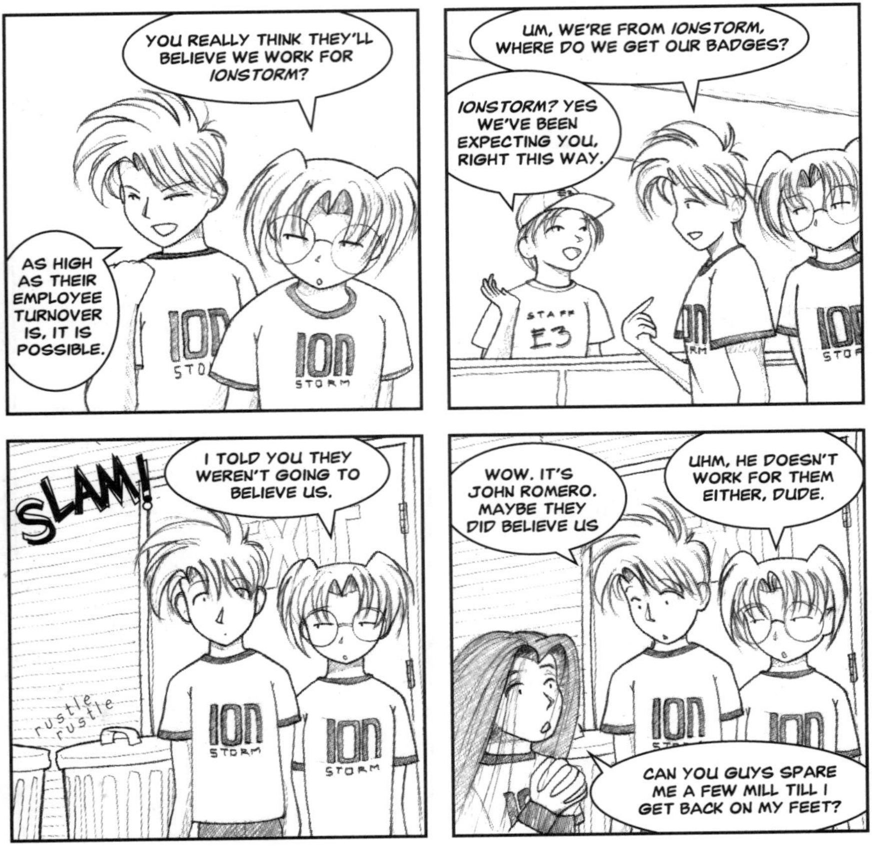
YOU REALLY THINK THEY'LL BELIEVE WE WORK FOR *IONSTORM*?
AS HIGH AS THEIR EMPLOYEE TURNOVER IS, IT IS POSSIBLE.
ION STORM
UM, WE'RE FROM *IONSTORM*, WHERE DO WE GET OUR BADGES?
IONSTORM? YES WE'VE BEEN EXPECTING YOU, RIGHT THIS WAY.
STAFF E3
SLAM!
I TOLD YOU THEY WEREN'T GOING TO BELIEVE US.
rustle rustle
ION STORM
WOW. IT'S JOHN ROMERO. MAYBE THEY DID BELIEVE US
UHM, HE DOESN'T WORK FOR THEM EITHER, DUDE.
CAN YOU GUYS SPARE ME A FEW MILL TILL I GET BACK ON MY FEET?

WHAT WOULD A GAMING COMIC BE WITHOUT POKING FUN AT JOHN ROMERO?

I THINK LARGO SPENT MOST OF HIS TIME THINKING OF HOW TO GET US INTO TROUBLE.

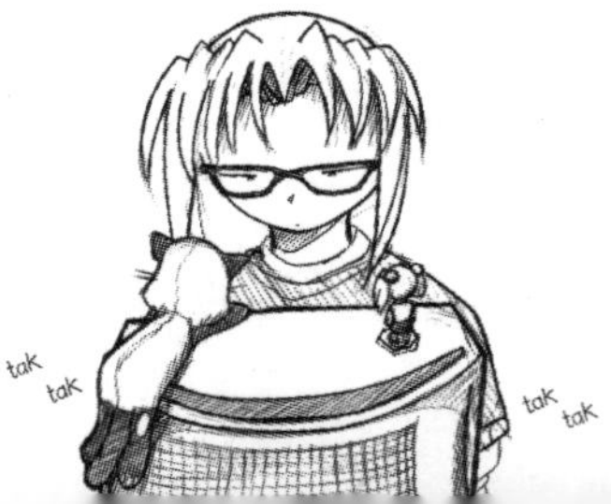
tak
tak
tak
tak

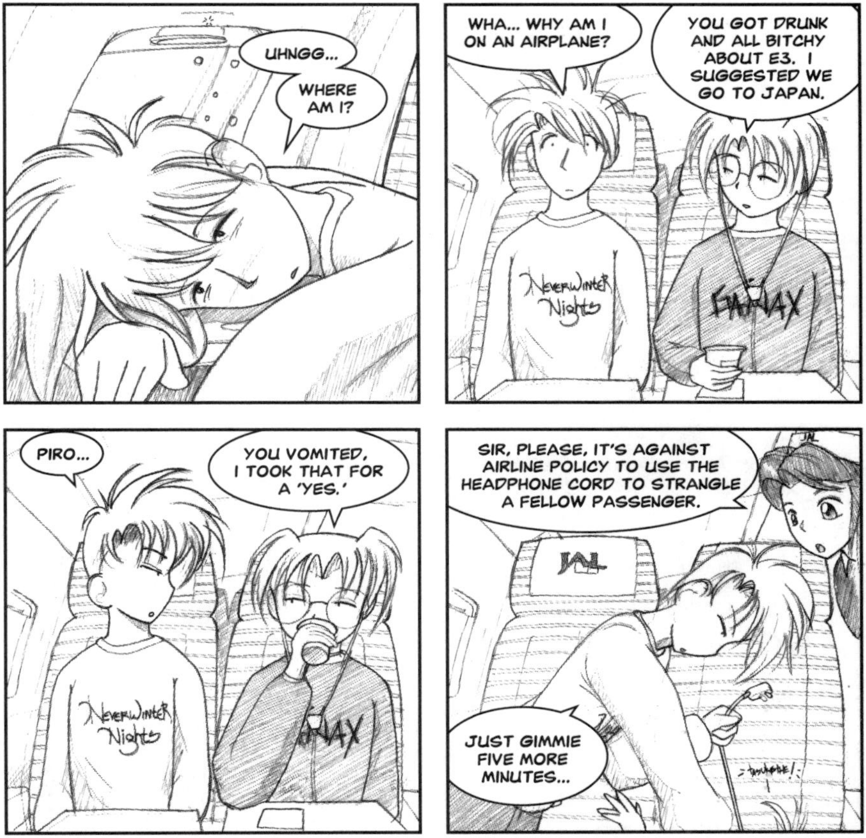
UHNGG...
WHERE AM I?
WHA... WHY AM I ON AN AIRPLANE?
YOU GOT DRUNK AND ALL BITCHY ABOUT E3. I SUGGESTED WE GO TO JAPAN.
PIRO...
YOU VOMITED, I TOOK THAT FOR A 'YES.'
SIR, PLEASE, IT'S AGAINST AIRLINE POLICY TO USE THE HEADPHONE CORD TO STRANGLE A FELLOW PASSENGER.
JUST GIMMIE FIVE MORE MINUTES...

"HEY, WE SHOULD HAVE THEM FLY TO JAPAN."

"SURE, OK."

AH, THE DAYS WHEN I DIDN'T WORRY ABOUT SETUP FOR DIRECTIONAL CHANGES IN THE PLOT.

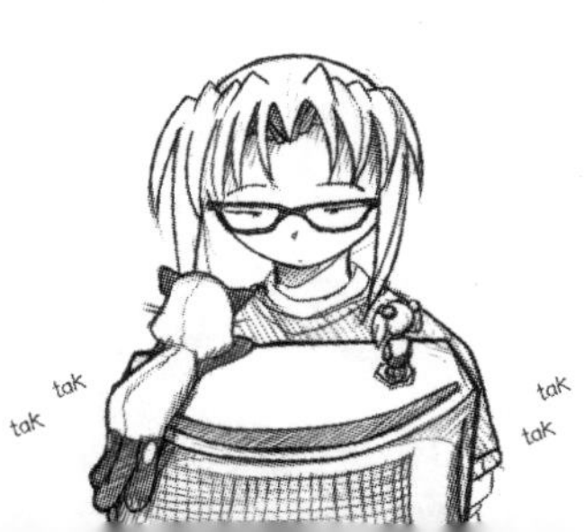
tak
tak
tak
tak

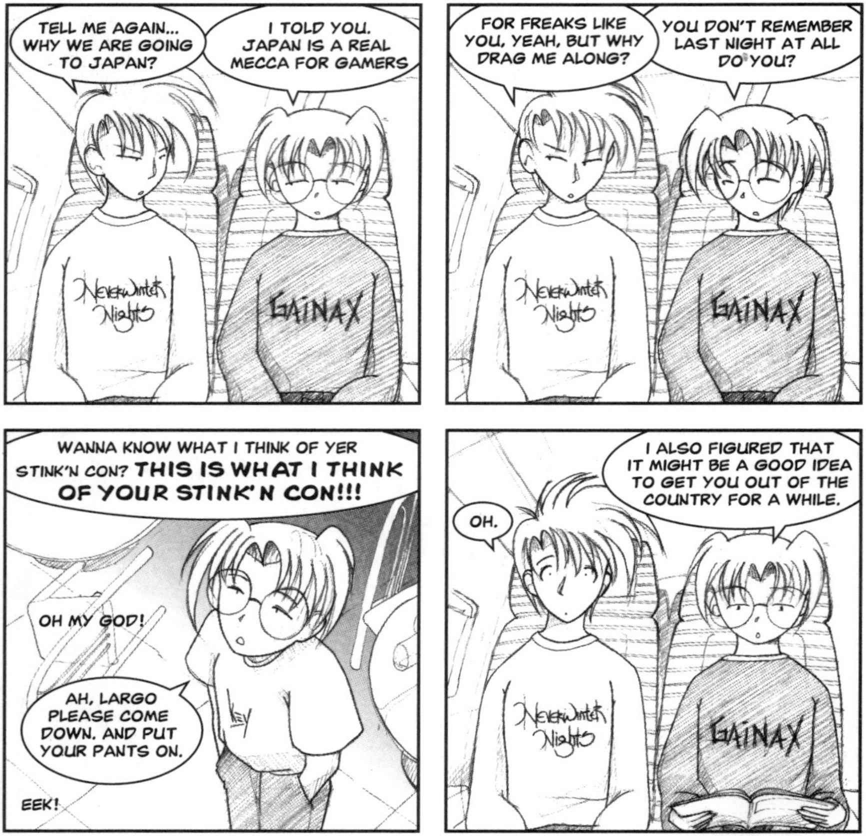
TELL ME AGAIN... WHY WE ARE GOING TO JAPAN?
I TOLD YOU. JAPAN IS A REAL MECCA FOR GAMERS
FOR FREAKS LIKE YOU, YEAH, BUT WHY DRAG ME ALONG?
YOU DON'T REMEMBER LAST NIGHT AT ALL DO YOU?
WANNA KNOW WHAT I THINK OF YER STINK'N CON? THIS IS WHAT I THINK OF YOUR STINK'N CON!!!
OH MY GOD!
AH, LARGO PLEASE COME DOWN. AND PUT YOUR PANTS ON.
EEK!
OH.
I ALSO FIGURED THAT IT MIGHT BE A GOOD IDEA TO GET YOU OUT OF THE COUNTRY FOR A WHILE.

EVEN THOUGH I WASN'T INKING THINGS, EACH COMIC STILL TOOK ABOUT SIX TO EIGHT HOURS TO COMPLETE. PART OF THE REASON IS THAT I SKETCHED EACH FRAME OF THE COMIC FIRST, AND THEN TRACED THE FINAL VERSIONS ON MARKER PAPER BEFORE I SCANNED THEM IN.

BASICALLY, IT WAS LIKE DRAWING EVERYTHING TWICE. MY SKETCHES WERE WAY TOO MESSY TO USE WITHOUT TRACING THEM FIRST.

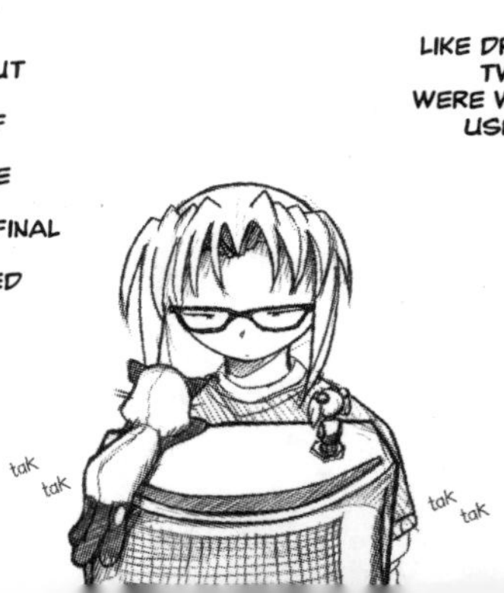
tak tak
tak tak

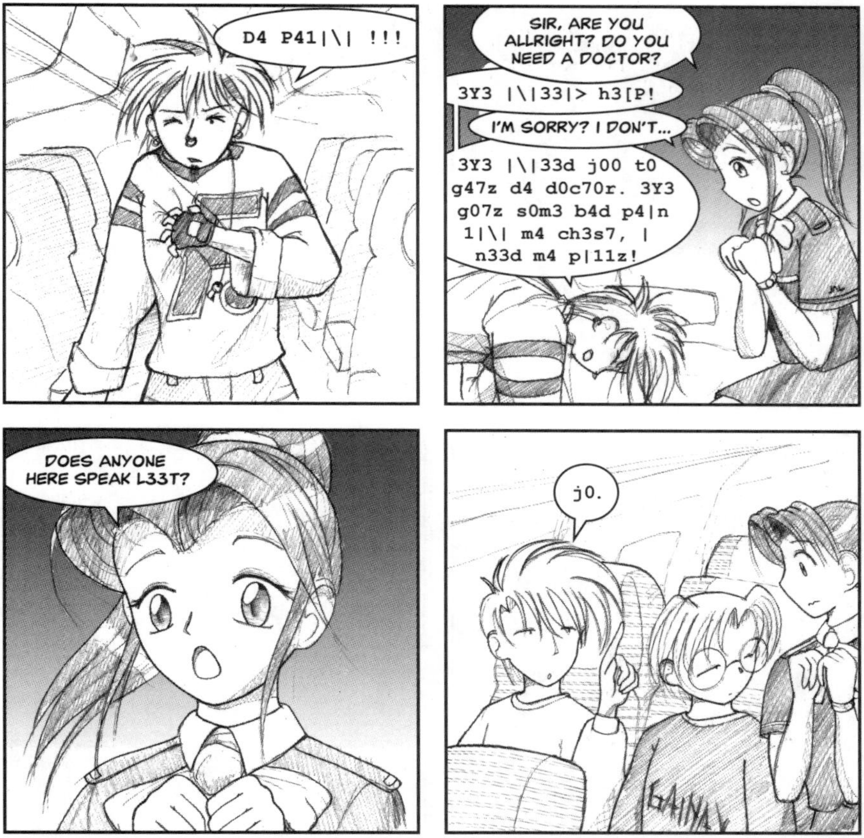
D4 P41|\| !!!
SIR, ARE YOU ALLRIGHT? DO YOU NEED A DOCTOR?
3Y3 |\|33|> h3[P!
I'M SORRY? I DON'T...
3Y3 |\|33d j00 t0 g47z d4 d0c70r. 3Y3 g07z s0m3 b4d p4|n 1|\| m4 ch3s7, | n33d m4 p|11z!
DOES ANYONE HERE SPEAK L33T?
j0.

THIS IS ARGUABLY THE MOST WELL-KNOW COMIC THAT WE'VE DONE.

IT ALSO MARKS THAT TERRIBLE DAY WHEN 'L33T SP34K' ENTERED MY LIFE.

I DIDN'T FULLY GET THE JOKE UNTIL SOMETIME THE FOLLOWING WEEK. I'M NOT WHAT YOU'D CALL "L33T."

IF YOU CAN'T READ WHAT L33T DUD3 SAYS–DON'T ASK ME, I HAVE NO IDEA. ASK LARGO.

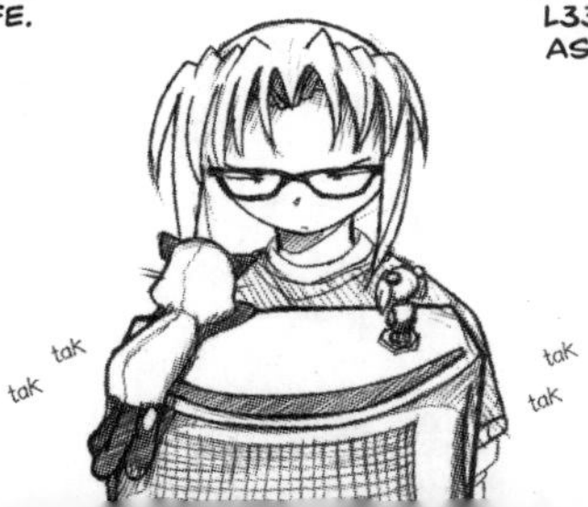
tak
tak
tak
tak

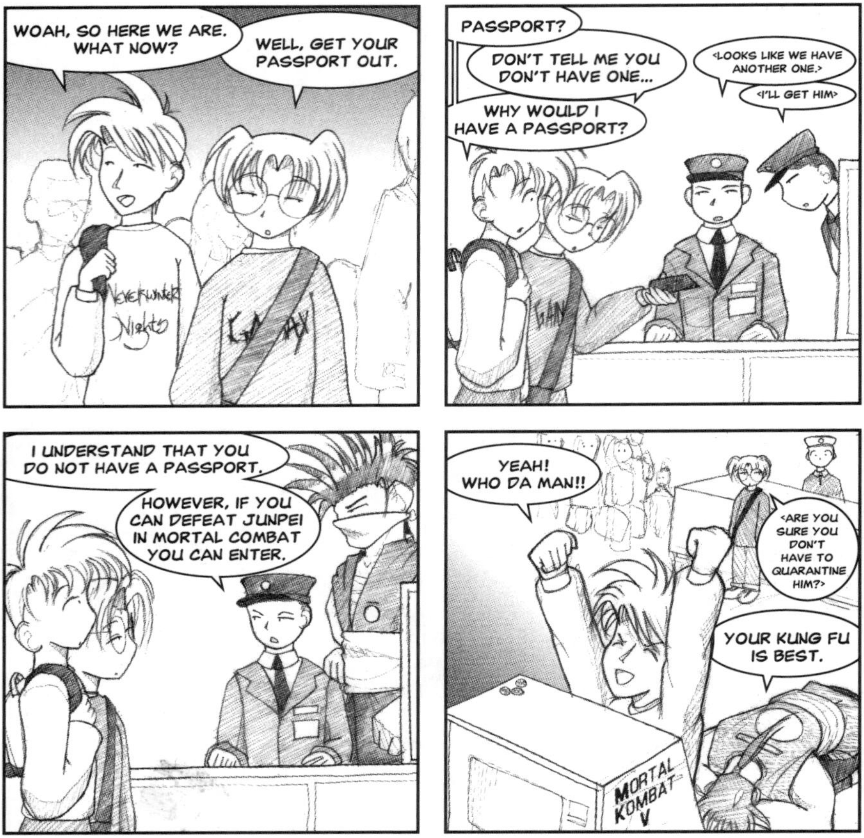
WOAH, SO HERE WE ARE. WHAT NOW?
WELL, GET YOUR PASSPORT OUT.
PASSPORT?
DON'T TELL ME YOU DON'T HAVE ONE...
WHY WOULD I HAVE A PASSPORT?
<LOOKS LIKE WE HAVE ANOTHER ONE.>
<I'LL GET HIM>
I UNDERSTAND THAT YOU DO NOT HAVE A PASSPORT.
HOWEVER, IF YOU CAN DEFEAT JUNPEI IN MORTAL COMBAT YOU CAN ENTER.
YEAH! WHO DA MAN!!
<ARE YOU SURE YOU DON'T HAVE TO QUARANTINE HIM?>
YOUR KUNG FU IS BEST.
MORTAL KOMBAT V

THIS EPISODE HAS HAUNTED ME EVER SINCE WE DID IT. I ALWAYS WANTED TO MAINTAIN SOME SORT OF LOOSE REALISM IN MEGATOKYO.

LARGO JUST GOT INTO JAPAN BY BEATING A NINJA AT A "MORTAL COMBAT" CONSOLE GAME.

THERE GOES THAT PLAN.

THIS WAS WHEN WE STARTED TO SEE THAT SOME OF OUR IDEAS WERE GOING TO CONFLICT WITH EACH OTHER'S STORY CONCEPTS. I WANTED TO LEAN TOWARDS A MORE STRUCTURED STORY, LARGO WANTED THINGS MORE FREE-FLOWING.

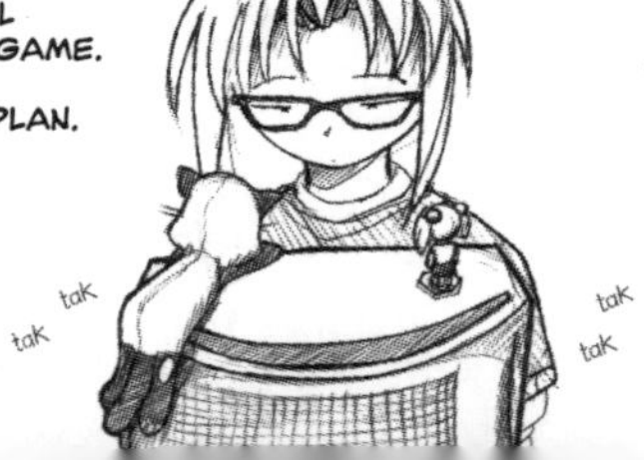
tak tak
tak tak

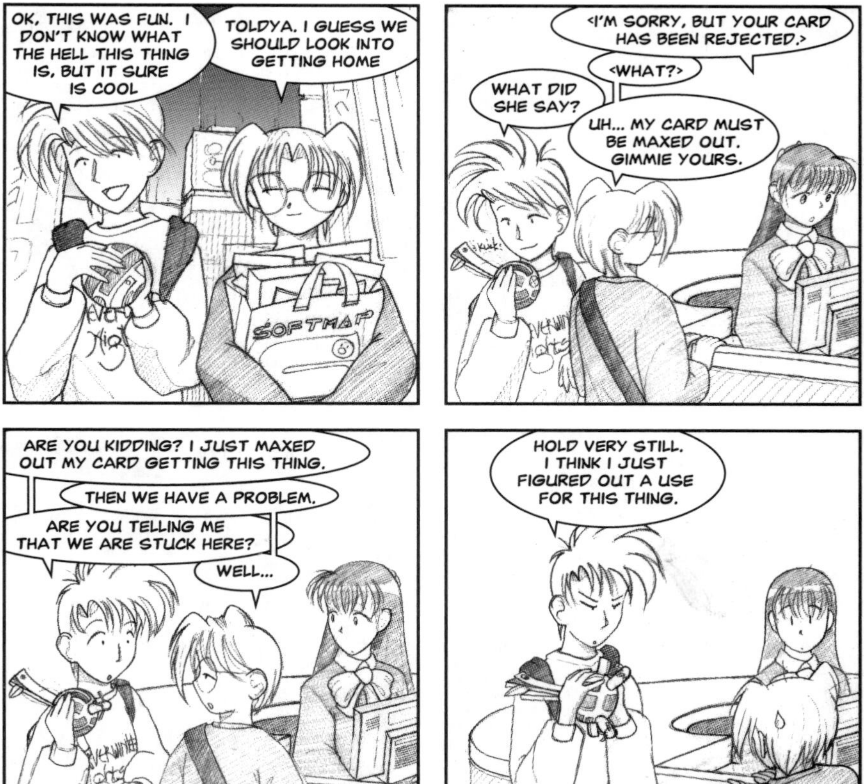
OK, THIS WAS FUN. I DON'T KNOW WHAT THE HELL THIS THING IS, BUT IT SURE IS COOL
TOLDYA. I GUESS WE SHOULD LOOK INTO GETTING HOME
SOFTMAP
<I'M SORRY, BUT YOUR CARD HAS BEEN REJECTED.>
<WHAT?>
WHAT DID SHE SAY?
UH... MY CARD MUST BE MAXED OUT. GIMMIE YOURS.
ARE YOU KIDDING? I JUST MAXED OUT MY CARD GETTING THIS THING.
THEN WE HAVE A PROBLEM.
ARE YOU TELLING ME THAT WE ARE STUCK HERE?
WELL...
HOLD VERY STILL. I THINK I JUST FIGURED OUT A USE FOR THIS THING.

HAVING SPENT A FEW WEEKS IN JAPAN MYSELF, I KNOW VERY WELL HOW EASY IT IS TO SPEND A LOT OF MONEY VERY QUICKLY.

ALSO, WE ARE INTRODUCED TO LARGO'S "COOL THING" WHICH IS... WELL...WE REALLY DON'T KNOW YET.

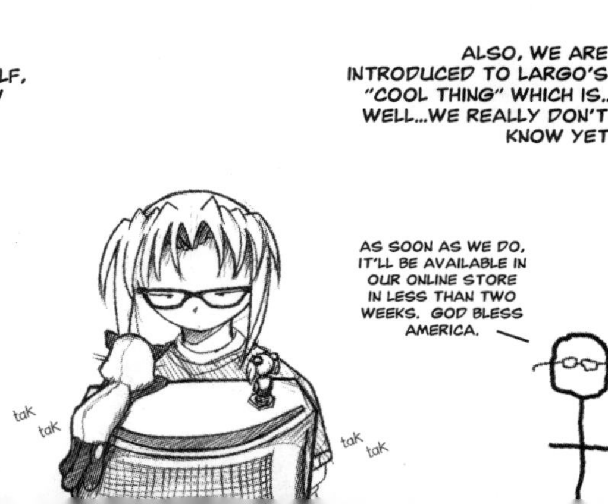
AS SOON AS WE DO, IT'LL BE AVAILABLE IN OUR ONLINE STORE IN LESS THAN TWO WEEKS. GOD BLESS AMERICA.
tak tak
tak tak

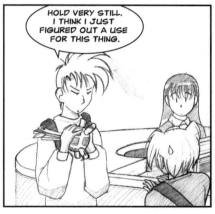

THIS IS JUST GREAT. THOUSANDS OF MILES FROM HOME, NO MONEY, NO PLACE TO STAY, AND WORST OF ALL I'M GOING TO MISS THE RELEASE OF BALDURS GATE 2... SOMEONE SHOOT ME.

DON'T FREAK ON ME, I KNOW A BUNCH OF PEOPLE HERE IN TOKYO. IT SHOULDN'T BE TOO HARD TO FIND SOMEWHERE TO CRASH.

THEN WHY ARE WE SITTING HERE? I'M STARVING, AND I NEED TO CHECK MY EMAIL.

WELL...

ON THE PLANE, I WAS FINALLY ABLE TO FINISH "WITH YOU MITSUMETEITAI" WITH MANAMI. UNFORTUNATELY, IT SEEMS TO HAVE DRAINED THE BATTERY ON MY PORTABLE. I CAN'T GET AT MY ADDRESS BOOK

YOU'RE DOING THIS ON PURPOSE, AREN'T YOU?

RELAX, I'M SURE WE'LL BE BACK BEFORE "NEVERWINTER NIGHTS" IS RELEASED.

GREAT. THAT'LL BE WHAT, THREE YEARS?

NIGHT SCENES ARE HARD TO DO IN PENCIL, SO I EXPERIMENTED WITH SHADING IN PHOTOSHOP TO GET THE RIGHT FEEL.

LARGO'S OBSESSION WITH A CERTAIN *BIOWARE* GAME STARTS TO SURFACE AGAIN, AND AGAIN.

tak tak

tak tak

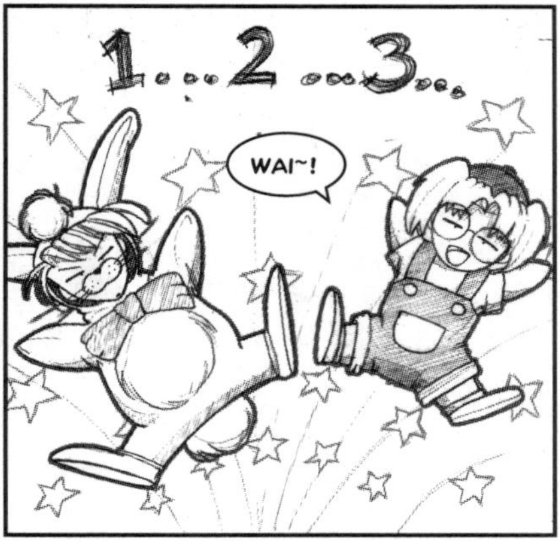
1...2...3...
WAI~!

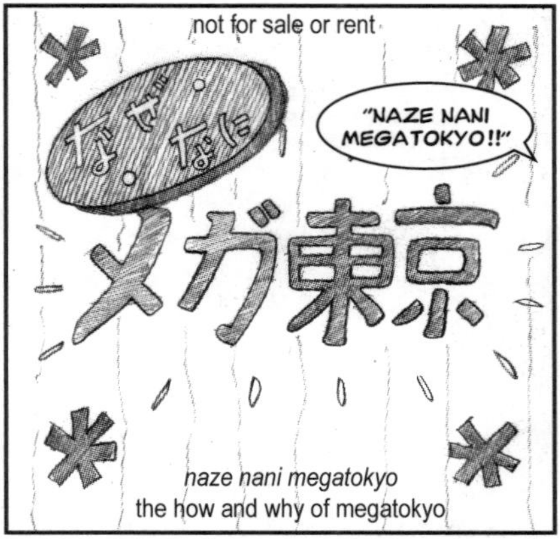
not for sale or rent
なぜなに
"NAZE NANI MEGATOKYO!!"
メガ東京
naze nani megatokyo
the how and why of megatokyo

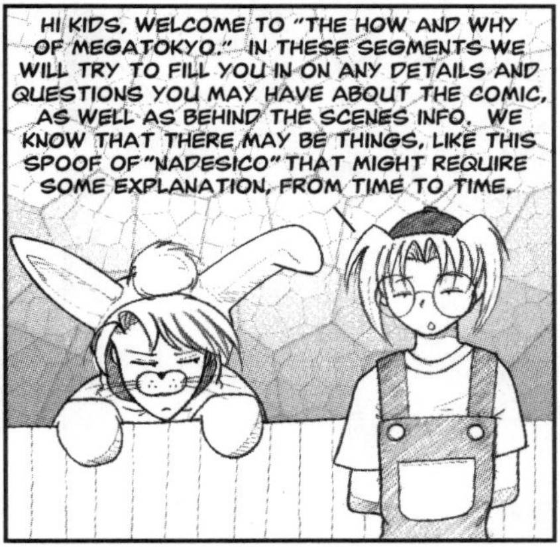
HI KIDS, WELCOME TO "THE HOW AND WHY OF MEGATOKYO." IN THESE SEGMENTS WE WILL TRY TO FILL YOU IN ON ANY DETAILS AND QUESTIONS YOU MAY HAVE ABOUT THE COMIC, AS WELL AS BEHIND THE SCENES INFO. WE KNOW THAT THERE MAY BE THINGS, LIKE THIS SPOOF OF "NADESICO" THAT MIGHT REQUIRE SOME EXPLANATION, FROM TIME TO TIME.

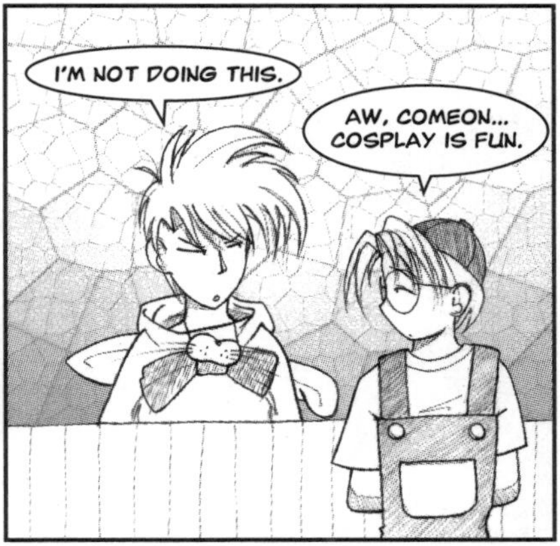
I'M NOT DOING THIS.
AW, COMEON... COSPLAY IS FUN.

THIS JOKE MAKES LITTLE SENSE UNLESS YOU'RE FAMILIAR WITH THE ANIME SERIES "MARTIAN SUCCESSOR NADESICO."

COSPLAY, IF YOU ARE NOT FAMILIAR WITH THE TERM, IS WHERE YOU DRESS UP AS YOUR FAVORITE ANIME OR GAME CHARACTER. IT'S A COMMON PRACTICE AT ANIME CONVENTIONS BOTH HERE AND IN JAPAN.

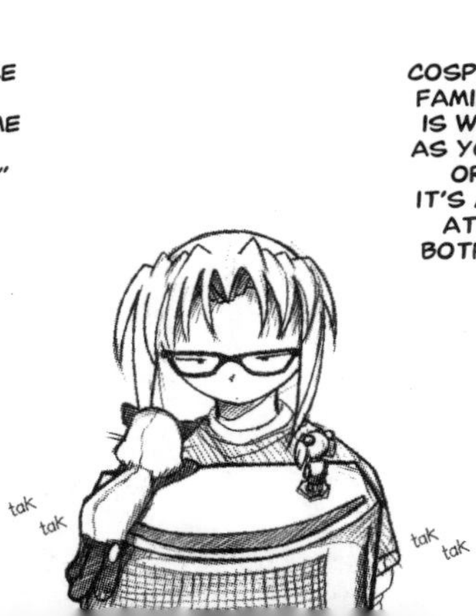
tak
tak
tak
tak

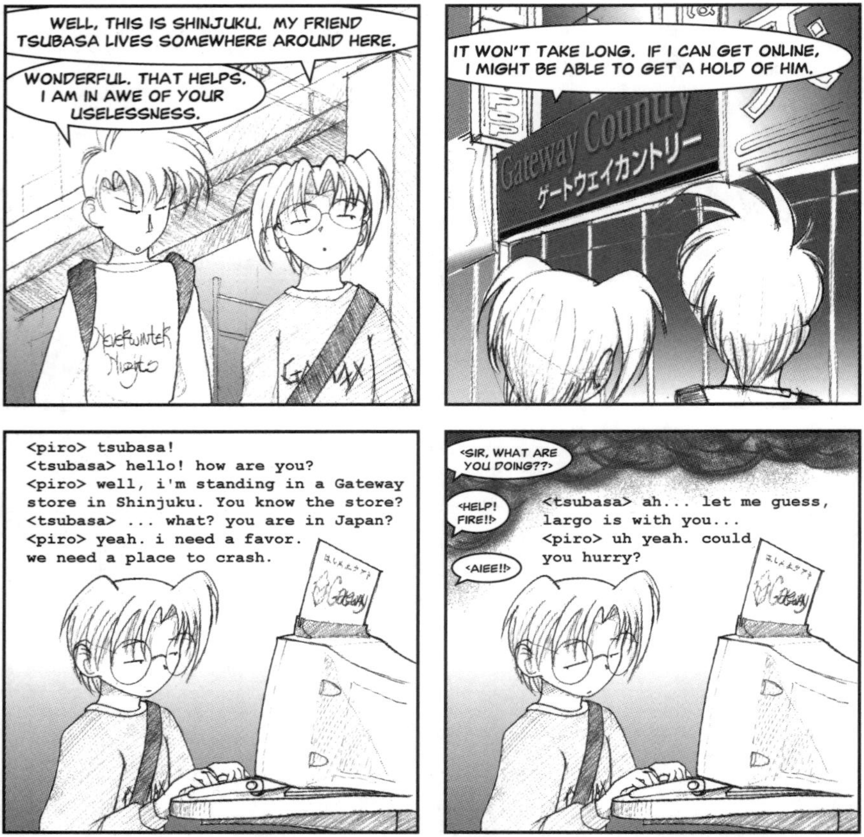
WELL, THIS IS SHINJUKU. MY FRIEND TSUBASA LIVES SOMEWHERE AROUND HERE.
WONDERFUL. THAT HELPS. I AM IN AWE OF YOUR USELESSNESS.
IT WON'T TAKE LONG. IF I CAN GET ONLINE, I MIGHT BE ABLE TO GET A HOLD OF HIM.
Gateway Country
ゲートウェイカントリー
<piro> tsubasa!
<tsubasa> hello! how are you?
<piro> well, i'm standing in a Gateway store in Shinjuku. You know the store?
<tsubasa> ... what? you are in Japan?
<piro> yeah. i need a favor. we need a place to crash.
<SIR, WHAT ARE YOU DOING??>
<HELP! FIRE!!>
<AIEE!!>
<tsubasa> ah... let me guess, largo is with you...
<piro> uh yeah. could you hurry?

TSUBASA, A FRIEND OF MINE IN JAPAN, HELPED ME WORK OUT WHERE MOST OF THE EVENTS IN MEGATOKYO TAKE PLACE.

LIKE MANY PEOPLE WHO SPEND A LOT OF TIME ONLINE, A GOOD CHUNK OF MY SOCIAL INTERACTION WITH PEOPLE IS ON IRC. IN FACT, LARGO AND I DO NOT LIVE ANYWHERE NEAR EACH OTHER, SO EVERYTHING WE DID WAS VIA IRC AND INSTANT MESSAGING.

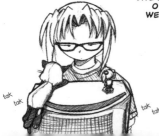

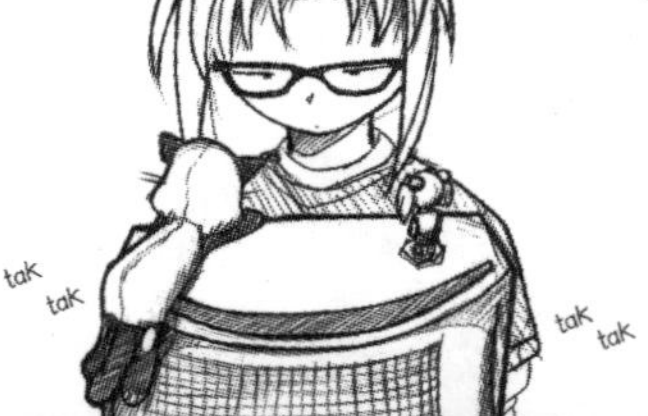
tak
tak
tak
tak

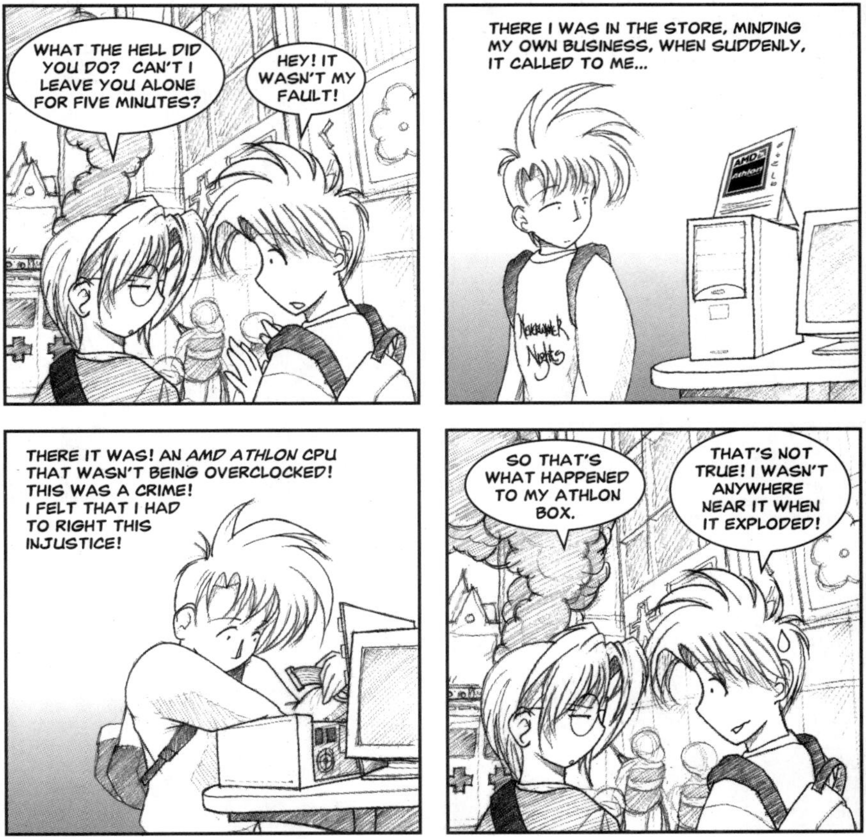
WHAT THE HELL DID YOU DO? CAN'T I LEAVE YOU ALONE FOR FIVE MINUTES?
HEY! IT WASN'T MY FAULT!
THERE I WAS IN THE STORE, MINDING MY OWN BUSINESS, WHEN SUDDENLY, IT CALLED TO ME...
THERE IT WAS! AN *AMD ATHLON* CPU THAT WASN'T BEING OVERCLOCKED! THIS WAS A CRIME! I FELT THAT I HAD TO RIGHT THIS INJUSTICE!
SO THAT'S WHAT HAPPENED TO MY ATHLON BOX.
THAT'S NOT TRUE! I WASN'T ANYWHERE NEAR IT WHEN IT EXPLODED!

HAVING AN AMD CHIP THAT USED TO OVERHEAT WITHOUT ANY OVERCLOCKING WHATSOEVER, I FOUND THIS COMIC TO BE PARTICULARLY HUMOROUS.

AND YES, LARGO HAS ACTUALLY HAD SMALL FIRES ERUPT INSIDE HIS COMPUTER CASES.

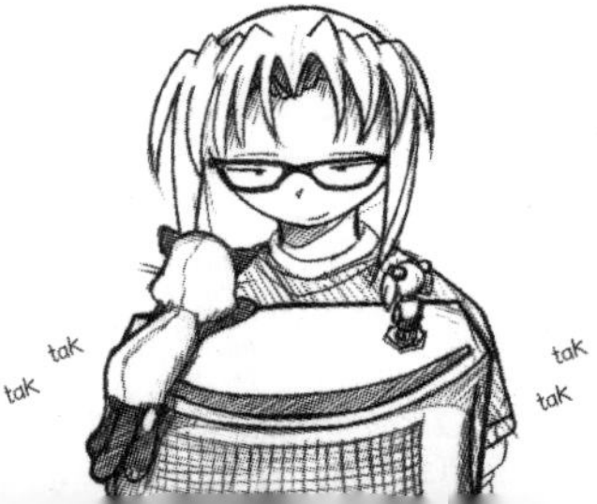
tak
tak
tak
tak

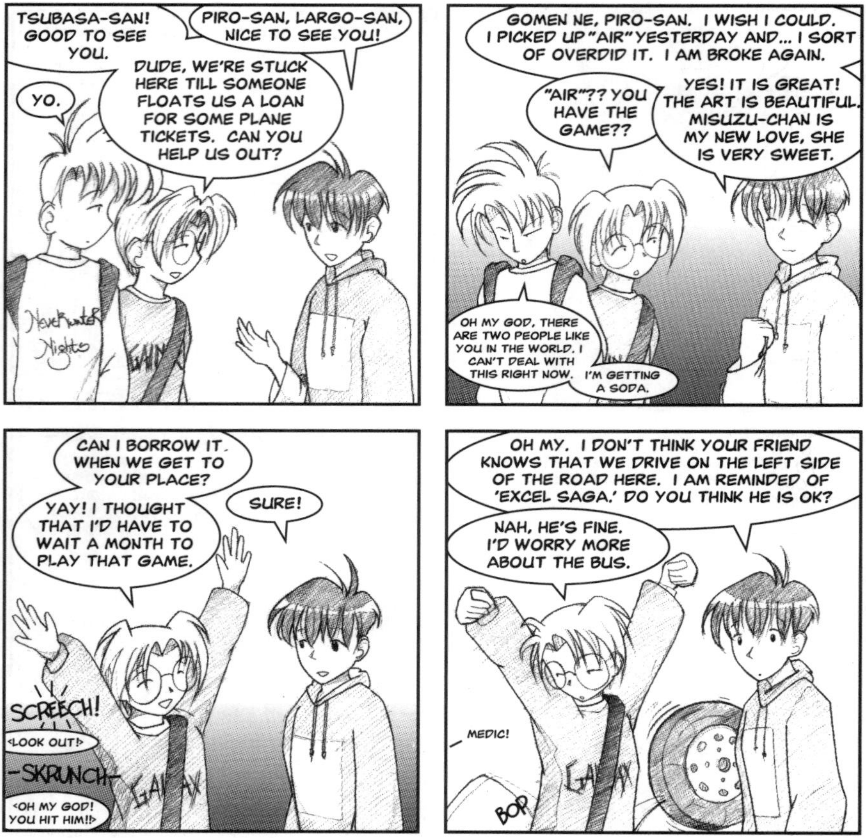
TSUBASA-SAN! GOOD TO SEE YOU.
PIRO-SAN, LARGO-SAN, NICE TO SEE YOU!
YO.
DUDE, WE'RE STUCK HERE TILL SOMEONE FLOATS US A LOAN FOR SOME PLANE TICKETS. CAN YOU HELP US OUT?
GOMEN NE, PIRO-SAN. I WISH I COULD. I PICKED UP "AIR" YESTERDAY AND... I SORT OF OVERDID IT. I AM BROKE AGAIN.
"AIR"?? YOU HAVE THE GAME??
YES! IT IS GREAT! THE ART IS BEAUTIFUL. MISUZU-CHAN IS MY NEW LOVE, SHE IS VERY SWEET.
OH MY GOD, THERE ARE TWO PEOPLE LIKE YOU IN THE WORLD. I CAN'T DEAL WITH THIS RIGHT NOW.
I'M GETTING A SODA.
CAN I BORROW IT WHEN WE GET TO YOUR PLACE?
SURE!
YAY! I THOUGHT THAT I'D HAVE TO WAIT A MONTH TO PLAY THAT GAME.
SCREECH!
<LOOK OUT!>
-SKRUNCH-
<OH MY GOD! YOU HIT HIM!!>
OH MY. I DON'T THINK YOUR FRIEND KNOWS THAT WE DRIVE ON THE LEFT SIDE OF THE ROAD HERE. I AM REMINDED OF 'EXCEL SAGA.' DO YOU THINK HE IS OK?
NAH, HE'S FINE. I'D WORRY MORE ABOUT THE BUS.
MEDIC!
BOP

I DON'T REALLY KNOW WHY, BUT I WAS OK WITH THE CONCEPT OF LARGO GETTING HIT BY A BUS.

LARGO'S ABILITY TO ABSORB ALMOST CARTOONISH LEVELS OF VIOLENCE WAS ONE OF THE BENEFITS OF THE DUAL NATURE OF THE WORLD THAT WAS STARTING TO DEVELOP.

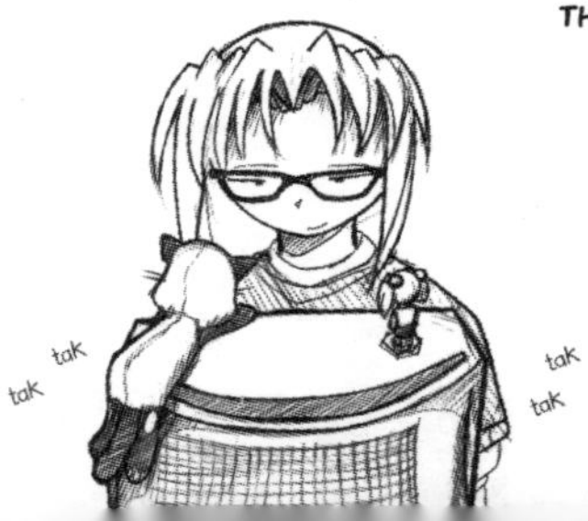
tak
tak
tak
tak

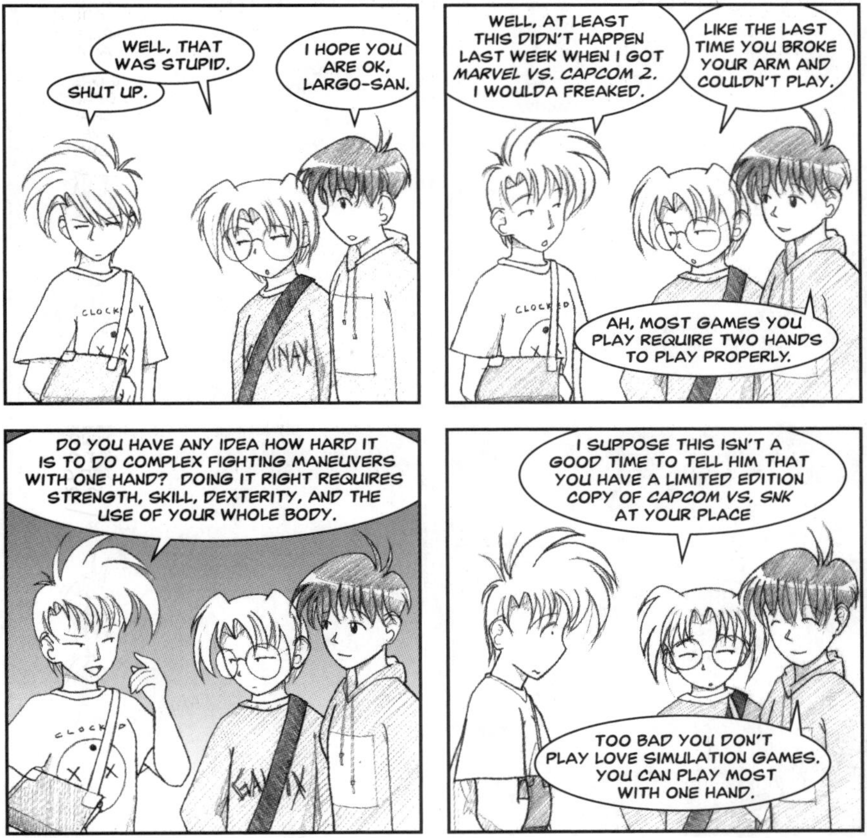
WELL, THAT WAS STUPID.
SHUT UP.
I HOPE YOU ARE OK, LARGO-SAN.
WELL, AT LEAST THIS DIDN'T HAPPEN LAST WEEK WHEN I GOT *MARVEL VS. CAPCOM 2*. I WOULDA FREAKED.
LIKE THE LAST TIME YOU BROKE YOUR ARM AND COULDN'T PLAY.
AH, MOST GAMES YOU PLAY REQUIRE TWO HANDS TO PLAY PROPERLY.
DO YOU HAVE ANY IDEA HOW HARD IT IS TO DO COMPLEX FIGHTING MANEUVERS WITH ONE HAND? DOING IT RIGHT REQUIRES STRENGTH, SKILL, DEXTERITY, AND THE USE OF YOUR WHOLE BODY.
I SUPPOSE THIS ISN'T A GOOD TIME TO TELL HIM THAT YOU HAVE A LIMITED EDITION COPY OF *CAPCOM VS. SNK* AT YOUR PLACE
TOO BAD YOU DON'T PLAY LOVE SIMULATION GAMES. YOU CAN PLAY MOST WITH ONE HAND.

ONE THING I WANTED TO MAKE SURE OF IN MEGATOKYO WAS THAT IF SOMEONE GETS HURT, THEY STAY HURT. LARGO'S ARM WON'T MAGICALLY HEAL ITSELF IN THE NEXT COMIC.

LARGO DOES MANAGE TO HEAL PRETTY FAST THOUGH. FAST, BUT NOT INSTANTLY.

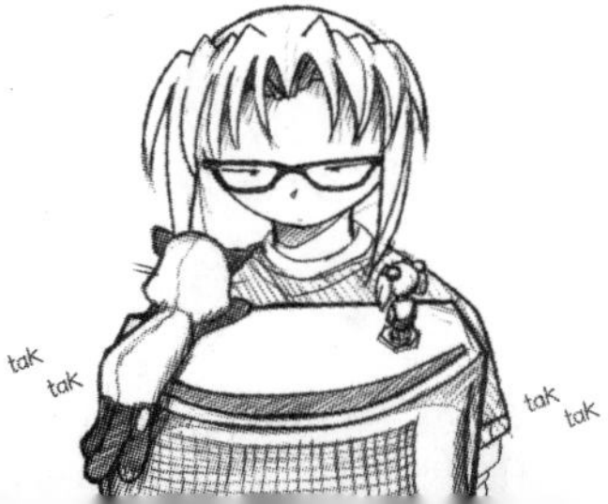
tak
tak
tak
tak

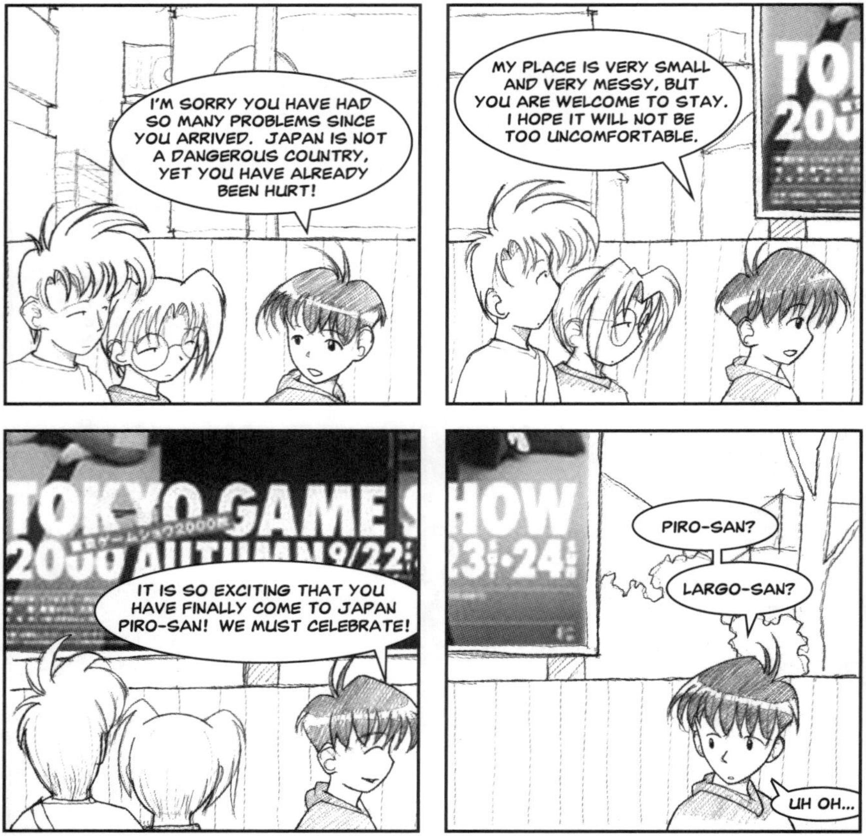
I'M SORRY YOU HAVE HAD SO MANY PROBLEMS SINCE YOU ARRIVED. JAPAN IS NOT A DANGEROUS COUNTRY, YET YOU HAVE ALREADY BEEN HURT!
MY PLACE IS VERY SMALL AND VERY MESSY, BUT YOU ARE WELCOME TO STAY. I HOPE IT WILL NOT BE TOO UNCOMFORTABLE.
IT IS SO EXCITING THAT YOU HAVE FINALLY COME TO JAPAN PIRO-SAN! WE MUST CELEBRATE!
PIRO-SAN?
LARGO-SAN?
UH OH...

JAPAN IS A PRETTY SAFE PLACE TO WANDER AROUND AIMLESSLY.

I ALWAYS FELT SAFE NO MATTER WHERE I WAS. BUT THEN AGAIN, I WASN'T LOOKING FOR TROUBLE WHEN I WAS THERE.

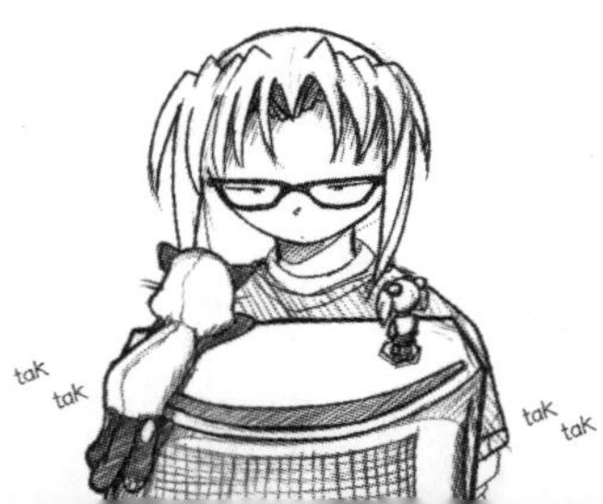
tak
tak
tak
tak

PIRO, I'VE BEEN THINKING.
AREN'T THERE LAWS AGAINST THAT?
I MEAN, HERE WE ARE AT YET ANOTHER GAMING TRADE SHOW. EVERY YEAR, ITS THE SAME THING. GAME SHOWS, LAN PARTIES NOTHING EVER CHANGES.
DON'T YOU EVER THINK THAT THERE MIGHT BE MORE TO LIFE THAN JUST GAMES?
YOU MEAN LIKE FINDING A GIRLFRIEND, GETTING OUT OF DEBT, MOVING AHEAD IN OUR CAREERS, STUFF LIKE THAT?
YEAH.
THERE WAS A SIM GAME ABOUT THAT, WASN'T THERE?
YEAH, IT SUCKED.
'NUFF SAID.

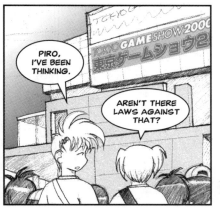

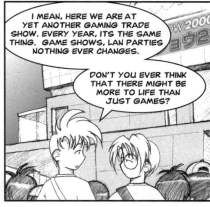

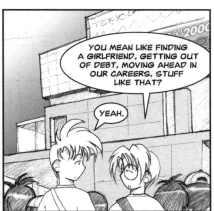

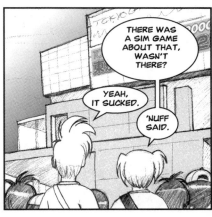

MUCH OF THE TIME, LARGO AND PIRO DON'T ACKNOWLEDGE THE EXISTENCE OF EACH OTHER, EXCEPT AS A SOURCE OF MINOR IRRITATION.

OTHER TIMES, THEY ARE VERY MUCH IN SYNCH WITH EACH OTHER'S THOUGHTS. IT'S AN INTERESTING RELATIONSHIP.

THE NUMBER OF PEOPLE WHO EMAIL ME SAYING, "MY FRIEND IS JUST LIKE LARGO AND I'M JUST LIKE PIRO!" MAKES ME WORRY ABOUT THE WORLD.

tak
tak
tak
tak

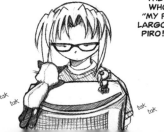

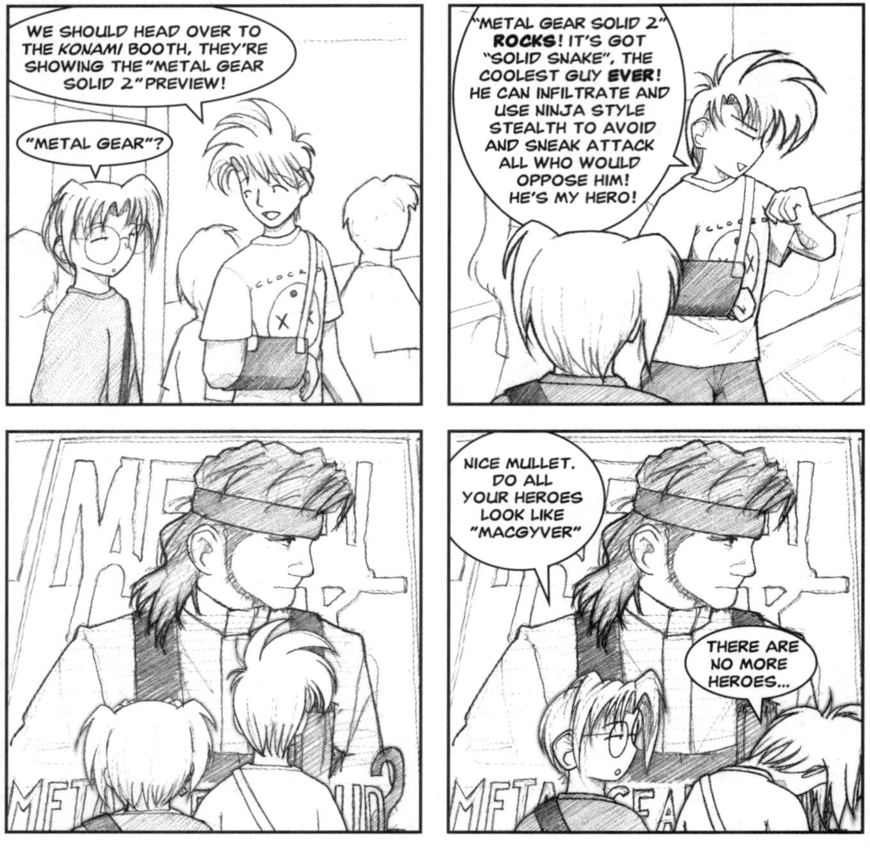
WE SHOULD HEAD OVER TO THE KONAMI BOOTH, THEY'RE SHOWING THE "METAL GEAR SOLID 2" PREVIEW!
"METAL GEAR"?
"METAL GEAR SOLID 2" ROCKS! IT'S GOT "SOLID SNAKE", THE COOLEST GUY EVER! HE CAN INFILTRATE AND USE NINJA STYLE STEALTH TO AVOID AND SNEAK ATTACK ALL WHO WOULD OPPOSE HIM! HE'S MY HERO!
NICE MULLET. DO ALL YOUR HEROES LOOK LIKE "MACGYVER"
THERE ARE NO MORE HEROES...

IT'S AMAZING HOW A BAD HAIR CUT CAN RUIN A COOL CHARACTER.

POOR LARGO, OF COURSE HIS HAIR IS BIGGER IN THE OPPOSITE DIRECTION. I WONDER WHAT THEY CALL THAT?

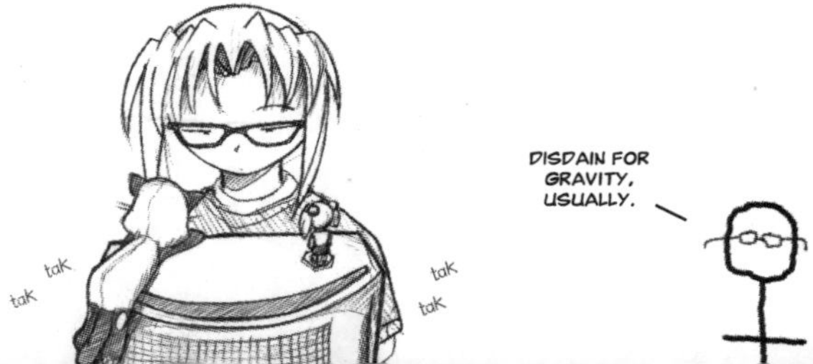
tak tak
tak tak
DISDAIN FOR GRAVITY, USUALLY.

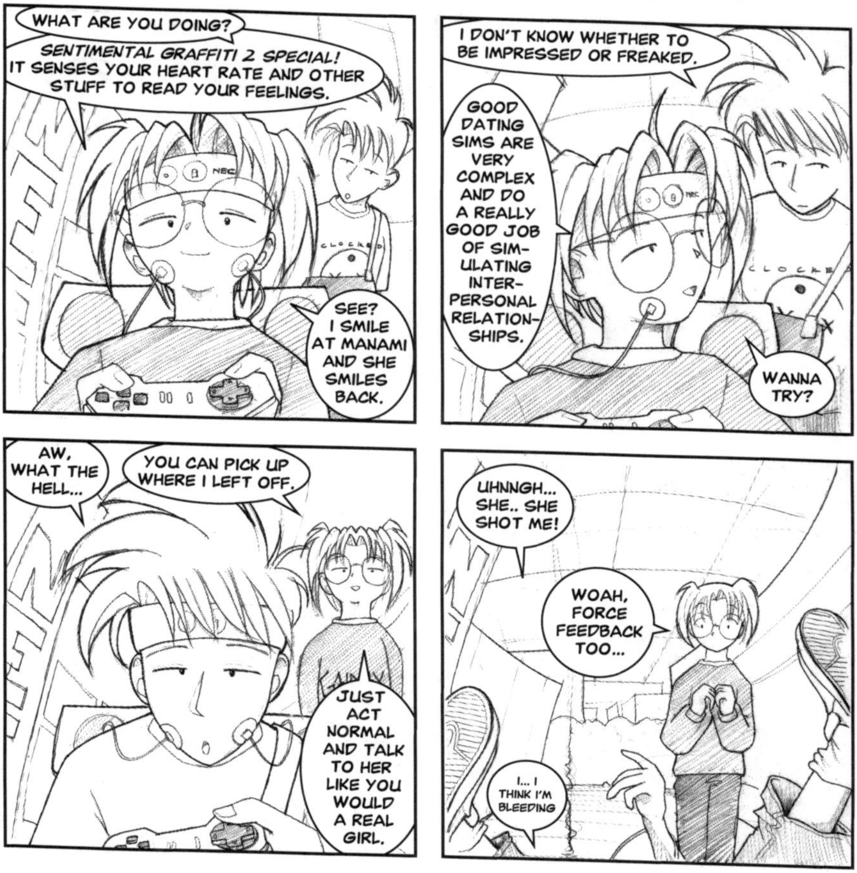
WHAT ARE YOU DOING?
SENTIMENTAL GRAFFITI 2 SPECIAL! IT SENSES YOUR HEART RATE AND OTHER STUFF TO READ YOUR FEELINGS.
SEE? I SMILE AT MANAMI AND SHE SMILES BACK.
I DON'T KNOW WHETHER TO BE IMPRESSED OR FREAKED.
GOOD DATING SIMS ARE VERY COMPLEX AND DO A REALLY GOOD JOB OF SIMULATING INTERPERSONAL RELATIONSHIPS.
WANNA TRY?
AW, WHAT THE HELL...
YOU CAN PICK UP WHERE I LEFT OFF.
JUST ACT NORMAL AND TALK TO HER LIKE YOU WOULD A REAL GIRL.
UHNNGH... SHE.. SHE SHOT ME!
WOAH, FORCE FEEDBACK TOO...
I... I THINK I'M BLEEDING

I CAN'T HELP BUT CHUCKLE AT THE CONCEPT OF A FORCE FEEDBACK "DATING SIM" GAME.

IMAGINE HOW BRUISED YOU'D GET.

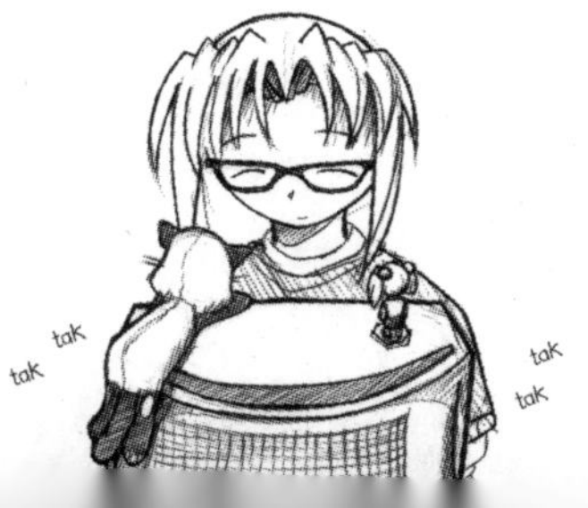
tak
tak
tak
tak

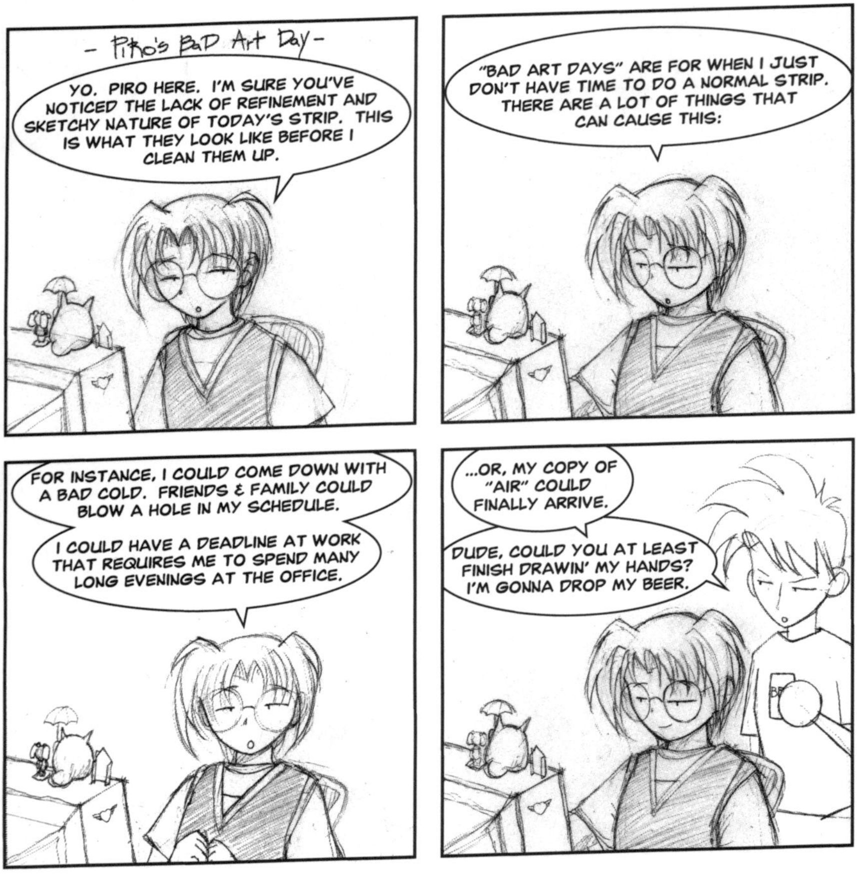
- PIRO'S BAD ART DAY -
YO. PIRO HERE. I'M SURE YOU'VE NOTICED THE LACK OF REFINEMENT AND SKETCHY NATURE OF TODAY'S STRIP. THIS IS WHAT THEY LOOK LIKE BEFORE I CLEAN THEM UP.
"BAD ART DAYS" ARE FOR WHEN I JUST DON'T HAVE TIME TO DO A NORMAL STRIP. THERE ARE A LOT OF THINGS THAT CAN CAUSE THIS:
FOR INSTANCE, I COULD COME DOWN WITH A BAD COLD. FRIENDS & FAMILY COULD BLOW A HOLE IN MY SCHEDULE.
I COULD HAVE A DEADLINE AT WORK THAT REQUIRES ME TO SPEND MANY LONG EVENINGS AT THE OFFICE.
...OR, MY COPY OF "AIR" COULD FINALLY ARRIVE.
DUDE, COULD YOU AT LEAST FINISH DRAWIN' MY HANDS? I'M GONNA DROP MY BEER.

MY FIRST DEAD PIRO DAY. YOU CAN SEE WHY I WAS TRACING MY SKETCHES AT THE TIME – EVEN THOUGH THEY WERE GETTING BETTER.

WITH ALL THE TIME IT TOOK TO MAKE THESE COMICS – SIX TO EIGHT HOURS – IT'S NO WONDER THAT I MISSED A DAY OR TWO.

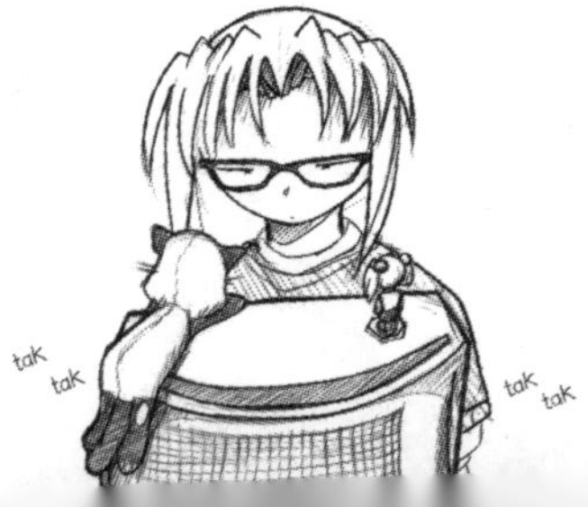
tak
tak
tak
tak

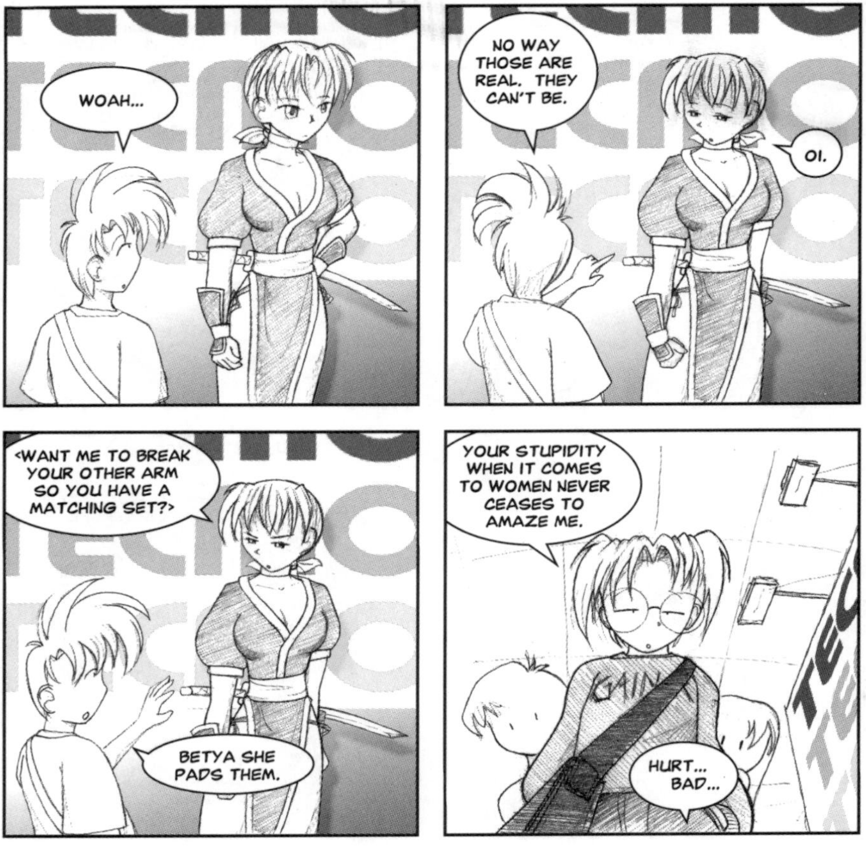
WOAH...
NO WAY THOSE ARE REAL. THEY CAN'T BE.
OI.
<WANT ME TO BREAK YOUR OTHER ARM SO YOU HAVE A MATCHING SET?>
BETYA SHE PADS THEM.
YOUR STUPIDITY WHEN IT COMES TO WOMEN NEVER CEASES TO AMAZE ME.
HURT... BAD...

A CLASSIC LARGO MOMENT.

NOTE THAT WHEN YOU SEE BRACKETS LIKE <THESE>, IT MEANS THE CHARACTER IS SPEAKING IN JAPANESE.

I DON'T THINK THAT ERIKA'S LINE WOULD BE VERY HARD TO UNDERSTAND IN ANY LANGUAGE.

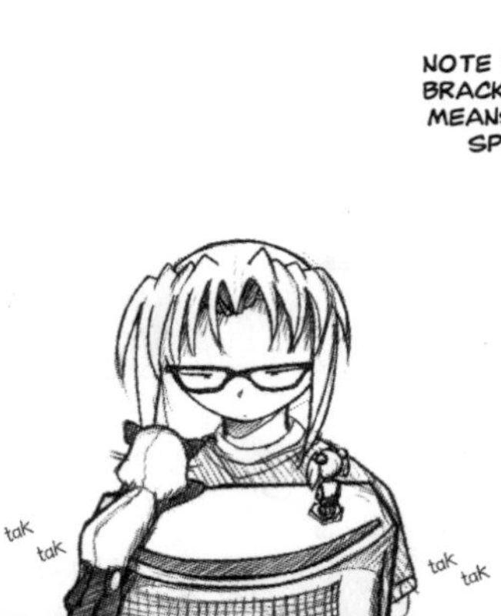
tak
tak
tak
tak

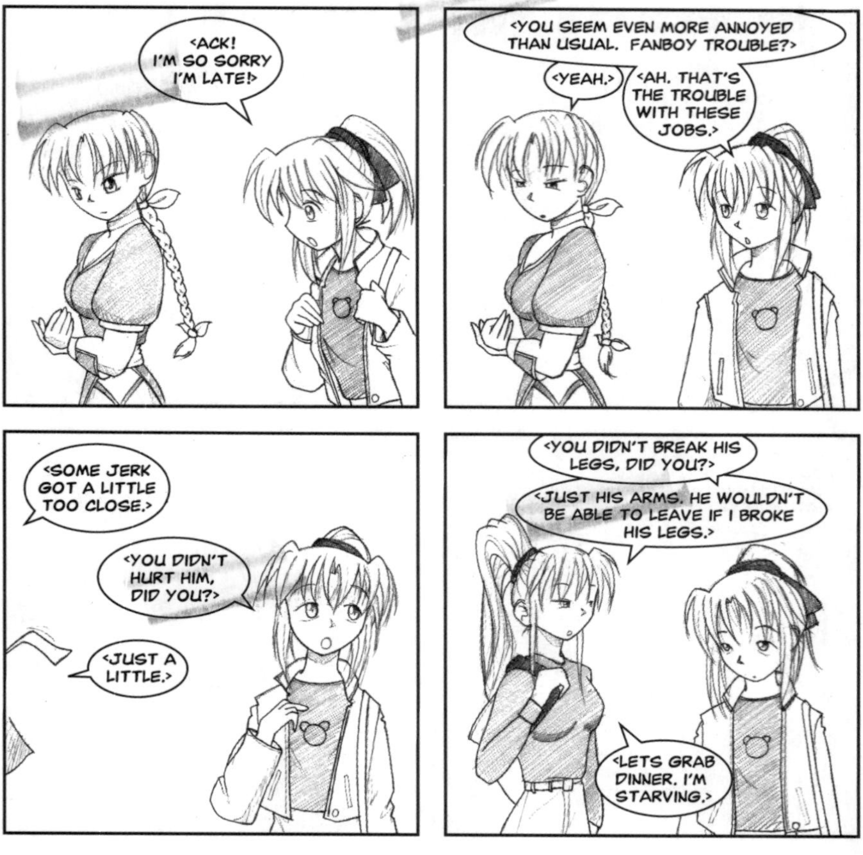
<ACK! I'M SO SORRY I'M LATE!>
<YOU SEEM EVEN MORE ANNOYED THAN USUAL. FANBOY TROUBLE?>
<YEAH.>
<AH. THAT'S THE TROUBLE WITH THESE JOBS.>
<SOME JERK GOT A LITTLE TOO CLOSE.>
<YOU DIDN'T HURT HIM, DID YOU?>
<JUST A LITTLE.>
<YOU DIDN'T BREAK HIS LEGS, DID YOU?>
<JUST HIS ARMS. HE WOULDN'T BE ABLE TO LEAVE IF I BROKE HIS LEGS.>
<LETS GRAB DINNER. I'M STARVING.>

IT TOOK A WHILE FOR THE GIRLS TO START SHOWING UP IN MEGATOKYO, MAINLY BECAUSE I FELT THAT I DIDN'T HAVE THE SKILLS TO DRAW THE FEMALE CAST PROPERLY.

IT WOULD BE ANOTHER SIX MONTHS BEFORE I FELT THAT I DID.

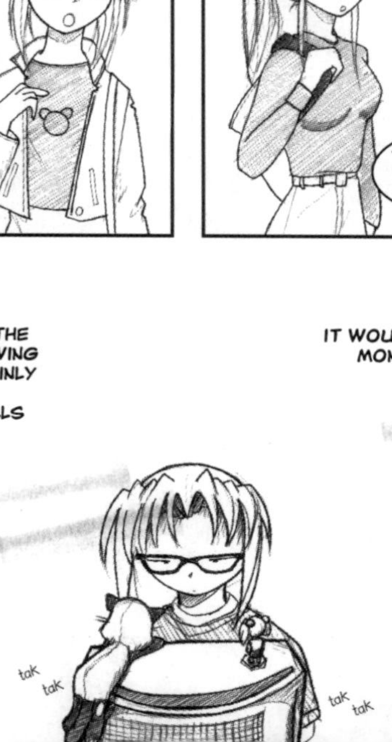
tak
tak
tak
tak

<THIS WAY, HURRY! WE CAN'T GET RID OF THEM!>
<I AM SO GLAD YOU FOUND THEM. I WAS VERY WORRIED.>
PIRO-SAN!
OH, HI TSUBASA. LOOK! *PIA CARROT 2.5 SUPER DX!*
OHH...
<AHEM.>
<OH, SORRY.>
PIRO-SAN, THE TOKYO GAME SHOW IS OVER. WE HAVE TO GO.
(SIGH) I GUESS YOU'RE RIGHT.
WHERE IS LARGO-SAN?
OVER THERE, IN THE SNK BOOTH.
AH... WHAT IS HE DOING?
SOME GIRL BROKE HIS OTHER ARM.
HE... HE CAN PLAY USING HIS TONGUE.
AMAZING.
AWW... AZUSA-CHAN, HIDOI...
<PLEASE TAKE THEM AWAY! THEY SCARE US!>

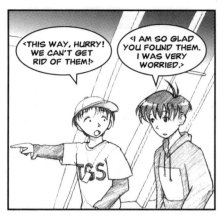

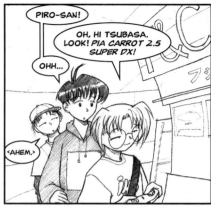

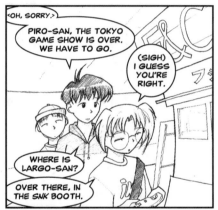

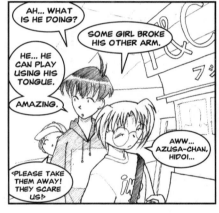

WHY DO I ALWAYS SHOW THE PEOPLE WHO WORK AT THESE SHOWS WEARING BASEBALL CAPS?

HMM, NO IDEA.

tak
tak
tak
tak

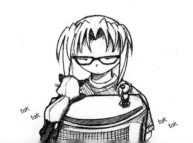

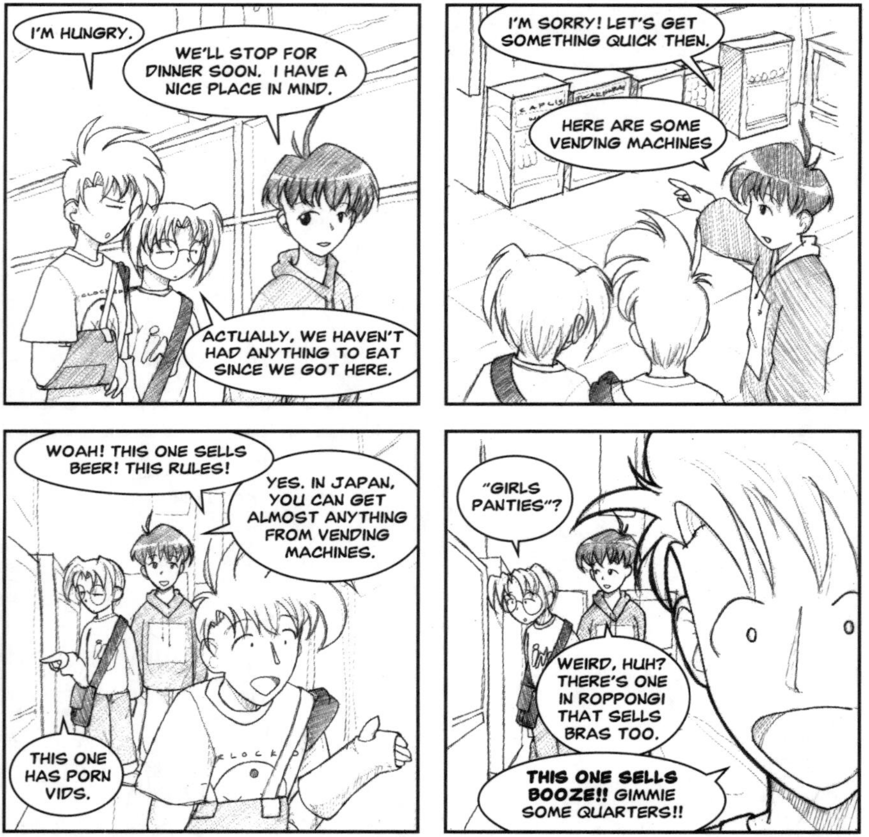
I'M HUNGRY.
WE'LL STOP FOR DINNER SOON. I HAVE A NICE PLACE IN MIND.
ACTUALLY, WE HAVEN'T HAD ANYTHING TO EAT SINCE WE GOT HERE.
I'M SORRY! LET'S GET SOMETHING QUICK THEN.
HERE ARE SOME VENDING MACHINES
WOAH! THIS ONE SELLS BEER! THIS RULES!
YES. IN JAPAN, YOU CAN GET ALMOST ANYTHING FROM VENDING MACHINES.
THIS ONE HAS PORN VIDS.
"GIRLS PANTIES"?
WEIRD, HUH? THERE'S ONE IN ROPPONGI THAT SELLS BRAS TOO.
THIS ONE SELLS BOOZE!! GIMMIE SOME QUARTERS!!

ODDLY ENOUGH, WE DIDN'T MAKE THIS UP.

YOU REALLY CAN GET THINGS LIKE THIS FROM VENDING MACHINES IN JAPAN. WE DIDN'T EVEN MENTION THE WEIRD STUFF.

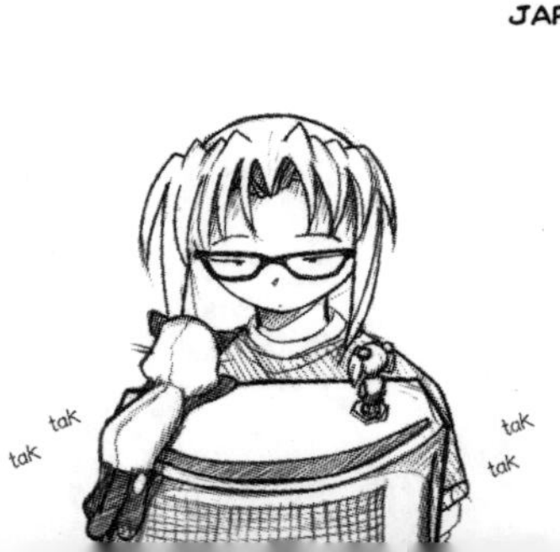
tak tak
tak tak

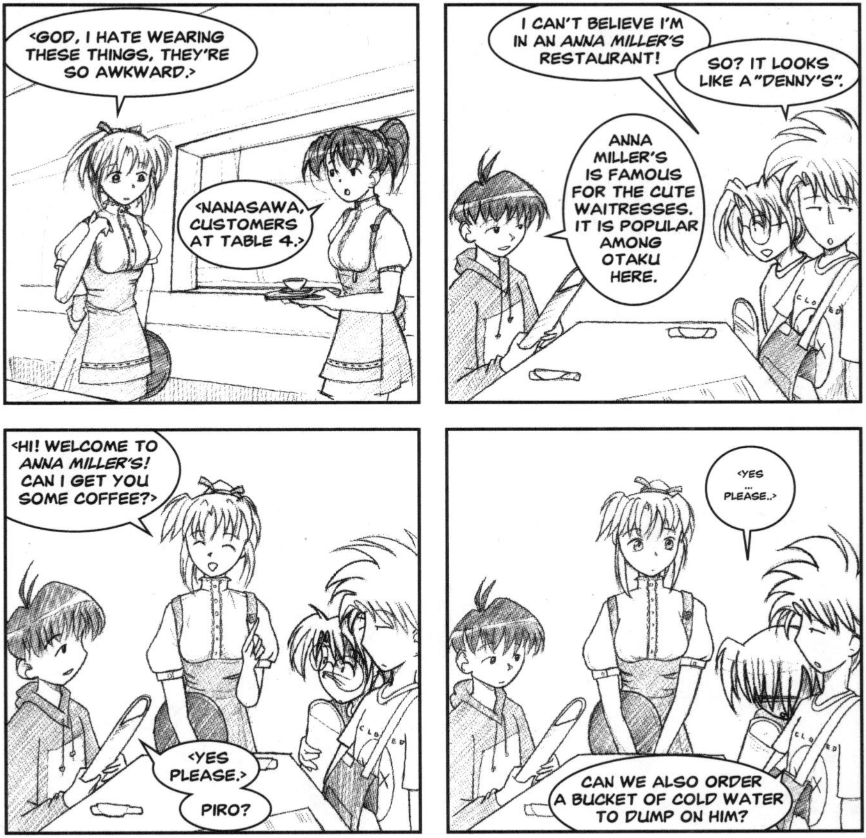
<GOD, I HATE WEARING THESE THINGS, THEY'RE SO AWKWARD.>
<NANASAWA, CUSTOMERS AT TABLE 4.>
I CAN'T BELIEVE I'M IN AN *ANNA MILLER'S* RESTAURANT!
SO? IT LOOKS LIKE A "DENNY'S".
ANNA MILLER'S IS FAMOUS FOR THE CUTE WAITRESSES. IT IS POPULAR AMONG OTAKU HERE.
<HI! WELCOME TO *ANNA MILLER'S!* CAN I GET YOU SOME COFFEE?>
<YES PLEASE.>
PIRO?
<YES ... PLEASE..>
CAN WE ALSO ORDER A BUCKET OF COLD WATER TO DUMP ON HIM?

KIMIKO'S COMMENT HERE IS A SETUP FOR THINGS THAT HAPPEN IN LATER STRIPS. WHEN WRITING SCRIPTS, YOU CAN DO SUBTLE THINGS NOW THAT LATER BECOME THE FOCUS OF A JOKE OR STORY ARC.

NOTE THAT THIS IS THE FIRST TIME PIRO MEETS KIMIKO.

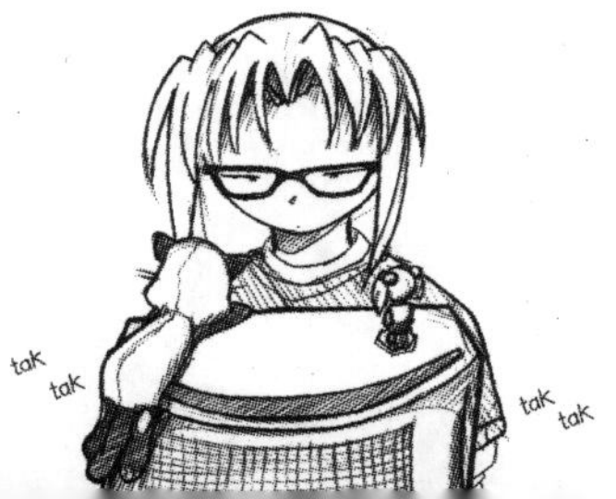
tak
tak
tak
tak

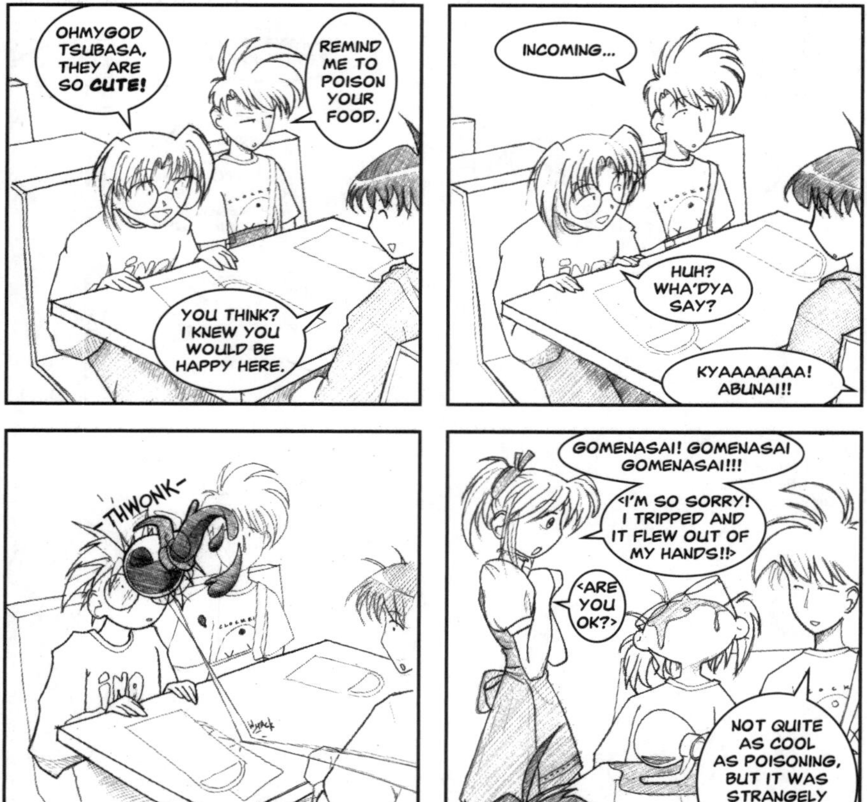
OHMYGOD TSUBASA, THEY ARE SO **CUTE!**
REMIND ME TO POISON YOUR FOOD.
YOU THINK? I KNEW YOU WOULD BE HAPPY HERE.
INCOMING...
HUH? WHA'DYA SAY?
KYAAAAAAA! ABUNAI!!
-THWONK-
GOMENASAI! GOMENASAI GOMENASAI!!!
<I'M SO SORRY! I TRIPPED AND IT FLEW OUT OF MY HANDS!!>
<ARE YOU OK?>
NOT QUITE AS COOL AS POISONING, BUT IT WAS STRANGELY SATISFYING.

IN MEGATOKYO, THE BASIC PREMISE IS THAT LARGO EXISTS TO ABSORB PHYSICAL DAMAGE, WHILE PIRO EXISTS TO TAKE EMOTIONAL DAMAGE.

AS THIS PARTICULAR COMIC DEMONSTRATES, THIS ISN'T ALWAYS THE CASE.

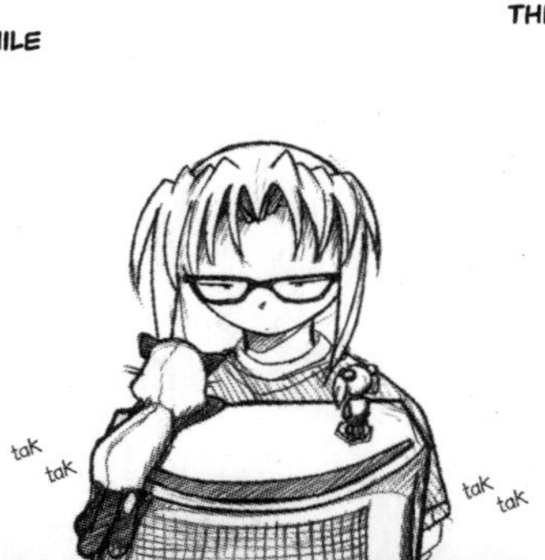
tak
tak
tak
tak

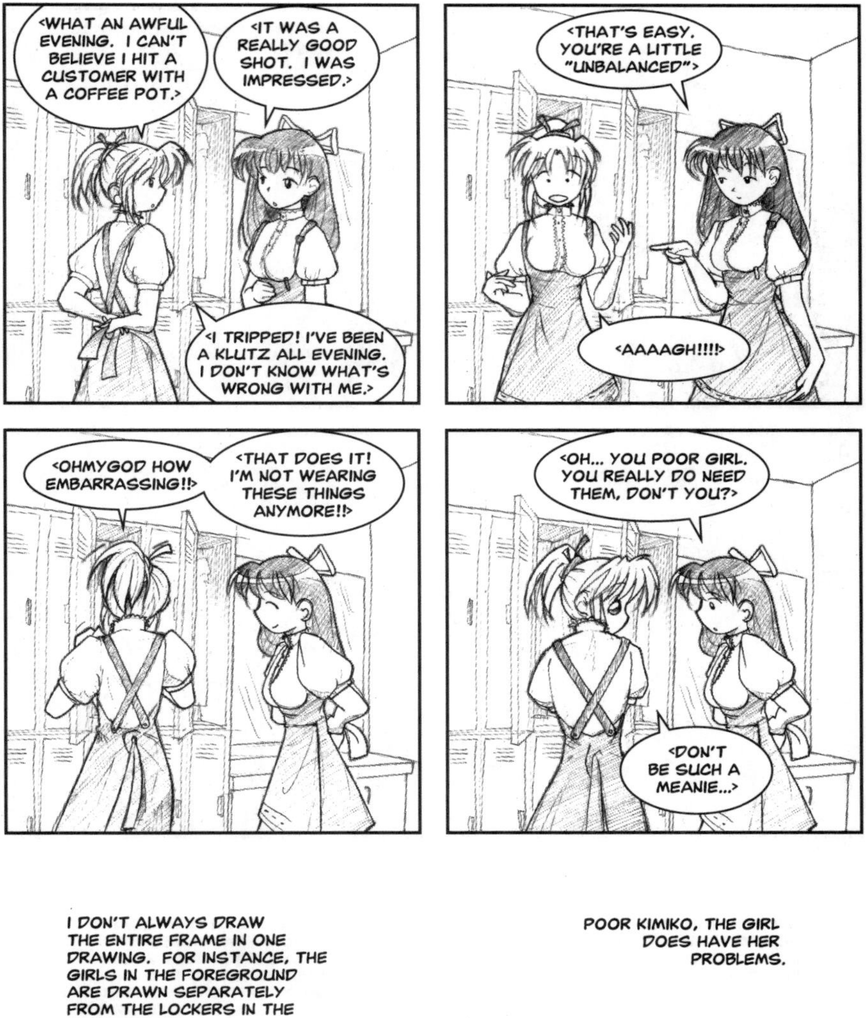
<WHAT AN AWFUL EVENING. I CAN'T BELIEVE I HIT A CUSTOMER WITH A COFFEE POT.>
<IT WAS A REALLY GOOD SHOT. I WAS IMPRESSED.>
<I TRIPPED! I'VE BEEN A KLUTZ ALL EVENING. I DON'T KNOW WHAT'S WRONG WITH ME.>
<THAT'S EASY. YOU'RE A LITTLE "UNBALANCED">
<AAAAGH!!!!>
<OHMYGOD HOW EMBARRASSING!!>
<THAT DOES IT! I'M NOT WEARING THESE THINGS ANYMORE!!>
<OH... YOU POOR GIRL. YOU REALLY DO NEED THEM, DON'T YOU?>
<DON'T BE SUCH A MEANIE...>

I DON'T ALWAYS DRAW THE ENTIRE FRAME IN ONE DRAWING. FOR INSTANCE, THE GIRLS IN THE FOREGROUND ARE DRAWN SEPARATELY FROM THE LOCKERS IN THE BACKGROUND.

POOR KIMIKO, THE GIRL DOES HAVE HER PROBLEMS.

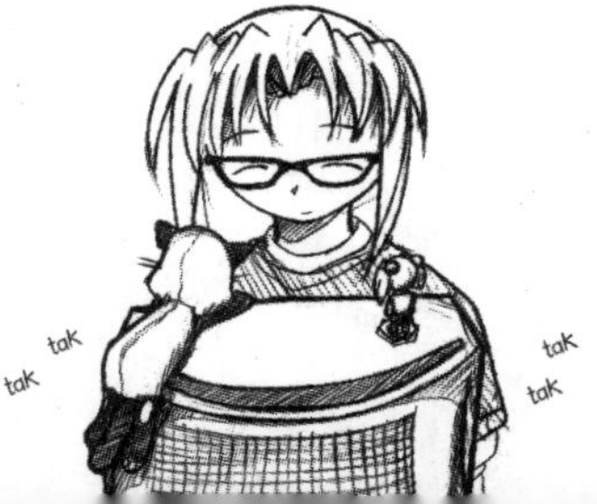
tak
tak
tak
tak

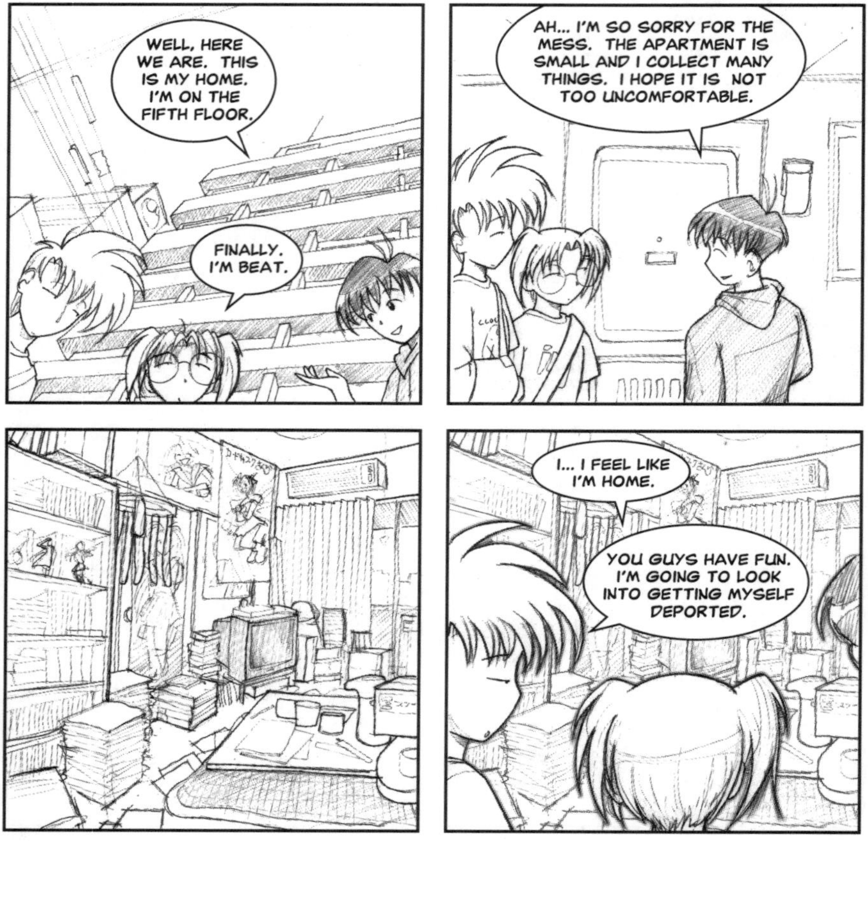
WELL, HERE WE ARE. THIS IS MY HOME. I'M ON THE FIFTH FLOOR.
FINALLY. I'M BEAT.
AH... I'M SO SORRY FOR THE MESS. THE APARTMENT IS SMALL AND I COLLECT MANY THINGS. I HOPE IT IS NOT TOO UNCOMFORTABLE.
I... I FEEL LIKE I'M HOME.
YOU GUYS HAVE FUN. I'M GOING TO LOOK INTO GETTING MYSELF DEPORTED.

SINCE I'M ACTUALLY AN ARCHITECT, NOT A COMIC ARTIST, DRAWING BUILDINGS AND STUFF COMES NATURALLY.

I LIKE TO USE DYNAMIC "CAMERA ANGLES" WHEN I CAN, ESPECIALLY WHEN IT HELPS CUT DOWN ON HOW MUCH OF THE CHARACTERS I HAVE TO DRAW.

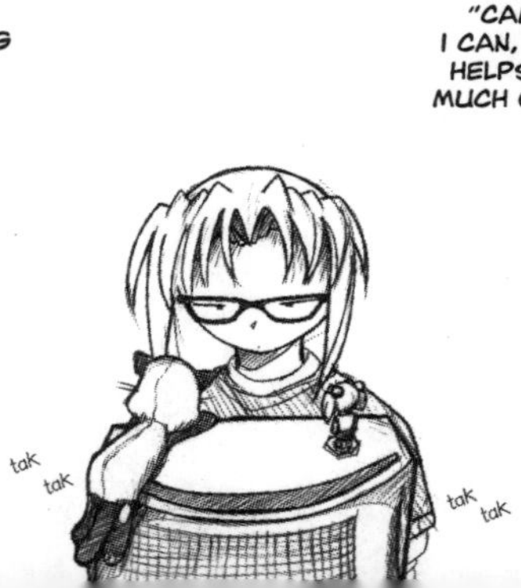
tak
tak
tak
tak

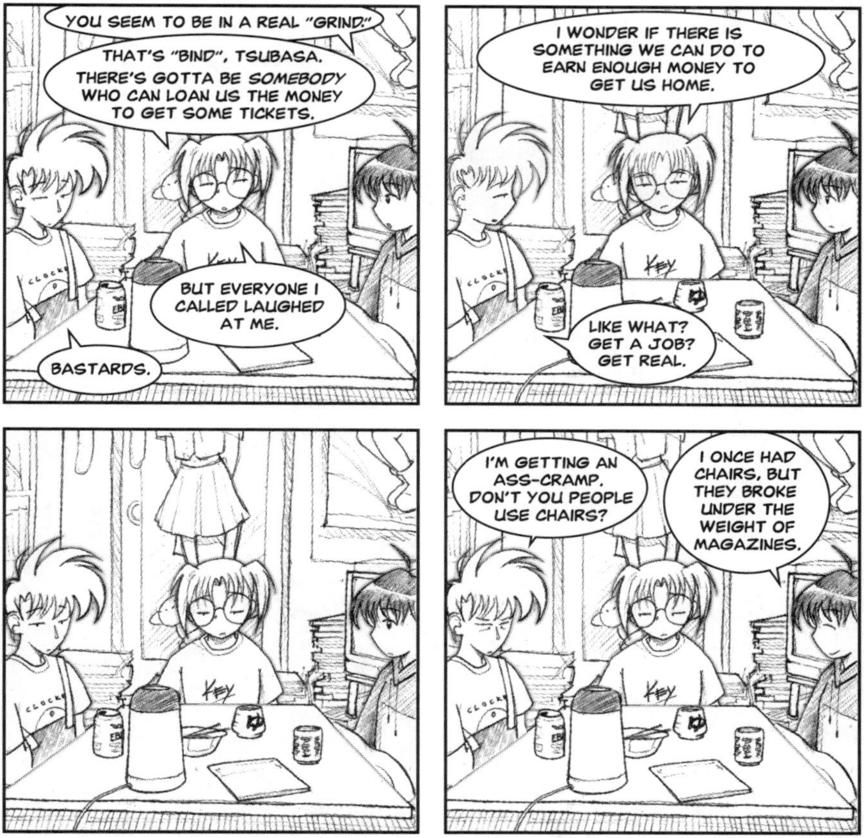
YOU SEEM TO BE IN A REAL "GRIND."
THAT'S "BIND", TSUBASA. THERE'S GOTTA BE SOMEBODY WHO CAN LOAN US THE MONEY TO GET SOME TICKETS.
BUT EVERYONE I CALLED LAUGHED AT ME.
BASTARDS.
I WONDER IF THERE IS SOMETHING WE CAN DO TO EARN ENOUGH MONEY TO GET US HOME.
LIKE WHAT? GET A JOB? GET REAL.
I'M GETTING AN ASS-CRAMP. DON'T YOU PEOPLE USE CHAIRS?
I ONCE HAD CHAIRS, BUT THEY BROKE UNDER THE WEIGHT OF MAGAZINES.

THE TABLE THEY ARE SITTING AT IS A "KOTATSU" - A FOLDING TABLE WITH A LITTLE ELECTRIC HEATER UNDER IT.

IF YOU AREN'T USED TO SITTING ON THE FLOOR LIKE THIS, IT REALLY DOES HURT AFTER AWHILE.

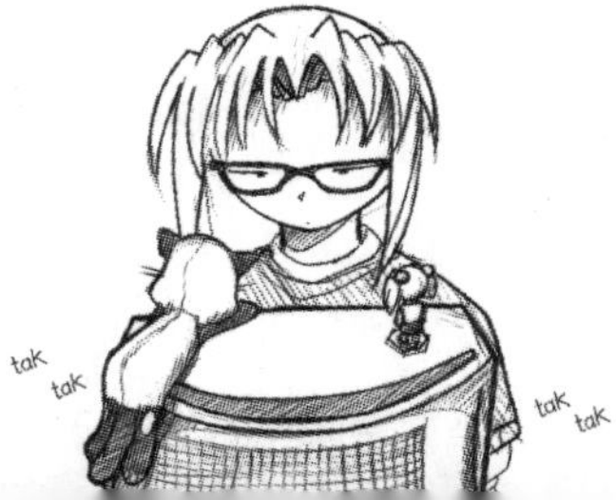
tak
tak
tak
tak

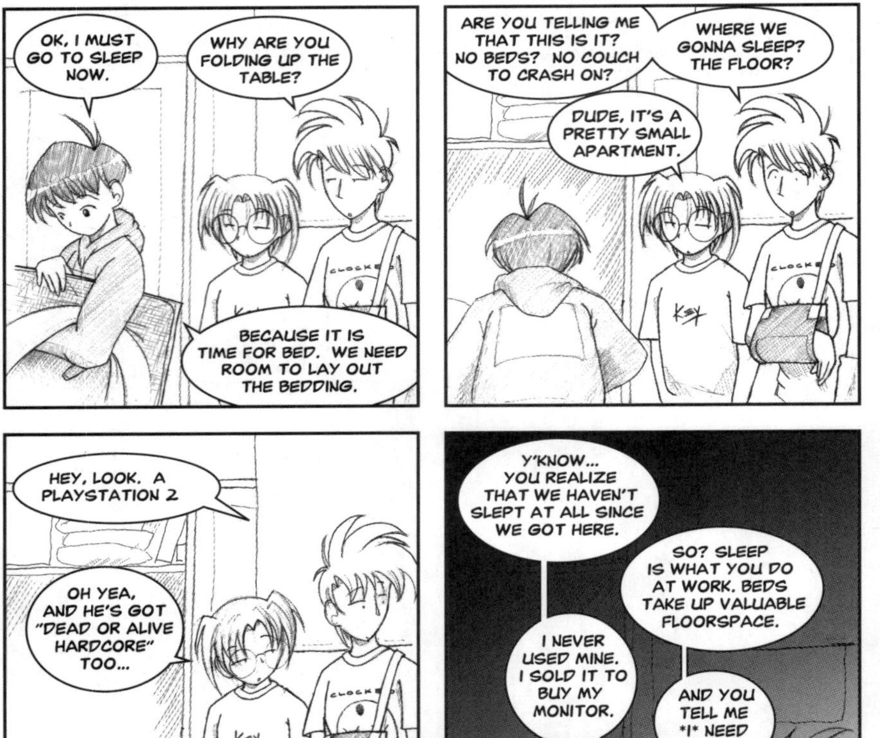
OK, I MUST GO TO SLEEP NOW.
WHY ARE YOU FOLDING UP THE TABLE?
BECAUSE IT IS TIME FOR BED. WE NEED ROOM TO LAY OUT THE BEDDING.
ARE YOU TELLING ME THAT THIS IS IT? NO BEDS? NO COUCH TO CRASH ON?
WHERE WE GONNA SLEEP? THE FLOOR?
DUDE, IT'S A PRETTY SMALL APARTMENT.
HEY, LOOK. A PLAYSTATION 2
OH YEA, AND HE'S GOT "DEAD OR ALIVE HARDCORE" TOO...
Y'KNOW... YOU REALIZE THAT WE HAVEN'T SLEPT AT ALL SINCE WE GOT HERE.
SO? SLEEP IS WHAT YOU DO AT WORK. BEDS TAKE UP VALUABLE FLOORSPACE.
I NEVER USED MINE. I SOLD IT TO BUY MY MONITOR.
AND YOU TELL ME *I* NEED HELP...

THIS IS THE FIRST COMIC WHERE I USED THE ORIGINAL SKETCHES AND DIDN'T TRACE OVER THEM. I WAS GETTING MUCH BETTER AT DRAWING THINGS WITH FEWER SCRIBBLES AND CONSTRUCTION LINES. I FIGURED THAT IF I COULD SKIP RE-TRACING, I COULD SPEND MORE TIME ON THE FRAMES THEMSELVES.

YOU ALWAYS LOSE SOMETHING WHEN YOU TRACE AN ORIGINAL SKETCH. BY ELIMINATING THIS STEP, IT GETS CLOSER TO THE DRAWING WHERE I FIRST PUT PENCIL TO PAPER.

I THINK THAT THIS EVENTUALLY LED TO BETTER LOOKING AND MORE EXPRESSIVE COMICS.

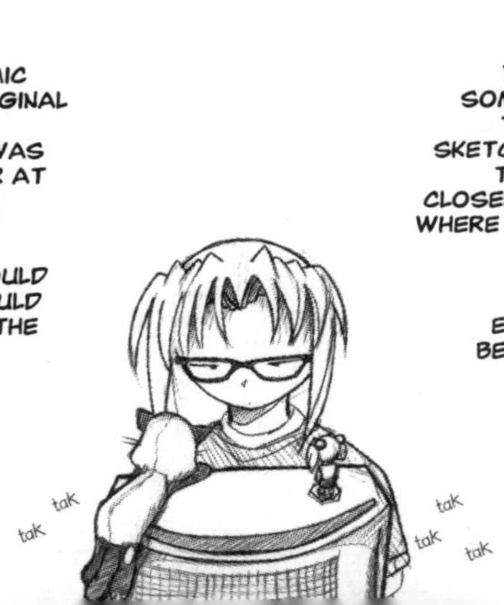
tak
tak
tak
tak
tak

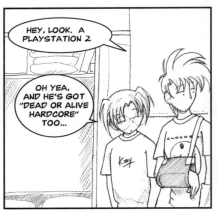

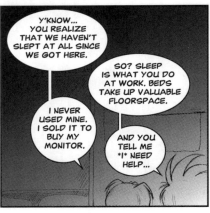

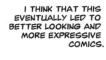

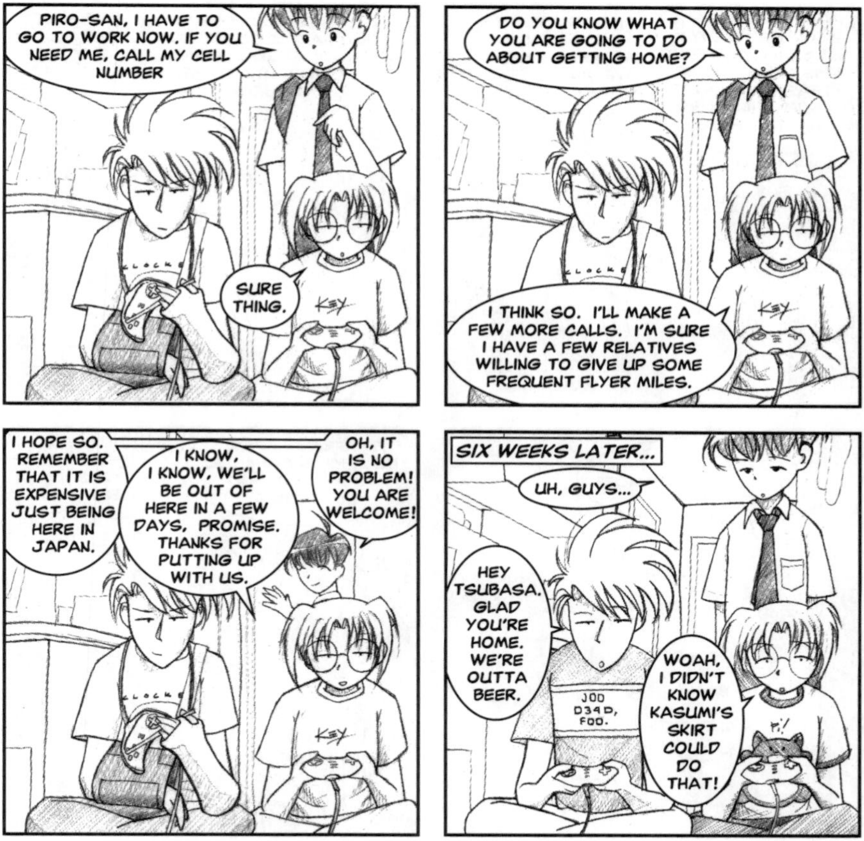
PIRO-SAN, I HAVE TO GO TO WORK NOW. IF YOU NEED ME, CALL MY CELL NUMBER
SURE THING.
DO YOU KNOW WHAT YOU ARE GOING TO DO ABOUT GETTING HOME?
I THINK SO. I'LL MAKE A FEW MORE CALLS. I'M SURE I HAVE A FEW RELATIVES WILLING TO GIVE UP SOME FREQUENT FLYER MILES.
I HOPE SO. REMEMBER THAT IT IS EXPENSIVE JUST BEING HERE IN JAPAN.
I KNOW, I KNOW, WE'LL BE OUT OF HERE IN A FEW DAYS, PROMISE. THANKS FOR PUTTING UP WITH US.
OH, IT IS NO PROBLEM! YOU ARE WELCOME!
SIX WEEKS LATER...
UH, GUYS...
HEY TSUBASA. GLAD YOU'RE HOME. WE'RE OUTTA BEER.
JOD D34D, FOO.
WOAH, I DIDN'T KNOW KASUMI'S SKIRT COULD DO THAT!

SERAPHIM, WHO HAS A MEDICAL BACKGROUND, TOLD ME THAT IT WOULD TAKE ABOUT SIX WEEKS FOR LARGO'S BROKEN ARM TO HEAL.

THAT SOUNDED LIKE A GOOD STRETCH OF TIME BEFORE TSUBASA'S PATIENCE WORE OUT. TSUBASA IS VERY PATIENT.

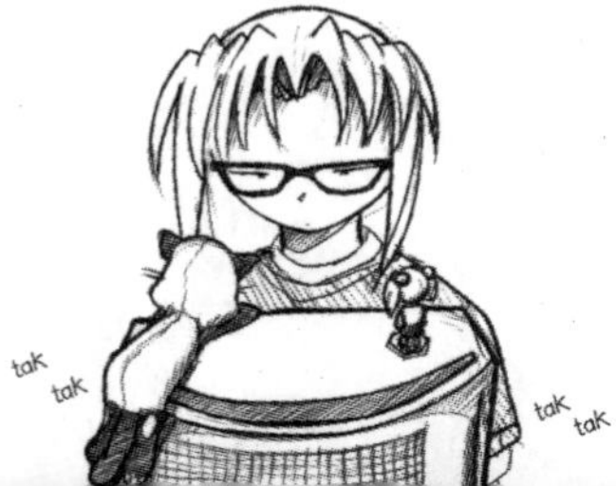
tak
tak
tak
tak

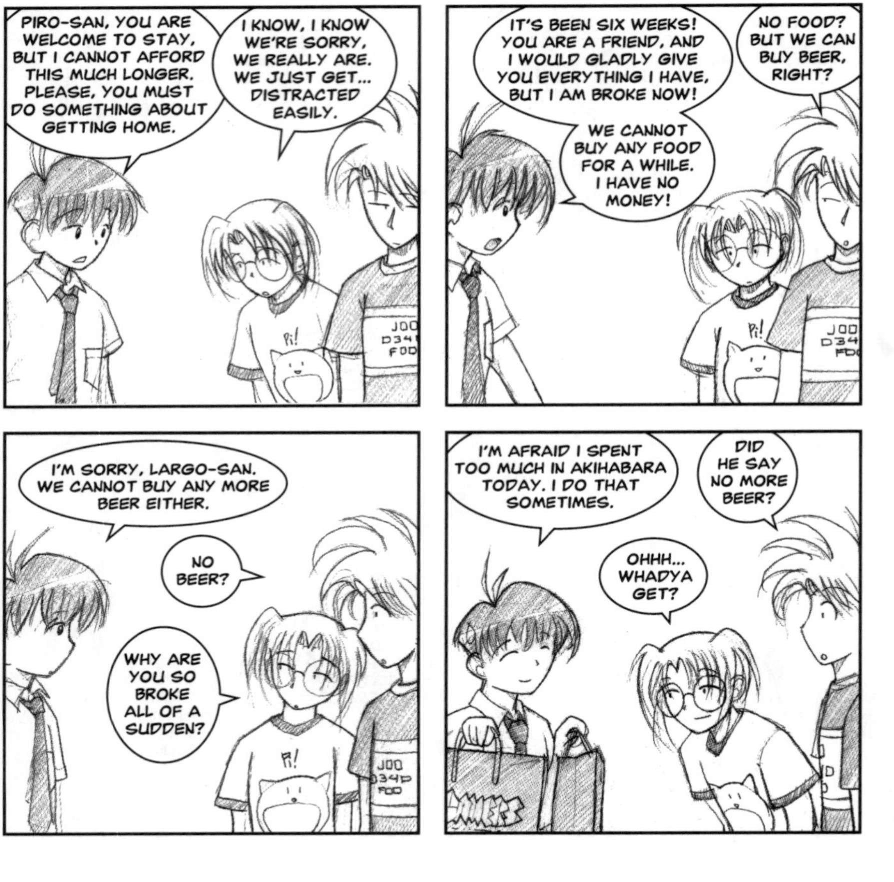
PIRO-SAN, YOU ARE WELCOME TO STAY, BUT I CANNOT AFFORD THIS MUCH LONGER. PLEASE, YOU MUST DO SOMETHING ABOUT GETTING HOME.
I KNOW, I KNOW WE'RE SORRY, WE REALLY ARE. WE JUST GET... DISTRACTED EASILY.
JOO D34D FOO
IT'S BEEN SIX WEEKS! YOU ARE A FRIEND, AND I WOULD GLADLY GIVE YOU EVERYTHING I HAVE, BUT I AM BROKE NOW!
NO FOOD? BUT WE CAN BUY BEER, RIGHT?
WE CANNOT BUY ANY FOOD FOR A WHILE. I HAVE NO MONEY!
I'M SORRY, LARGO-SAN. WE CANNOT BUY ANY MORE BEER EITHER.
NO BEER?
WHY ARE YOU SO BROKE ALL OF A SUDDEN?
JOO D34D FOO
I'M AFRAID I SPENT TOO MUCH IN AKIHABARA TODAY. I DO THAT SOMETIMES.
DID HE SAY NO MORE BEER?
OHHH... WHADYA GET?

SOMETIMES FRIENDS CAN'T TAKE SUBTLE HINTS, OR EVEN DIRECT ONES.

I HAVE HEARD STORIES FROM JAPANESE FRIENDS WHO REFER TO SOME OF THEIR AMERICAN VISITORS AS BEING "AS BAD AS PIRO AND LARGO."

YOU HAVE NO IDEA HOW BAD I FEEL FOR THEM.

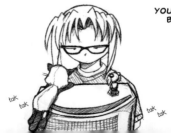

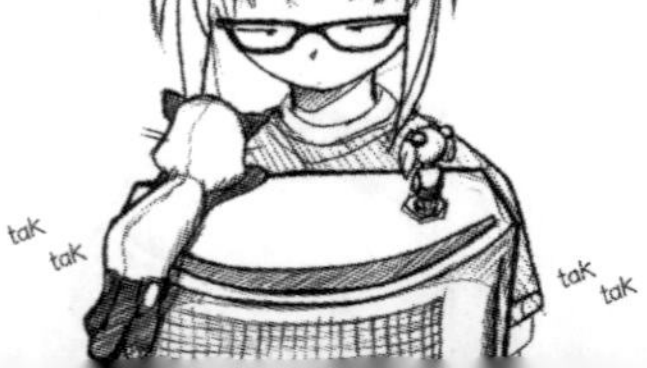
tak
tak
tak
tak

NOVEMBER 11, 2000 - IN LOVING MEMORY OF 'BULLITO' 1993-2000

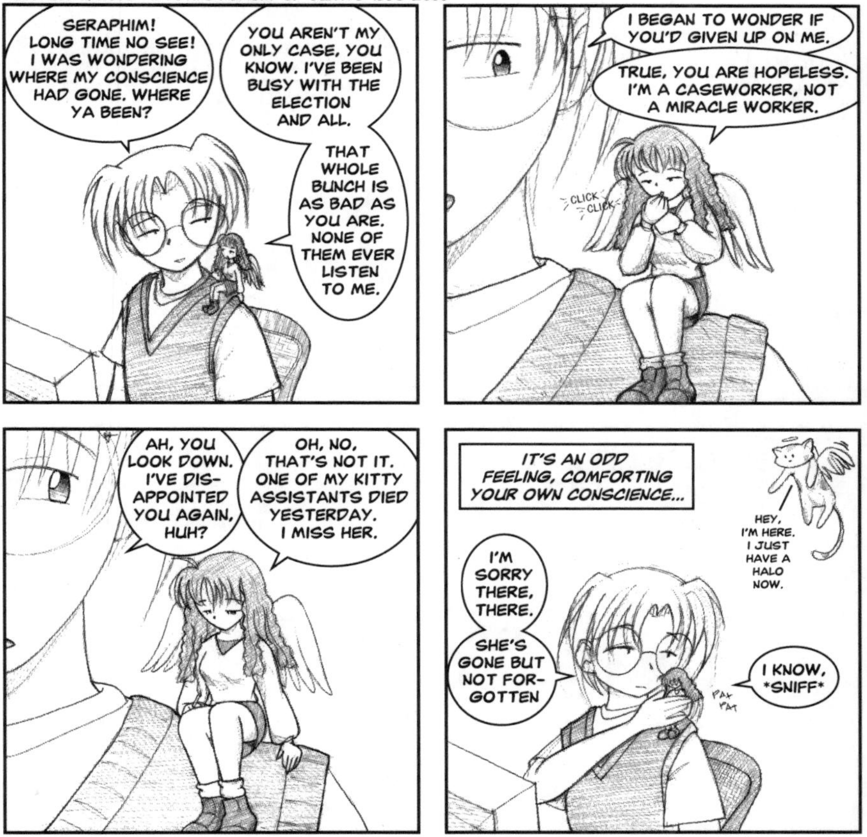
SERAPHIM! LONG TIME NO SEE! I WAS WONDERING WHERE MY CONSCIENCE HAD GONE. WHERE YA BEEN?
YOU AREN'T MY ONLY CASE, YOU KNOW. I'VE BEEN BUSY WITH THE ELECTION AND ALL.
THAT WHOLE BUNCH IS AS BAD AS YOU ARE. NONE OF THEM EVER LISTEN TO ME.
I BEGAN TO WONDER IF YOU'D GIVEN UP ON ME.
TRUE, YOU ARE HOPELESS. I'M A CASEWORKER, NOT A MIRACLE WORKER.
CLICK CLICK
AH, YOU LOOK DOWN. I'VE DIS-APPOINTED YOU AGAIN, HUH?
OH, NO, THAT'S NOT IT. ONE OF MY KITTY ASSISTANTS DIED YESTERDAY. I MISS HER.
IT'S AN ODD FEELING, COMFORTING YOUR OWN CONSCIENCE...
HEY, I'M HERE. I JUST HAVE A HALO NOW.
I'M SORRY THERE, THERE.
SHE'S GONE BUT NOT FOR-GOTTEN
PAT PAT
I KNOW, *SNIFF*

IT WAS SERAPHIM'S IDEA THAT SHE WOULD MAKE A GOOD CONSCIENCE FOR PIRO IN THE COMIC. SHE'S A TOUGH TALKING LITTLE ANGEL THAT TRIES TO KEEP PIRO STRAIGHT, BUT HAS AS MUCH LUCK AS THE REAL SERAPHIM HAS WITH ME.

SERAPHIM IS MY GIRLFRIEND (ACTUALLY, MY WIFE NOW) IN REAL LIFE IN CASE YOU DIDN'T GUESS.

THIS WAS A RATHER SAD COMIC BECAUSE ONE OF SERAPHIM'S CATS, BULLITO, HAD DIED THE PREVIOUS DAY. I WANTED TO HAVE SOME SORT OF MEMORIAL FOR HER, SO THIS IS WHAT I DID.

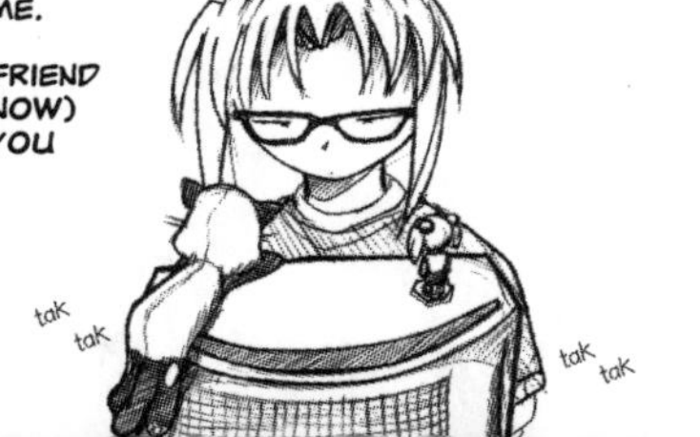
tak tak
tak tak

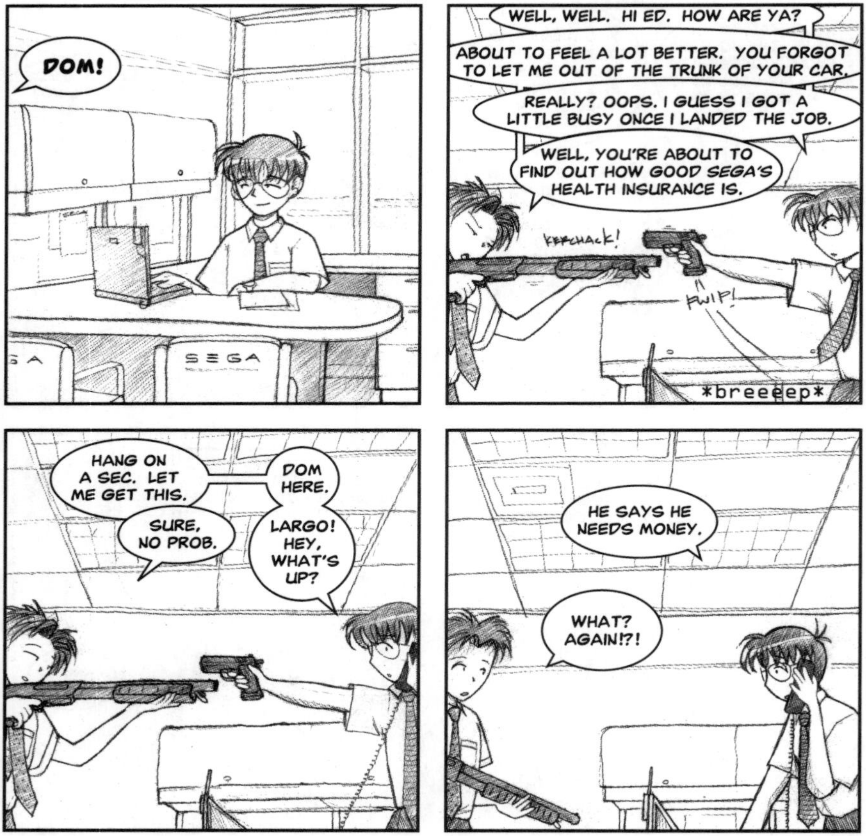
DOM!
WELL, WELL. HI ED. HOW ARE YA?
ABOUT TO FEEL A LOT BETTER. YOU FORGOT TO LET ME OUT OF THE TRUNK OF YOUR CAR.
REALLY? OOPS. I GUESS I GOT A LITTLE BUSY ONCE I LANDED THE JOB.
WELL, YOU'RE ABOUT TO FIND OUT HOW GOOD SEGA'S HEALTH INSURANCE IS.
KERCHACK!
FWIP!
breeeep
HANG ON A SEC. LET ME GET THIS.
DOM HERE.
SURE, NO PROB.
LARGO! HEY, WHAT'S UP?
HE SAYS HE NEEDS MONEY.
WHAT? AGAIN!?!

AH, RANDOM SENSELESS VIOLENCE.

SINCE SO MUCH VIOLENCE ON TV AND IN THE MOVIES IS SENSELESS, DOESN'T IT MAKE SENSE THAT DOM AND ED CAN PRACTICE VIOLENCE THAT MAKES NO SENSE?

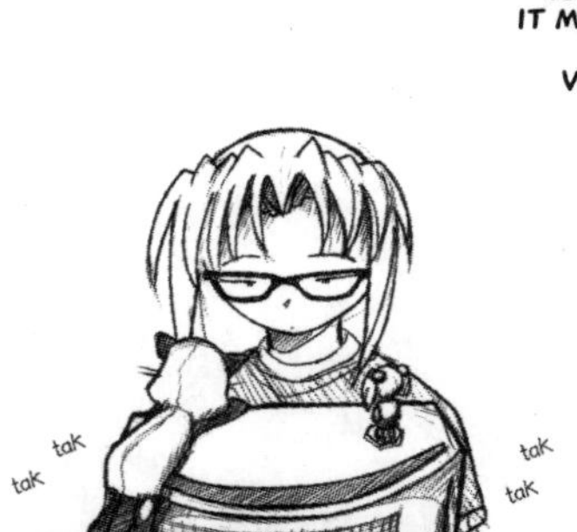
tak
tak
tak
tak

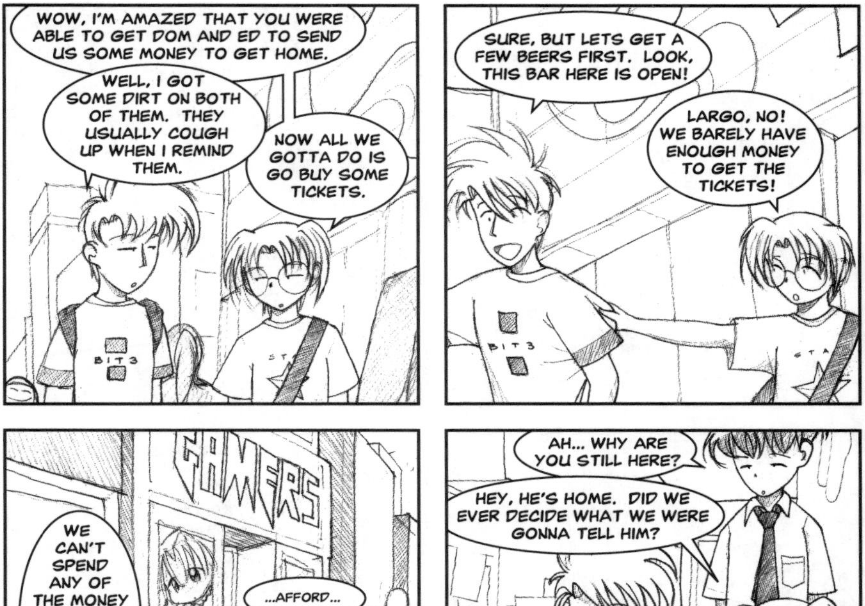
WOW, I'M AMAZED THAT YOU WERE ABLE TO GET DOM AND ED TO SEND US SOME MONEY TO GET HOME.
WELL, I GOT SOME DIRT ON BOTH OF THEM. THEY USUALLY COUGH UP WHEN I REMIND THEM.
NOW ALL WE GOTTA DO IS GO BUY SOME TICKETS.
SURE, BUT LETS GET A FEW BEERS FIRST. LOOK, THIS BAR HERE IS OPEN!
LARGO, NO! WE BARELY HAVE ENOUGH MONEY TO GET THE TICKETS!
GAMERS
WE CAN'T SPEND ANY OF THE MONEY ED AND DOM SENT US, OR WE WON'T BE ABLE TO...
...AFFORD...
...TICKETS...
AH... WHY ARE YOU STILL HERE?
HEY, HE'S HOME. DID WE EVER DECIDE WHAT WE WERE GONNA TELL HIM?
AWW, JUST GET HIM A FEW BEERS AND SHOW HIM SOME OF THE CRAP YOU GOT IN THAT GAME STORE. HE'LL BE FINE.
TRUE.

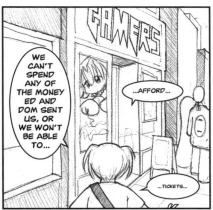

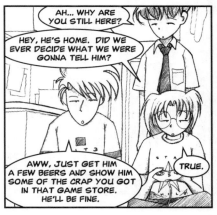

I SOMETIMES WONDER WHAT IT IS THAT LARGO HAS ON DOM AND ED THAT CAN MAKE THEM PONY UP CASH LIKE THAT.

WAIT, THOSE TWO PHOTOGRAPHS... OK, NEVER MIND.

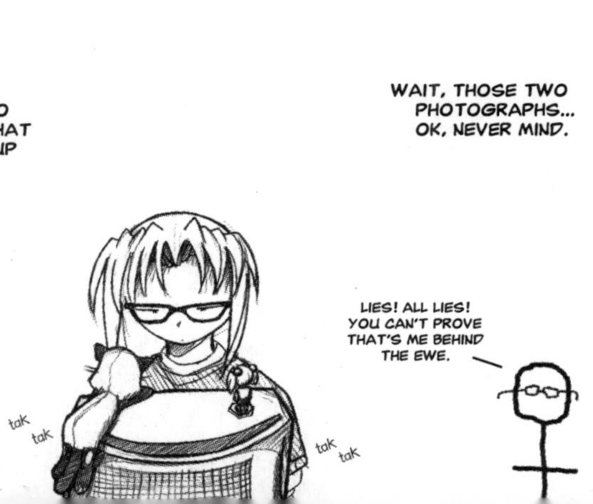
LIES! ALL LIES! YOU CAN'T PROVE THAT'S ME BEHIND THE EWE.
tak tak
tak tak

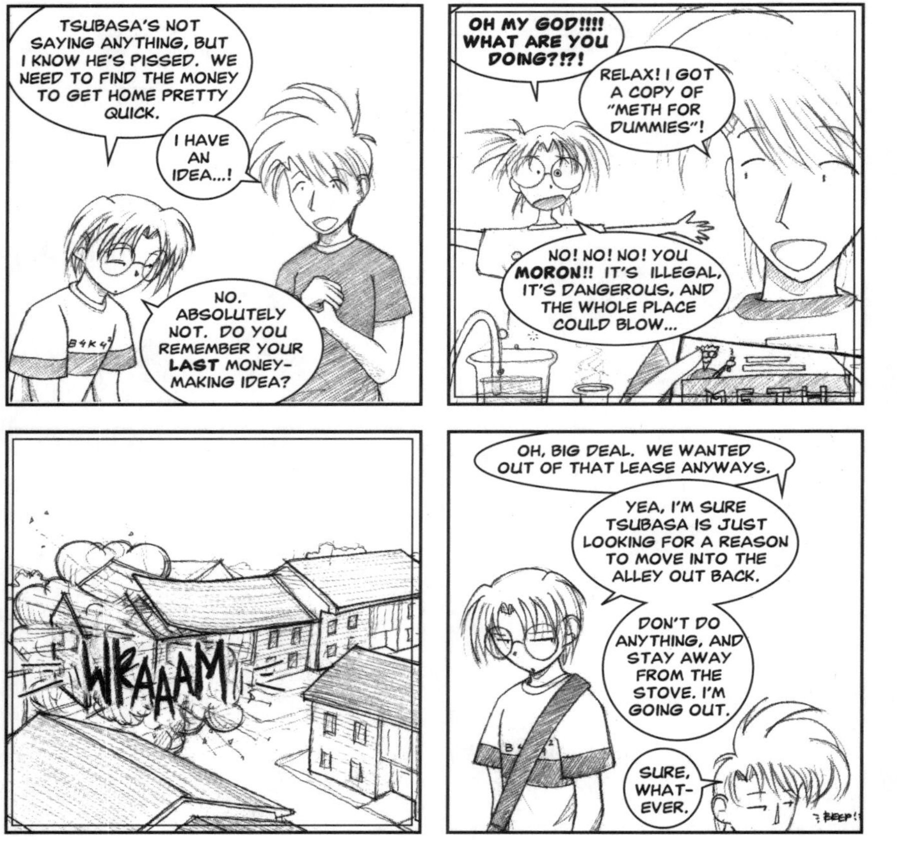
TSUBASA'S NOT SAYING ANYTHING, BUT I KNOW HE'S PISSED. WE NEED TO FIND THE MONEY TO GET HOME PRETTY QUICK.
I HAVE AN IDEA...!
NO. ABSOLUTELY NOT. DO YOU REMEMBER YOUR LAST MONEY-MAKING IDEA?
OH MY GOD!!!! WHAT ARE YOU DOING?!?!
RELAX! I GOT A COPY OF "METH FOR DUMMIES"!
NO! NO! NO! YOU MORON!! IT'S ILLEGAL, IT'S DANGEROUS, AND THE WHOLE PLACE COULD BLOW...
WRAAAM
OH, BIG DEAL. WE WANTED OUT OF THAT LEASE ANYWAYS.
YEA, I'M SURE TSUBASA IS JUST LOOKING FOR A REASON TO MOVE INTO THE ALLEY OUT BACK.
DON'T DO ANYTHING, AND STAY AWAY FROM THE STOVE. I'M GOING OUT.
SURE, WHAT-EVER.
BEEP!

I RESISTED DOING THIS COMIC BECAUSE I DIDN'T WANT TO CONDONE DRUG USE OF ANY SORT. I DON'T CONSIDER IT A LAUGHING MATTER.

IT DOES, HOWEVER, MAKE SOCIAL COMMENTARY ON VARIOUS LEVELS, SO I WENT WITH IT.

NOTE THAT THIS IS THE FIRST TIME THAT PIRO AND LARGO SEPARATE - PIRO GOES OUT AND LEAVES LARGO BEHIND.

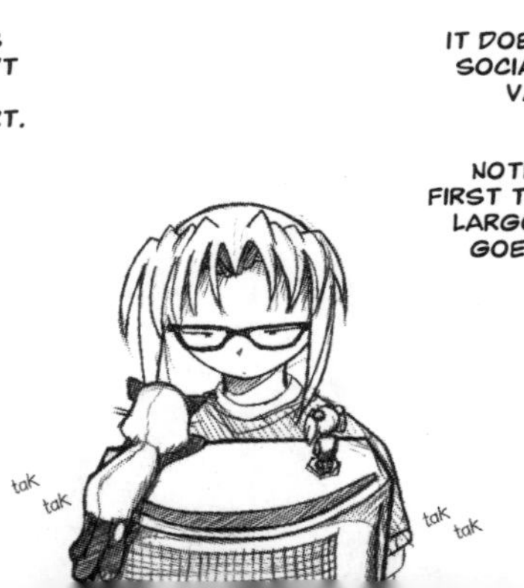
tak
tak
tak
tak

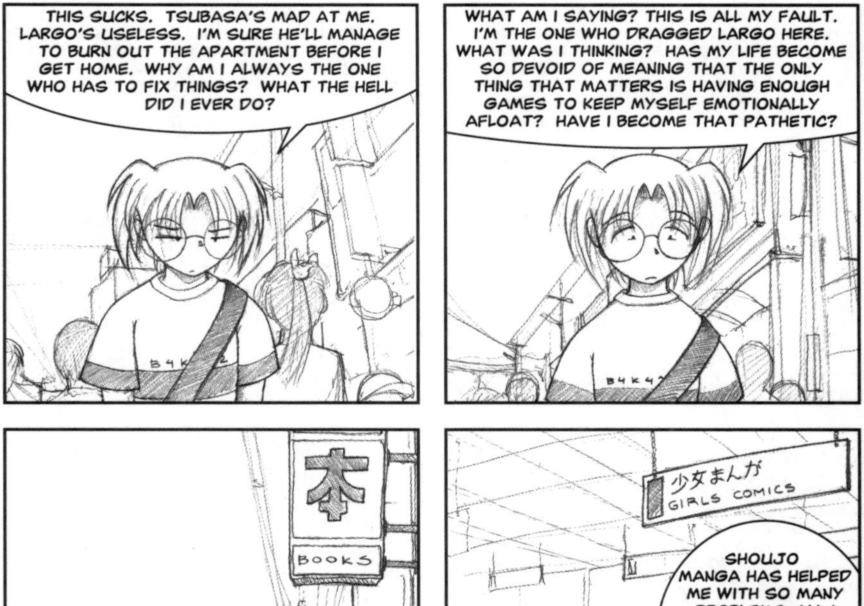
THIS SUCKS. TSUBASA'S MAD AT ME. LARGO'S USELESS. I'M SURE HE'LL MANAGE TO BURN OUT THE APARTMENT BEFORE I GET HOME. WHY AM I ALWAYS THE ONE WHO HAS TO FIX THINGS? WHAT THE HELL DID I EVER DO?
B4K42
WHAT AM I SAYING? THIS IS ALL MY FAULT. I'M THE ONE WHO DRAGGED LARGO HERE. WHAT WAS I THINKING? HAS MY LIFE BECOME SO DEVOID OF MEANING THAT THE ONLY THING THAT MATTERS IS HAVING ENOUGH GAMES TO KEEP MYSELF EMOTIONALLY AFLOAT? HAVE I BECOME THAT PATHETIC?
B4K42
本
BOOKS
少女まんが
GIRLS COMICS
SHOUJO MANGA HAS HELPED ME WITH SO MANY PROBLEMS. ALL I NEED TO DO IS READ UNTIL I FIND A SIMILAR SITUATION AND IT WILL TELL ME EVERYTHING I NEED TO KNOW.

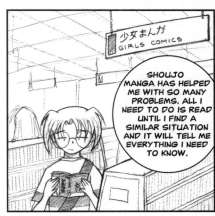

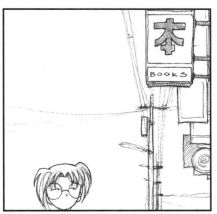

SHOUJO MANGA, OR "GIRLS COMICS," TEND TO HAVE LESS VIOLENCE AND DEEPER STORYLINES THAN SHOUNEN MANGA OR "BOYS COMICS."

IT'S NOT UNSUAL FOR GUYS TO READ SHOUJO MANGA. BUT MOST WOULDN'T BE CAUGHT DEAD BROWSING THE SHOUJO MANGA SECTION OF THE LOCAL BOOKSTORE.

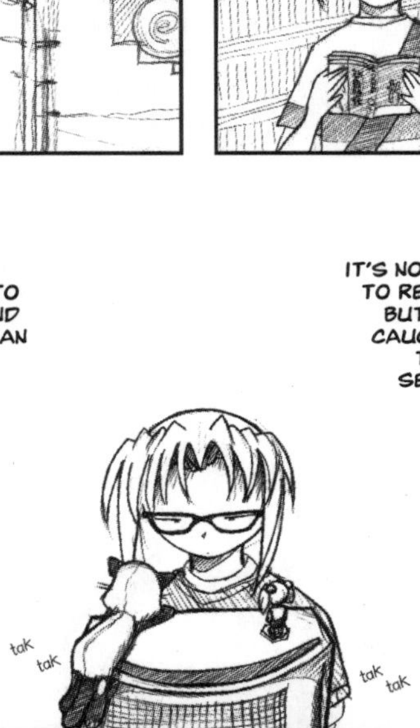
tak
tak
tak
tak

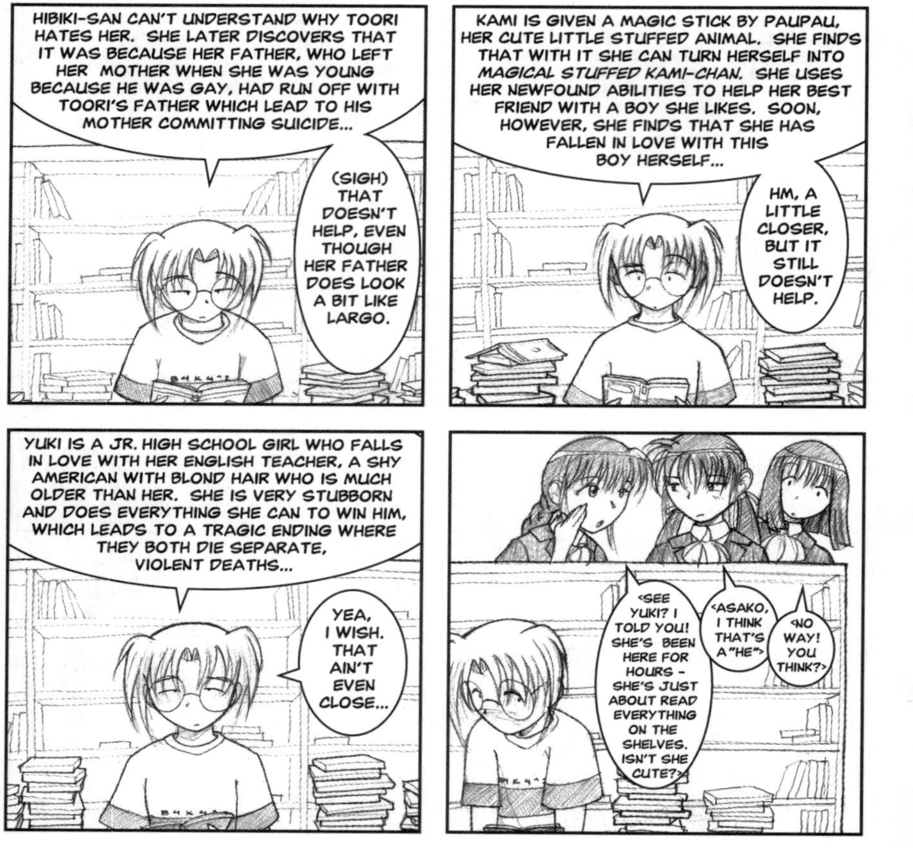
HIBIKI-SAN CAN'T UNDERSTAND WHY TOORI HATES HER. SHE LATER DISCOVERS THAT IT WAS BECAUSE HER FATHER, WHO LEFT HER MOTHER WHEN SHE WAS YOUNG BECAUSE HE WAS GAY, HAD RUN OFF WITH TOORI'S FATHER WHICH LEAD TO HIS MOTHER COMMITTING SUICIDE...
(SIGH) THAT DOESN'T HELP, EVEN THOUGH HER FATHER DOES LOOK A BIT LIKE LARGO.
KAMI IS GIVEN A MAGIC STICK BY PAUPAU, HER CUTE LITTLE STUFFED ANIMAL. SHE FINDS THAT WITH IT SHE CAN TURN HERSELF INTO *MAGICAL STUFFED KAMI-CHAN*. SHE USES HER NEWFOUND ABILITIES TO HELP HER BEST FRIEND WITH A BOY SHE LIKES. SOON, HOWEVER, SHE FINDS THAT SHE HAS FALLEN IN LOVE WITH THIS BOY HERSELF...
HM, A LITTLE CLOSER, BUT IT STILL DOESN'T HELP.
YUKI IS A JR. HIGH SCHOOL GIRL WHO FALLS IN LOVE WITH HER ENGLISH TEACHER, A SHY AMERICAN WITH BLOND HAIR WHO IS MUCH OLDER THAN HER. SHE IS VERY STUBBORN AND DOES EVERYTHING SHE CAN TO WIN HIM, WHICH LEADS TO A TRAGIC ENDING WHERE THEY BOTH DIE SEPARATE, VIOLENT DEATHS...
YEA, I WISH. THAT AIN'T EVEN CLOSE...
<SEE YUKI? I TOLD YOU! SHE'S BEEN HERE FOR HOURS - SHE'S JUST ABOUT READ EVERYTHING ON THE SHELVES. ISN'T SHE CUTE?>
<ASAKO, I THINK THAT'S A "HE">
<NO WAY! YOU THINK?>

WHAT'S SCARY ABOUT THIS COMIC IS THAT THESE SCENARIOS ARE NOT VERY OUTSIDE OF WHAT YOU REALLY FIND IN SOME SHOUJO MANGA STORIES.

FOR THE RECORD, PIRO IS A GUY. HE ALWAYS HAS BEEN, ALWAYS WILL BE. SHEESH

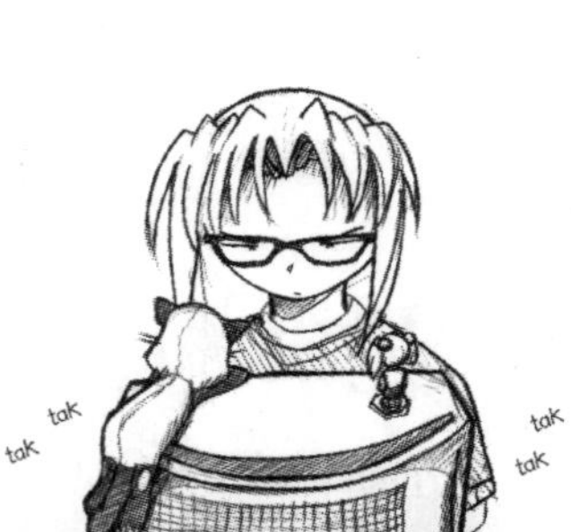
tak
tak
tak
tak

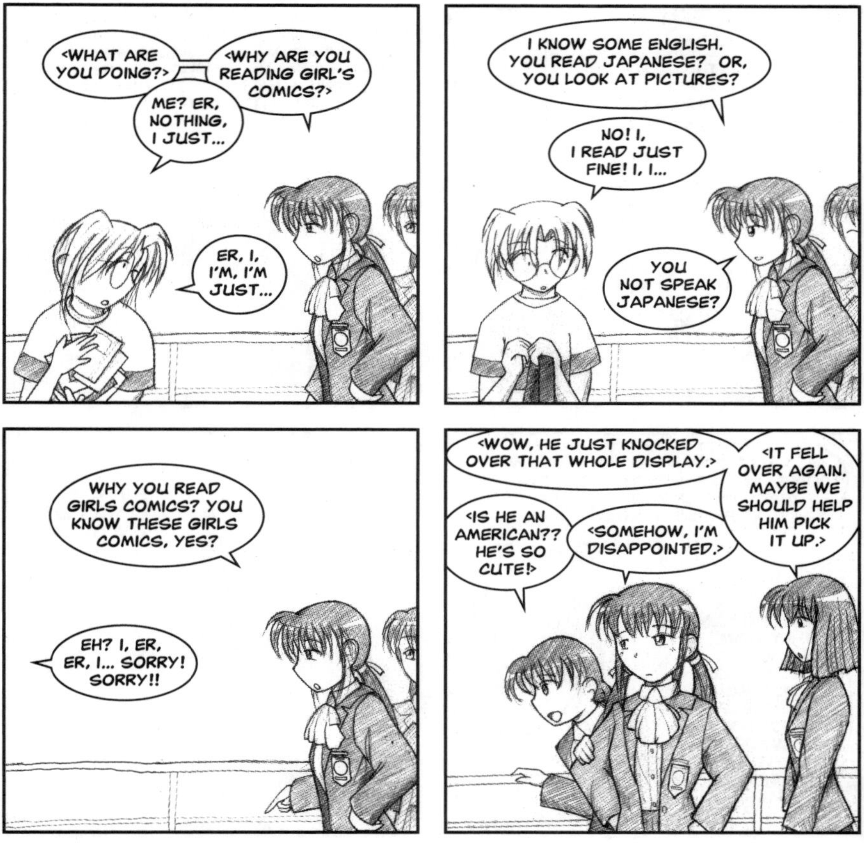
<WHAT ARE YOU DOING?>
<WHY ARE YOU READING GIRL'S COMICS?>
ME? ER, NOTHING, I JUST...
ER, I, I'M, I'M JUST...
I KNOW SOME ENGLISH. YOU READ JAPANESE? OR, YOU LOOK AT PICTURES?
NO! I, I READ JUST FINE! I, I...
YOU NOT SPEAK JAPANESE?
WHY YOU READ GIRLS COMICS? YOU KNOW THESE GIRLS COMICS, YES?
EH? I, ER, ER, I... SORRY! SORRY!!
<WOW, HE JUST KNOCKED OVER THAT WHOLE DISPLAY.>
<IT FELL OVER AGAIN. MAYBE WE SHOULD HELP HIM PICK IT UP.>
<IS HE AN AMERICAN?? HE'S SO CUTE!>
<SOMEHOW, I'M DISAPPOINTED.>

YUKI IS A FUN CHARACTER. I WANTED HER TO BE A 'JAPANESE SCHOOL GIRL' THAT WAS CLOSER TO BEING A REAL JAPANESE SCHOOL GIRL THAN THE SORT OF FANCIFUL CHARACTERS YOU SEE IN MOST ANIME AND GAMES.

WHEN I WAS IN JAPAN, I ACTUALLY DID KNOCK OVER A DISPLAY IN THE SHOUJO MANGA SECTION OF A BOOKSTORE WITH MY BOOK BAG. NO ONE HELPED ME PICK IT UP, THOUGH.

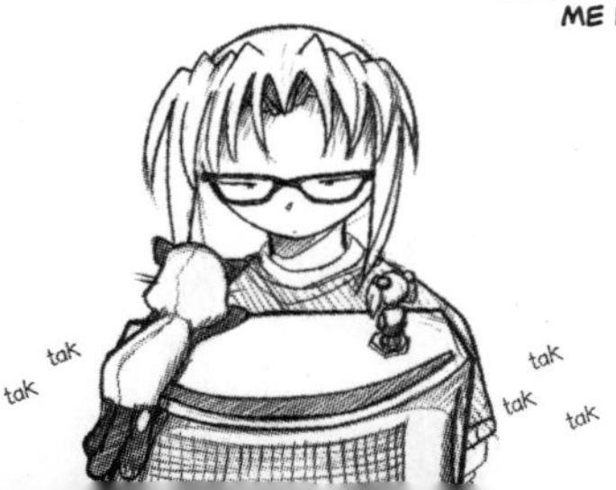
tak
tak
tak
tak
tak

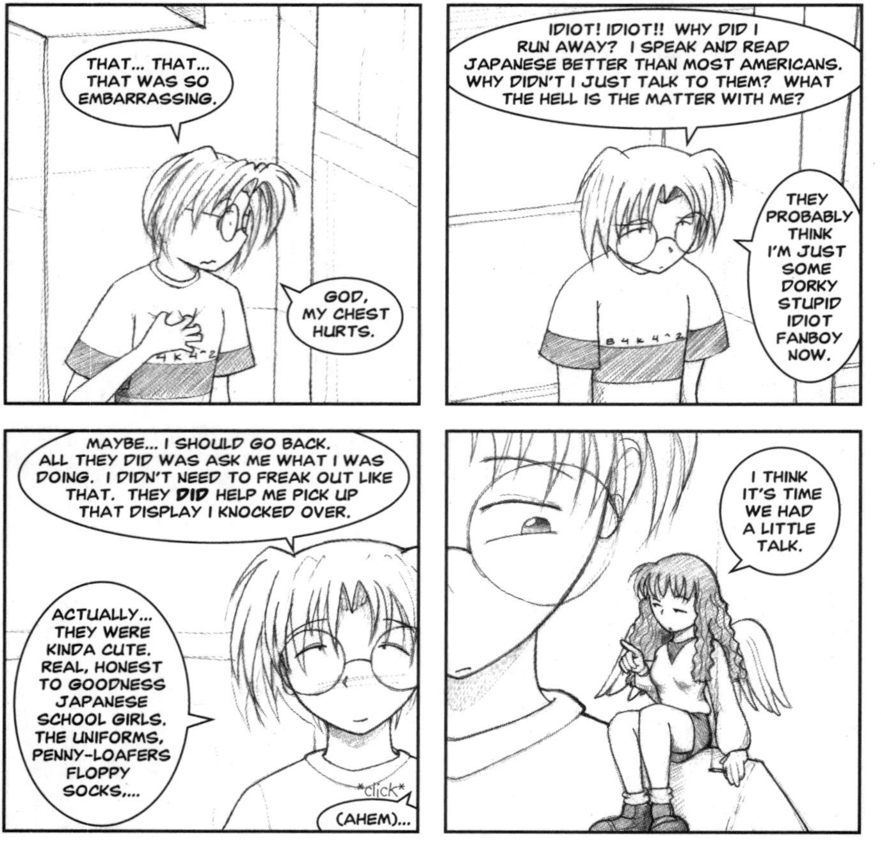
THAT... THAT... THAT WAS SO EMBARRASSING.
GOD, MY CHEST HURTS.
IDIOT! IDIOT!! WHY DID I RUN AWAY? I SPEAK AND READ JAPANESE BETTER THAN MOST AMERICANS. WHY DIDN'T I JUST TALK TO THEM? WHAT THE HELL IS THE MATTER WITH ME?
THEY PROBABLY THINK I'M JUST SOME DORKY STUPID IDIOT FANBOY NOW.
MAYBE... I SHOULD GO BACK. ALL THEY DID WAS ASK ME WHAT I WAS DOING. I DIDN'T NEED TO FREAK OUT LIKE THAT. THEY DID HELP ME PICK UP THAT DISPLAY I KNOCKED OVER.
ACTUALLY... THEY WERE KINDA CUTE. REAL, HONEST TO GOODNESS JAPANESE SCHOOL GIRLS. THE UNIFORMS, PENNY-LOAFERS FLOPPY SOCKS,...
click
(AHEM)...
I THINK IT'S TIME WE HAD A LITTLE TALK.

LARGO IS THE KIND OF PERSON WHO WILL FALL DOWN A FLIGHT OF STAIRS, RUN BACK UP AND FALL RIGHT DOWN AGAIN.

PIRO SITS AT THE BOTTOM OF THE STAIRS AND WONDERS IF THEY ARE SAFE TO CLIMB OR NOT.

HE'S A LOT LIKE ME, HE THINKS TOO MUCH.

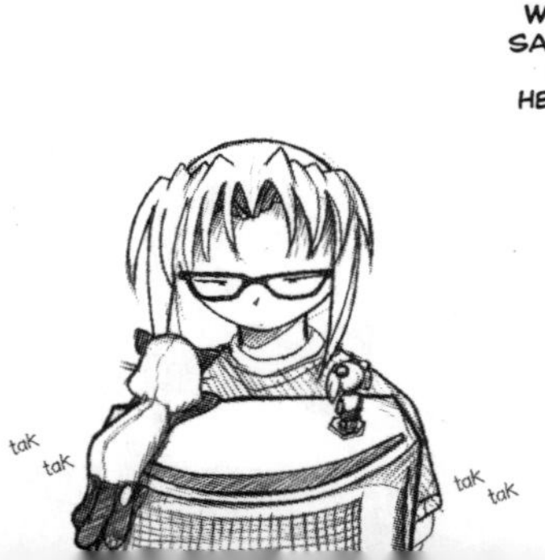
tak
tak
tak
tak

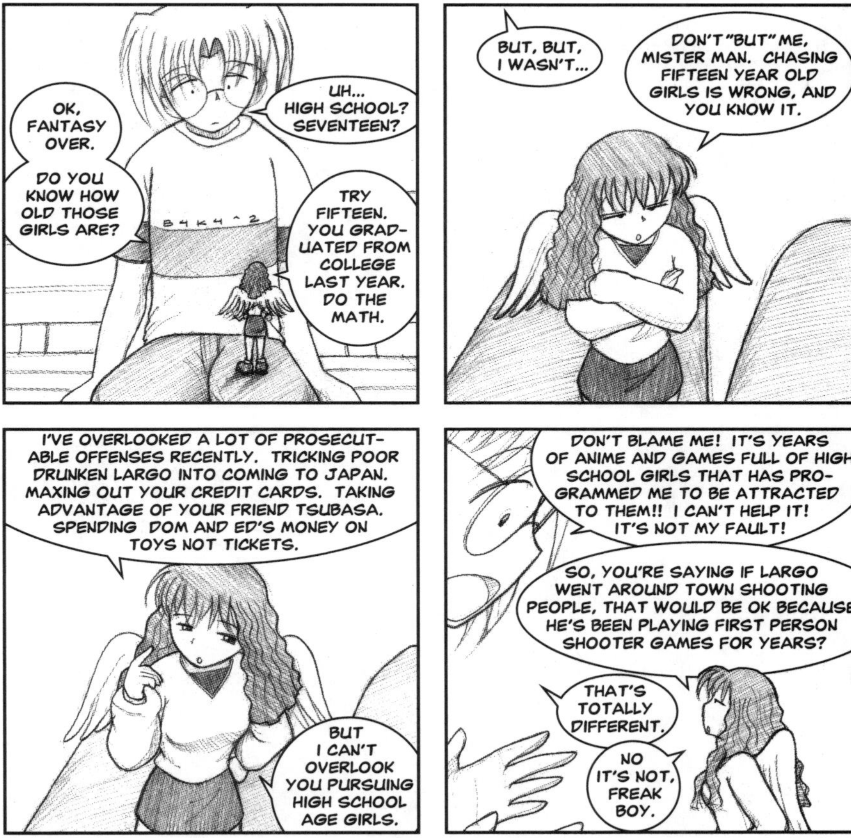
OK, FANTASY OVER.
DO YOU KNOW HOW OLD THOSE GIRLS ARE?
UH... HIGH SCHOOL? SEVENTEEN?
B4K4^2
TRY FIFTEEN. YOU GRADUATED FROM COLLEGE LAST YEAR. DO THE MATH.
BUT, BUT, I WASN'T...
DON'T "BUT" ME, MISTER MAN. CHASING FIFTEEN YEAR OLD GIRLS IS WRONG, AND YOU KNOW IT.
I'VE OVERLOOKED A LOT OF PROSECUTABLE OFFENSES RECENTLY. TRICKING POOR DRUNKEN LARGO INTO COMING TO JAPAN. MAXING OUT YOUR CREDIT CARDS. TAKING ADVANTAGE OF YOUR FRIEND TSUBASA. SPENDING DOM AND ED'S MONEY ON TOYS NOT TICKETS.
BUT I CAN'T OVERLOOK YOU PURSUING HIGH SCHOOL AGE GIRLS.
DON'T BLAME ME! IT'S YEARS OF ANIME AND GAMES FULL OF HIGH SCHOOL GIRLS THAT HAS PROGRAMMED ME TO BE ATTRACTED TO THEM!! I CAN'T HELP IT! IT'S NOT MY FAULT!
SO, YOU'RE SAYING IF LARGO WENT AROUND TOWN SHOOTING PEOPLE, THAT WOULD BE OK BECAUSE HE'S BEEN PLAYING FIRST PERSON SHOOTER GAMES FOR YEARS?
THAT'S TOTALLY DIFFERENT.
NO IT'S NOT, FREAK BOY.

THE ARGUEMENT THAT VIOLENT VIDEO GAMES LEAD TO VIOLENT BEHAVIOR ALSO EXISTS IN JAPAN WHERE IT IS SOMETIMES APPLIED TO 'DATING SIM' STYLE GAMES.

TO ME, YOU CAN NEITHER CONDONE NOR EXCUSE YOUR BEHAVIOR BASED ON THE GAMES YOU PLAY.

THERE IS NOTHING WRONG WITH ESCAPISM AS LONG AS IT DOESN'T GO TO FAR. IN FACT, YOU CAN ARGUE THAT A CERTAIN AMOUNT OF IT IS HEALTHY AND NORMAL.

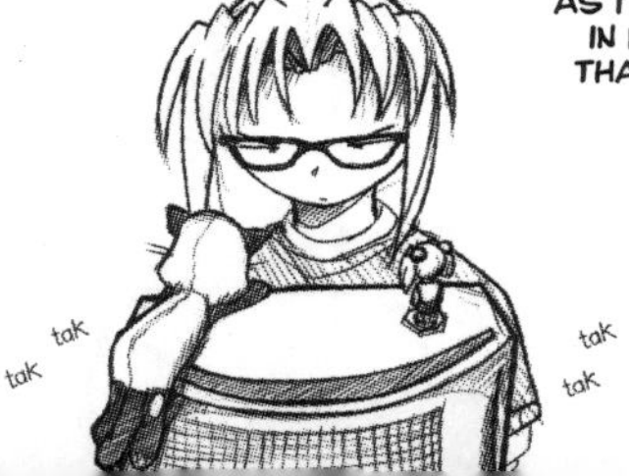
tak
tak
tak
tak

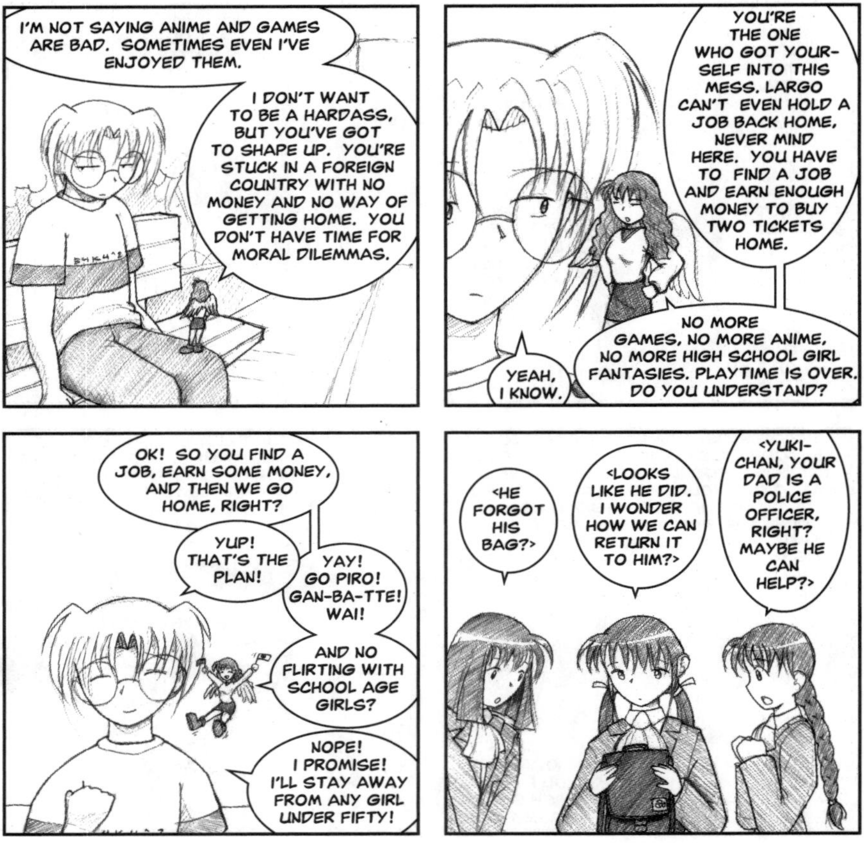
I'M NOT SAYING ANIME AND GAMES ARE BAD. SOMETIMES EVEN I'VE ENJOYED THEM.
I DON'T WANT TO BE A HARDASS, BUT YOU'VE GOT TO SHAPE UP. YOU'RE STUCK IN A FOREIGN COUNTRY WITH NO MONEY AND NO WAY OF GETTING HOME. YOU DON'T HAVE TIME FOR MORAL DILEMMAS.
YOU'RE THE ONE WHO GOT YOURSELF INTO THIS MESS. LARGO CAN'T EVEN HOLD A JOB BACK HOME, NEVER MIND HERE. YOU HAVE TO FIND A JOB AND EARN ENOUGH MONEY TO BUY TWO TICKETS HOME.
NO MORE GAMES, NO MORE ANIME, NO MORE HIGH SCHOOL GIRL FANTASIES. PLAYTIME IS OVER. DO YOU UNDERSTAND?
YEAH, I KNOW.
OK! SO YOU FIND A JOB, EARN SOME MONEY, AND THEN WE GO HOME, RIGHT?
YUP! THAT'S THE PLAN!
YAY! GO PIRO! GAN-BA-TTE! WAI!
AND NO FLIRTING WITH SCHOOL AGE GIRLS?
NOPE! I PROMISE! I'LL STAY AWAY FROM ANY GIRL UNDER FIFTY!
<HE FORGOT HIS BAG?>
<LOOKS LIKE HE DID. I WONDER HOW WE CAN RETURN IT TO HIM?>
<YUKI-CHAN, YOUR DAD IS A POLICE OFFICER, RIGHT? MAYBE HE CAN HELP?>

YOU HAVE TO BE CAREFUL TO REMEMBER WHERE YOUR FANTASIES LIE IN RELATION TO REALITY.

BECAUSE YOU NEVER KNOW WHEN SOMEONE ELSE'S FANTASY MIGHT INVOLVE *YOU*.

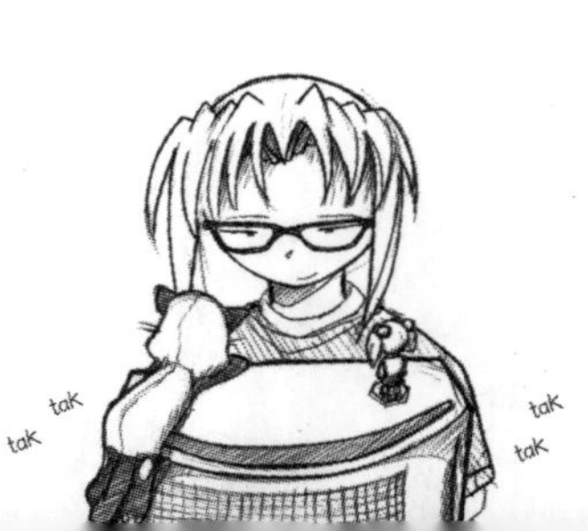
tak
tak
tak
tak

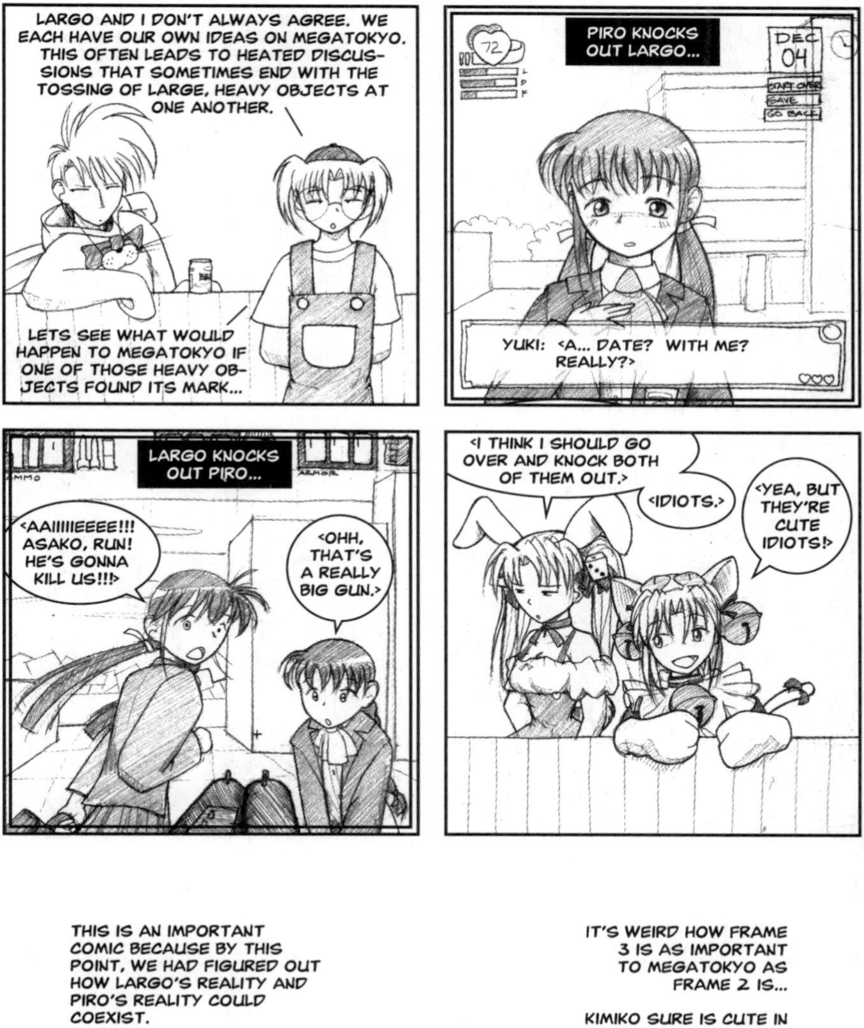
LARGO AND I DON'T ALWAYS AGREE. WE EACH HAVE OUR OWN IDEAS ON MEGATOKYO. THIS OFTEN LEADS TO HEATED DISCUSSIONS THAT SOMETIMES END WITH THE TOSSING OF LARGE, HEAVY OBJECTS AT ONE ANOTHER.
LETS SEE WHAT WOULD HAPPEN TO MEGATOKYO IF ONE OF THOSE HEAVY OBJECTS FOUND ITS MARK...
PIRO KNOCKS OUT LARGO...
72
DEC
04
START OVER
SAVE
GO BACK
YUKI: <A... DATE? WITH ME? REALLY?>
LARGO KNOCKS OUT PIRO...
AMMO
ARMOR
<AAIIIIIEEEE!!! ASAKO, RUN! HE'S GONNA KILL US!!!>
<OHH, THAT'S A REALLY BIG GUN.>
<I THINK I SHOULD GO OVER AND KNOCK BOTH OF THEM OUT.>
<IDIOTS.>
<YEA, BUT THEY'RE CUTE IDIOTS!>

THIS IS AN IMPORTANT COMIC BECAUSE BY THIS POINT, WE HAD FIGURED OUT HOW LARGO'S REALITY AND PIRO'S REALITY COULD COEXIST.

TWO YEARS LATER, WE ACTUALLY TESTED THE "HEAVY OBJECT" THEORY WHEN LARGO AND I PARTED WAYS AND I WENT SOLO WITH MEGATOKYO.

IT'S WEIRD HOW FRAME 3 IS AS IMPORTANT TO MEGATOKYO AS FRAME 2 IS...

KIMIKO SURE IS CUTE IN THAT DEJIKO OUTFIT...

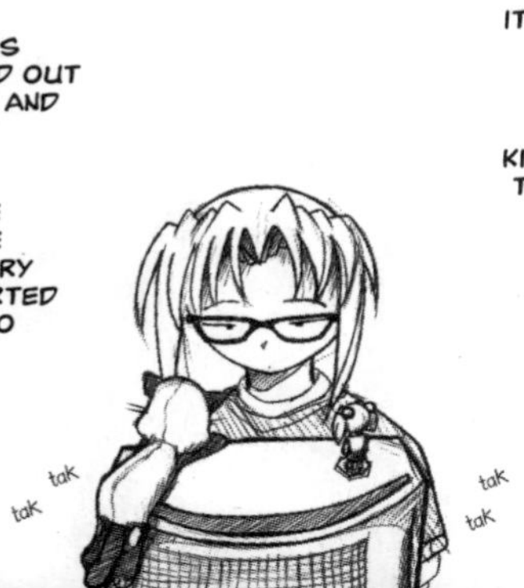
tak
tak
tak
tak

YO DUDE, WHAT'S UP?
NOTHING.
SLAM!
MOO MILK
I GOT BORED AND STARTED PLAYING THAT "NAPPLE TALE" GAME. YOU AND TSUBASA WERE PLAYIN' YESTERDAY.
WHERE'S MY BOOK BAG? **OHMYGOD**!!
CRUNCH CRUNCH
IT WAS KINDA LAME AT FIRST, BUT ONCE I GOT INTO IT, IT WAS PRETTY COOL. SORTA LIKE *CANDYLAND* ON CRACK, ISNT IT?
I MUST HAVE LEFT IT SOMEWHERE!! I GOTTA FIND IT!
I'M NOT SAYING THAT I REALLY LIKED IT, SMACKING THINGS WITH A WAND IS MORE YOUR KINDA THING.
OH YEA, AND PICK UP SOME MORE BEER WHILE YOU'RE OUT.
click

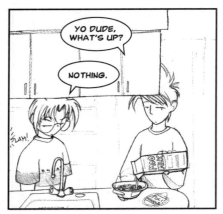

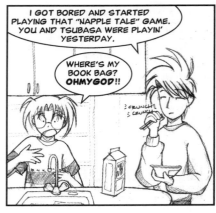

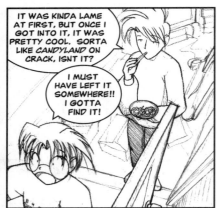

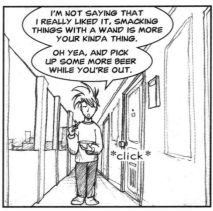

TO ANSWER A LONG STANDING QUESTION ABOUT THIS EPISODE:

YES, THAT IS MILK. NO THAT ISN'T CEREAL. IT'S RAMEN. LARGO IS POURING MILK OVER A BOWL OF INSTANT RAMEN. I THINK HE BLEW OUT HIS TASTE BUDS YEARS AGO.

tak tak
tak tak

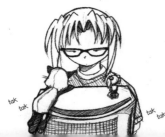

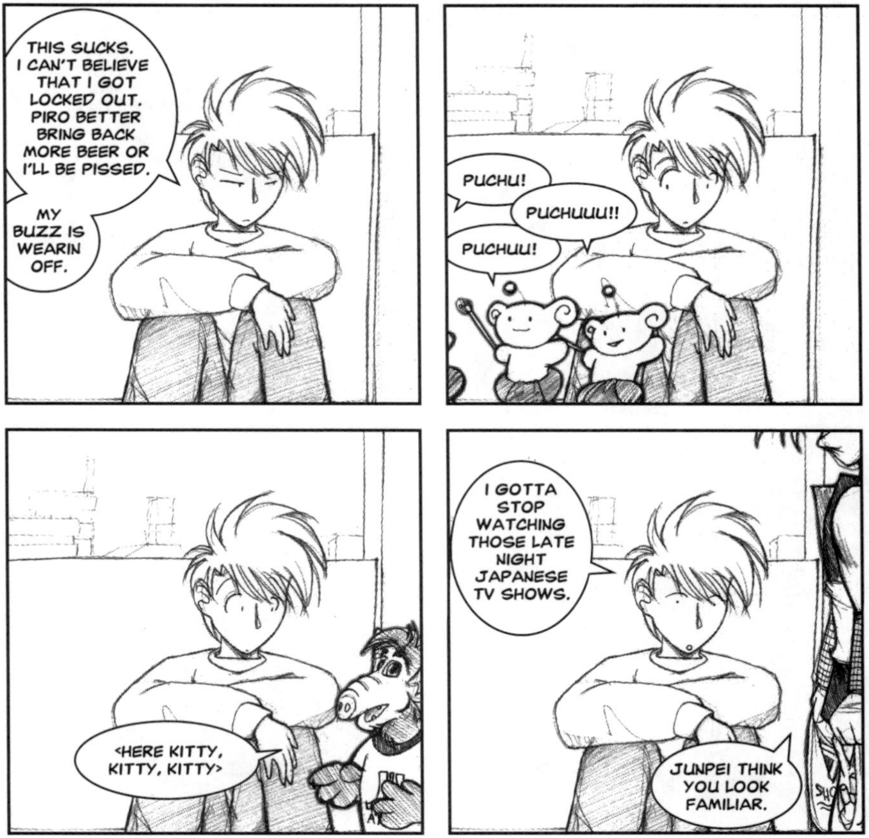
THIS SUCKS. I CAN'T BELIEVE THAT I GOT LOCKED OUT. PIRO BETTER BRING BACK MORE BEER OR I'LL BE PISSED.
MY BUZZ IS WEARIN OFF.
PUCHU!
PUCHUUU!!
PUCHUU!
<HERE KITTY, KITTY, KITTY>
I GOTTA STOP WATCHING THOSE LATE NIGHT JAPANESE TV SHOWS.
JUNPEI THINK YOU LOOK FAMILIAR.

OK, THIS ONE IS JUST WEIRD.

I DON'T KNOW HOW I GOT TALKED INTO PUTTING ALF IN THERE...

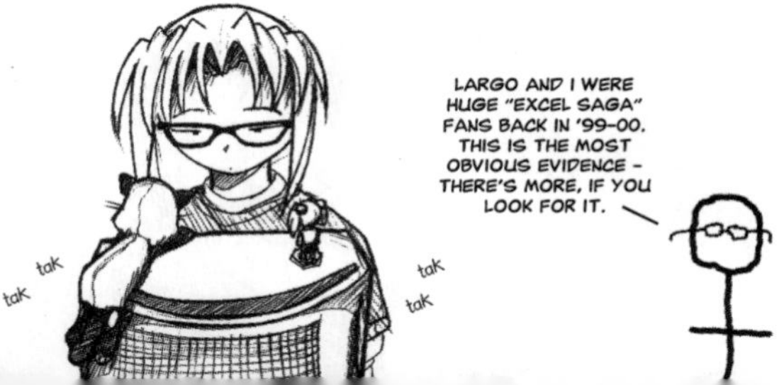
LARGO AND I WERE HUGE "EXCEL SAGA" FANS BACK IN '99-00. THIS IS THE MOST OBVIOUS EVIDENCE - THERE'S MORE, IF YOU LOOK FOR IT.
tak
tak
tak
tak

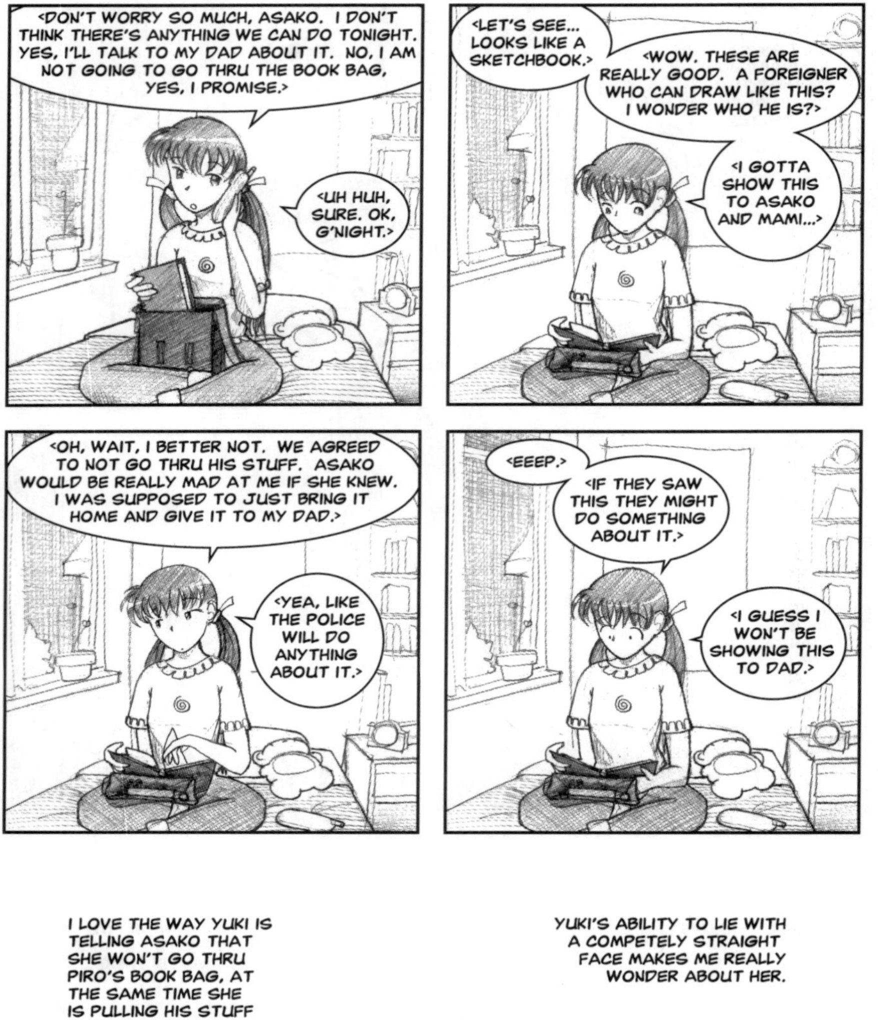
<DON'T WORRY SO MUCH, ASAKO. I DON'T THINK THERE'S ANYTHING WE CAN DO TONIGHT. YES, I'LL TALK TO MY DAD ABOUT IT. NO, I AM NOT GOING TO GO THRU THE BOOK BAG, YES, I PROMISE.>
<UH HUH, SURE. OK, G'NIGHT.>
<LET'S SEE... LOOKS LIKE A SKETCHBOOK.>
<WOW. THESE ARE REALLY GOOD. A FOREIGNER WHO CAN DRAW LIKE THIS? I WONDER WHO HE IS?>
<I GOTTA SHOW THIS TO ASAKO AND MAMI...>
<OH, WAIT, I BETTER NOT. WE AGREED TO NOT GO THRU HIS STUFF. ASAKO WOULD BE REALLY MAD AT ME IF SHE KNEW. I WAS SUPPOSED TO JUST BRING IT HOME AND GIVE IT TO MY DAD.>
<YEA, LIKE THE POLICE WILL DO ANYTHING ABOUT IT.>
<EEEP.>
<IF THEY SAW THIS THEY MIGHT DO SOMETHING ABOUT IT.>
<I GUESS I WON'T BE SHOWING THIS TO DAD.>

I LOVE THE WAY YUKI IS TELLING ASAKO THAT SHE WON'T GO THRU PIRO'S BOOK BAG, AT THE SAME TIME SHE IS PULLING HIS STUFF OUT TO LOOK AT IT.

YUKI'S ABILITY TO LIE WITH A COMPETELY STRAIGHT FACE MAKES ME REALLY WONDER ABOUT HER.

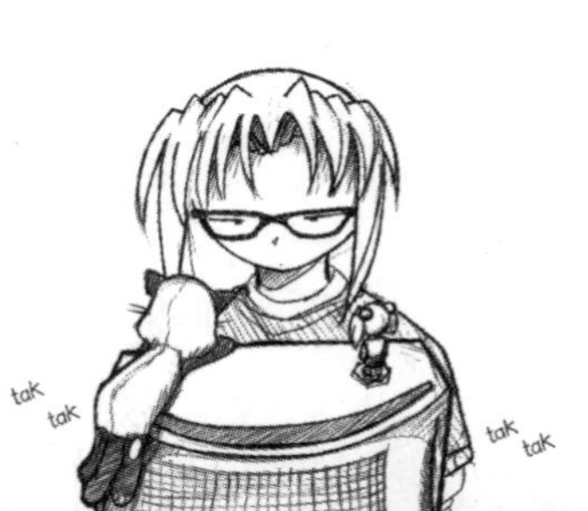
tak
tak
tak
tak

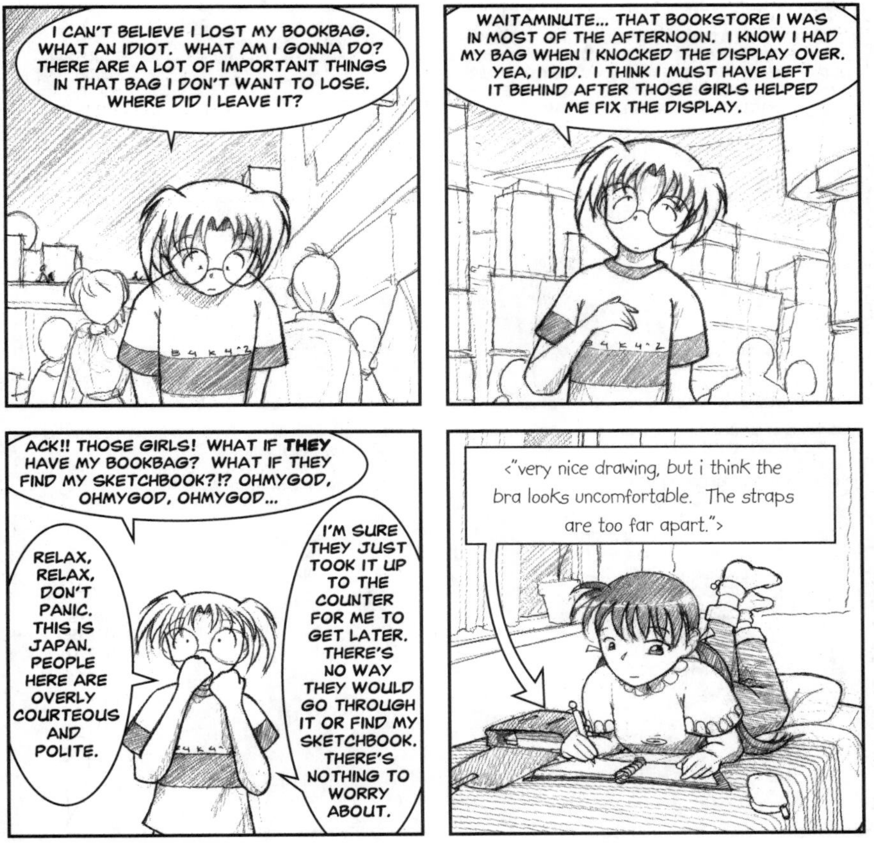
I CAN'T BELIEVE I LOST MY BOOKBAG. WHAT AN IDIOT. WHAT AM I GONNA DO? THERE ARE A LOT OF IMPORTANT THINGS IN THAT BAG I DON'T WANT TO LOSE. WHERE DID I LEAVE IT?
WAITAMINUTE... THAT BOOKSTORE I WAS IN MOST OF THE AFTERNOON. I KNOW I HAD MY BAG WHEN I KNOCKED THE DISPLAY OVER. YEA, I DID. I THINK I MUST HAVE LEFT IT BEHIND AFTER THOSE GIRLS HELPED ME FIX THE DISPLAY.
ACK!! THOSE GIRLS! WHAT IF **THEY** HAVE MY BOOKBAG? WHAT IF THEY FIND MY SKETCHBOOK?!? OHMYGOD, OHMYGOD, OHMYGOD...
RELAX, RELAX, DON'T PANIC. THIS IS JAPAN. PEOPLE HERE ARE OVERLY COURTEOUS AND POLITE.
I'M SURE THEY JUST TOOK IT UP TO THE COUNTER FOR ME TO GET LATER. THERE'S NO WAY THEY WOULD GO THROUGH IT OR FIND MY SKETCHBOOK. THERE'S NOTHING TO WORRY ABOUT.
<"very nice drawing, but i think the bra looks uncomfortable. The straps are too far apart.">

HEHEH.

I'D BE HORRIFIED IF ANYONE GOT A HOLD OF ONE OF MY SKETCHBOOKS.

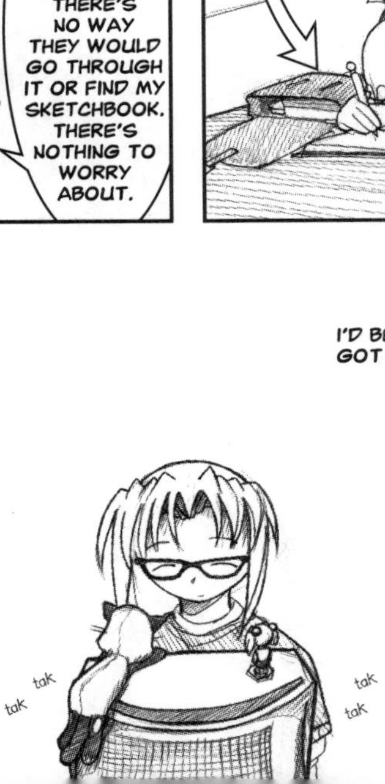
tak tak
tak tak

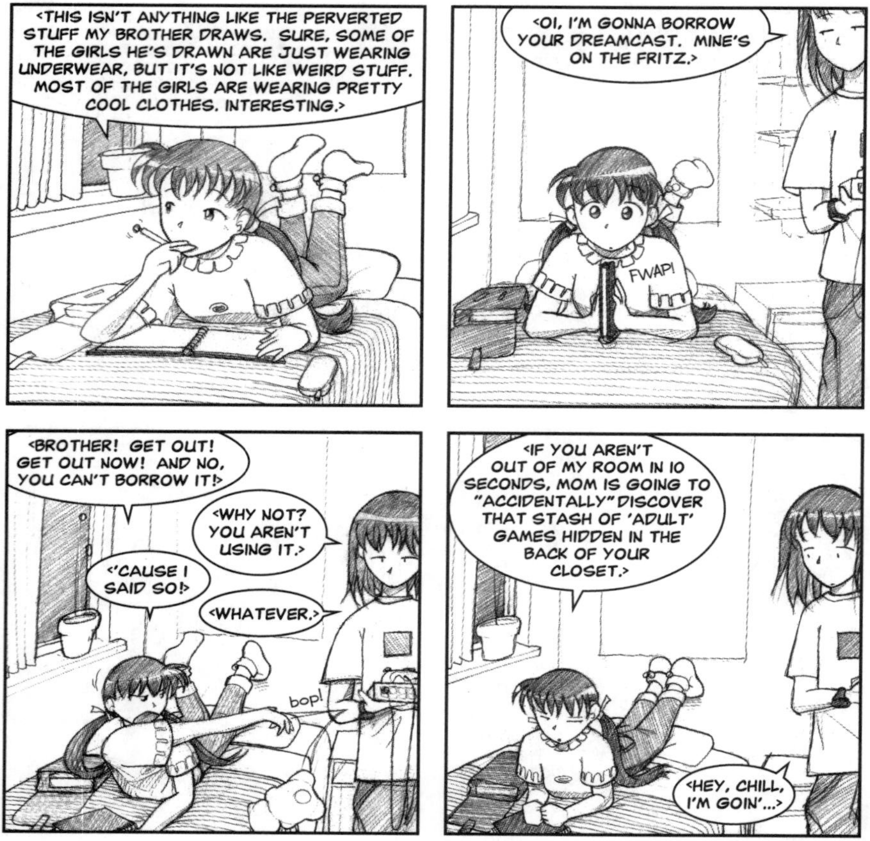
<THIS ISN'T ANYTHING LIKE THE PERVERTED STUFF MY BROTHER DRAWS. SURE, SOME OF THE GIRLS HE'S DRAWN ARE JUST WEARING UNDERWEAR, BUT IT'S NOT LIKE WEIRD STUFF. MOST OF THE GIRLS ARE WEARING PRETTY COOL CLOTHES. INTERESTING.>
<OI, I'M GONNA BORROW YOUR DREAMCAST. MINE'S ON THE FRITZ.>
FWAP!
<BROTHER! GET OUT! GET OUT NOW! AND NO, YOU CAN'T BORROW IT!>
<WHY NOT? YOU AREN'T USING IT.>
<'CAUSE I SAID SO!>
<WHATEVER.>
bop!
<IF YOU AREN'T OUT OF MY ROOM IN 10 SECONDS, MOM IS GOING TO "ACCIDENTALLY" DISCOVER THAT STASH OF 'ADULT' GAMES HIDDEN IN THE BACK OF YOUR CLOSET.>
<HEY, CHILL, I'M GOIN'...>

I WANTED YUKI'S BROTHER TO BE MORE INTERESTING THAN JUST SOME FACELESS BACKGROUND CHARACTER.

OF COURSE, ONCE THEY WERE DEVELOPED, THE ENTIRE SONODA FAMILY TURNED OUT RATHER INTERESTING.

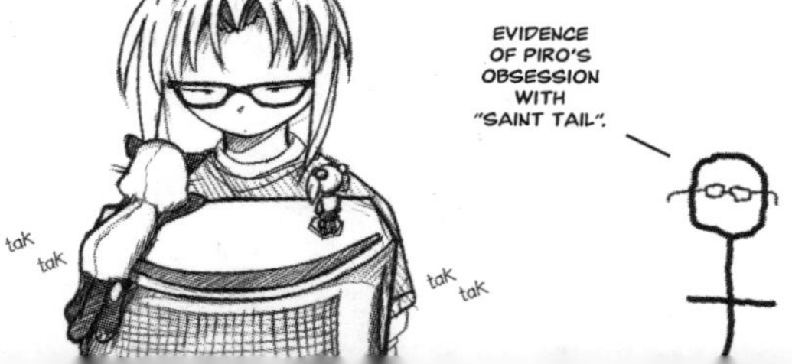
tak
tak
tak
tak
EVIDENCE OF PIRO'S OBSESSION WITH "SAINT TAIL".

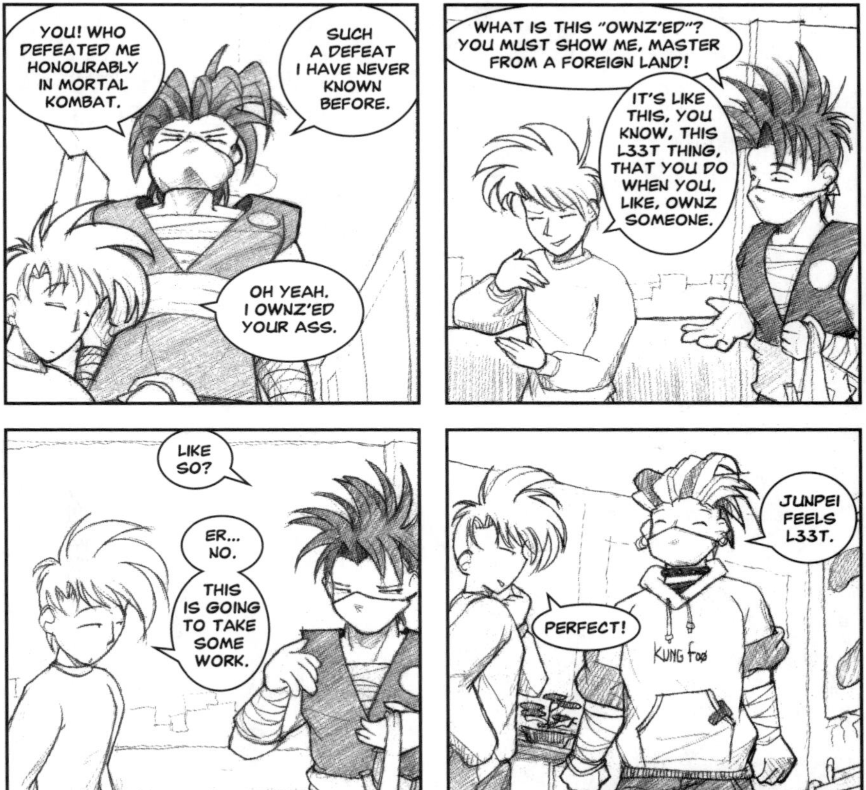
YOU! WHO DEFEATED ME HONOURABLY IN MORTAL KOMBAT.
SUCH A DEFEAT I HAVE NEVER KNOWN BEFORE.
OH YEAH. I OWNZ'ED YOUR ASS.
WHAT IS THIS "OWNZ'ED"? YOU MUST SHOW ME, MASTER FROM A FOREIGN LAND!
IT'S LIKE THIS, YOU KNOW, THIS L33T THING, THAT YOU DO WHEN YOU, LIKE, OWNZ SOMEONE.
LIKE SO?
ER... NO.
THIS IS GOING TO TAKE SOME WORK.
JUNPEI FEELS L33T.
PERFECT!
KUNG FOØ

JUNPEI WAS JUST TOO COOL A CHARACTER TO NOT BRING BACK AT SOME POINT.

JUNPEI, THE L33T NINJA. YOU KNOW IT HAD TO HAPPEN.

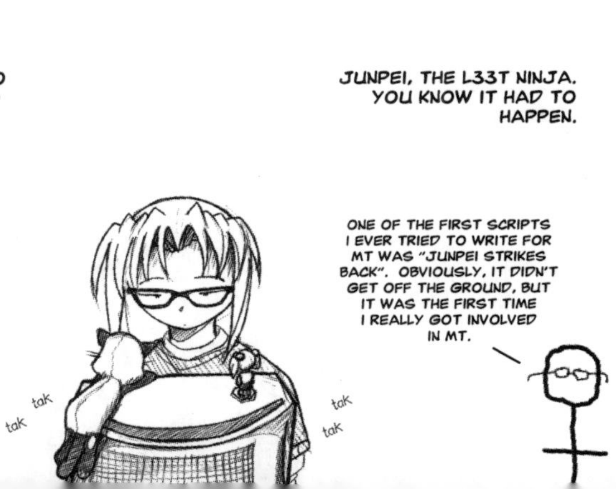
ONE OF THE FIRST SCRIPTS I EVER TRIED TO WRITE FOR MT WAS "JUNPEI STRIKES BACK". OBVIOUSLY, IT DIDN'T GET OFF THE GROUND, BUT IT WAS THE FIRST TIME I REALLY GOT INVOLVED IN MT.
tak tak
tak
tak
tak

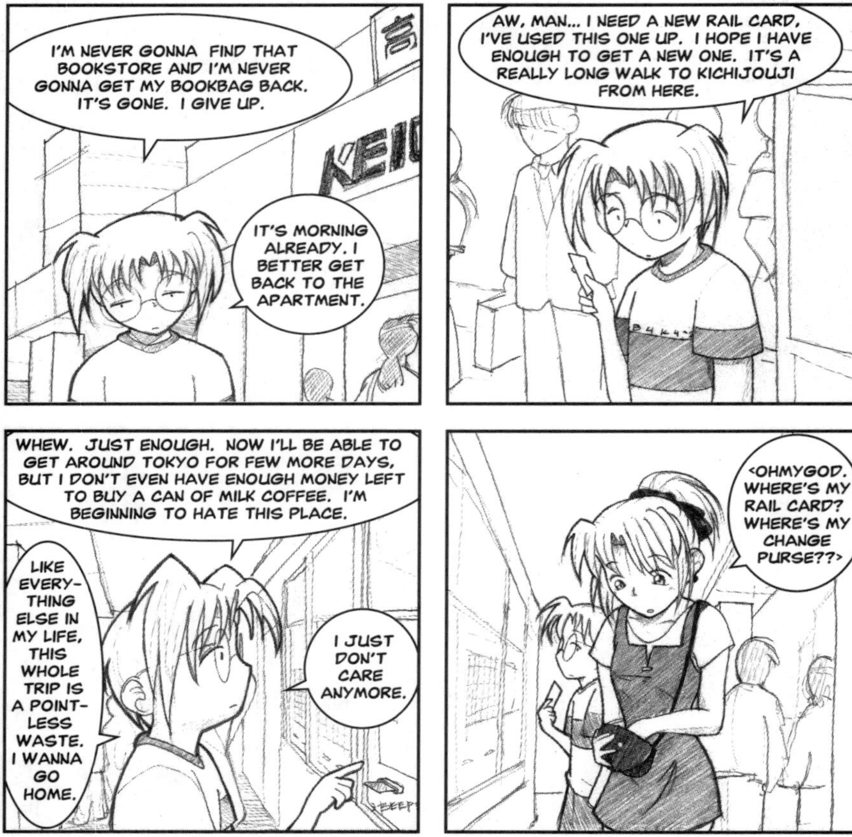
I'M NEVER GONNA FIND THAT BOOKSTORE AND I'M NEVER GONNA GET MY BOOKBAG BACK. IT'S GONE. I GIVE UP.
IT'S MORNING ALREADY. I BETTER GET BACK TO THE APARTMENT.
AW, MAN... I NEED A NEW RAIL CARD, I'VE USED THIS ONE UP. I HOPE I HAVE ENOUGH TO GET A NEW ONE. IT'S A REALLY LONG WALK TO KICHIJOUJI FROM HERE.
WHEW. JUST ENOUGH. NOW I'LL BE ABLE TO GET AROUND TOKYO FOR FEW MORE DAYS, BUT I DON'T EVEN HAVE ENOUGH MONEY LEFT TO BUY A CAN OF MILK COFFEE. I'M BEGINNING TO HATE THIS PLACE.
LIKE EVERY-THING ELSE IN MY LIFE, THIS WHOLE TRIP IS A POINT-LESS WASTE. I WANNA GO HOME.
I JUST DON'T CARE ANYMORE.
<OHMYGOD. WHERE'S MY RAIL CARD? WHERE'S MY CHANGE PURSE??>

THIS IS THE POINT WHERE I STARTED TO GET INTO TROUBLE.

LIFE ISN'T ALWAYS FUNNY. USUALLY YOU CAN FIND HUMOR IN JUST ABOUT EVERYTHING.

WHEN I STARTED MEGATOKYO, I FELT THAT THERE WOULD BE TIMES WHEN IT WOULD NOT BE PARTICULARLY FUNNY.

BUT SOMETIMES THINGS AREN'T FUNNY AT ALL.

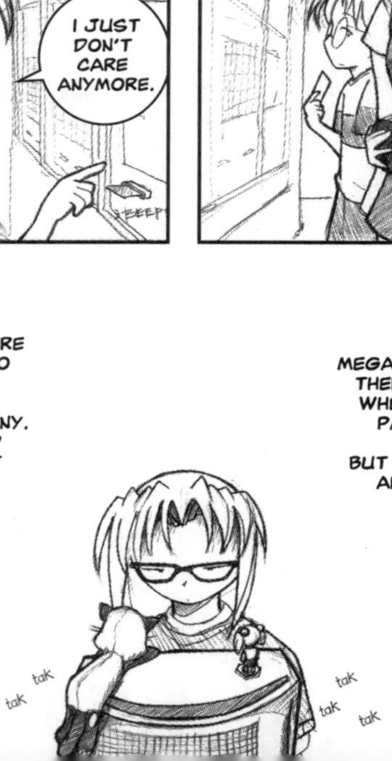
tak
tak
tak
tak
tak

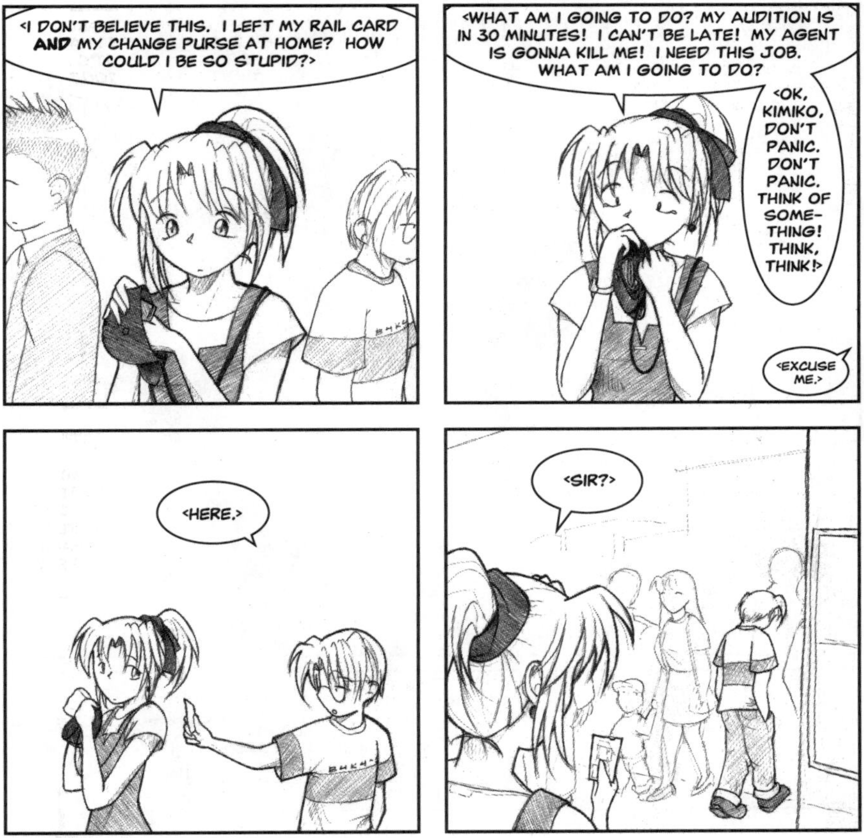
<I DON'T BELIEVE THIS. I LEFT MY RAIL CARD **AND** MY CHANGE PURSE AT HOME? HOW COULD I BE SO STUPID?>
<WHAT AM I GOING TO DO? MY AUDITION IS IN 30 MINUTES! I CAN'T BE LATE! MY AGENT IS GONNA KILL ME! I NEED THIS JOB. WHAT AM I GOING TO DO?
<OK, KIMIKO, DON'T PANIC. DON'T PANIC. THINK OF SOME-THING! THINK, THINK!>
<EXCUSE ME.>
<HERE.>
<SIR?>

LIFE DOESN'T ALWAYS HAVE A PUNCHLINE.

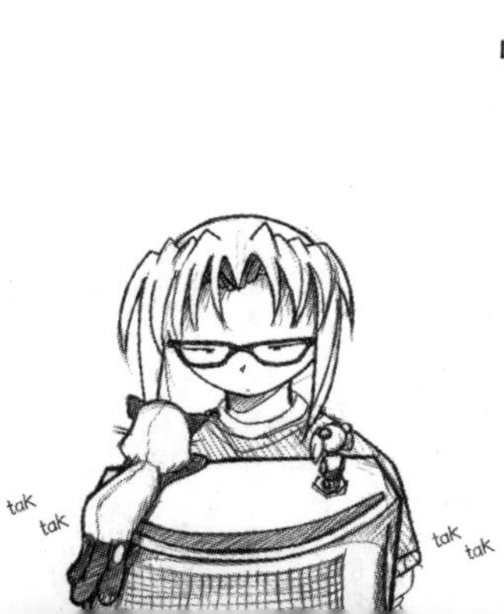
tak
tak
tak
tak

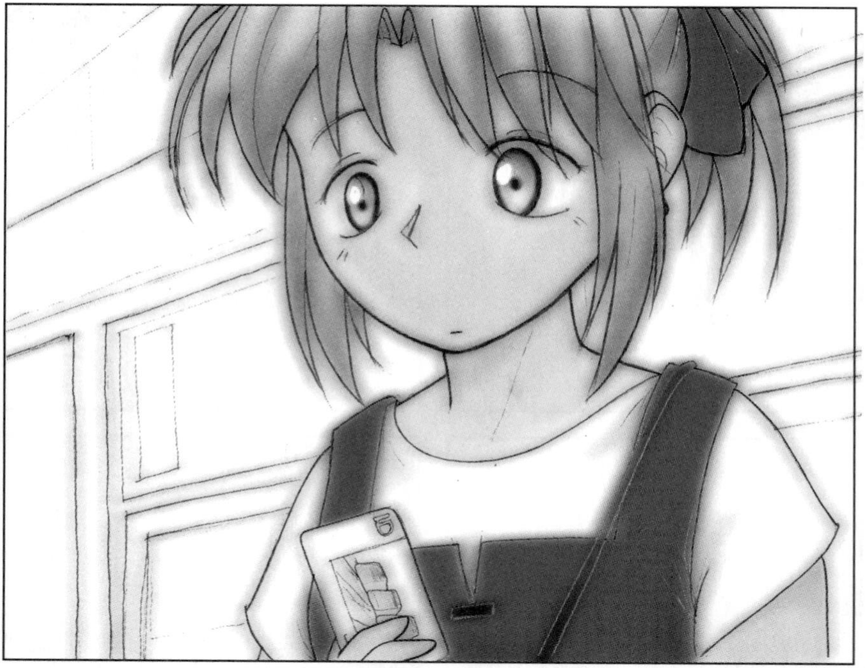

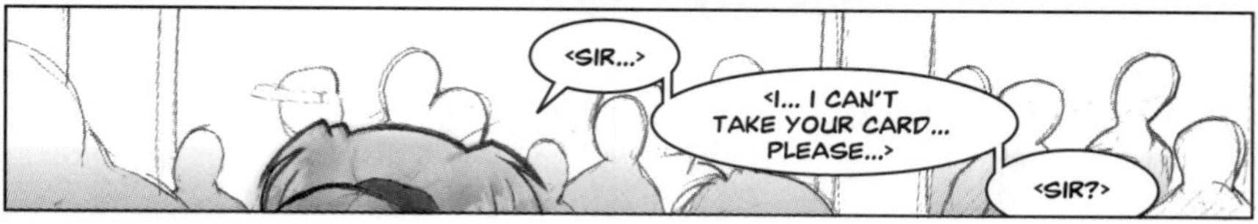
<SIR...>
<I... I CAN'T TAKE YOUR CARD... PLEASE...>
<SIR?>

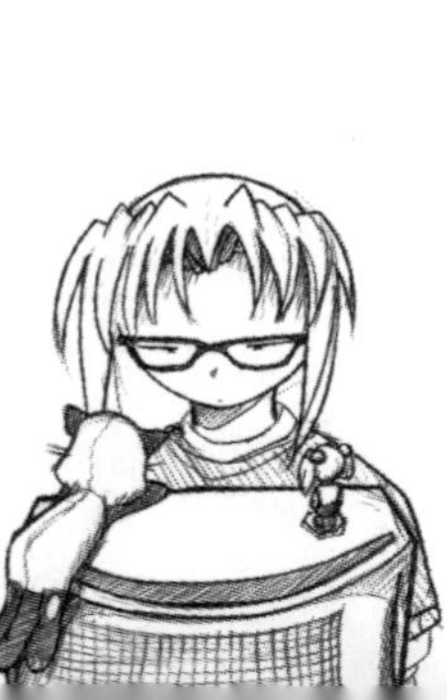

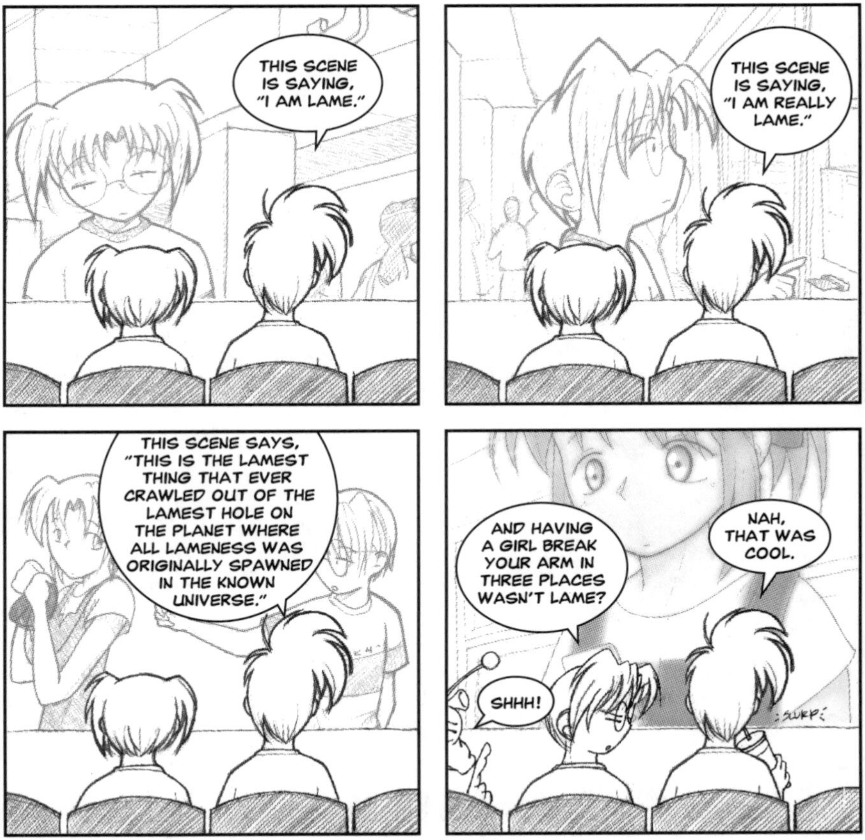
THIS SCENE IS SAYING, "I AM LAME."
THIS SCENE IS SAYING, "I AM REALLY LAME."
THIS SCENE SAYS, "THIS IS THE LAMEST THING THAT EVER CRAWLED OUT OF THE LAMEST HOLE ON THE PLANET WHERE ALL LAMENESS WAS ORIGINALLY SPAWNED IN THE KNOWN UNIVERSE."
AND HAVING A GIRL BREAK YOUR ARM IN THREE PLACES WASN'T LAME?
NAH, THAT WAS COOL.
SHHH!
:SLURP:

A LOT OF PEOPLE EMAILED ME WONDERING WHAT THE JOKE WAS IN THE PREVIOUS COMIC. IT WAS VERY FRUSTRATING.

I WAS TRYING TO BREAK OUT OF THE MOLD THAT WEBCOMICS HAD TO BE LIKE NEWSPAPER COMICS - SOMETHING FUNNY, EVERY DAY

SOME PEOPLE WERE UNWILLING TO ACCEPT THAT, AND EVEN THREATENED TO STOP READING IF I PULLED SOMETHING LIKE THAT AGAIN.

MY RESPONSE WAS SIMPLE - FINE, DON'T READ IT. NO ONE IS FORCING YOU.

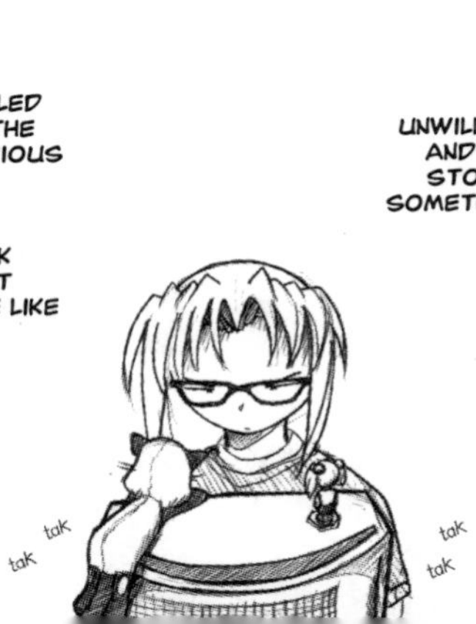
tak
tak
tak
tak

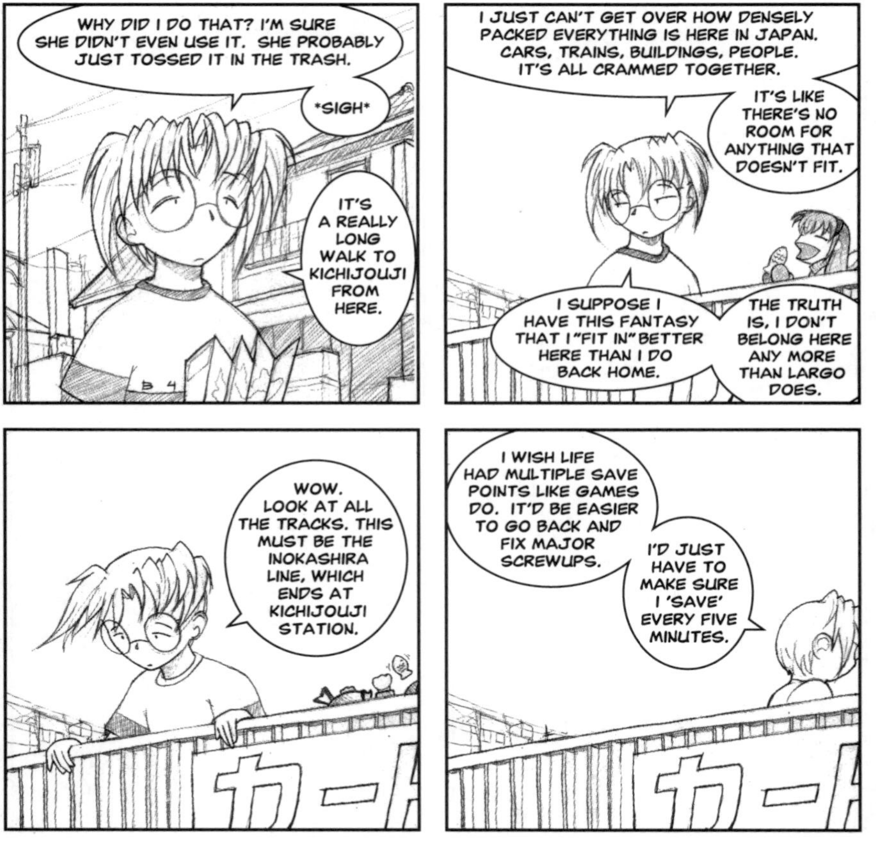
WHY DID I DO THAT? I'M SURE SHE DIDN'T EVEN USE IT. SHE PROBABLY JUST TOSSED IT IN THE TRASH.
SIGH
IT'S A REALLY LONG WALK TO KICHIJOUJI FROM HERE.
I JUST CAN'T GET OVER HOW DENSELY PACKED EVERYTHING IS HERE IN JAPAN. CARS, TRAINS, BUILDINGS, PEOPLE. IT'S ALL CRAMMED TOGETHER.
IT'S LIKE THERE'S NO ROOM FOR ANYTHING THAT DOESN'T FIT.
I SUPPOSE I HAVE THIS FANTASY THAT I "FIT IN" BETTER HERE THAN I DO BACK HOME.
THE TRUTH IS, I DON'T BELONG HERE ANY MORE THAN LARGO DOES.
WOW. LOOK AT ALL THE TRACKS. THIS MUST BE THE INOKASHIRA LINE, WHICH ENDS AT KICHIJOUJI STATION.
I WISH LIFE HAD MULTIPLE SAVE POINTS LIKE GAMES DO. IT'D BE EASIER TO GO BACK AND FIX MAJOR SCREWUPS.
I'D JUST HAVE TO MAKE SURE I 'SAVE' EVERY FIVE MINUTES.

LARGO WAS GETTING ON MY CASE ABOUT THE FACT THAT PIRO WAS GETTING WAY TOO MOPEY AND INTROSPECTIVE.

WELL, THAT'S JUST HOW PIRO IS. IT'S ALMOST AS ANNOYING AS LARGO AND HIS "L33T SP33K."

THE LITTLE CHARACTER IN THE UPPER RIGHT FRAME IS HOMAGE TO A JAPANESE WEBCOMIC CALLED "QUARTER ICESHOP" WHICH PARTLY INSPIRED ME TO START MEGATOKYO. THAT LITTLE FISH THING IS A "TAIYAKI," A KIND OF HOT PASTRY.

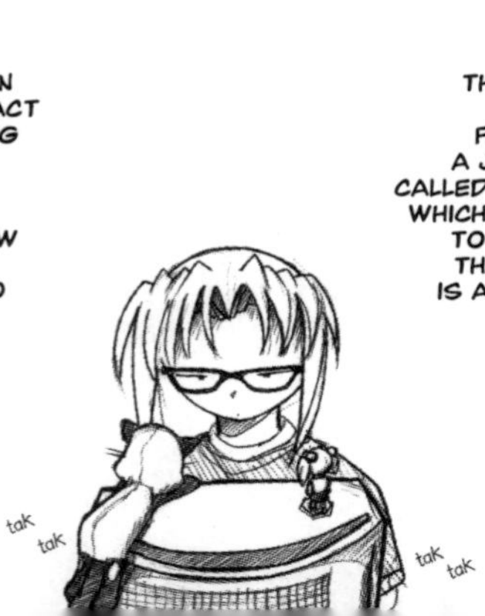
tak
tak
tak
tak

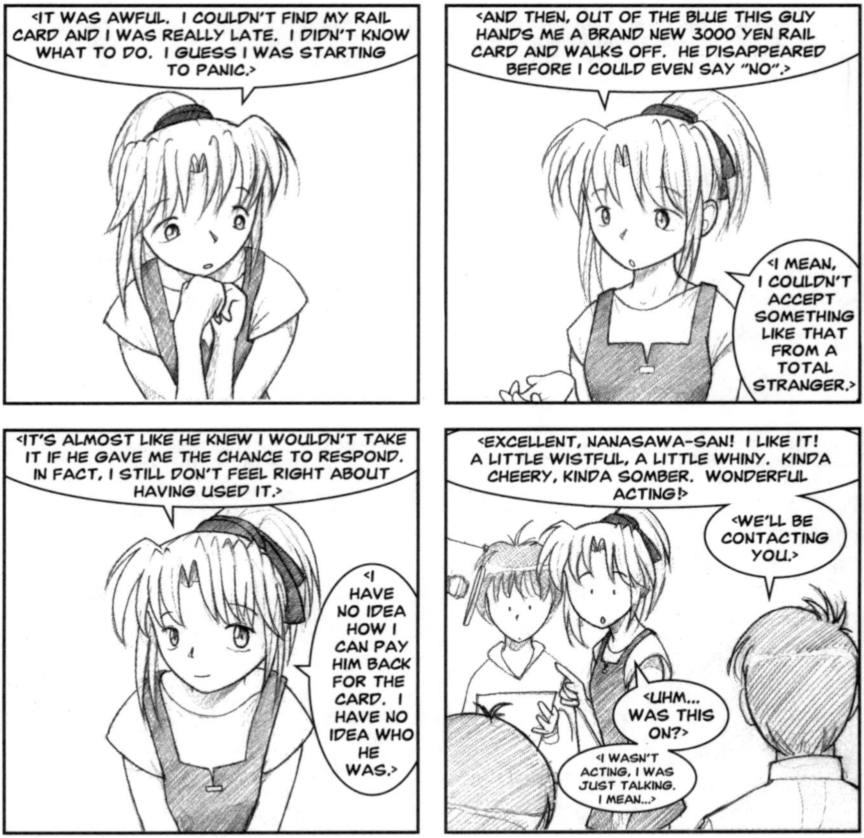
<IT WAS AWFUL. I COULDN'T FIND MY RAIL CARD AND I WAS REALLY LATE. I DIDN'T KNOW WHAT TO DO. I GUESS I WAS STARTING TO PANIC.>
<AND THEN, OUT OF THE BLUE THIS GUY HANDS ME A BRAND NEW 3000 YEN RAIL CARD AND WALKS OFF. HE DISAPPEARED BEFORE I COULD EVEN SAY "NO".>
<I MEAN, I COULDN'T ACCEPT SOMETHING LIKE THAT FROM A TOTAL STRANGER.>
<IT'S ALMOST LIKE HE KNEW I WOULDN'T TAKE IT IF HE GAVE ME THE CHANCE TO RESPOND. IN FACT, I STILL DON'T FEEL RIGHT ABOUT HAVING USED IT.>
<I HAVE NO IDEA HOW I CAN PAY HIM BACK FOR THE CARD. I HAVE NO IDEA WHO HE WAS.>
<EXCELLENT, NANASAWA-SAN! I LIKE IT! A LITTLE WISTFUL, A LITTLE WHINY. KINDA CHEERY, KINDA SOMBER. WONDERFUL ACTING!>
<WE'LL BE CONTACTING YOU.>
<UHM... WAS THIS ON?>
<I WASN'T ACTING, I WAS JUST TALKING. I MEAN...>

KIMIKO IS AN ASPIRING "SEIYUU", OR VOICE ACTRESS. IN JAPAN, ANIME FANS OFTEN WORSHIP SEIYUU MORE THAN THE CHARACTERS THEY PLAY.

OF COURSE, KIMIKO IS STILL TRYING TO BREAK INTO THE BUSINESS. IT'S A COMPETITIVE INDUSTRY, AND I'VE BEEN DOING A LOT OF RESEARCH INTO HOW THE INDUSTRY WORKS SO THAT I CAN REPRESENT IT ACCURATELY.

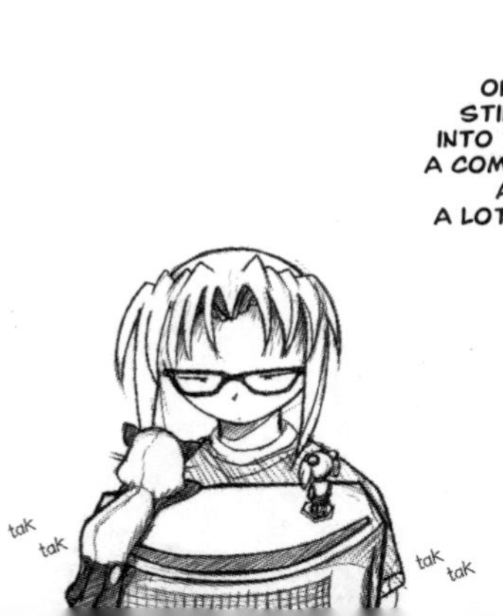
tak
tak
tak
tak

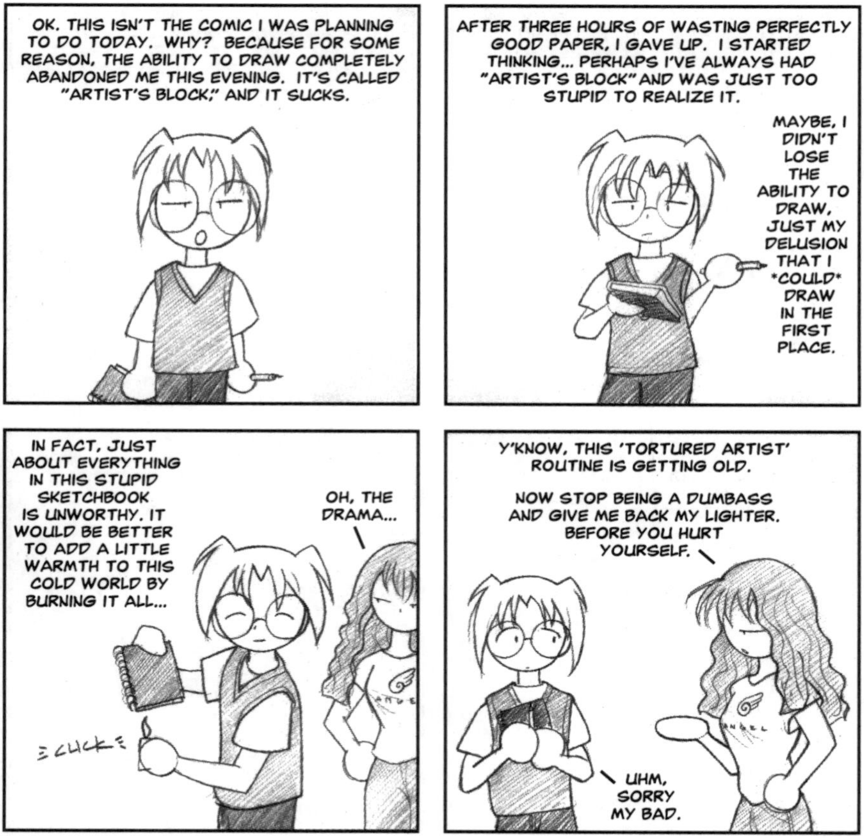
OK. THIS ISN'T THE COMIC I WAS PLANNING TO DO TODAY. WHY? BECAUSE FOR SOME REASON, THE ABILITY TO DRAW COMPLETELY ABANDONED ME THIS EVENING. IT'S CALLED "ARTIST'S BLOCK," AND IT SUCKS.
AFTER THREE HOURS OF WASTING PERFECTLY GOOD PAPER, I GAVE UP. I STARTED THINKING... PERHAPS I'VE ALWAYS HAD "ARTIST'S BLOCK" AND WAS JUST TOO STUPID TO REALIZE IT.
MAYBE, I DIDN'T LOSE THE ABILITY TO DRAW, JUST MY DELUSION THAT I *COULD* DRAW IN THE FIRST PLACE.
IN FACT, JUST ABOUT EVERYTHING IN THIS STUPID SKETCHBOOK IS UNWORTHY. IT WOULD BE BETTER TO ADD A LITTLE WARMTH TO THIS COLD WORLD BY BURNING IT ALL...
OH, THE DRAMA...
CLICK
Y'KNOW, THIS 'TORTURED ARTIST' ROUTINE IS GETTING OLD.
NOW STOP BEING A DUMBASS AND GIVE ME BACK MY LIGHTER. BEFORE YOU HURT YOURSELF.
UHM, SORRY MY BAD.

I STARTED TO USE THIS DRAWING STYLE FOR "REAL LIFE ADVENTURES OF PIRO AND SERAPHIM" COMICS.

OFTEN OUR OWN EXPERIENCES AND INTERACTIONS CAN BE FAR MORE ENTERTAINING THAN ANYTHING I CAN MAKE UP. YES, WE ARE REALLY LIKE THAT.

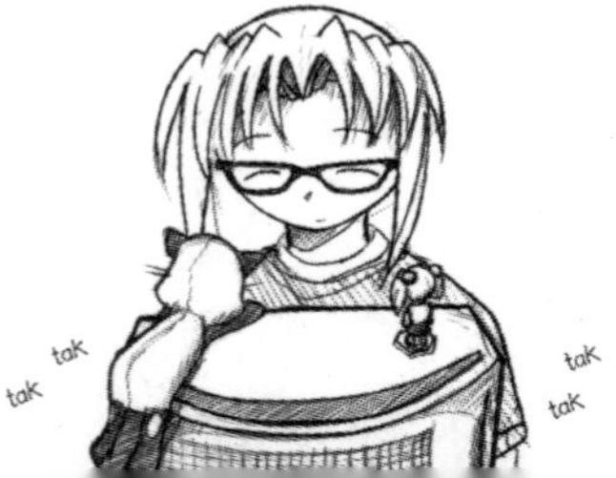
tak
tak
tak
tak

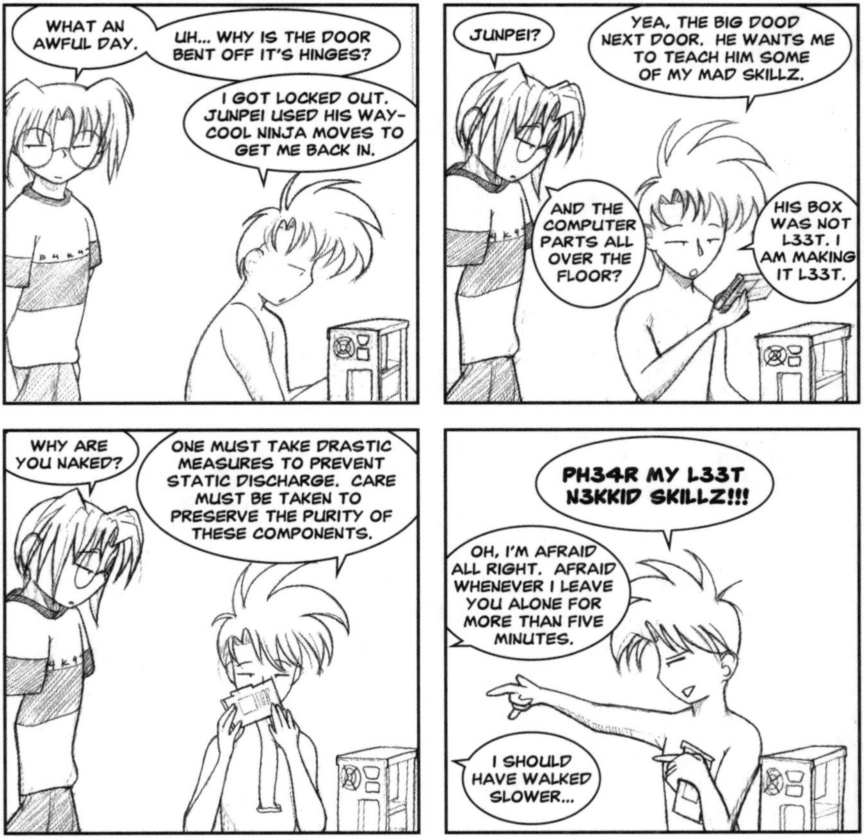
WHAT AN AWFUL DAY.
UH... WHY IS THE DOOR BENT OFF IT'S HINGES?
I GOT LOCKED OUT. JUNPEI USED HIS WAY-COOL NINJA MOVES TO GET ME BACK IN.
JUNPEI?
YEA, THE BIG DOOD NEXT DOOR. HE WANTS ME TO TEACH HIM SOME OF MY MAD SKILLZ.
AND THE COMPUTER PARTS ALL OVER THE FLOOR?
HIS BOX WAS NOT L33T. I AM MAKING IT L33T.
WHY ARE YOU NAKED?
ONE MUST TAKE DRASTIC MEASURES TO PREVENT STATIC DISCHARGE. CARE MUST BE TAKEN TO PRESERVE THE PURITY OF THESE COMPONENTS.
PH34R MY L33T N3KKID SKILLZ!!!
OH, I'M AFRAID ALL RIGHT. AFRAID WHENEVER I LEAVE YOU ALONE FOR MORE THAN FIVE MINUTES.
I SHOULD HAVE WALKED SLOWER...

GOD, THIS ONE SCARES ME.

I'M SORRY, BUT IT DOES. I CAN'T DEAL WITH THE IMAGERY.

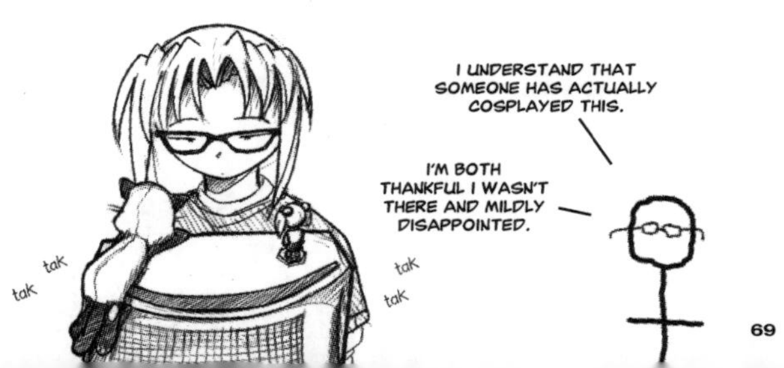
I UNDERSTAND THAT SOMEONE HAS ACTUALLY COSPLAYED THIS.
I'M BOTH THANKFUL I WASN'T THERE AND MILDLY DISAPPOINTED.
tak tak
tak tak

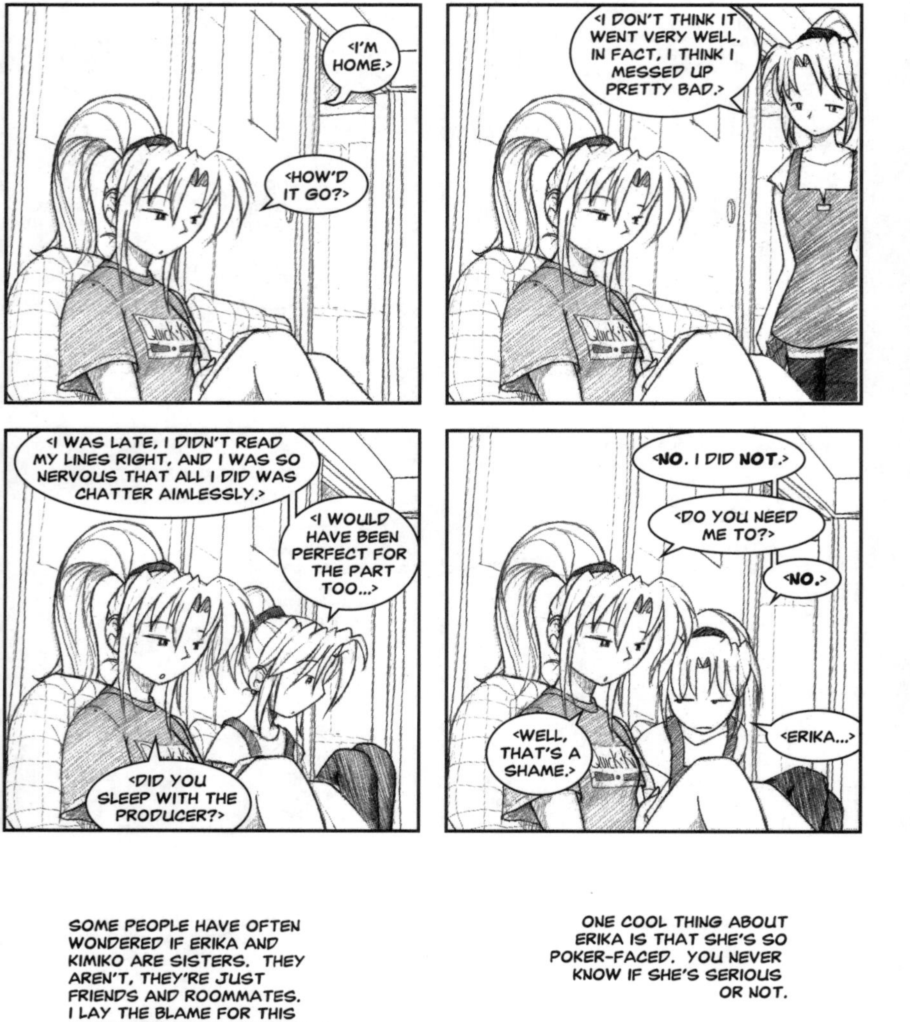
<I'M HOME.>
<HOW'D IT GO?>
<I DON'T THINK IT WENT VERY WELL. IN FACT, I THINK I MESSED UP PRETTY BAD.>
<I WAS LATE, I DIDN'T READ MY LINES RIGHT, AND I WAS SO NERVOUS THAT ALL I DID WAS CHATTER AIMLESSLY.>
<I WOULD HAVE BEEN PERFECT FOR THE PART TOO...>
<DID YOU SLEEP WITH THE PRODUCER?>
<**NO**. I DID **NOT**.>
<DO YOU NEED ME TO?>
<**NO.**>
<WELL, THAT'S A SHAME.>
<ERIKA...>

SOME PEOPLE HAVE OFTEN WONDERED IF ERIKA AND KIMIKO ARE SISTERS. THEY AREN'T, THEY'RE JUST FRIENDS AND ROOMMATES. I LAY THE BLAME FOR THIS CONFUSION ON THE PROBLEMS I HAD DRAWING THEM TOO SIMILARLY IN EARLY COMICS LIKE THIS ONE.

ONE COOL THING ABOUT ERIKA IS THAT SHE'S SO POKER-FACED. YOU NEVER KNOW IF SHE'S SERIOUS OR NOT.

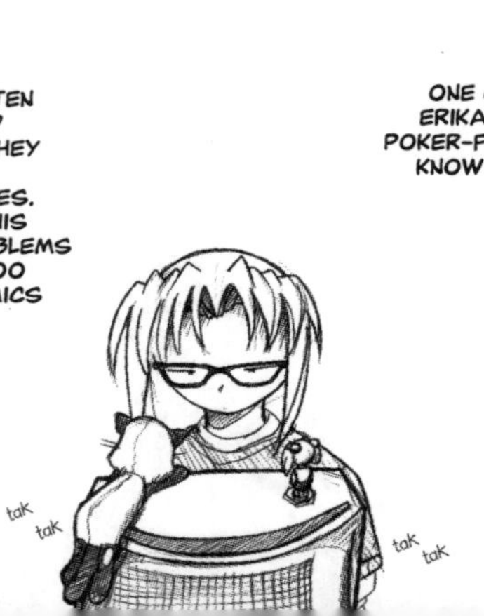
tak
tak
tak
tak

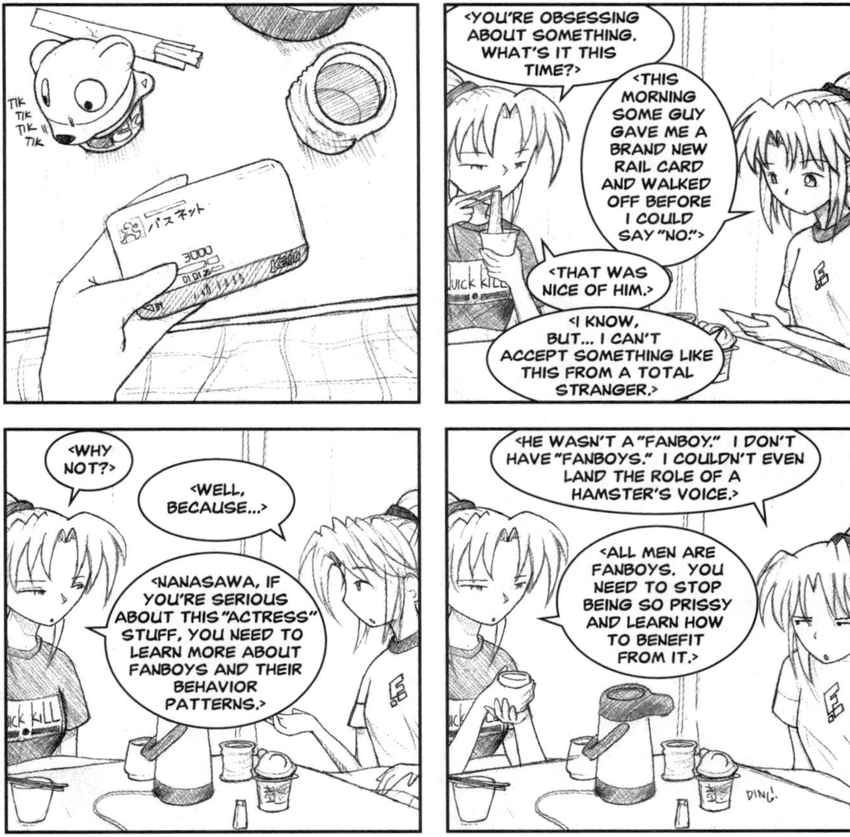
TIK
TIK
TIK
TIK
パスネット
<YOU'RE OBSESSING ABOUT SOMETHING. WHAT'S IT THIS TIME?>
<THIS MORNING SOME GUY GAVE ME A BRAND NEW RAIL CARD AND WALKED OFF BEFORE I COULD SAY "NO.">
<THAT WAS NICE OF HIM.>
<I KNOW, BUT... I CAN'T ACCEPT SOMETHING LIKE THIS FROM A TOTAL STRANGER.>
<WHY NOT?>
<WELL, BECAUSE...>
<NANASAWA, IF YOU'RE SERIOUS ABOUT THIS "ACTRESS" STUFF, YOU NEED TO LEARN MORE ABOUT FANBOYS AND THEIR BEHAVIOR PATTERNS.>
<HE WASN'T A "FANBOY." I DON'T HAVE "FANBOYS." I COULDN'T EVEN LAND THE ROLE OF A HAMSTER'S VOICE.>
<ALL MEN ARE FANBOYS. YOU NEED TO STOP BEING SO PRISSY AND LEARN HOW TO BENEFIT FROM IT.>
DING!

PIRO AND LARGO AREN'T THE ONLY CHARACTERS IN MEGATOKYO THAT ARE OBSESSIVE. KIMIKO HAS PLENTY OF HER OWN LITTLE QUIRKS.

SHE HAS A LOT OF TROUBLE ACCEPTING THINGS FROM OTHER PEOPLE. MOST PEOPLE WOULD SHRUG THIS OFF, BUT KIMIKO IS THE TYPE THAT JUST WON'T LET GO.

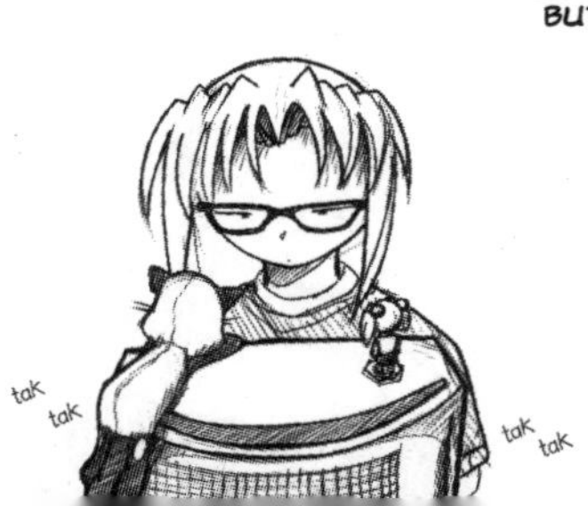
tak
tak
tak
tak

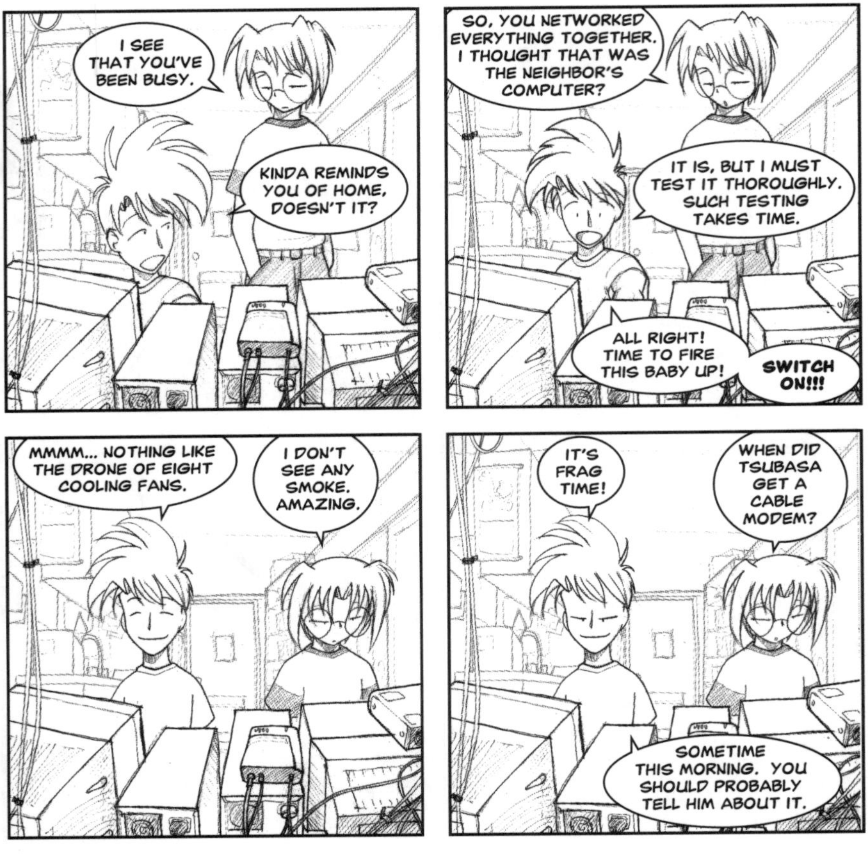
I SEE THAT YOU'VE BEEN BUSY.
KINDA REMINDS YOU OF HOME, DOESN'T IT?
SO, YOU NETWORKED EVERYTHING TOGETHER. I THOUGHT THAT WAS THE NEIGHBOR'S COMPUTER?
IT IS, BUT I MUST TEST IT THOROUGHLY. SUCH TESTING TAKES TIME.
ALL RIGHT! TIME TO FIRE THIS BABY UP!
SWITCH ON!!!
MMMM... NOTHING LIKE THE DRONE OF EIGHT COOLING FANS.
I DON'T SEE ANY SMOKE. AMAZING.
IT'S FRAG TIME!
WHEN DID TSUBASA GET A CABLE MODEM?
SOMETIME THIS MORNING. YOU SHOULD PROBABLY TELL HIM ABOUT IT.

LOOK FAMILIAR? MOST OF MY FRIENDS HAVE A ROOM OR TWO THAT LOOK LIKE THIS.

IT'S HARD DOING A COMIC ABOUT GAMERS WHEN THEY DON'T HAVE A COMPUTER TO PLAY ON, SO WE TOOK SOME LIBERTIES TO GET LARGO AND PIRO "GEARED UP".

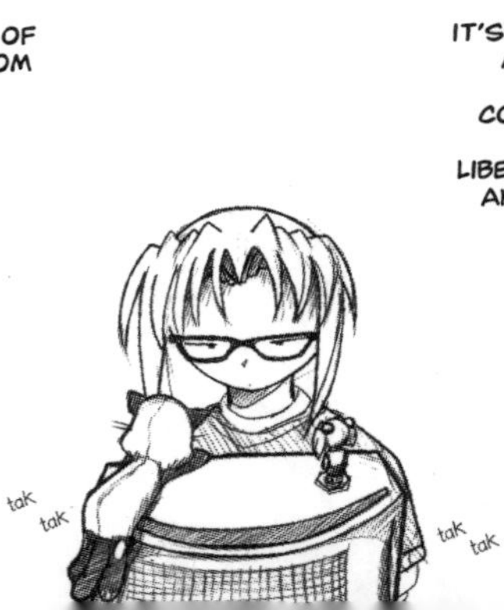
tak
tak
tak
tak

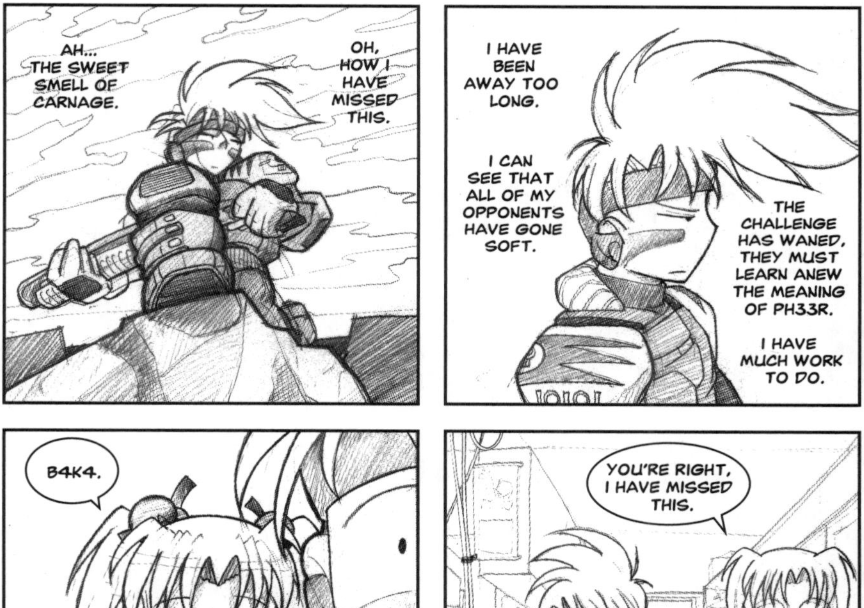
AH... THE SWEET SMELL OF CARNAGE.
OH, HOW I HAVE MISSED THIS.
I HAVE BEEN AWAY TOO LONG.
I CAN SEE THAT ALL OF MY OPPONENTS HAVE GONE SOFT.
THE CHALLENGE HAS WANED, THEY MUST LEARN ANEW THE MEANING OF PH33R.
I HAVE MUCH WORK TO DO.
B4K4.
HUH?
YOU'RE RIGHT, I HAVE MISSED THIS.
WHEN I RESPAWN YOU ARE SOOOO FSCKING DEAD.

SOMETIMES OUR EXPERIENCES IN A GAME CAN BE JUST AS IMPORTANT AS OUR REAL LIFE EXPERIENCES, SO IT'S ONLY NATURAL TO SHOW PIRO AND LARGO IN THE GAMES THEY PLAY.

PIRO IS ONE OF THOSE GAMERS WHO PREFERS TO USE FEMALE CHARACTERS WHEN PLAYING. "PIROKO" CAN KICK LARGO'S ASS IN QUAKE 3 - A FACT THAT IRRITATES LARGO TO NO END.

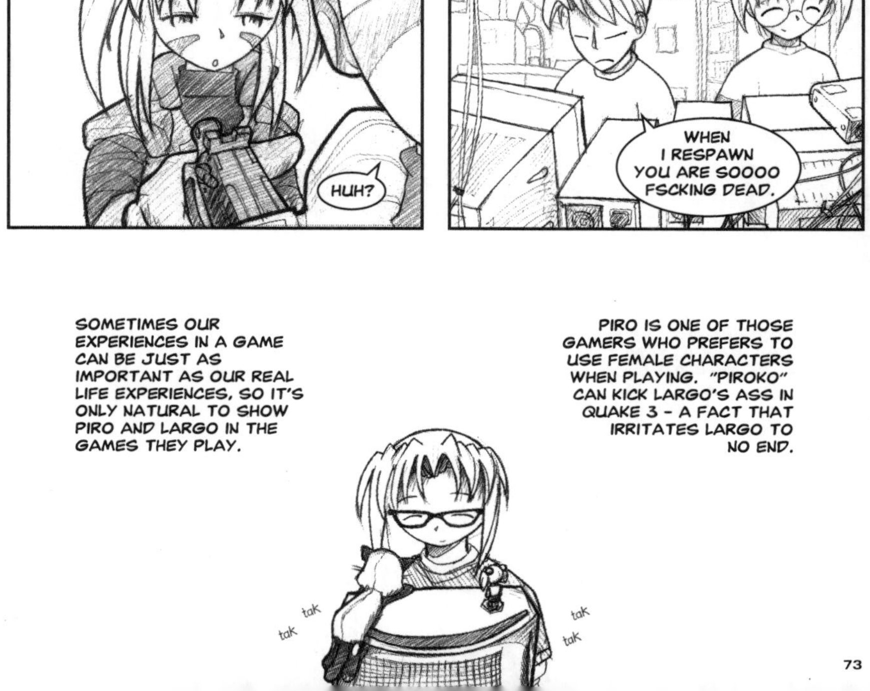
tak
tak
tak
tak

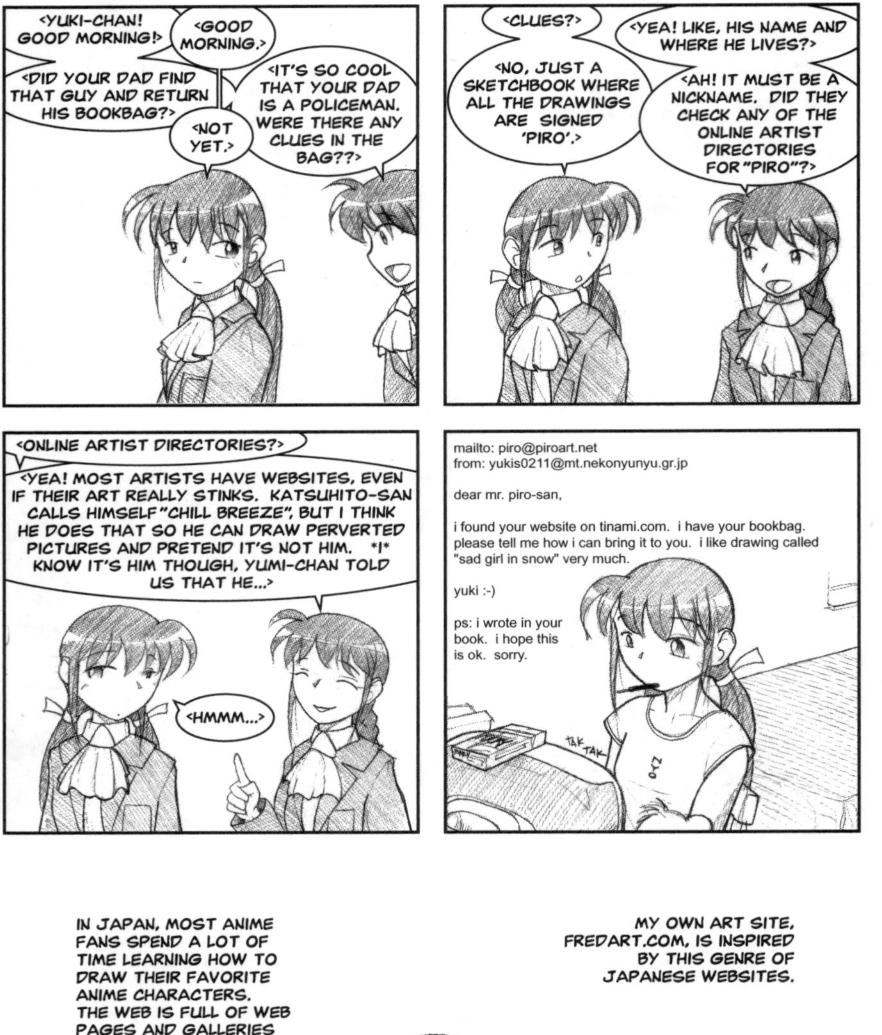
<YUKI-CHAN! GOOD MORNING!>
<GOOD MORNING.>
<DID YOUR DAD FIND THAT GUY AND RETURN HIS BOOKBAG?>
<NOT YET.>
<IT'S SO COOL THAT YOUR DAD IS A POLICEMAN. WERE THERE ANY CLUES IN THE BAG??>
<CLUES?>
<NO, JUST A SKETCHBOOK WHERE ALL THE DRAWINGS ARE SIGNED 'PIRO'.>
<YEA! LIKE, HIS NAME AND WHERE HE LIVES?>
<AH! IT MUST BE A NICKNAME. DID THEY CHECK ANY OF THE ONLINE ARTIST DIRECTORIES FOR "PIRO"?>
<ONLINE ARTIST DIRECTORIES?>
<YEA! MOST ARTISTS HAVE WEBSITES, EVEN IF THEIR ART REALLY STINKS. KATSUHITO-SAN CALLS HIMSELF "CHILL BREEZE", BUT I THINK HE DOES THAT SO HE CAN DRAW PERVERTED PICTURES AND PRETEND IT'S NOT HIM. *I* KNOW IT'S HIM THOUGH, YUMI-CHAN TOLD US THAT HE...>
<HMMM...>
mailto: piro@piroart.net
from: yukis0211@mt.nekonyunyu.gr.jp
dear mr. piro-san,
i found your website on tinami.com. i have your bookbag. please tell me how i can bring it to you. i like drawing called "sad girl in snow" very much.
yuki :-)
ps: i wrote in your book. i hope this is ok. sorry.
TAK TAK

IN JAPAN, MOST ANIME FANS SPEND A LOT OF TIME LEARNING HOW TO DRAW THEIR FAVORITE ANIME CHARACTERS. THE WEB IS FULL OF WEB PAGES AND GALLERIES OF THEIR WORK.

MY OWN ART SITE, FREDART.COM, IS INSPIRED BY THIS GENRE OF JAPANESE WEBSITES.

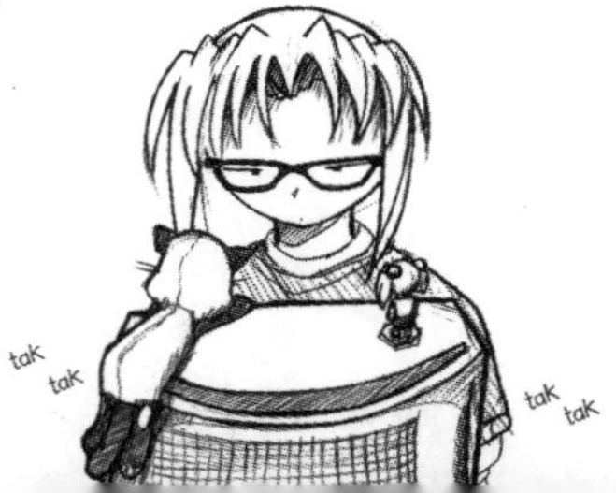
tak
tak
tak
tak

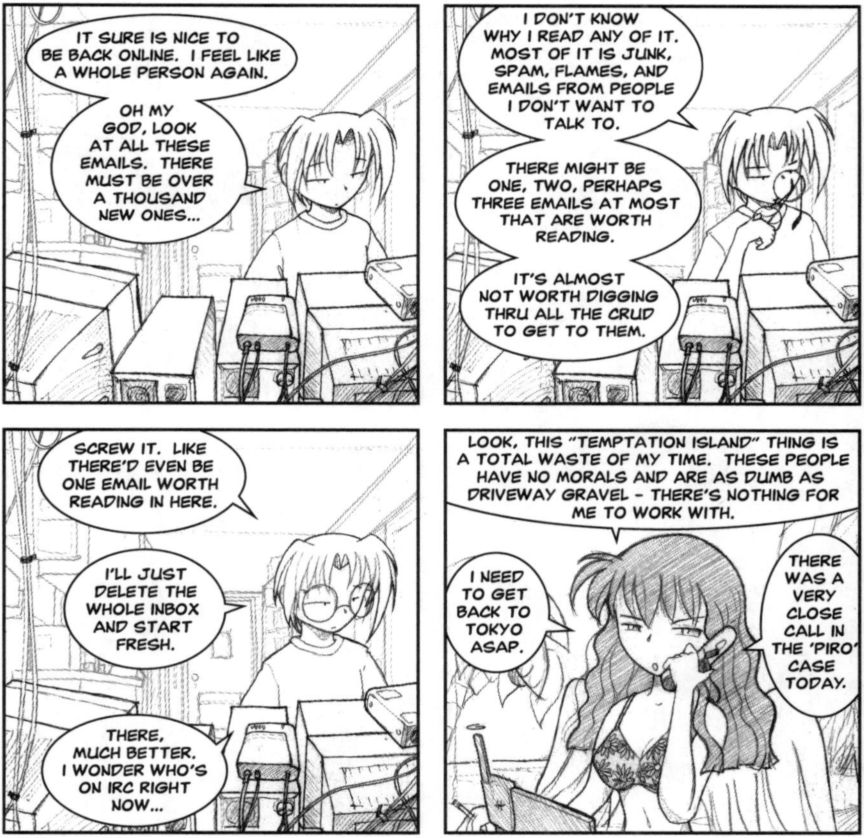
IT SURE IS NICE TO BE BACK ONLINE. I FEEL LIKE A WHOLE PERSON AGAIN.
OH MY GOD, LOOK AT ALL THESE EMAILS. THERE MUST BE OVER A THOUSAND NEW ONES...
I DON'T KNOW WHY I READ ANY OF IT. MOST OF IT IS JUNK, SPAM, FLAMES, AND EMAILS FROM PEOPLE I DON'T WANT TO TALK TO.
THERE MIGHT BE ONE, TWO, PERHAPS THREE EMAILS AT MOST THAT ARE WORTH READING.
IT'S ALMOST NOT WORTH DIGGING THRU ALL THE CRUD TO GET TO THEM.
SCREW IT. LIKE THERE'D EVEN BE ONE EMAIL WORTH READING IN HERE.
I'LL JUST DELETE THE WHOLE INBOX AND START FRESH.
THERE, MUCH BETTER. I WONDER WHO'S ON IRC RIGHT NOW...
LOOK, THIS "TEMPTATION ISLAND" THING IS A TOTAL WASTE OF MY TIME. THESE PEOPLE HAVE NO MORALS AND ARE AS DUMB AS DRIVEWAY GRAVEL - THERE'S NOTHING FOR ME TO WORK WITH.
I NEED TO GET BACK TO TOKYO ASAP.
THERE WAS A VERY CLOSE CALL IN THE 'PIRO' CASE TODAY.

EMAIL HAS ALWAYS BEEN A PROBLEM FOR ME. EVEN WHEN I USED TO GET A REASONABLE AMOUNT OF IT, I WAS BAD AT RESPONDING.

THESE DAYS, I CAN'T EVEN KEEP UP WITH READING IT AS IT COMES IN.

"DUMB AS DRIVEWAY GRAVEL."...HEHEH. I KNOW PEOPLE LIKE THAT.

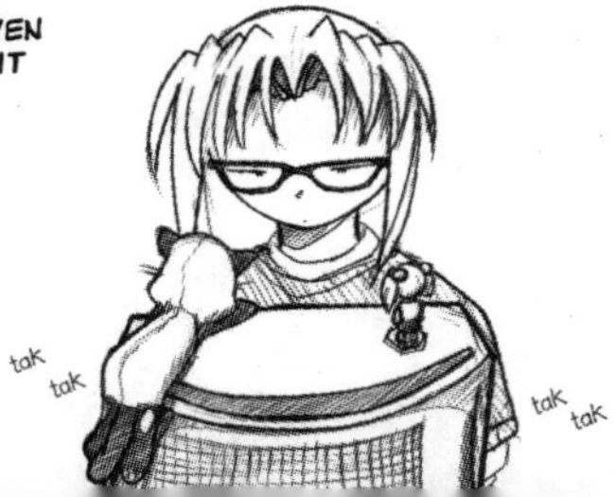
tak tak
tak tak

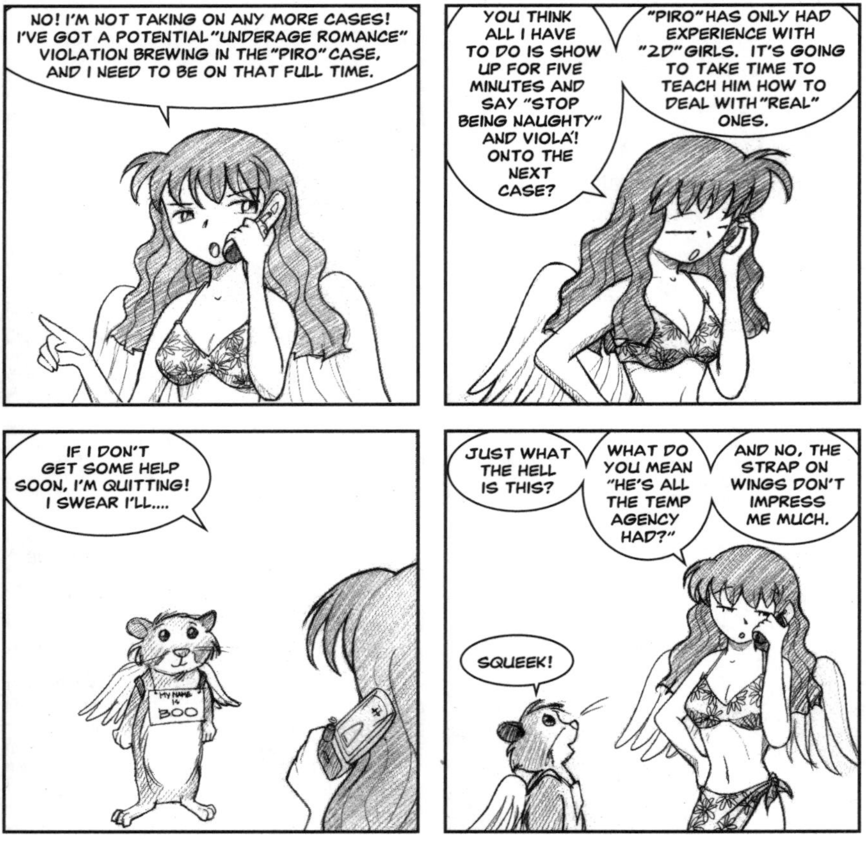
NO! I'M NOT TAKING ON ANY MORE CASES! I'VE GOT A POTENTIAL "UNDERAGE ROMANCE" VIOLATION BREWING IN THE "PIRO" CASE, AND I NEED TO BE ON THAT FULL TIME.
YOU THINK ALL I HAVE TO DO IS SHOW UP FOR FIVE MINUTES AND SAY "STOP BEING NAUGHTY" AND VIOLA'! ONTO THE NEXT CASE?
"PIRO" HAS ONLY HAD EXPERIENCE WITH "2D" GIRLS. IT'S GOING TO TAKE TIME TO TEACH HIM HOW TO DEAL WITH "REAL" ONES.
IF I DON'T GET SOME HELP SOON, I'M QUITTING! I SWEAR I'LL....
MY NAME IS BOO
JUST WHAT THE HELL IS THIS?
WHAT DO YOU MEAN "HE'S ALL THE TEMP AGENCY HAD?"
AND NO, THE STRAP ON WINGS DON'T IMPRESS ME MUCH.
SQUEEK!

LARGO THOUGHT THAT IT WASN'T FAIR THAT PIRO HAD A CONSCIENCE BUT LARGO DID NOT. HE SUGGESTED THAT HIS CONSCIENCE COULD BE A LOT LIKE THE LITTLE SPACE HAMPSTER STAR FROM ONE OF *BIOWARE'S* POPULAR GAMES. (IT'S AN OBSESSION, I TELL YOU!)

SINCE A HAMSTER REALLY DID SEEM APPROPRIATE FOR LARGO'S CONSCIENCE, BOO - COMPLETE WITH STRAP-ON WINGS AND FRESH FROM A TEMP AGENCY - ARRIVED TO SEE WHAT HE COULD DO.

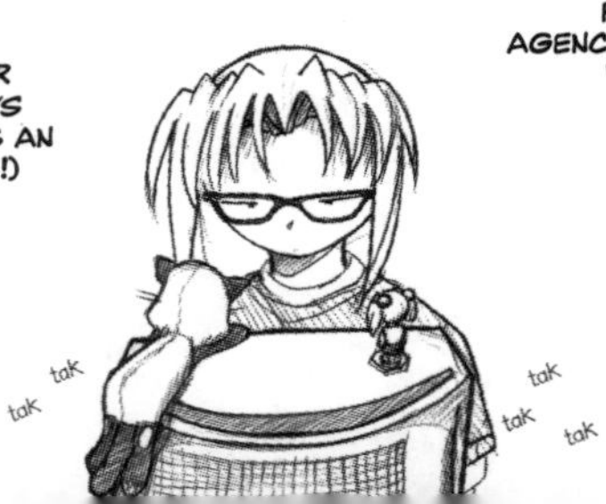
tak tak
tak tak tak

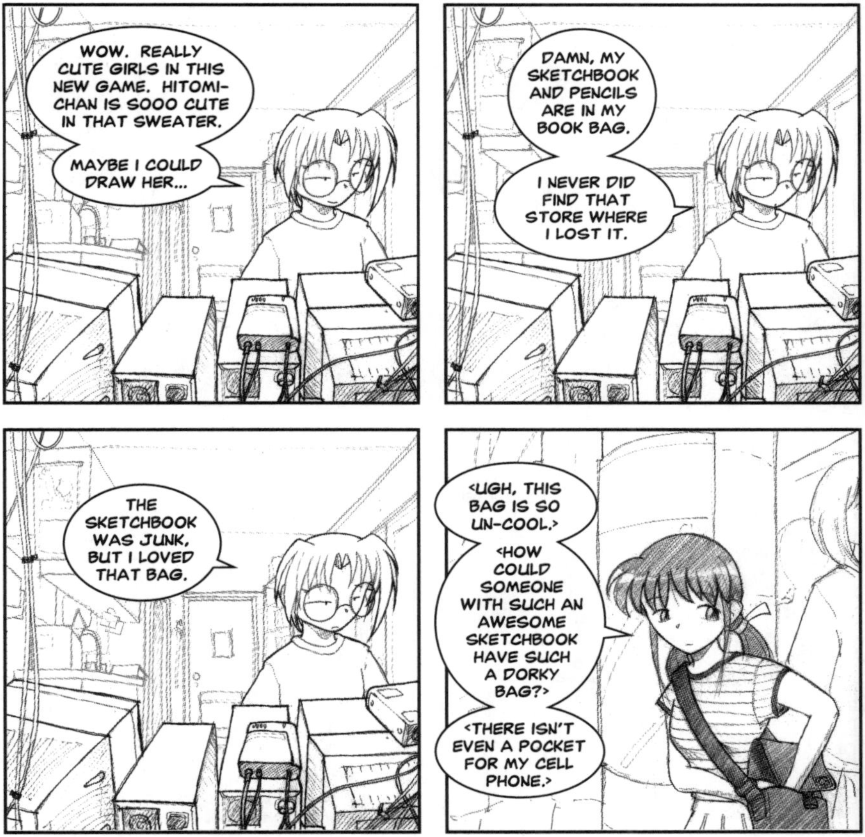
WOW. REALLY CUTE GIRLS IN THIS NEW GAME. HITOMI-CHAN IS SOOO CUTE IN THAT SWEATER.
MAYBE I COULD DRAW HER...
DAMN, MY SKETCHBOOK AND PENCILS ARE IN MY BOOK BAG.
I NEVER DID FIND THAT STORE WHERE I LOST IT.
THE SKETCHBOOK WAS JUNK, BUT I LOVED THAT BAG.
<UGH, THIS BAG IS SO UN-COOL.>
<HOW COULD SOMEONE WITH SUCH AN AWESOME SKETCHBOOK HAVE SUCH A DORKY BAG?>
<THERE ISN'T EVEN A POCKET FOR MY CELL PHONE.>

A LOT OF YOU ARE PROBABLY WONDERING "WHAT IS YUKI THINKING?"

NEVER UNDERESTIMATE A PLUCKY 15 YEAR OLD. SHE PROBABLY DOESN'T KNOW EITHER.

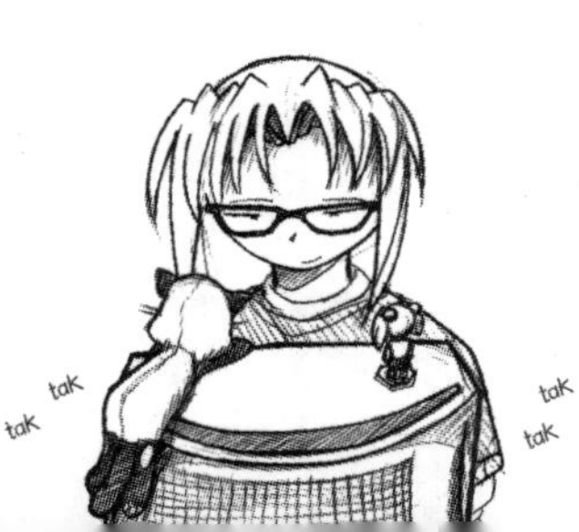
tak
tak
tak
tak

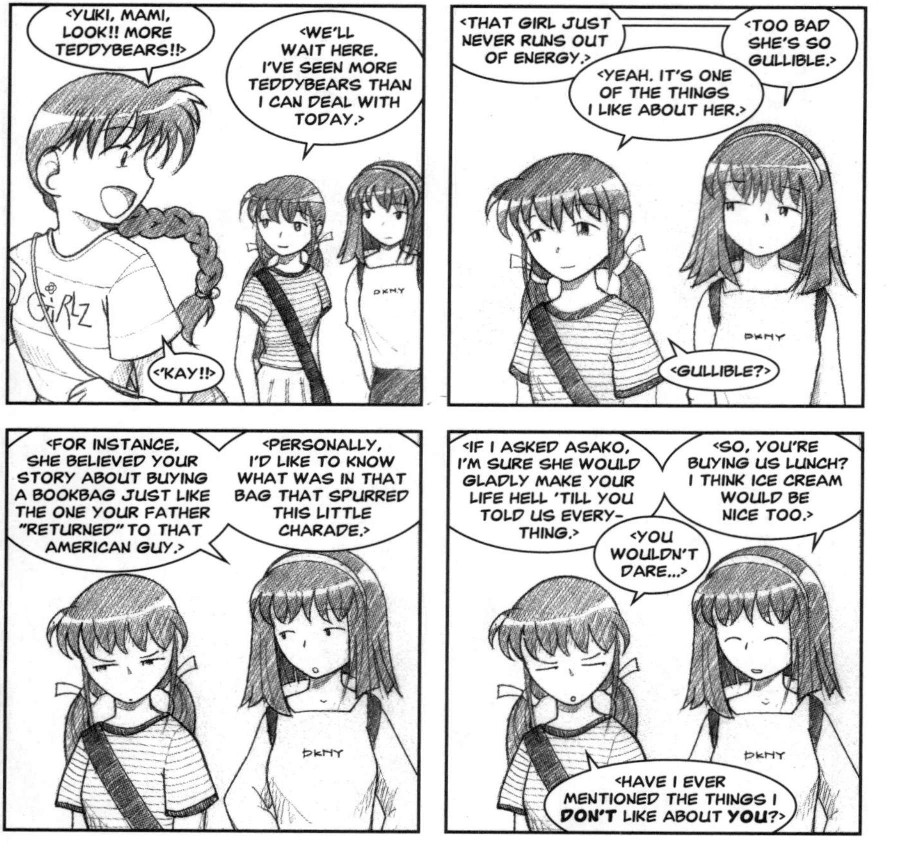
<YUKI, MAMI, LOOK!! MORE TEDDYBEARS!!>
<WE'LL WAIT HERE. I'VE SEEN MORE TEDDYBEARS THAN I CAN DEAL WITH TODAY.>
<'KAY!!>
<THAT GIRL JUST NEVER RUNS OUT OF ENERGY.>
<TOO BAD SHE'S SO GULLIBLE.>
<YEAH, IT'S ONE OF THE THINGS I LIKE ABOUT HER.>
<GULLIBLE?>
<FOR INSTANCE, SHE BELIEVED YOUR STORY ABOUT BUYING A BOOKBAG JUST LIKE THE ONE YOUR FATHER "RETURNED" TO THAT AMERICAN GUY.>
<PERSONALLY, I'D LIKE TO KNOW WHAT WAS IN THAT BAG THAT SPURRED THIS LITTLE CHARADE.>
<IF I ASKED ASAKO, I'M SURE SHE WOULD GLADLY MAKE YOUR LIFE HELL 'TILL YOU TOLD US EVERY-THING.>
<SO, YOU'RE BUYING US LUNCH? I THINK ICE CREAM WOULD BE NICE TOO.>
<YOU WOULDN'T DARE...>
<HAVE I EVER MENTIONED THE THINGS I DON'T LIKE ABOUT YOU?>

WE ALL HAVE FRIENDS WE CAN HIDE THINGS FROM, AND FRIENDS WHO CAN SEE RIGHT THOUGH US.

I FEEL FOR YOU IF YOU HAVE TOO MANY OF THE LATTER.

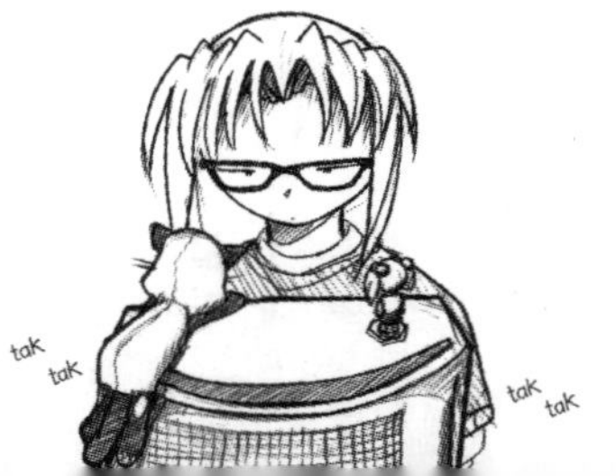
tak tak
tak tak

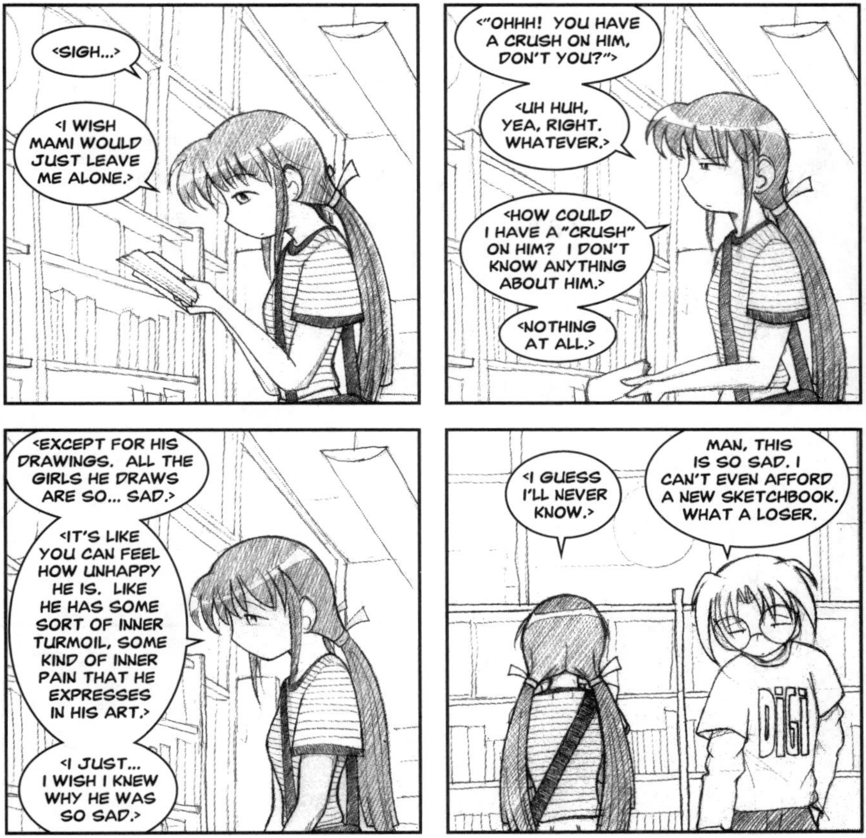
<SIGH...>
<I WISH MAMI WOULD JUST LEAVE ME ALONE.>
<"OHHH! YOU HAVE A CRUSH ON HIM, DON'T YOU?">
<UH HUH, YEA, RIGHT. WHATEVER.>
<HOW COULD I HAVE A "CRUSH" ON HIM? I DON'T KNOW ANYTHING ABOUT HIM.>
<NOTHING AT ALL.>
<EXCEPT FOR HIS DRAWINGS. ALL THE GIRLS HE DRAWS ARE SO... SAD.>
<IT'S LIKE YOU CAN FEEL HOW UNHAPPY HE IS. LIKE HE HAS SOME SORT OF INNER TURMOIL, SOME KIND OF INNER PAIN THAT HE EXPRESSES IN HIS ART.>
<I JUST... I WISH I KNEW WHY HE WAS SO SAD.>
<I GUESS I'LL NEVER KNOW.>
MAN, THIS IS SO SAD. I CAN'T EVEN AFFORD A NEW SKETCHBOOK. WHAT A LOSER.
DiGi

CHARACTER PLACEMENT IS PROBABLY ONE OF THE HARDEST THINGS ABOUT WRITING A COMIC LIKE THIS.

YOU HAVE TO PLAN FAR IN ADVANCE TO GET CHARACTERS TO BE IN THE RIGHT PLACE AT THE RIGHT TIME.

WRITING IS AN ORGANIC PROCESS, AND THE STORY CAN TAKE ON A LIFE OF ITS OWN IF YOU AREN'T CAREFUL.

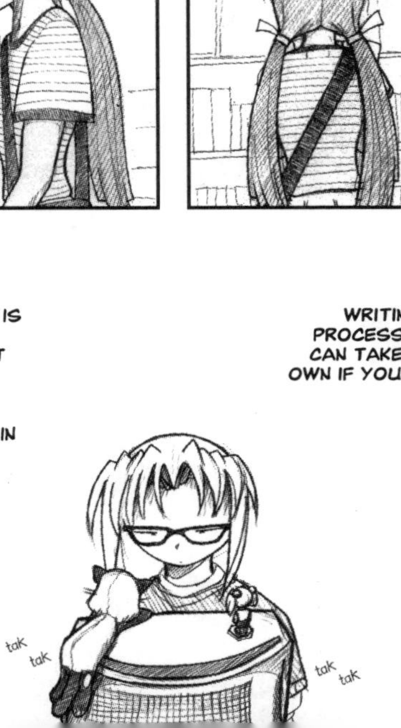
tak
tak
tak
tak

WHAT THE...
THAT'S MY BOOKBAG!
AND... ISN'T THAT THE SAME GIRL?
WHY... WHY IS SHE WEARING IT??
SHE JUST KEPT IT?
WHY WOULD SHE DO THAT?
I CAN'T JUST GO UP TO HER AND ASK FOR IT BACK.
AND MY SKETCH-BOOK...
IF SHE'S SEEN THAT, THEN THERE IS NO WAY I CAN ASK HER...
(SIGH)
DAMMNIT, SHE'S LEAVING THE STORE.

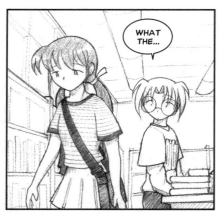

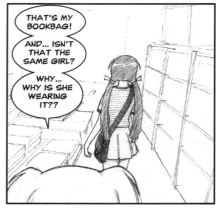

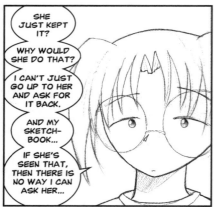

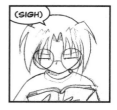

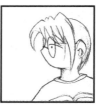

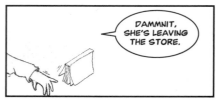

NOTE THAT WE ARE STARTING TO SEE THE BREAKDOWN OF THE FOUR-PANEL SETUP.

ONE OF THE HARDEST THINGS ABOUT DOING MEGATOKYO IS THAT I'M TRYING TO DO SEQUENTIAL COMICS WHERE EACH EPISODE HAS TO STAND ON ITS OWN. THE LATEST COMIC IS ALWAYS A STOPPING POINT.

AT ABOUT THIS TIME I WAS REALLY STARTING TO HAVE TOUBLE WITH THE LIMITATIONS OF THE ONE-TWO-THREE-FOUR COMIC SETUP.

I STARTED THINKING ABOUT CHANGING FORMAT.

tak
tak
tak
tak
tak

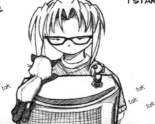

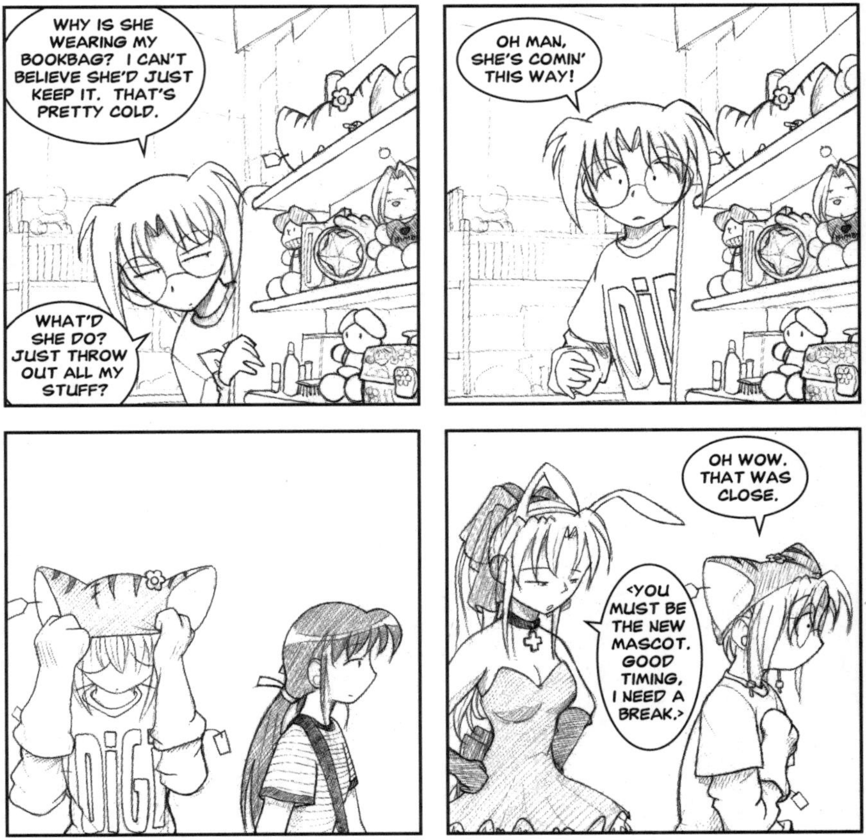
WHY IS SHE WEARING MY BOOKBAG? I CAN'T BELIEVE SHE'D JUST KEEP IT. THAT'S PRETTY COLD.
WHAT'D SHE DO? JUST THROW OUT ALL MY STUFF?
OH MAN, SHE'S COMIN' THIS WAY!
OH WOW. THAT WAS CLOSE.
<YOU MUST BE THE NEW MASCOT. GOOD TIMING, I NEED A BREAK.>

WHAT'S SAD IS THE REAL VERSION OF THAT HAT IS WAY TOO SMALL TO ACTUALLY FIT ON A GROWN UP'S HEAD.

HALF THE FUN OF THIS COMIC WAS DRAWING ALL THE LITTLE DOLLS ON THE SHELF. OH, AND ERIKA'S OUTFIT, TOO.

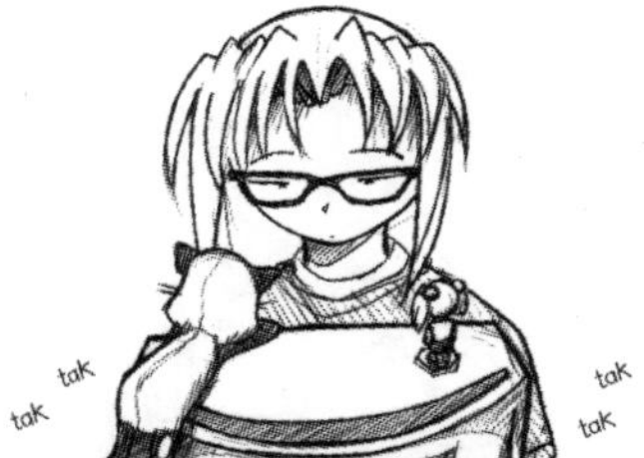
tak
tak
tak
tak

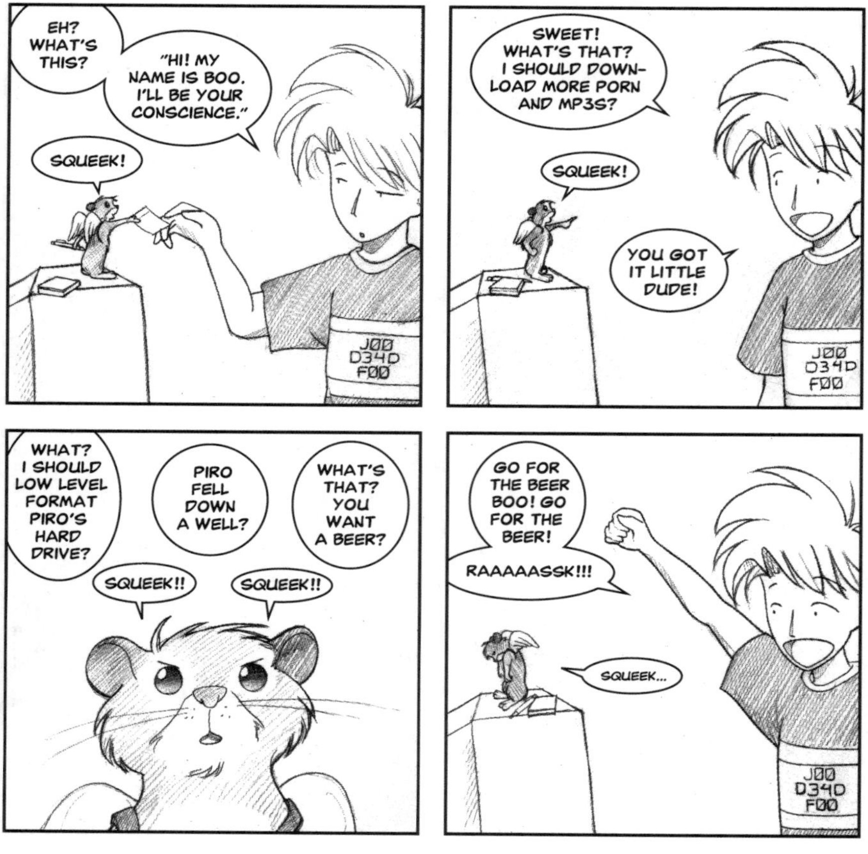
EH? WHAT'S THIS?
"HI! MY NAME IS BOO. I'LL BE YOUR CONSCIENCE."
SQUEEK!
J00 D34D F00
SWEET! WHAT'S THAT? I SHOULD DOWN-LOAD MORE PORN AND MP3S?
SQUEEK!
YOU GOT IT LITTLE DUDE!
J00 D34D F00
WHAT? I SHOULD LOW LEVEL FORMAT PIRO'S HARD DRIVE?
PIRO FELL DOWN A WELL?
WHAT'S THAT? YOU WANT A BEER?
SQUEEK!!
SQUEEK!!
GO FOR THE BEER BOO! GO FOR THE BEER!
RAAAAAASSK!!!
SQUEEK...
J00 D34D F00

PERSONALLY, I THINK THAT BOO IS ABOUT AS EFFECTIVE WITH LARGO AS ANY CONSCIENCE WOULD BE.

POOR BOO. HE TRIES.

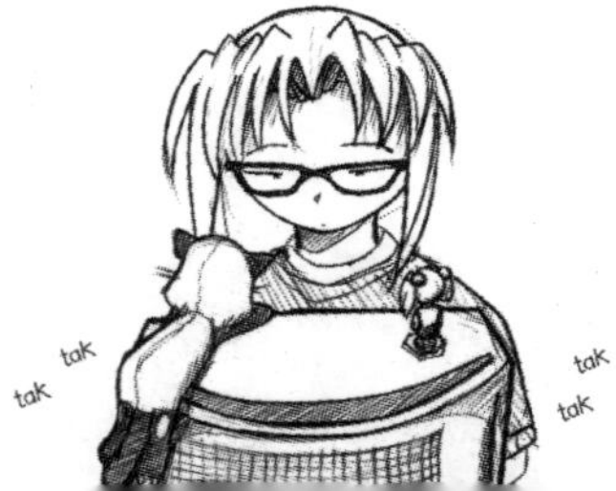
tak
tak
tak
tak

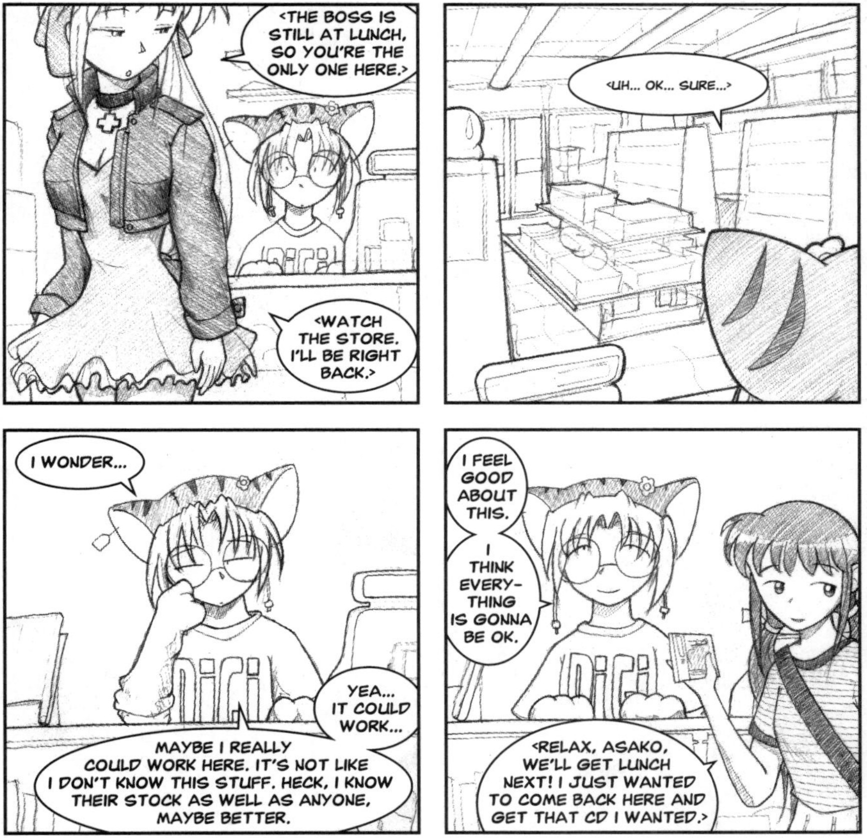
<THE BOSS IS STILL AT LUNCH, SO YOU'RE THE ONLY ONE HERE.>
<WATCH THE STORE. I'LL BE RIGHT BACK.>
<UH... OK... SURE...>
I WONDER...
MAYBE I REALLY COULD WORK HERE. IT'S NOT LIKE I DON'T KNOW THIS STUFF. HECK, I KNOW THEIR STOCK AS WELL AS ANYONE, MAYBE BETTER.
YEA... IT COULD WORK...
I FEEL GOOD ABOUT THIS.
I THINK EVERYTHING IS GONNA BE OK.
<RELAX, ASAKO, WE'LL GET LUNCH NEXT! I JUST WANTED TO COME BACK HERE AND GET THAT CD I WANTED.>

I PATTERNED THE "MEGAGAMERS" STORE AFTER SOME OF THE SMALL ANIME AND GAME SHOPS YOU CAN FIND IN AND AROUND TOKYO.

THE STORE IS ACTUALLY TWO LEVELS IN A SMALL BUILDING WITH A STORAGE ROOM ON THE TOP FLOOR.

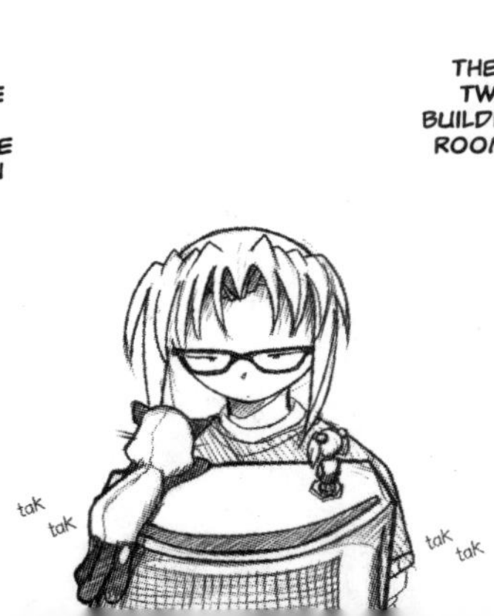
tak
tak
tak
tak

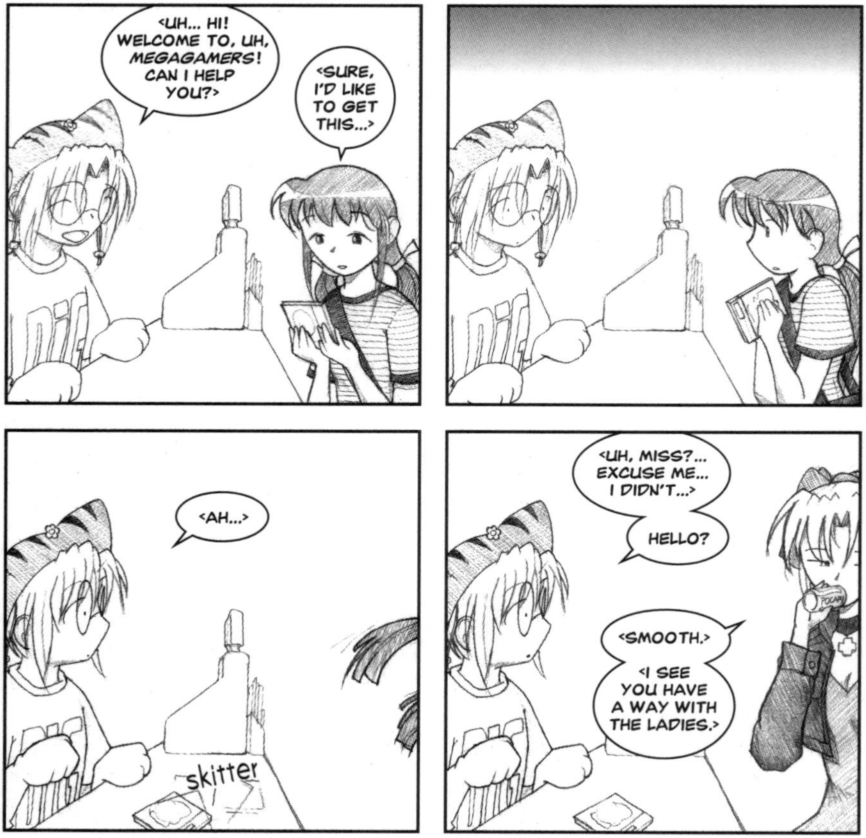

<UH... HI! WELCOME TO, UH, MEGAGAMERS! CAN I HELP YOU?>
<SURE, I'D LIKE TO GET THIS...>
<AH...>
skitter
<UH, MISS?... EXCUSE ME... I DIDN'T...>
HELLO?
<SMOOTH.>
<I SEE YOU HAVE A WAY WITH THE LADIES.>

GIVEN THE REAL LIFE RELEASE SCHEDULE OF THE COMIC BEING TWO TO THREE COMICS PER WEEK, PEOPLE WERE GETTING IRRITATED WITH HOW LONG IT TOOK FOR THINGS TO HAPPEN.

MOST READERS FOLLOWING THE COMIC BACK THEN DIDN'T HAVE THE LUXURY OF READING ALL OF THE EARILER COMICS IN A ROW LIKE THIS.

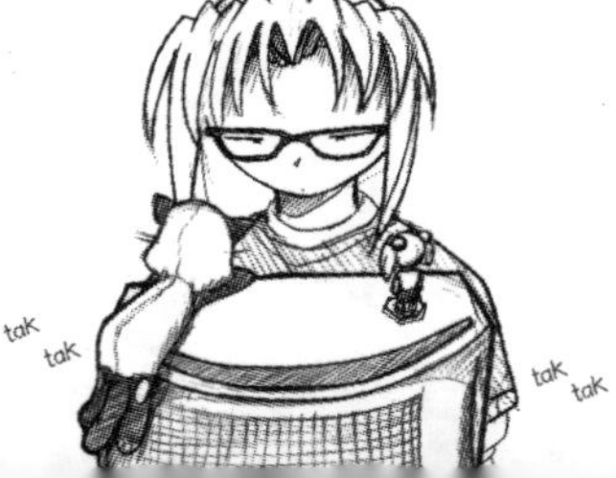

tak
tak
tak
tak

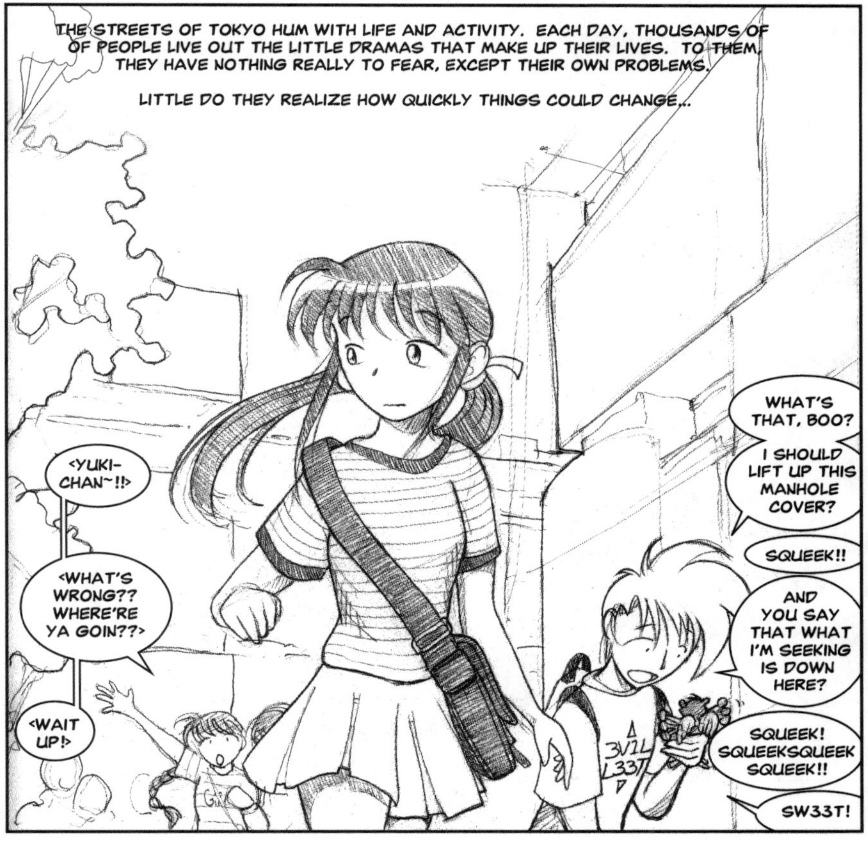
THE STREETS OF TOKYO HUM WITH LIFE AND ACTIVITY. EACH DAY, THOUSANDS OF OF PEOPLE LIVE OUT THE LITTLE DRAMAS THAT MAKE UP THEIR LIVES. TO THEM, THEY HAVE NOTHING REALLY TO FEAR, EXCEPT THEIR OWN PROBLEMS.
LITTLE DO THEY REALIZE HOW QUICKLY THINGS COULD CHANGE...
<YUKI-CHAN~!!>
<WHAT'S WRONG?? WHERE'RE YA GOIN??>
<WAIT UP!>
WHAT'S THAT, BOO?
I SHOULD LIFT UP THIS MANHOLE COVER?
SQUEEK!!
AND YOU SAY THAT WHAT I'M SEEKING IS DOWN HERE?
SQUEEK! SQUEEKSQUEEK SQUEEK!!
SW33T!
3VIL L33T

ABOUT THIS TIME I STARTED TO GET REALLY BUSY AT WORK, AND I WAS FINDING MYSELF SHORT ON TIME, SO I EXPERIMENTED WITH SOME SINGLE FRAME STRIPS.

THE MOST AMUSING THING ABOUT THIS COMIC IS LARGO'S T-SHIRT, WHICH WAS JUST A RANDOM SKETCH AT THE TIME. PEOPLE ALMOST THREATENED BODILY HARM IF WE DIDN'T MAKE T-SHIRTS WITH "3VIL L33T" ON THEM.

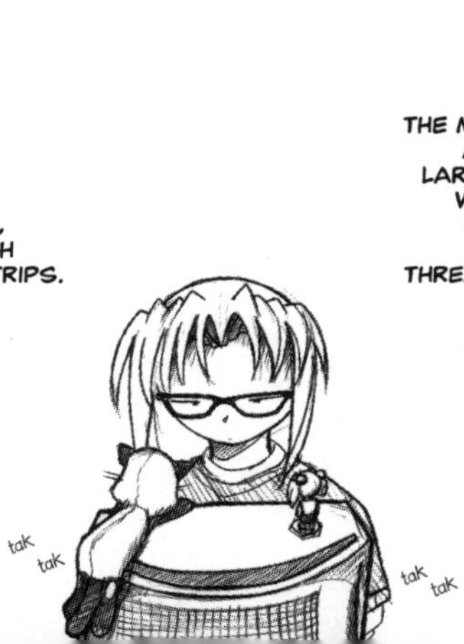
tak
tak
tak
tak

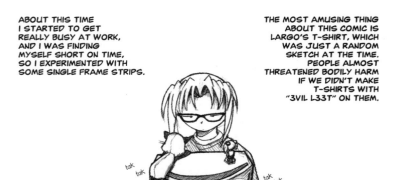

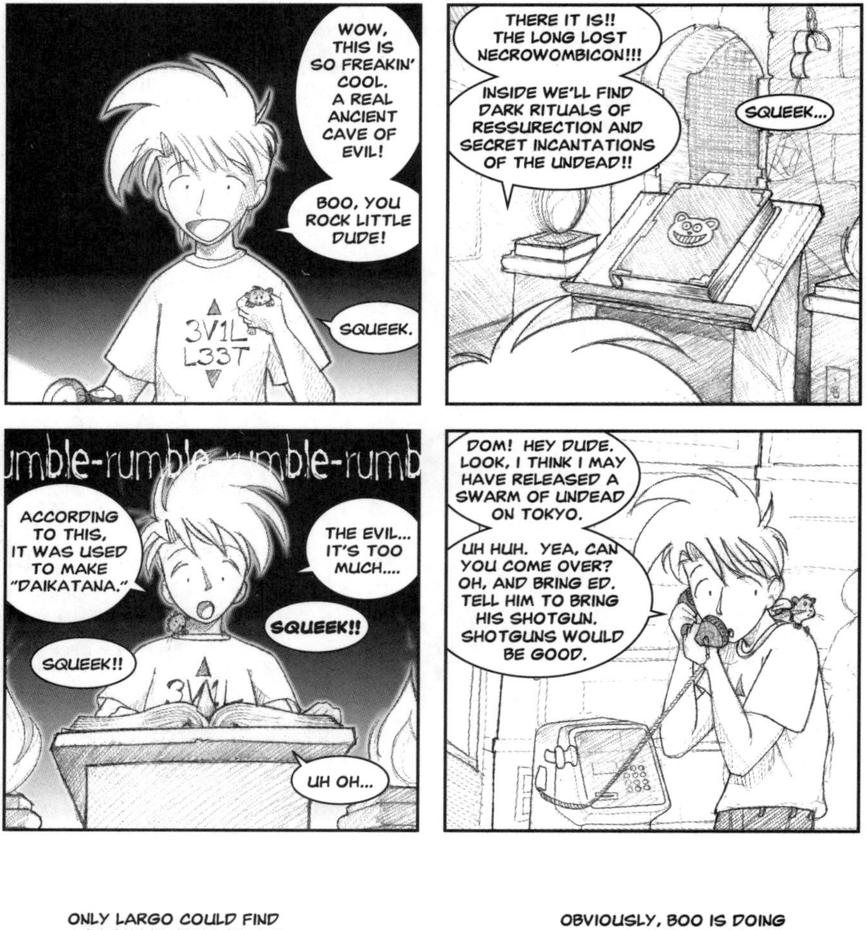
WOW, THIS IS SO FREAKIN' COOL. A REAL ANCIENT CAVE OF EVIL!
BOO, YOU ROCK LITTLE DUDE!
3V1L L33T
SQUEEK.
THERE IT IS!! THE LONG LOST NECROWOMBICON!!!
INSIDE WE'LL FIND DARK RITUALS OF RESSURECTION AND SECRET INCANTATIONS OF THE UNDEAD!!
SQUEEK...
umble-rumble rumble-rumb
ACCORDING TO THIS, IT WAS USED TO MAKE "DAIKATANA."
THE EVIL... IT'S TOO MUCH....
SQUEEK!!
SQUEEK!!
UH OH...
DOM! HEY DUDE. LOOK, I THINK I MAY HAVE RELEASED A SWARM OF UNDEAD ON TOKYO.
UH HUH. YEA, CAN YOU COME OVER? OH, AND BRING ED. TELL HIM TO BRING HIS SHOTGUN. SHOTGUNS WOULD BE GOOD.

ONLY LARGO COULD FIND AN ANCIENT CAVE OF EVIL IN DOWNTOWN TOKYO.

OBVIOUSLY, BOO IS DOING A STELLAR JOB OF KEEPING LARGO OUT OF TROUBLE.

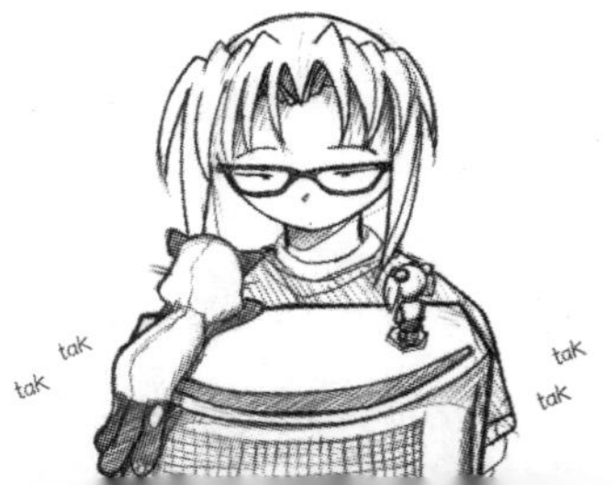
tak tak
tak tak

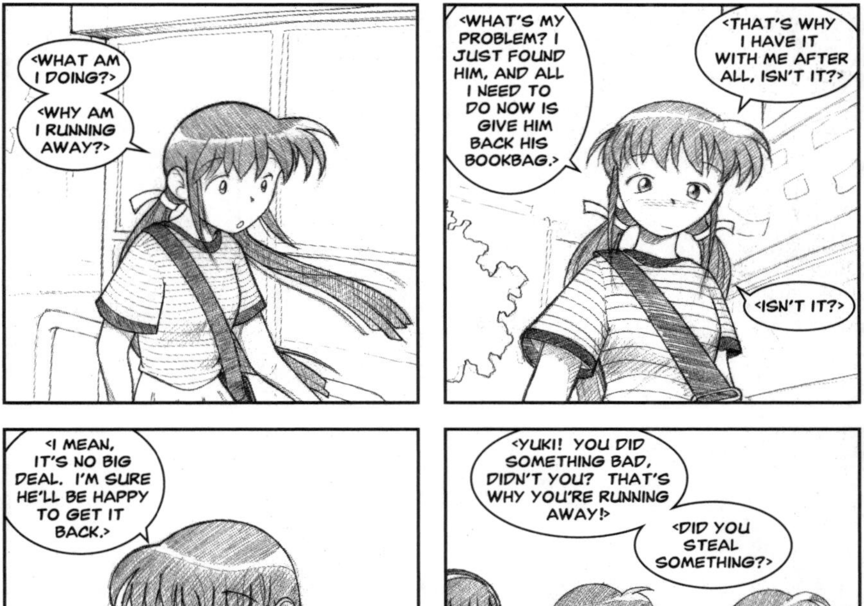
<WHAT AM I DOING?>
<WHY AM I RUNNING AWAY?>
<WHAT'S MY PROBLEM? I JUST FOUND HIM, AND ALL I NEED TO DO NOW IS GIVE HIM BACK HIS BOOKBAG.>
<THAT'S WHY I HAVE IT WITH ME AFTER ALL, ISN'T IT?>
<ISN'T IT?>
<I MEAN, IT'S NO BIG DEAL. I'M SURE HE'LL BE HAPPY TO GET IT BACK.>
<ALL I HAVE TO DO IS GO BACK TO THE STORE, GIVE HIM HIS SKETCHBOOK AND SAY...>
<...AND SAY...>
<YUKI! YOU DID SOMETHING BAD, DIDN'T YOU? THAT'S WHY YOU'RE RUNNING AWAY!>
<DID YOU STEAL SOMETHING?>
GIRLZ
<ASAKO...>

I COULD PROBABLY DO A WHOLE SERIES OF COMICS ABOUT YUKI AND HER FRIENDS.

YUKI IS THE LEADER OF THIS LITTLE CLUSTER, BUT THE ARRIVAL OF PIRO AND HIS BOOK BAG HAS STIRRED THINGS UP. THIS IS WHY HER FRIENDS AREN'T GIVING HER ANY SLACK.

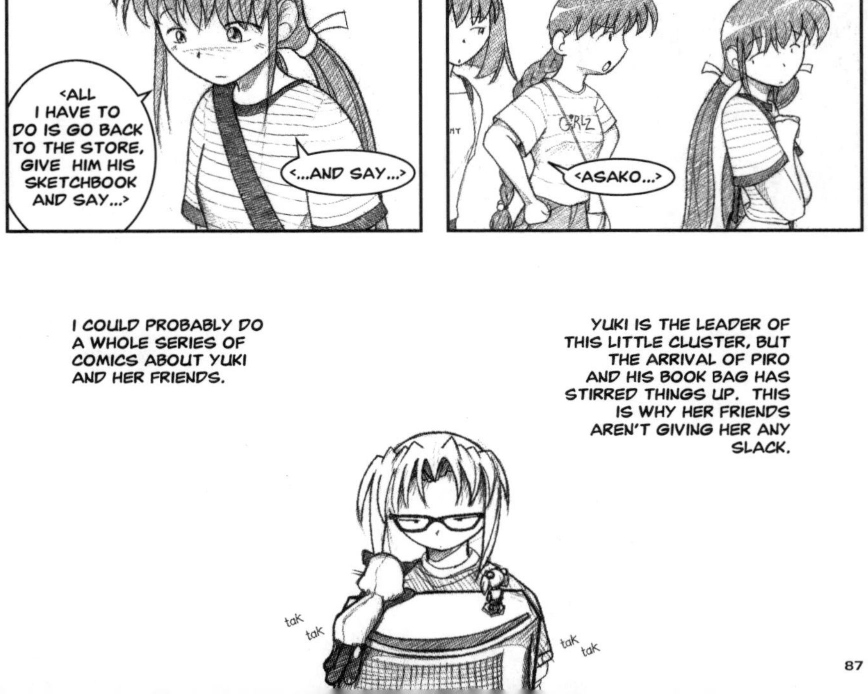
tak
tak
tak
tak

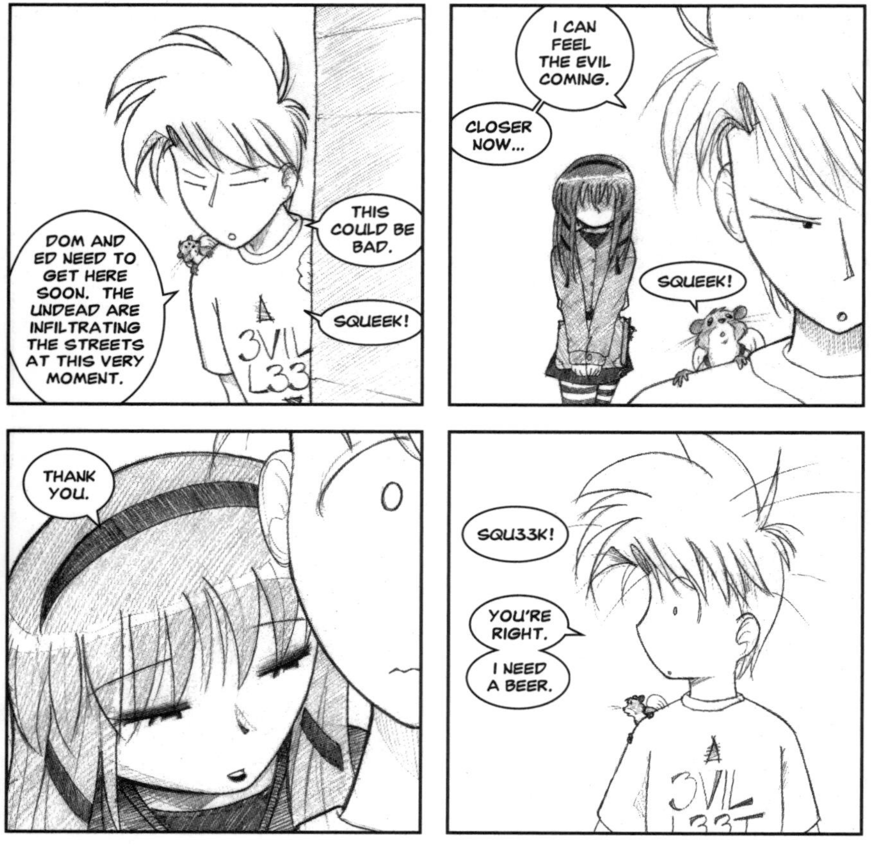
DOM AND ED NEED TO GET HERE SOON. THE UNDEAD ARE INFILTRATING THE STREETS AT THIS VERY MOMENT.
THIS COULD BE BAD.
SQUEEK!
3VIL L33
I CAN FEEL THE EVIL COMING.
CLOSER NOW...
SQUEEK!
THANK YOU.
SQU33K!
YOU'RE RIGHT.
I NEED A BEER.
3VIL

SOMETHING DARKLY CUTE THIS WAY COMES.

PEOPLE ON THE FORUMS SPENT MONTHS JUST WONDERING WHAT HER NAME WAS.

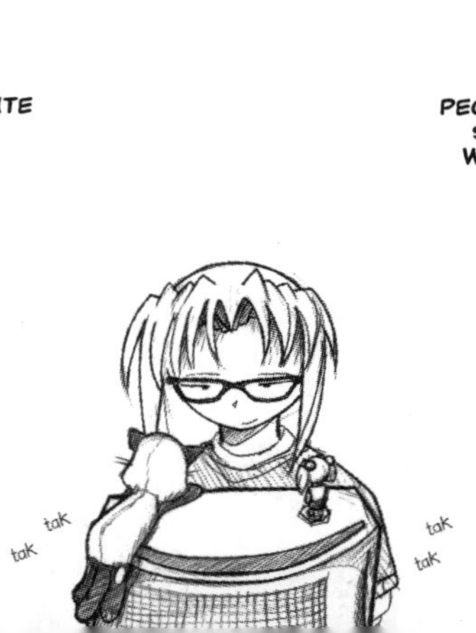
tak
tak
tak
tak

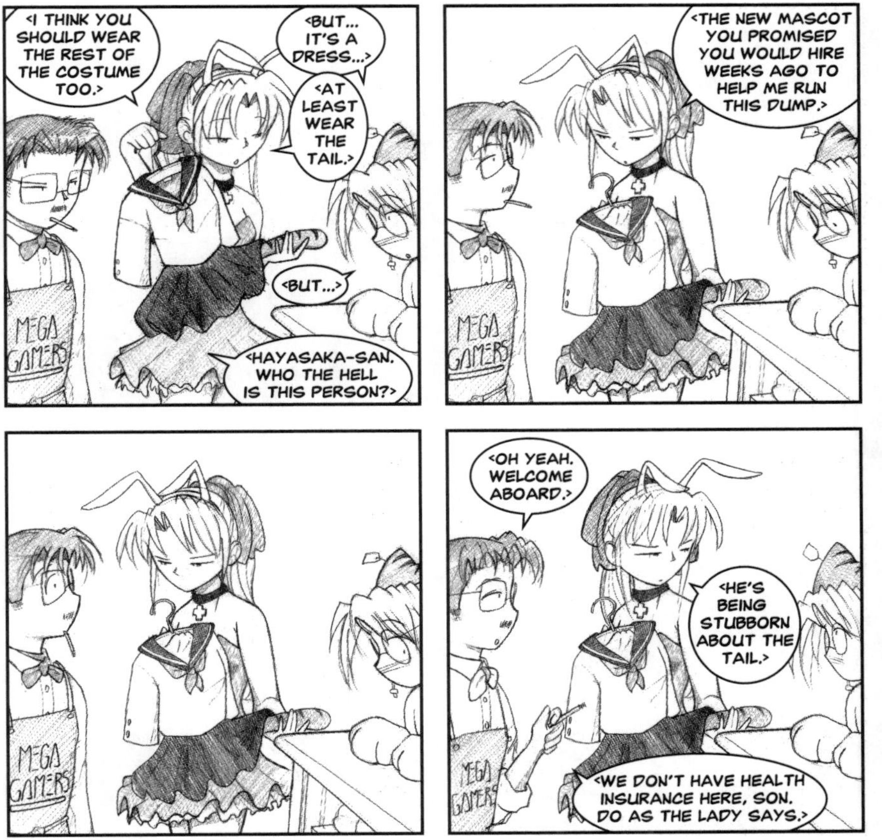
<I THINK YOU SHOULD WEAR THE REST OF THE COSTUME TOO.>
<BUT... IT'S A DRESS...>
<AT LEAST WEAR THE TAIL.>
<BUT...>
<HAYASAKA-SAN. WHO THE HELL IS THIS PERSON?>
<THE NEW MASCOT YOU PROMISED YOU WOULD HIRE WEEKS AGO TO HELP ME RUN THIS DUMP.>
MEGA GAMERS
<OH YEAH. WELCOME ABOARD.>
<HE'S BEING STUBBORN ABOUT THE TAIL.>
<WE DON'T HAVE HEALTH INSURANCE HERE, SON. DO AS THE LADY SAYS.>

YOU WILL NEVER SEE PIRO IN A DRESS.

CROSSDRESSING COSPLAY == THE EVIL.

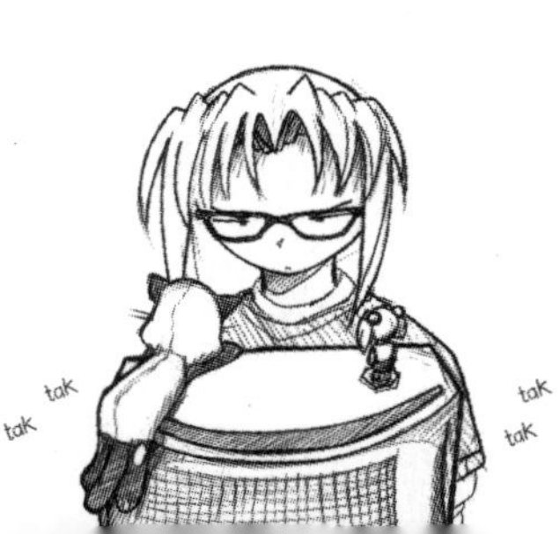
tak
tak
tak
tak

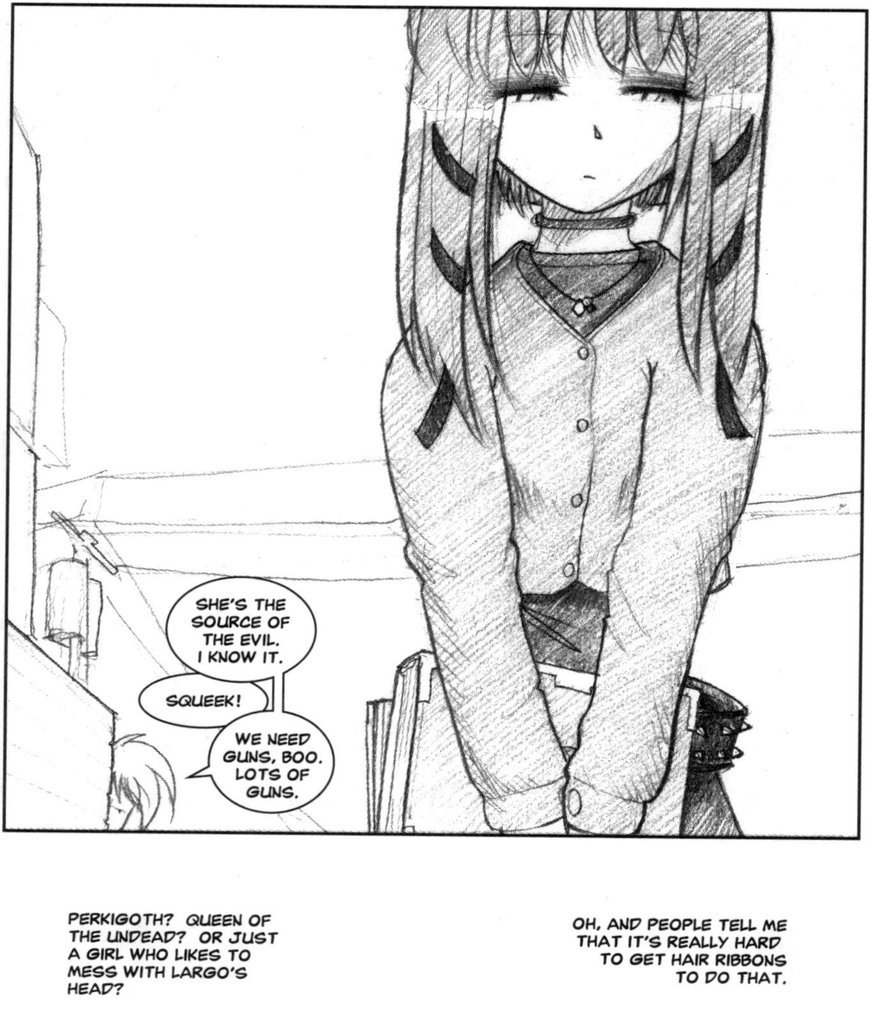
SHE'S THE SOURCE OF THE EVIL. I KNOW IT.
SQUEEK!
WE NEED GUNS, BOO. LOTS OF GUNS.

PERKIGOTH? QUEEN OF THE UNDEAD? OR JUST A GIRL WHO LIKES TO MESS WITH LARGO'S HEAD?

OH, AND PEOPLE TELL ME THAT IT'S REALLY HARD TO GET HAIR RIBBONS TO DO THAT.

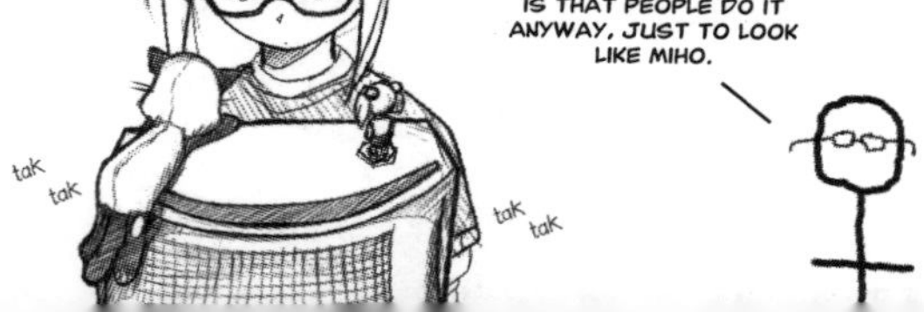
THE AMAZING THING IS THAT PEOPLE DO IT ANYWAY, JUST TO LOOK LIKE MIHO.
tak
tak
tak
tak

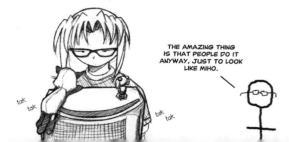

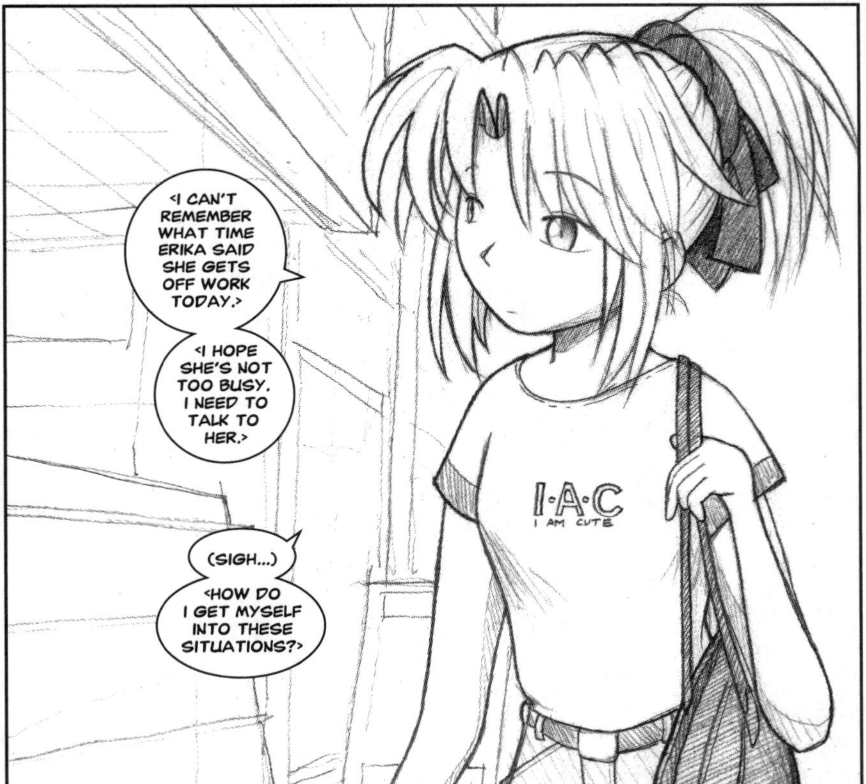
<I CAN'T REMEMBER WHAT TIME ERIKA SAID SHE GETS OFF WORK TODAY.>
<I HOPE SHE'S NOT TOO BUSY. I NEED TO TALK TO HER.>
I·A·C
I AM CUTE
(SIGH...)
<HOW DO I GET MYSELF INTO THESE SITUATIONS?>

MOST "ONE PANEL" COMICS DIDN'T WORK AS WELL AS "THE LITTLE DRAMAS" STRIP DID, SO I TRIED TO THINK OF OTHER WAYS TO SAVE TIME WHEN I WAS SWAMPED.

THERE IS SOMETHING REALLY WRONG WITH THIS DRAWING, THE PROPORTIONS ARE ALL SCREWED UP.

I REALLY HAVE TO REDRAW THIS STRIP SOMEDAY.

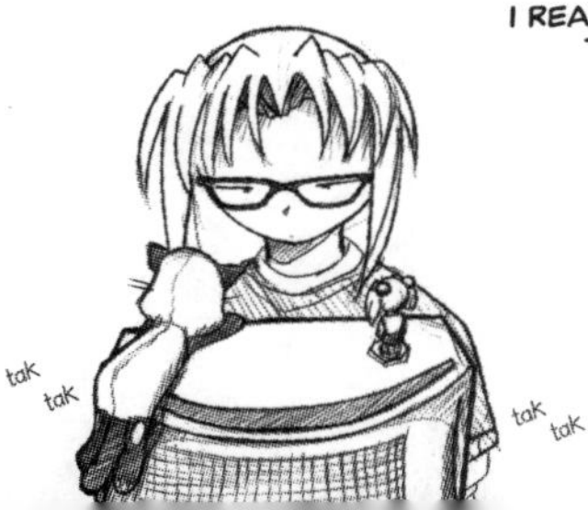
tak
tak
tak
tak

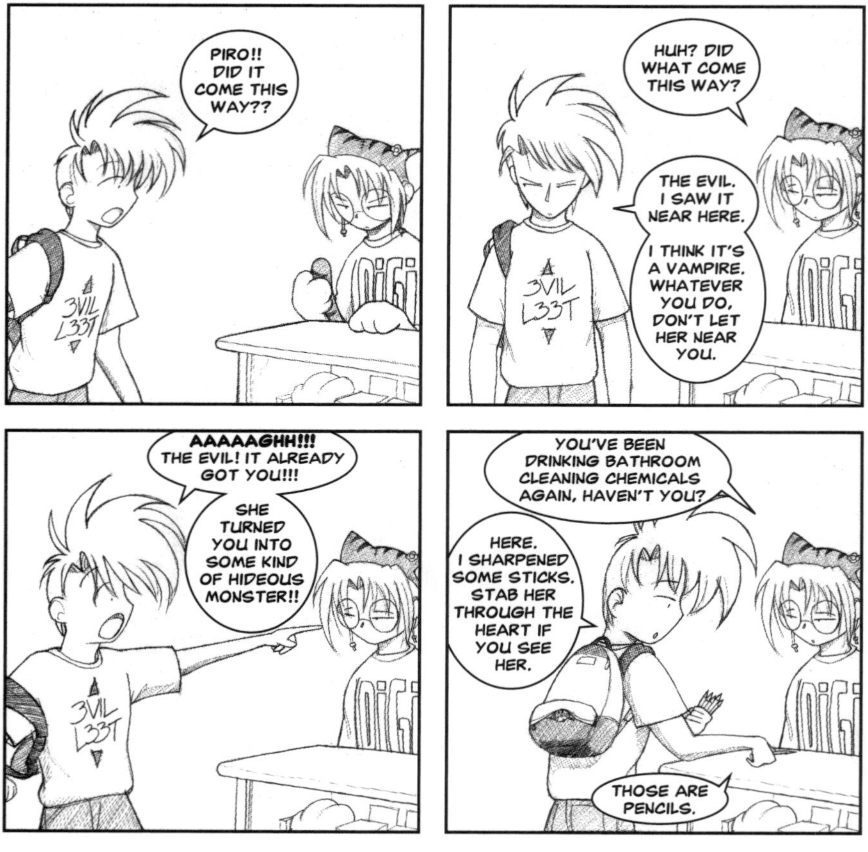
PIRO!! DID IT COME THIS WAY??
HUH? DID WHAT COME THIS WAY?
THE EVIL. I SAW IT NEAR HERE.
I THINK IT'S A VAMPIRE. WHATEVER YOU DO, DON'T LET HER NEAR YOU.
AAAAAGHH!!! THE EVIL! IT ALREADY GOT YOU!!!
SHE TURNED YOU INTO SOME KIND OF HIDEOUS MONSTER!!
YOU'VE BEEN DRINKING BATHROOM CLEANING CHEMICALS AGAIN, HAVEN'T YOU?
HERE. I SHARPENED SOME STICKS. STAB HER THROUGH THE HEART IF YOU SEE HER.
THOSE ARE PENCILS.

THIS WAS A FUN STRIP. I LIKE THE WAY LARGO'S MIND JUMPS FROM THOUGHT TO THOUGHT.

I GUESS A SHARPENED PENCIL COULD TECHNICALLY BE CONSIDERED A "WOODEN STAKE" IN A PINCH.

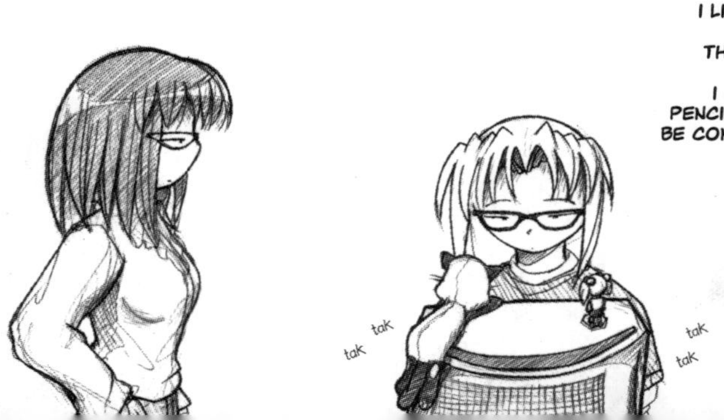
tak
tak
tak
tak

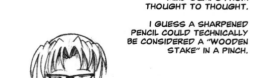

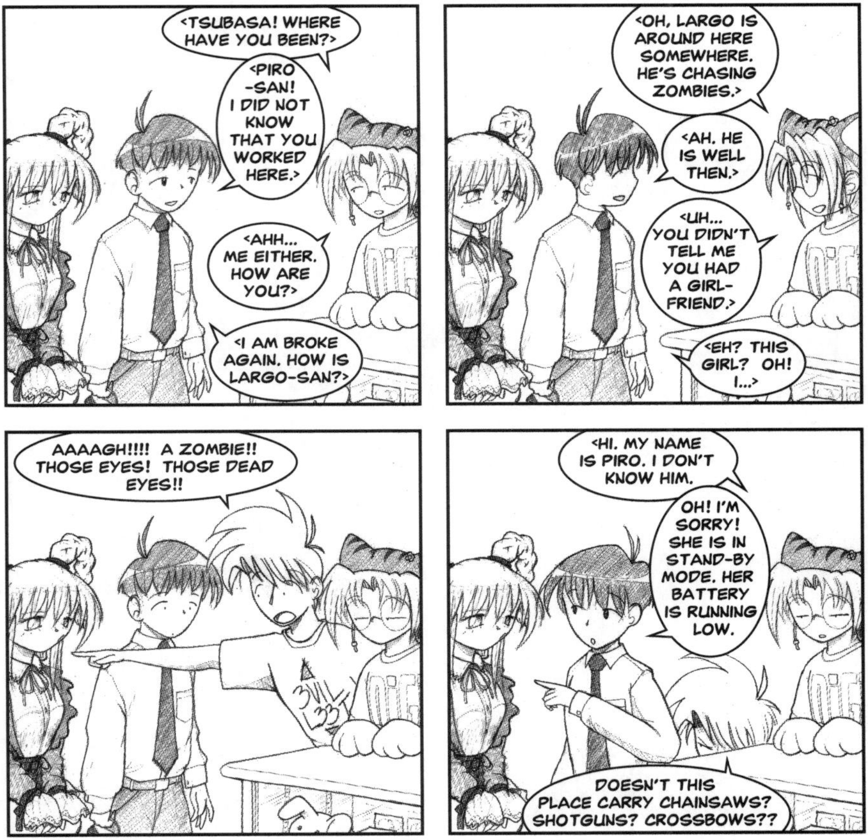
<TSUBASA! WHERE HAVE YOU BEEN?>
<PIRO -SAN! I DID NOT KNOW THAT YOU WORKED HERE.>
<AHH... ME EITHER. HOW ARE YOU?>
<I AM BROKE AGAIN. HOW IS LARGO-SAN?>
<OH, LARGO IS AROUND HERE SOMEWHERE. HE'S CHASING ZOMBIES.>
<AH. HE IS WELL THEN.>
<UH... YOU DIDN'T TELL ME YOU HAD A GIRL-FRIEND.>
<EH? THIS GIRL? OH! I...>
AAAAGH!!!! A ZOMBIE!! THOSE EYES! THOSE DEAD EYES!!
<HI. MY NAME IS PIRO. I DON'T KNOW HIM.
OH! I'M SORRY! SHE IS IN STAND-BY MODE. HER BATTERY IS RUNNING LOW.
DOESN'T THIS PLACE CARRY CHAINSAWS? SHOTGUNS? CROSSBOWS??

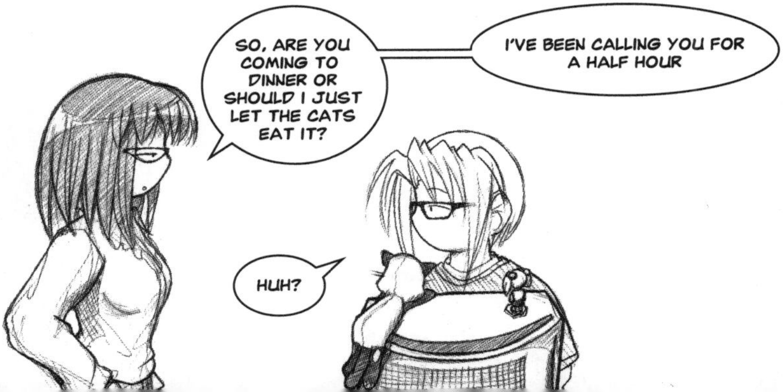
SO, ARE YOU COMING TO DINNER OR SHOULD I JUST LET THE CATS EAT IT?
I'VE BEEN CALLING YOU FOR A HALF HOUR
HUH?

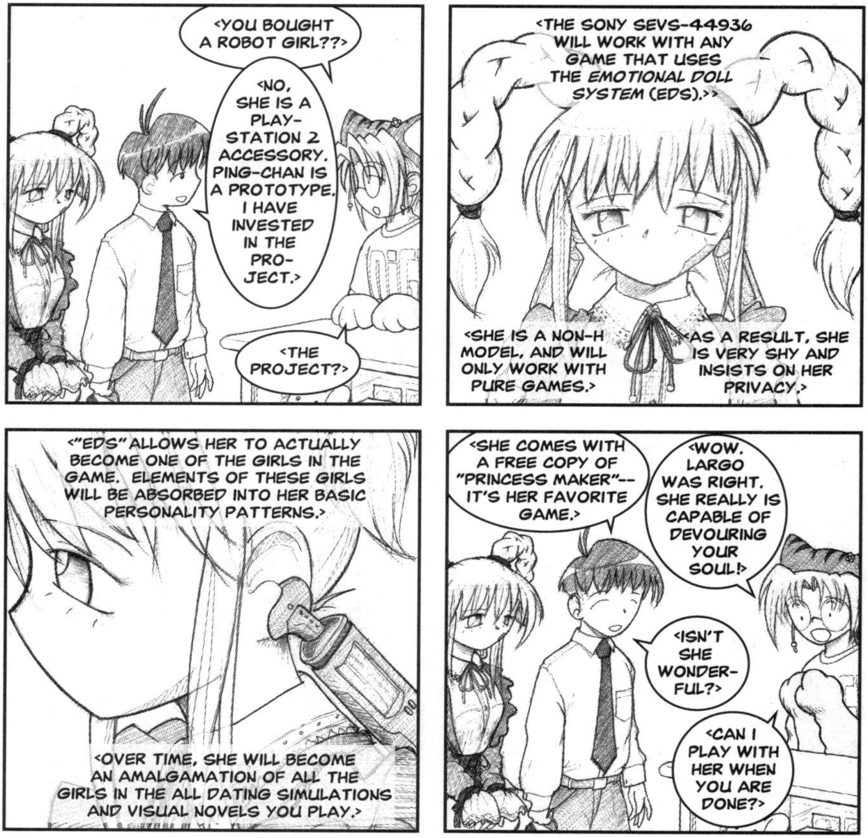
<YOU BOUGHT A ROBOT GIRL??>
<NO, SHE IS A PLAY-STATION 2 ACCESSORY. PING-CHAN IS A PROTOTYPE. I HAVE INVESTED IN THE PRO-JECT.>
<THE PROJECT?>
<THE SONY SEVS-44936 WILL WORK WITH ANY GAME THAT USES THE *EMOTIONAL DOLL SYSTEM* (EDS).>
<SHE IS A NON-H MODEL, AND WILL ONLY WORK WITH PURE GAMES.>
<AS A RESULT, SHE IS VERY SHY AND INSISTS ON HER PRIVACY.>
<"EDS" ALLOWS HER TO ACTUALLY BECOME ONE OF THE GIRLS IN THE GAME. ELEMENTS OF THESE GIRLS WILL BE ABSORBED INTO HER BASIC PERSONALITY PATTERNS.>
<OVER TIME, SHE WILL BECOME AN AMALGAMATION OF ALL THE GIRLS IN THE ALL DATING SIMULATIONS AND VISUAL NOVELS YOU PLAY.>
<SHE COMES WITH A FREE COPY OF "PRINCESS MAKER"-- IT'S HER FAVORITE GAME.>
<WOW. LARGO WAS RIGHT. SHE REALLY IS CAPABLE OF DEVOURING YOUR SOUL!>
<ISN'T SHE WONDER-FUL?>
<CAN I PLAY WITH HER WHEN YOU ARE DONE?>

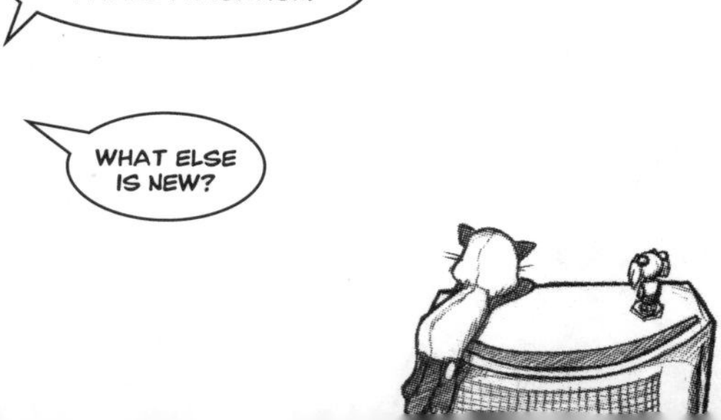
I'M SORRY, I WASN'T PAYING ATTENTION.
WHAT ELSE IS NEW?

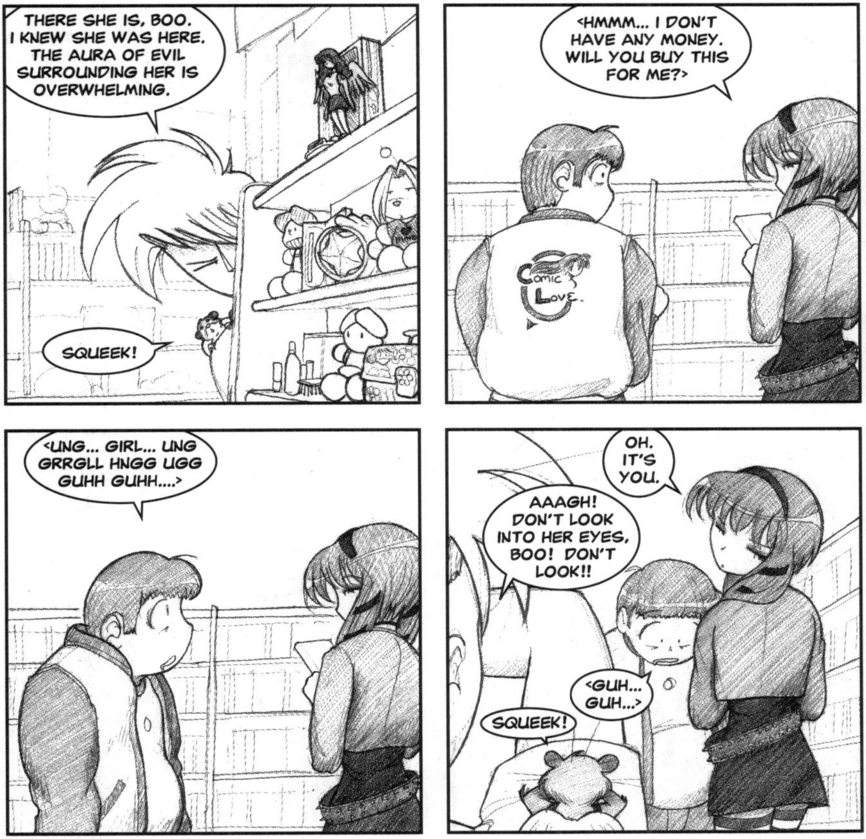
THERE SHE IS, BOO. I KNEW SHE WAS HERE. THE AURA OF EVIL SURROUNDING HER IS OVERWHELMING.
SQUEEK!
<HMMM... I DON'T HAVE ANY MONEY. WILL YOU BUY THIS FOR ME?>
COMIC LOVE
<UNG... GIRL... UNG GRRGLL HNGG UGG GUHH GUHH....>
OH. IT'S YOU.
AAAGH! DON'T LOOK INTO HER EYES, BOO! DON'T LOOK!!
<GUH... GUH...>
SQUEEK!

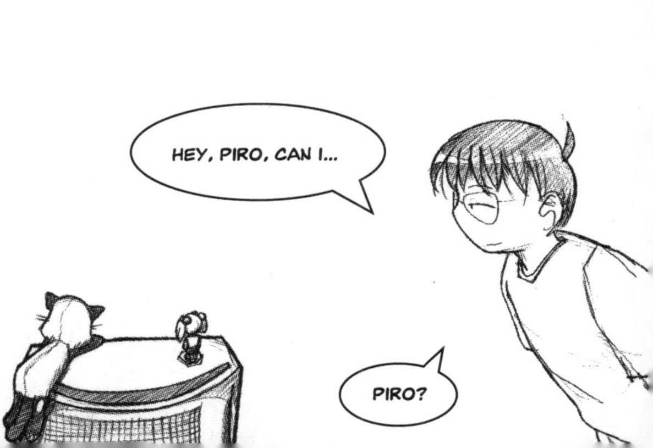
HEY, PIRO, CAN I...
PIRO?

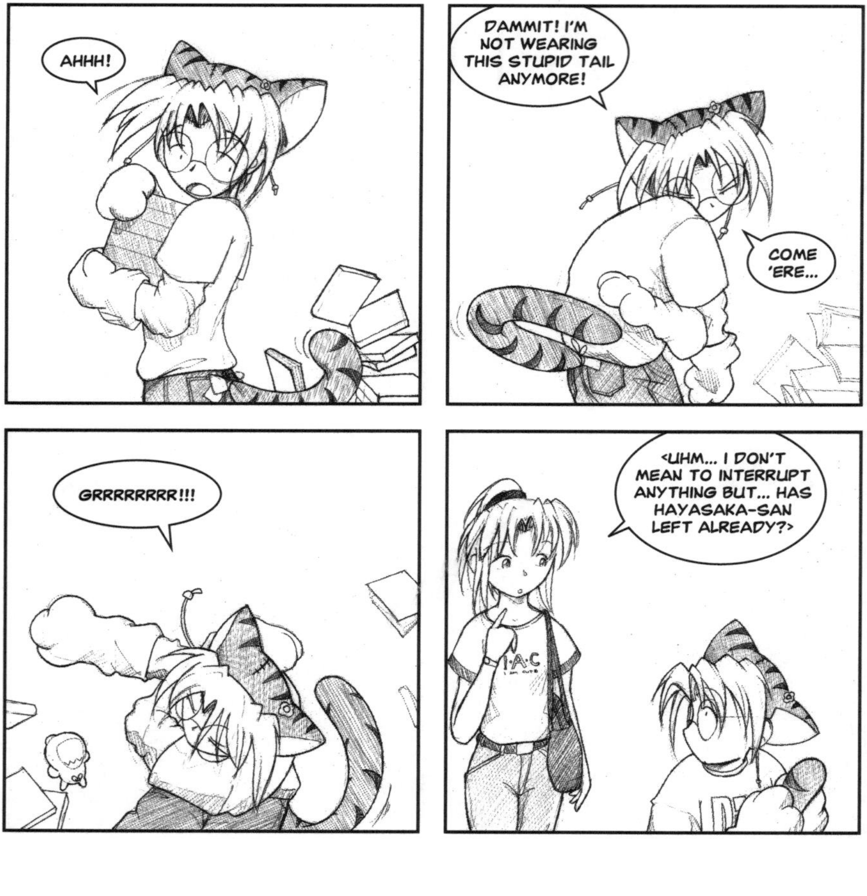
AHHH!
DAMMIT! I'M NOT WEARING THIS STUPID TAIL ANYMORE!
COME 'ERE...
GRRRRRRRR!!!
<UHM... I DON'T MEAN TO INTERRUPT ANYTHING BUT... HAS HAYASAKA-SAN LEFT ALREADY?>
I·A·C

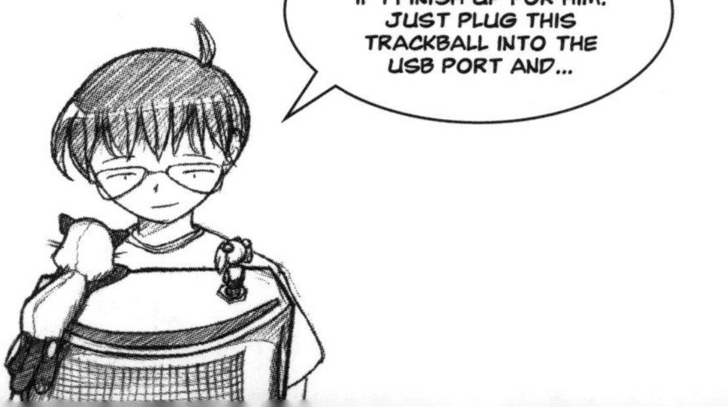
I GUESS HE WON'T MIND IF I FINISH UP FOR HIM. JUST PLUG THIS TRACKBALL INTO THE USB PORT AND...

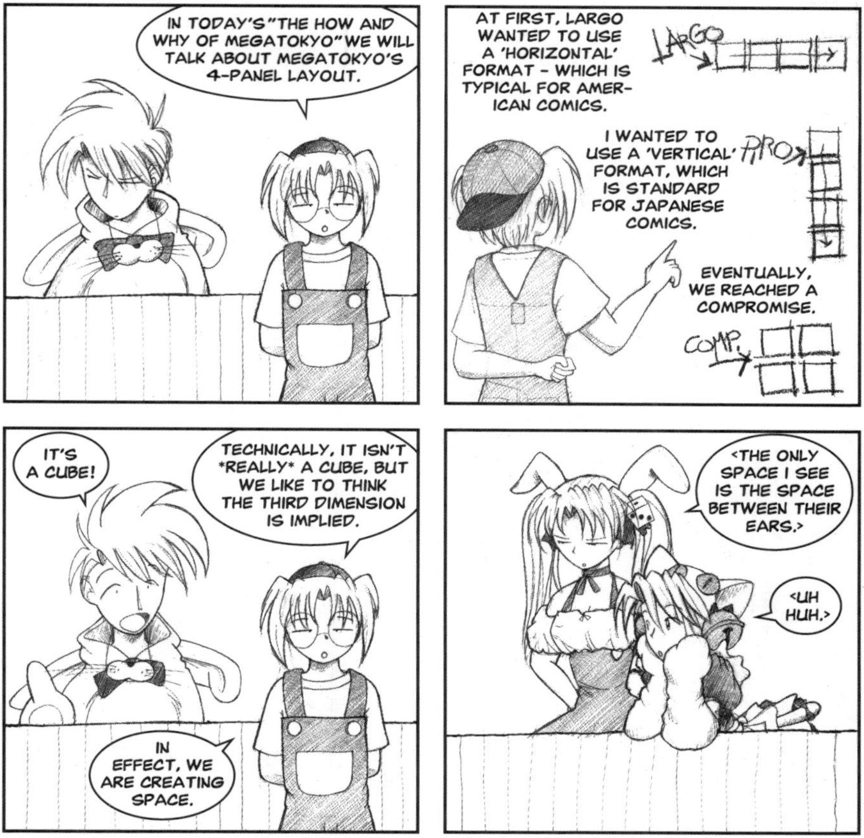
IN TODAY'S "THE HOW AND WHY OF MEGATOKYO" WE WILL TALK ABOUT MEGATOKYO'S 4-PANEL LAYOUT.
AT FIRST, LARGO WANTED TO USE A 'HORIZONTAL' FORMAT - WHICH IS TYPICAL FOR AMERICAN COMICS.
LARGO
I WANTED TO USE A 'VERTICAL' FORMAT, WHICH IS STANDARD FOR JAPANESE COMICS.
PRO
EVENTUALLY, WE REACHED A COMPROMISE.
COMP.
IT'S A CUBE!
TECHNICALLY, IT ISN'T *REALLY* A CUBE, BUT WE LIKE TO THINK THE THIRD DIMENSION IS IMPLIED.
IN EFFECT, WE ARE CREATING SPACE.
<THE ONLY SPACE I SEE IS THE SPACE BETWEEN THEIR EARS.>
<UH HUH.>

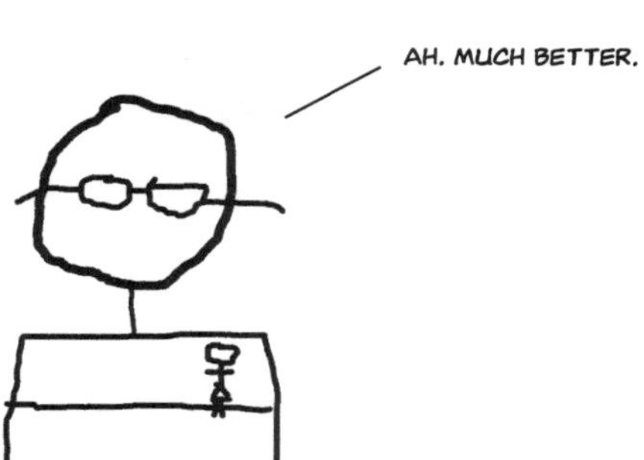
AH. MUCH BETTER.

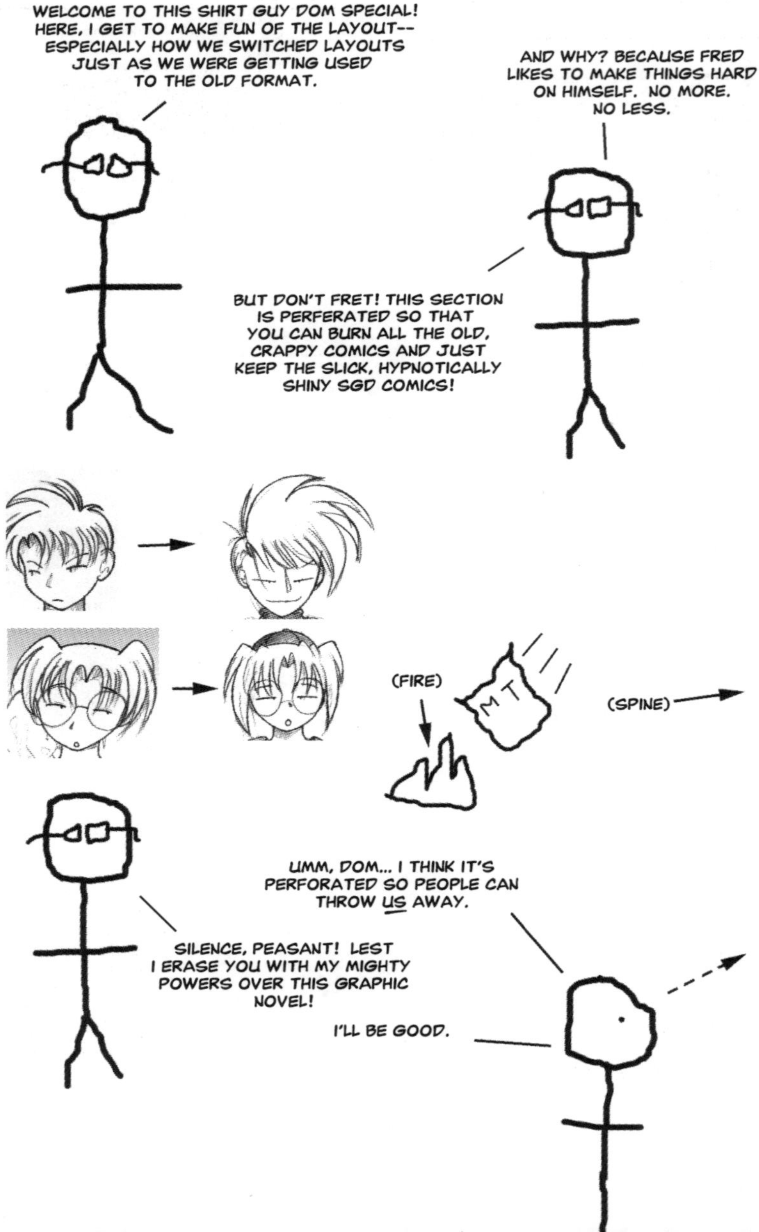
WELCOME TO THIS SHIRT GUY DOM SPECIAL! HERE, I GET TO MAKE FUN OF THE LAYOUT-- ESPECIALLY HOW WE SWITCHED LAYOUTS JUST AS WE WERE GETTING USED TO THE OLD FORMAT.
AND WHY? BECAUSE FRED LIKES TO MAKE THINGS HARD ON HIMSELF. NO MORE. NO LESS.
BUT DON'T FRET! THIS SECTION IS PERFERATED SO THAT YOU CAN BURN ALL THE OLD, CRAPPY COMICS AND JUST KEEP THE SLICK, HYPNOTICALLY SHINY SGD COMICS!
(FIRE)
MT
(SPINE)
UMM, DOM... I THINK IT'S PERFORATED SO PEOPLE CAN THROW US AWAY.
SILENCE, PEASANT! LEST I ERASE YOU WITH MY MIGHTY POWERS OVER THIS GRAPHIC NOVEL!
I'LL BE GOOD.

FOR A LIMITED ENGAGEMENT ONLY –
SHIRT GUY DOM'S EMERGENCY STICK
FIGURE ART DAY!

HEY, DOM HERE.
SORRY THIS EPISODE
LOOKS SO CRAPPY,
BUT THERE'S NOTHING
TO BE DONE.

(THESE ARE GLASSES)

SEE, PIRO IS STILL RECOVERING, AND HAS
PERSONAL BUSINESS TO TAKE CARE OF.

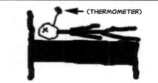

(THERMOMETER)

MEANWHILE, LARGO HAS PERSONAL
BUSINESS OF HIS OWN.

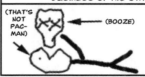

(THAT'S
NOT
PAC-
MAN)

(BOOZE)

WHICH LEAVES IT UP TO
ME TO DO SOMETHING
FUNNY TODAY.

(BUNNY
EARS)

(SWEAT
DROPLET)

I WOULD PERSONALLY LIKE TO
APOLOGIZE FOR TODAY'S STRIP. I HAVE
TAKEN STEPS TO ENSURE THAT THIS
WILL NEVER HAPPEN AGAIN.

IF YOU SEE DOM, TELL HIM THAT I KNOW
WHERE HE LIVES, AND THAT HE CAN'T
HIDE FROM ME FOREVER.

AH, THE EARLY DAYS OF
MT. THE SAGA OF THE
SHIRT GUY STARTS WITH
LARGO, WHO GETS TIRED
OF PEOPLE ASKING HIM
ABOUT OUR NEWLY OPENED
T-SHIRT STORE, AND
SAYS "ALL QUESTIONS
GO TO SHIRT GUY DOM".
SO, I'M THE SHIRT GUY.
I SHRUG IT OFF, SINCE IT
DOESN'T MATTER TO ME.

THEN ONE NIGHT PIRO CAN'T
FINISH THE COMIC ON TIME, AND
I GET A MESSAGE FROM LARGO
AROUND AN HOUR BEFORE WE'RE
SCHEDULED TO UPDATE.
"WE NEED THE SHIRT GUY TO DO
STICK FIGURES", IT SAYS.
I REALIZED THAT IT WOULD
MAKE PEOPLE SUFFER, AND THE
REST IS HISTORY. WE HAVEN'T
BEEN SUED BY SLUGGY
FREELANCE YET, SO I'D
CONSIDER IT A SUCCESS.

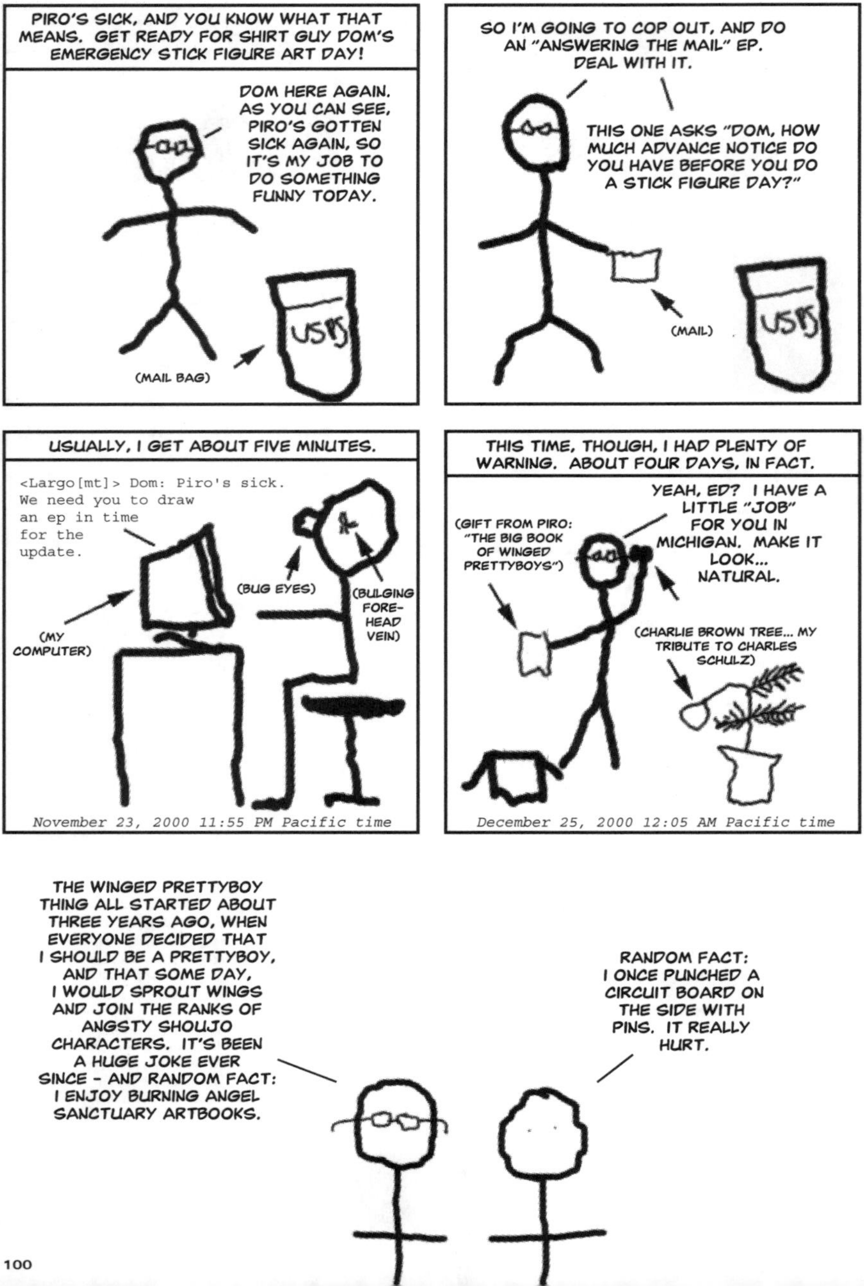
PIRO'S SICK, AND YOU KNOW WHAT THAT MEANS. GET READY FOR SHIRT GUY DOM'S EMERGENCY STICK FIGURE ART DAY!
DOM HERE AGAIN. AS YOU CAN SEE, PIRO'S GOTTEN SICK AGAIN, SO IT'S MY JOB TO DO SOMETHING FUNNY TODAY.
(MAIL BAG)
USPS
SO I'M GOING TO COP OUT, AND DO AN "ANSWERING THE MAIL" EP. DEAL WITH IT.
THIS ONE ASKS "DOM, HOW MUCH ADVANCE NOTICE DO YOU HAVE BEFORE YOU DO A STICK FIGURE DAY?"
(MAIL)
USPS
USUALLY, I GET ABOUT FIVE MINUTES.
<Largo[mt]> Dom: Piro's sick. We need you to draw an ep in time for the update.
(MY COMPUTER)
(BUG EYES)
(BULGING FORE-HEAD VEIN)
November 23, 2000 11:55 PM Pacific time
THIS TIME, THOUGH, I HAD PLENTY OF WARNING. ABOUT FOUR DAYS, IN FACT.
YEAH, ED? I HAVE A LITTLE "JOB" FOR YOU IN MICHIGAN. MAKE IT LOOK... NATURAL.
(GIFT FROM PIRO: "THE BIG BOOK OF WINGED PRETTYBOYS")
(CHARLIE BROWN TREE... MY TRIBUTE TO CHARLES SCHULZ)
December 25, 2000 12:05 AM Pacific time
THE WINGED PRETTYBOY THING ALL STARTED ABOUT THREE YEARS AGO, WHEN EVERYONE DECIDED THAT I SHOULD BE A PRETTYBOY, AND THAT SOME DAY, I WOULD SPROUT WINGS AND JOIN THE RANKS OF ANGSTY SHOUJO CHARACTERS. IT'S BEEN A HUGE JOKE EVER SINCE - AND RANDOM FACT: I ENJOY BURNING ANGEL SANCTUARY ARTBOOKS.
RANDOM FACT: I ONCE PUNCHED A CIRCUIT BOARD ON THE SIDE WITH PINS. IT REALLY HURT.

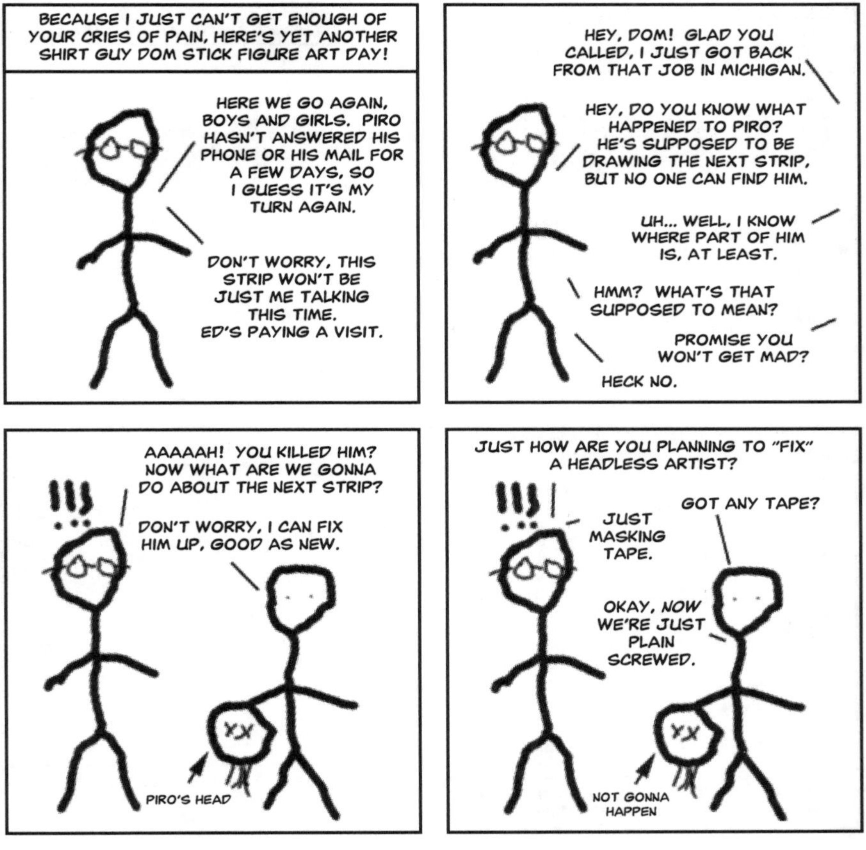
BECAUSE I JUST CAN'T GET ENOUGH OF YOUR CRIES OF PAIN, HERE'S YET ANOTHER SHIRT GUY DOM STICK FIGURE ART DAY!
HERE WE GO AGAIN, BOYS AND GIRLS. PIRO HASN'T ANSWERED HIS PHONE OR HIS MAIL FOR A FEW DAYS, SO I GUESS IT'S MY TURN AGAIN.
DON'T WORRY, THIS STRIP WON'T BE JUST ME TALKING THIS TIME. ED'S PAYING A VISIT.
HEY, DOM! GLAD YOU CALLED, I JUST GOT BACK FROM THAT JOB IN MICHIGAN.
HEY, DO YOU KNOW WHAT HAPPENED TO PIRO? HE'S SUPPOSED TO BE DRAWING THE NEXT STRIP, BUT NO ONE CAN FIND HIM.
UH... WELL, I KNOW WHERE PART OF HIM IS, AT LEAST.
HMM? WHAT'S THAT SUPPOSED TO MEAN?
PROMISE YOU WON'T GET MAD?
HECK NO.
!!!
...
AAAAAH! YOU KILLED HIM? NOW WHAT ARE WE GONNA DO ABOUT THE NEXT STRIP?
DON'T WORRY, I CAN FIX HIM UP, GOOD AS NEW.
PIRO'S HEAD
JUST HOW ARE YOU PLANNING TO "FIX" A HEADLESS ARTIST?
!!!
...
GOT ANY TAPE?
JUST MASKING TAPE.
OKAY, NOW WE'RE JUST PLAIN SCREWED.
NOT GONNA HAPPEN

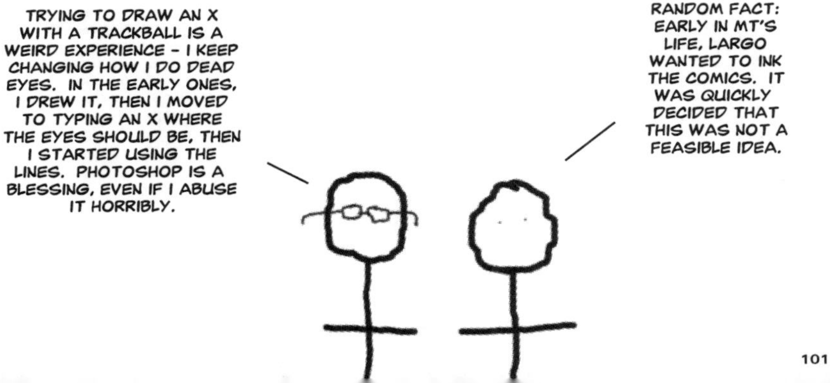
TRYING TO DRAW AN X WITH A TRACKBALL IS A WEIRD EXPERIENCE - I KEEP CHANGING HOW I DO DEAD EYES. IN THE EARLY ONES, I DREW IT, THEN I MOVED TO TYPING AN X WHERE THE EYES SHOULD BE, THEN I STARTED USING THE LINES. PHOTOSHOP IS A BLESSING, EVEN IF I ABUSE IT HORRIBLY.
RANDOM FACT: EARLY IN MT'S LIFE, LARGO WANTED TO INK THE COMICS. IT WAS QUICKLY DECIDED THAT THIS WAS NOT A FEASIBLE IDEA.

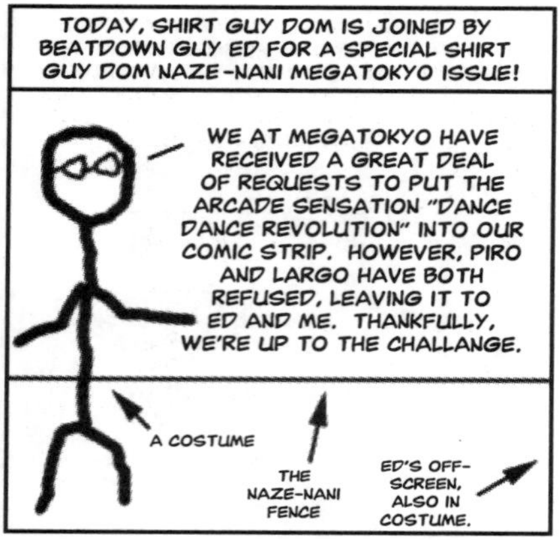
TODAY, SHIRT GUY DOM IS JOINED BY BEATDOWN GUY ED FOR A SPECIAL SHIRT GUY DOM NAZE-NANI MEGATOKYO ISSUE!
WE AT MEGATOKYO HAVE RECEIVED A GREAT DEAL OF REQUESTS TO PUT THE ARCADE SENSATION "DANCE DANCE REVOLUTION" INTO OUR COMIC STRIP. HOWEVER, PIRO AND LARGO HAVE BOTH REFUSED, LEAVING IT TO ED AND ME. THANKFULLY, WE'RE UP TO THE CHALLANGE.
A COSTUME
THE NAZE-NANI FENCE
ED'S OFF-SCREEN, ALSO IN COSTUME.
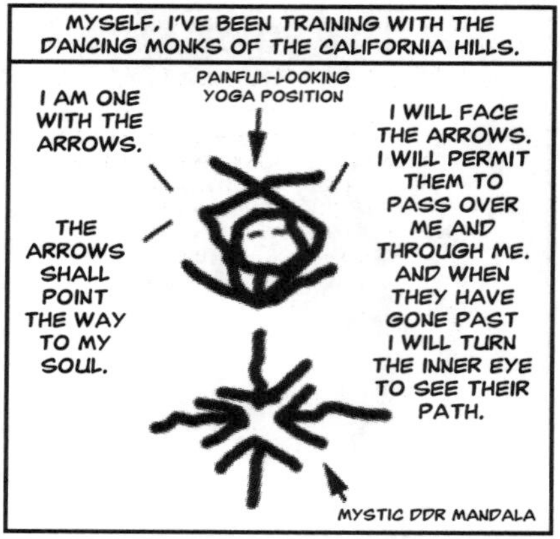
MYSELF, I'VE BEEN TRAINING WITH THE DANCING MONKS OF THE CALIFORNIA HILLS.
I AM ONE WITH THE ARROWS.
PAINFUL-LOOKING YOGA POSITION
I WILL FACE THE ARROWS. I WILL PERMIT THEM TO PASS OVER ME AND THROUGH ME. AND WHEN THEY HAVE GONE PAST I WILL TURN THE INNER EYE TO SEE THEIR PATH.
THE ARROWS SHALL POINT THE WAY TO MY SOUL.
MYSTIC DDR MANDALA
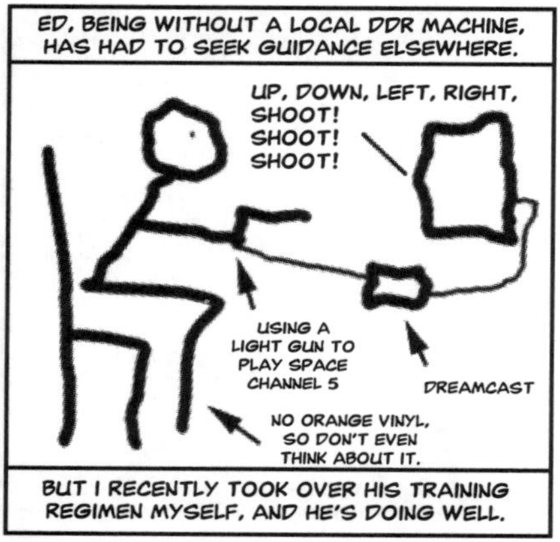
ED, BEING WITHOUT A LOCAL DDR MACHINE, HAS HAD TO SEEK GUIDANCE ELSEWHERE.
UP, DOWN, LEFT, RIGHT, SHOOT! SHOOT! SHOOT!
USING A LIGHT GUN TO PLAY SPACE CHANNEL 5
DREAMCAST
NO ORANGE VINYL, SO DON'T EVEN THINK ABOUT IT.
BUT I RECENTLY TOOK OVER HIS TRAINING REGIMEN MYSELF, AND HE'S DOING WELL.
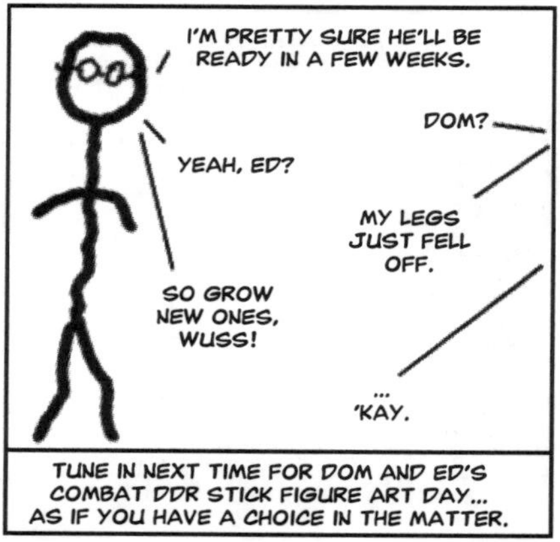
I'M PRETTY SURE HE'LL BE READY IN A FEW WEEKS.
DOM?
YEAH, ED?
MY LEGS JUST FELL OFF.
SO GROW NEW ONES, WUSS!
...
'KAY.
TUNE IN NEXT TIME FOR DOM AND ED'S COMBAT DDR STICK FIGURE ART DAY... AS IF YOU HAVE A CHOICE IN THE MATTER.
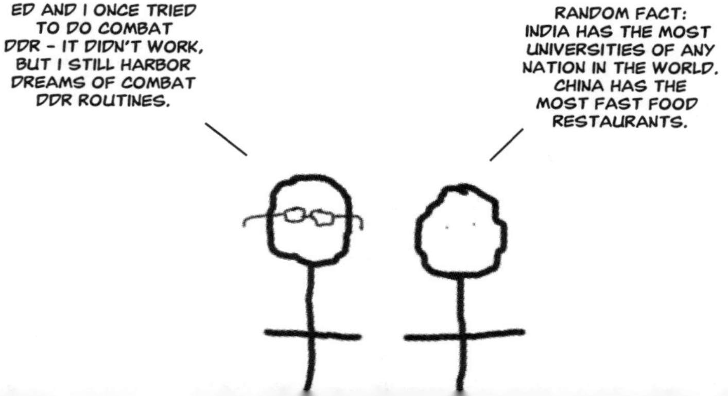
ED AND I ONCE TRIED TO DO COMBAT DDR – IT DIDN'T WORK, BUT I STILL HARBOR DREAMS OF COMBAT DDR ROUTINES.
RANDOM FACT: INDIA HAS THE MOST UNIVERSITIES OF ANY NATION IN THE WORLD. CHINA HAS THE MOST FAST FOOD RESTAURANTS.

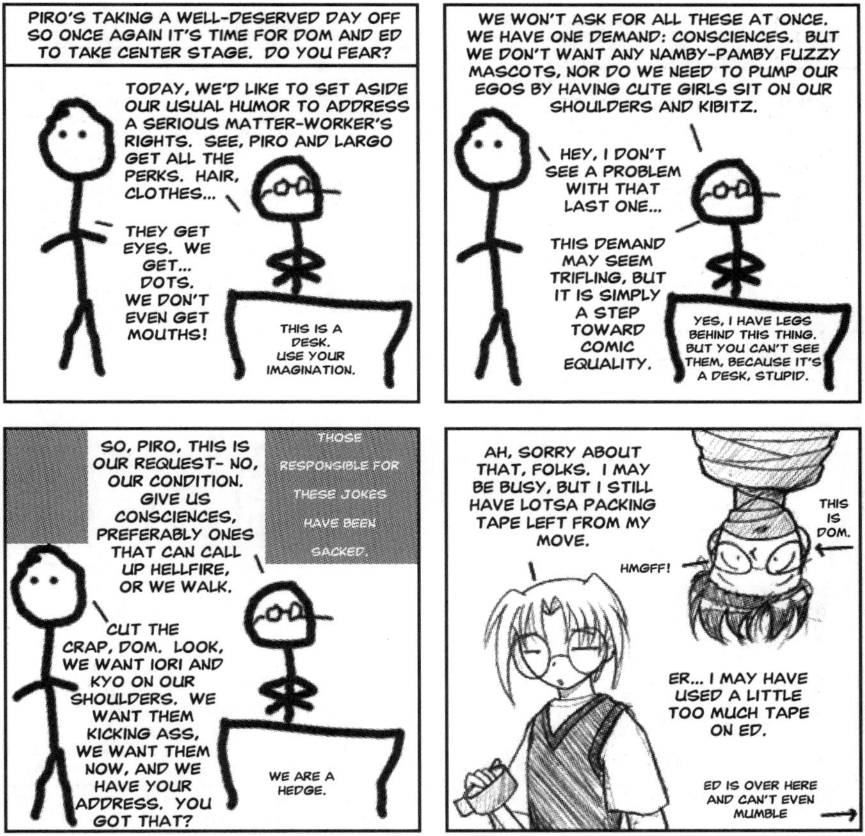
PIRO'S TAKING A WELL-DESERVED DAY OFF SO ONCE AGAIN IT'S TIME FOR DOM AND ED TO TAKE CENTER STAGE. DO YOU FEAR?
TODAY, WE'D LIKE TO SET ASIDE OUR USUAL HUMOR TO ADDRESS A SERIOUS MATTER-WORKER'S RIGHTS. SEE, PIRO AND LARGO GET ALL THE PERKS. HAIR, CLOTHES...
THEY GET EYES. WE GET... DOTS. WE DON'T EVEN GET MOUTHS!
THIS IS A DESK. USE YOUR IMAGINATION.
WE WON'T ASK FOR ALL THESE AT ONCE. WE HAVE ONE DEMAND: CONSCIENCES. BUT WE DON'T WANT ANY NAMBY-PAMBY FUZZY MASCOTS, NOR DO WE NEED TO PUMP OUR EGOS BY HAVING CUTE GIRLS SIT ON OUR SHOULDERS AND KIBITZ.
HEY, I DON'T SEE A PROBLEM WITH THAT LAST ONE...
THIS DEMAND MAY SEEM TRIFLING, BUT IT IS SIMPLY A STEP TOWARD COMIC EQUALITY.
YES, I HAVE LEGS BEHIND THIS THING. BUT YOU CAN'T SEE THEM, BECAUSE IT'S A DESK, STUPID.
SO, PIRO, THIS IS OUR REQUEST- NO, OUR CONDITION. GIVE US CONSCIENCES, PREFERABLY ONES THAT CAN CALL UP HELLFIRE, OR WE WALK.
THOSE RESPONSIBLE FOR THESE JOKES HAVE BEEN SACKED.
CUT THE CRAP, DOM. LOOK, WE WANT IORI AND KYO ON OUR SHOULDERS. WE WANT THEM KICKING ASS, WE WANT THEM NOW, AND WE HAVE YOUR ADDRESS. YOU GOT THAT?
WE ARE A HEDGE.
AH, SORRY ABOUT THAT, FOLKS. I MAY BE BUSY, BUT I STILL HAVE LOTSA PACKING TAPE LEFT FROM MY MOVE.
THIS IS DOM.
HMGFF!
ER... I MAY HAVE USED A LITTLE TOO MUCH TAPE ON ED.
ED IS OVER HERE AND CAN'T EVEN MUMBLE

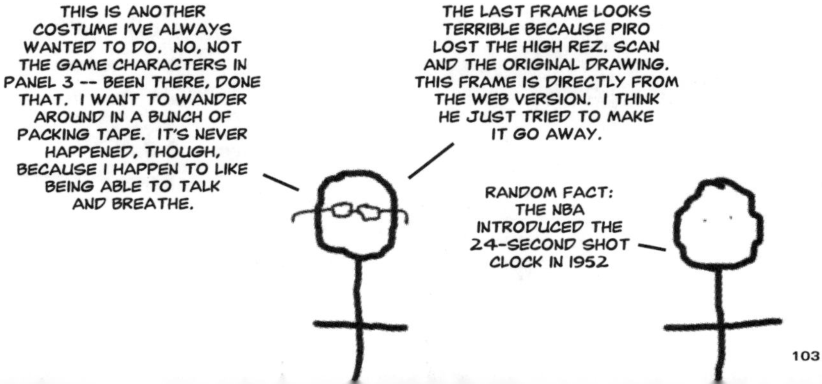
THIS IS ANOTHER COSTUME I'VE ALWAYS WANTED TO DO. NO, NOT THE GAME CHARACTERS IN PANEL 3 -- BEEN THERE, DONE THAT. I WANT TO WANDER AROUND IN A BUNCH OF PACKING TAPE. IT'S NEVER HAPPENED, THOUGH, BECAUSE I HAPPEN TO LIKE BEING ABLE TO TALK AND BREATHE.
THE LAST FRAME LOOKS TERRIBLE BECAUSE PIRO LOST THE HIGH REZ. SCAN AND THE ORIGINAL DRAWING. THIS FRAME IS DIRECTLY FROM THE WEB VERSION. I THINK HE JUST TRIED TO MAKE IT GO AWAY.
RANDOM FACT: THE NBA INTRODUCED THE 24-SECOND SHOT CLOCK IN 1952

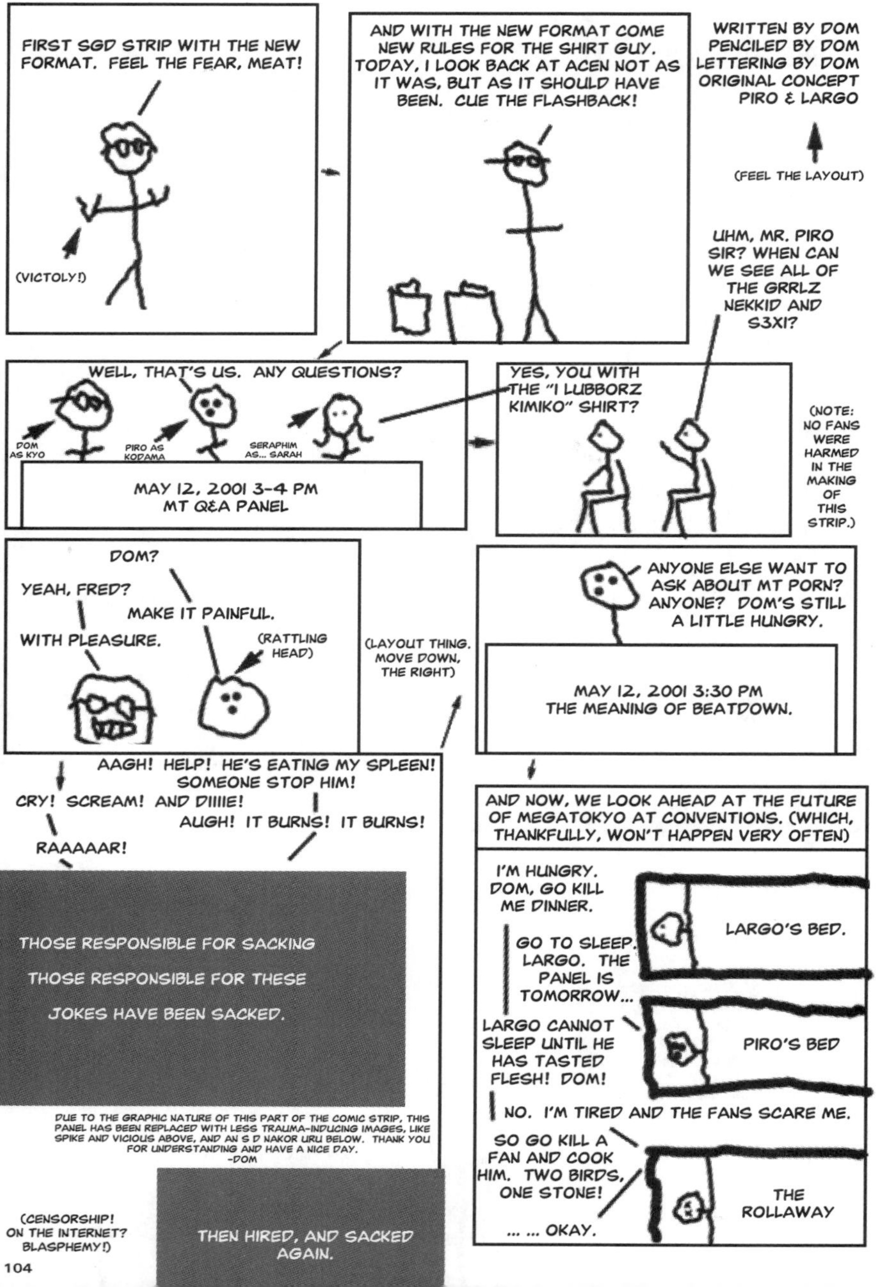
FIRST SGD STRIP WITH THE NEW FORMAT. FEEL THE FEAR, MEAT!
(VICTOLY!)
AND WITH THE NEW FORMAT COME NEW RULES FOR THE SHIRT GUY. TODAY, I LOOK BACK AT ACEN NOT AS IT WAS, BUT AS IT SHOULD HAVE BEEN. CUE THE FLASHBACK!
WRITTEN BY DOM
PENCILED BY DOM
LETTERING BY DOM
ORIGINAL CONCEPT
PIRO & LARGO
(FEEL THE LAYOUT)
WELL, THAT'S US. ANY QUESTIONS?
DOM AS KYO
PIRO AS KODAMA
SERAPHIM AS... SARAH
MAY 12, 2001 3-4 PM
MT Q&A PANEL
UHM, MR. PIRO SIR? WHEN CAN WE SEE ALL OF THE GRRLZ NEKKID AND S3XI?
YES, YOU WITH THE "I LUBBORZ KIMIKO" SHIRT?
(NOTE: NO FANS WERE HARMED IN THE MAKING OF THIS STRIP.)
DOM?
YEAH, FRED?
MAKE IT PAINFUL.
WITH PLEASURE.
(RATTLING HEAD)
(LAYOUT THING. MOVE DOWN, THE RIGHT)
ANYONE ELSE WANT TO ASK ABOUT MT PORN? ANYONE? DOM'S STILL A LITTLE HUNGRY.
MAY 12, 2001 3:30 PM
THE MEANING OF BEATDOWN.
AAGH! HELP! HE'S EATING MY SPLEEN! SOMEONE STOP HIM!
CRY! SCREAM! AND DIIIIE!
AUGH! IT BURNS! IT BURNS!
RAAAAAR!
THOSE RESPONSIBLE FOR SACKING
THOSE RESPONSIBLE FOR THESE
JOKES HAVE BEEN SACKED.
DUE TO THE GRAPHIC NATURE OF THIS PART OF THE COMIC STRIP, THIS PANEL HAS BEEN REPLACED WITH LESS TRAUMA-INDUCING IMAGES, LIKE SPIKE AND VICIOUS ABOVE, AND AN S D NAKOR URU BELOW. THANK YOU FOR UNDERSTANDING AND HAVE A NICE DAY.
-DOM
(CENSORSHIP! ON THE INTERNET? BLASPHEMY!)
THEN HIRED, AND SACKED AGAIN.
AND NOW, WE LOOK AHEAD AT THE FUTURE OF MEGATOKYO AT CONVENTIONS. (WHICH, THANKFULLY, WON'T HAPPEN VERY OFTEN)
I'M HUNGRY. DOM, GO KILL ME DINNER.
LARGO'S BED.
GO TO SLEEP. LARGO. THE PANEL IS TOMORROW...
LARGO CANNOT SLEEP UNTIL HE HAS TASTED FLESH! DOM!
PIRO'S BED
NO. I'M TIRED AND THE FANS SCARE ME.
SO GO KILL A FAN AND COOK HIM. TWO BIRDS, ONE STONE!
THE ROLLAWAY
... ... OKAY.

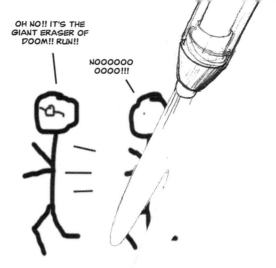

OH NO!! IT'S THE GIANT ERASER OF DOOM!! RUN!!

NOOOOOO OOOO!!!

SORRY ABOUT THAT.

AS I HAD MENTIONED EARLIER, I WAS STARTING TO FEEL CONSTRAINED BY THE FOUR PANEL FORMAT. WHEN WE STARTED MEGATOKYO, THE FORMAT WORKED GREAT BECAUSE IT SET REALISTIC BOUNDS ON WHAT I COULD DRAW IN A GIVEN EVENING.

AS THE STORY PROGRESSED, I REALIZED THAT THERE WERE THINGS THAT I JUST COULDN'T DO IN FOUR PANELS.

SINCE MY GOAL WAS TO ONE DAY DO A REAL MANGA, I DECIDED IT WAS TIME TO SWITCH TO A FULL PAGE FORMAT. MY DRAWING SPEED HAD INCREASED SO THAT THE COMIC WAS NO LONGER TAKING EIGHT HOURS TO PRODUCE. IT MADE SENSE IN SOME SORT OF TWISTED, MASOCHISTIC WAY, THAT I COULD USE THAT EXTRA TIME TO DRAW MORE FOR EACH COMIC.

IT WAS ALSO AT THIS TIME THAT WE DECIDED TO START DIVIDING THINGS INTO CHAPTERS. EVERYTHING WE HAD DONE SO FAR WE CALLED 'CHAPTER 0', AND ALL WE NEEDED TO DO WAS WRAP THINGS UP SO WE COULD START CHAPTER 1 AND START BEING A LITTLE MORE ORGANIZED.

YEAH, LIKE THAT COULD EVER HAPPEN. SO, WITHOUT FURTHER INTERRUPTION, I PRESENT THE LAST PART OF 'CHAPTER 0' IN ITS FULL PAGE GLORY.

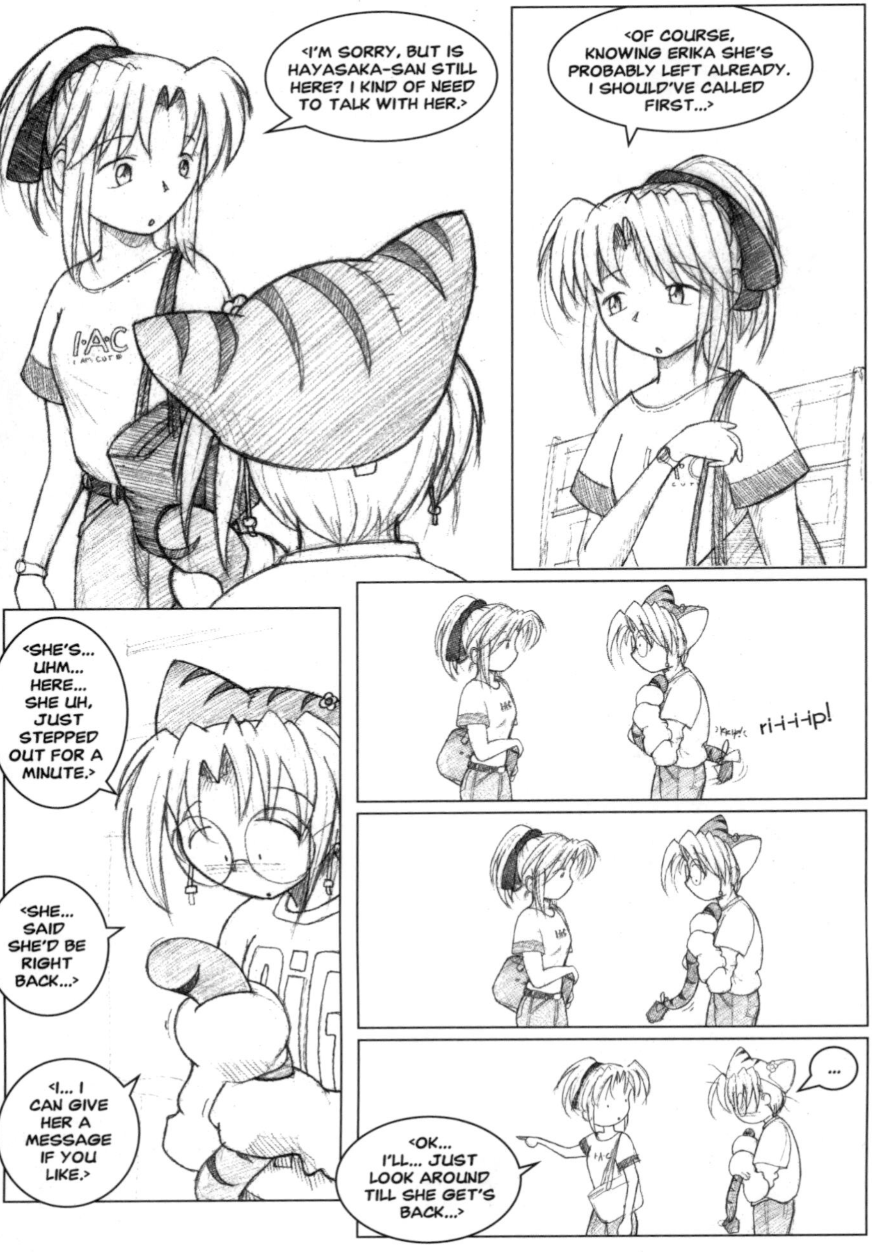

<I'M SORRY, BUT IS HAYASAKA-SAN STILL HERE? I KIND OF NEED TO TALK WITH HER.>
I·A·C
<OF COURSE, KNOWING ERIKA SHE'S PROBABLY LEFT ALREADY. I SHOULD'VE CALLED FIRST...>
<SHE'S... UHM... HERE... SHE UH, JUST STEPPED OUT FOR A MINUTE.>
<SHE... SAID SHE'D BE RIGHT BACK...>
<I... I CAN GIVE HER A MESSAGE IF YOU LIKE.>
ri-i-i-ip!
<OK... I'LL... JUST LOOK AROUND TILL SHE GET'S BACK...>
...

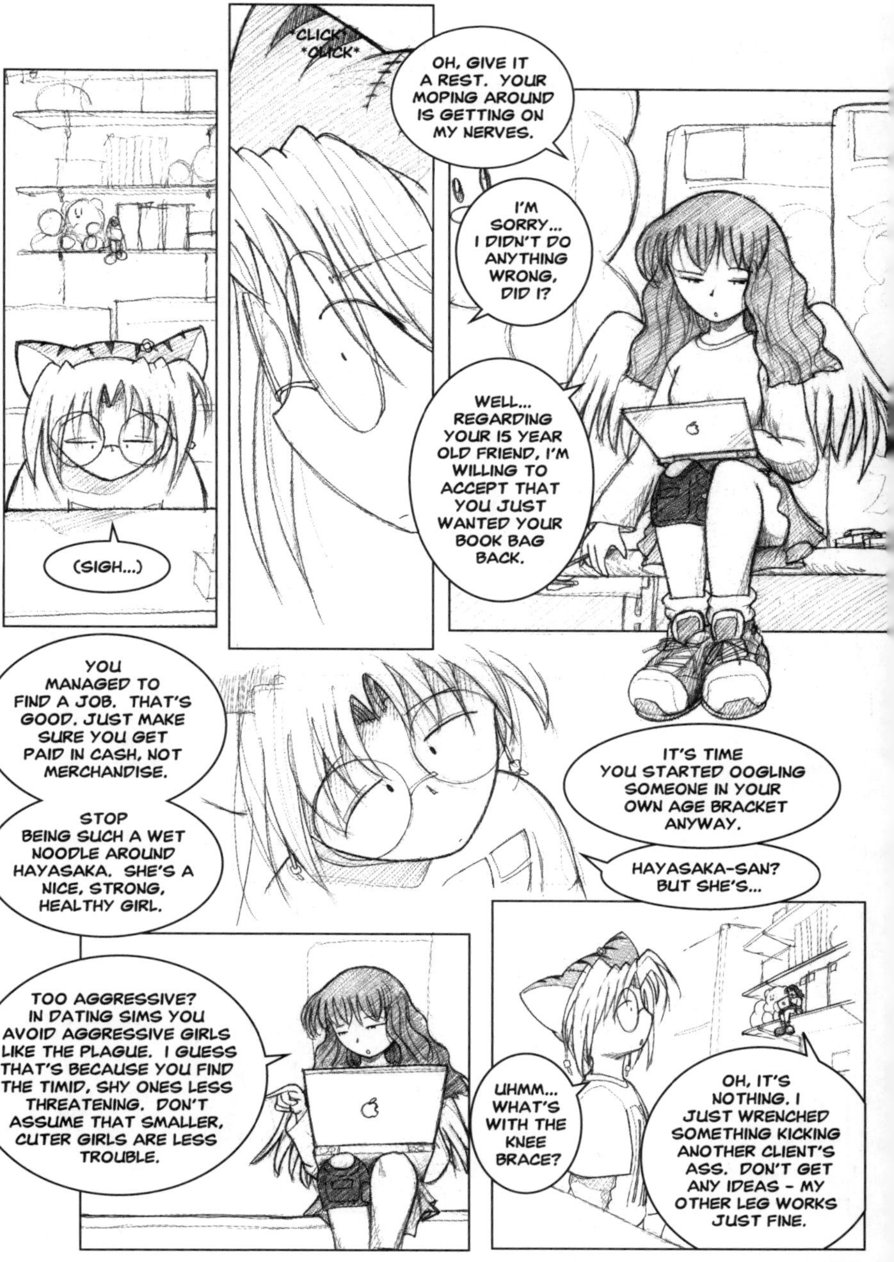
(SIGH...)
CLICK *CLICK*
OH, GIVE IT A REST. YOUR MOPING AROUND IS GETTING ON MY NERVES.
I'M SORRY... I DIDN'T DO ANYTHING WRONG, DID I?
WELL... REGARDING YOUR 15 YEAR OLD FRIEND, I'M WILLING TO ACCEPT THAT YOU JUST WANTED YOUR BOOK BAG BACK.
YOU MANAGED TO FIND A JOB. THAT'S GOOD. JUST MAKE SURE YOU GET PAID IN CASH, NOT MERCHANDISE.
STOP BEING SUCH A WET NOODLE AROUND HAYASAKA. SHE'S A NICE, STRONG, HEALTHY GIRL.
IT'S TIME YOU STARTED OOGLING SOMEONE IN YOUR OWN AGE BRACKET ANYWAY.
HAYASAKA-SAN? BUT SHE'S...
TOO AGGRESSIVE? IN DATING SIMS YOU AVOID AGGRESSIVE GIRLS LIKE THE PLAGUE. I GUESS THAT'S BECAUSE YOU FIND THE TIMID, SHY ONES LESS THREATENING. DON'T ASSUME THAT SMALLER, CUTER GIRLS ARE LESS TROUBLE.
UHMM... WHAT'S WITH THE KNEE BRACE?
OH, IT'S NOTHING. I JUST WRENCHED SOMETHING KICKING ANOTHER CLIENT'S ASS. DON'T GET ANY IDEAS - MY OTHER LEG WORKS JUST FINE.

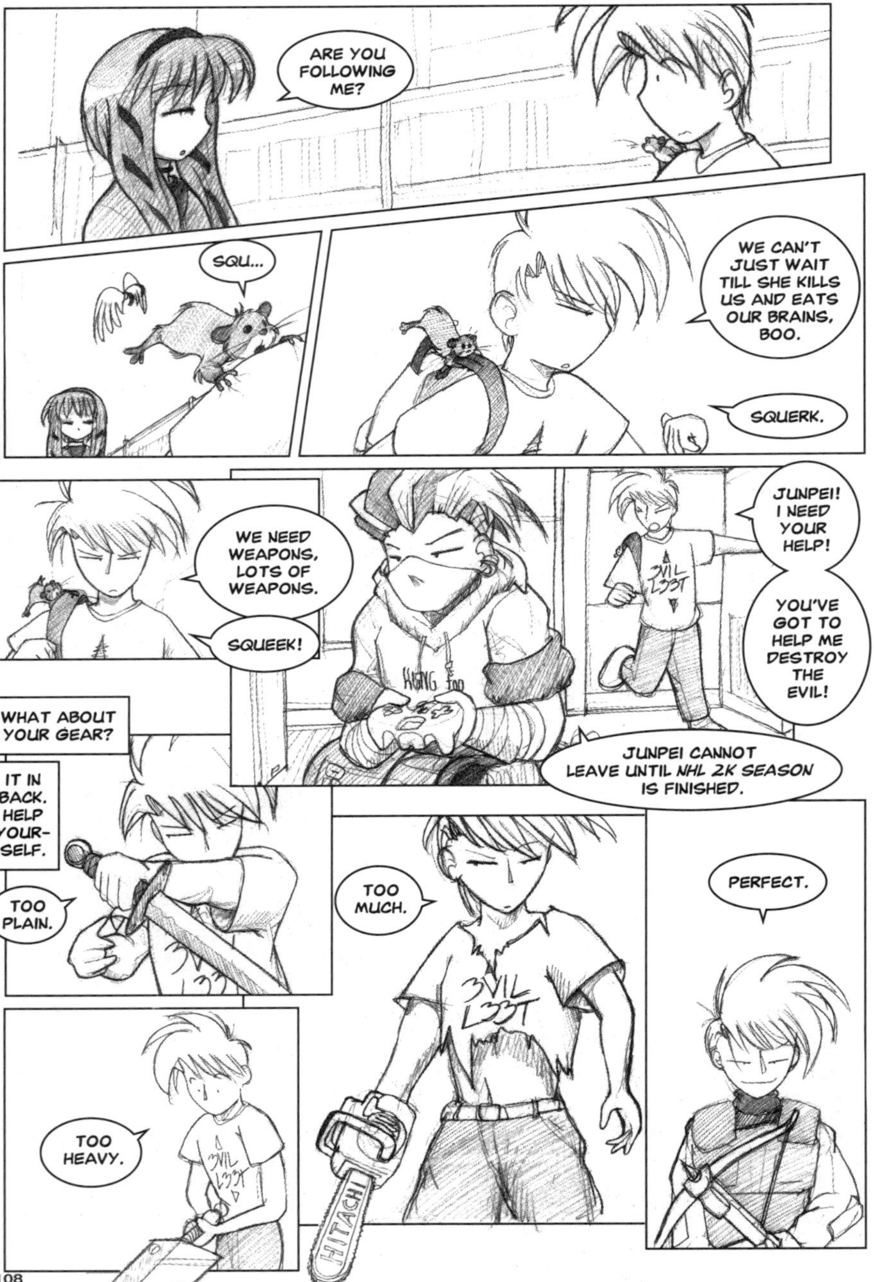
ARE YOU FOLLOWING ME?
SQU...
WE CAN'T JUST WAIT TILL SHE KILLS US AND EATS OUR BRAINS, BOO.
SQUERK.
WE NEED WEAPONS, LOTS OF WEAPONS.
SQUEEK!
JUNPEI! I NEED YOUR HELP!
YOU'VE GOT TO HELP ME DESTROY THE EVIL!
JUNPEI CANNOT LEAVE UNTIL *NHL 2K SEASON* IS FINISHED.
WHAT ABOUT YOUR GEAR?
IT IN BACK. HELP YOURSELF.
TOO PLAIN.
TOO HEAVY.
TOO MUCH.
HITACHI
PERFECT.

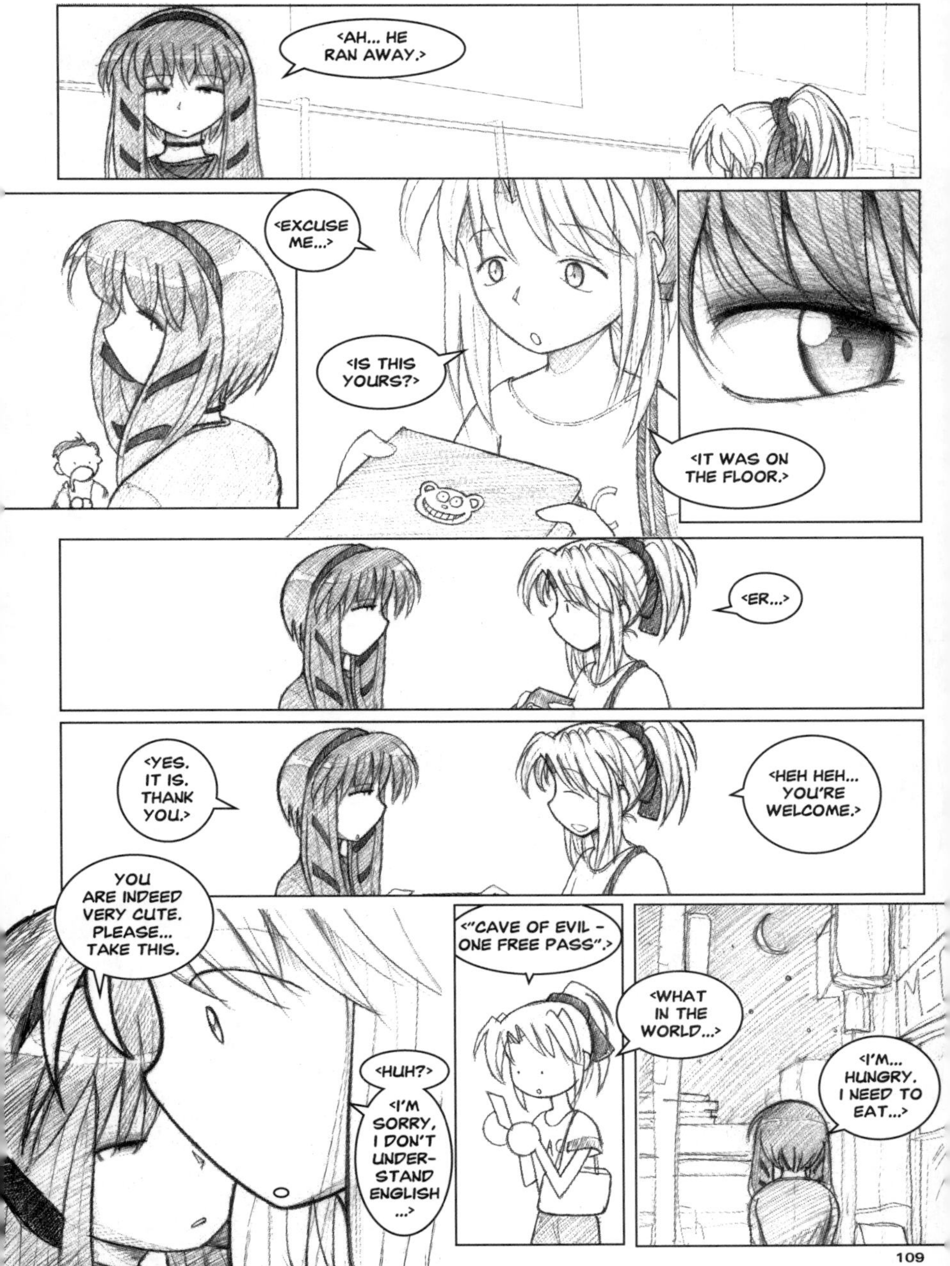
<AH... HE RAN AWAY.>
<EXCUSE ME...>
<IS THIS YOURS?>
<IT WAS ON THE FLOOR.>
<ER...>
<YES. IT IS. THANK YOU.>
<HEH HEH... YOU'RE WELCOME.>
YOU ARE INDEED VERY CUTE. PLEASE... TAKE THIS.
<HUH?>
<I'M SORRY, I DON'T UNDER-STAND ENGLISH...>
<"CAVE OF EVIL - ONE FREE PASS".>
<WHAT IN THE WORLD...>
<I'M... HUNGRY. I NEED TO EAT...>

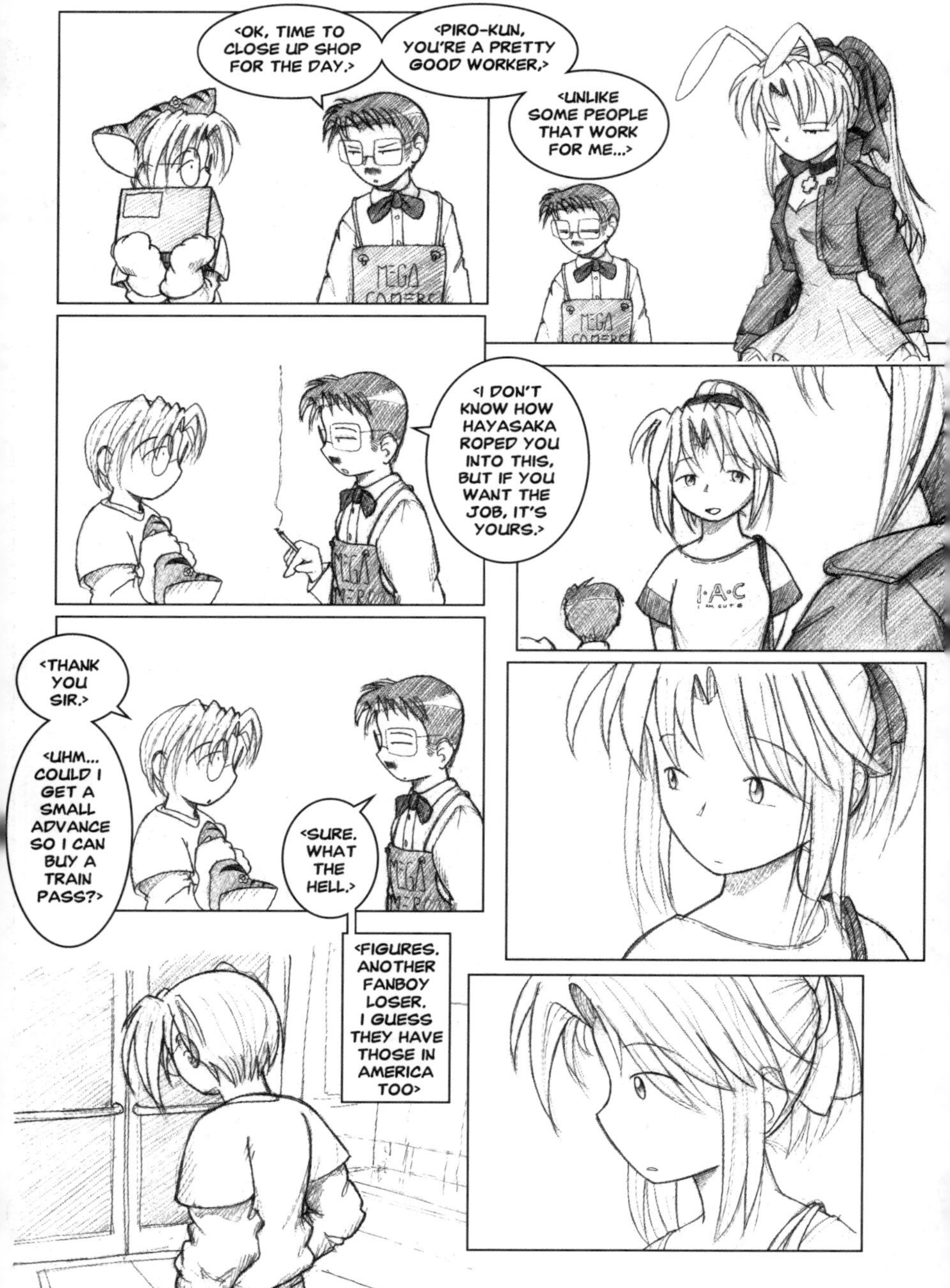
<OK, TIME TO CLOSE UP SHOP FOR THE DAY.>
<PIRO-KUN, YOU'RE A PRETTY GOOD WORKER,>
<UNLIKE SOME PEOPLE THAT WORK FOR ME...>
MEGA COMERC
<I DON'T KNOW HOW HAYASAKA ROPED YOU INTO THIS, BUT IF YOU WANT THE JOB, IT'S YOURS.>
I·A·C
<THANK YOU SIR.>
<UHM... COULD I GET A SMALL ADVANCE SO I CAN BUY A TRAIN PASS?>
<SURE. WHAT THE HELL.>
<FIGURES. ANOTHER FANBOY LOSER. I GUESS THEY HAVE THOSE IN AMERICA TOO>

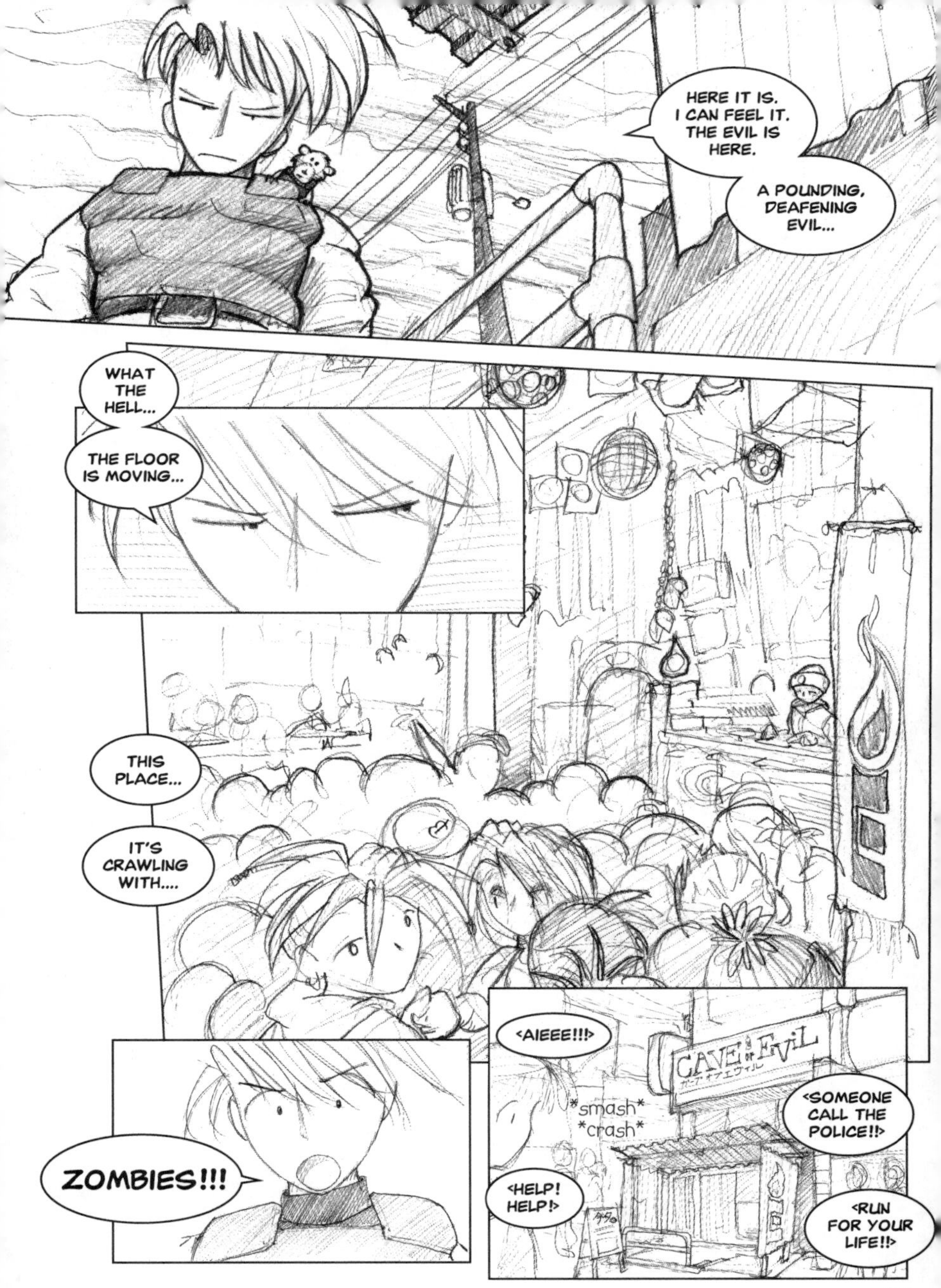
HERE IT IS. I CAN FEEL IT. THE EVIL IS HERE.
A POUNDING, DEAFENING EVIL...
WHAT THE HELL...
THE FLOOR IS MOVING...
THIS PLACE...
IT'S CRAWLING WITH....
ZOMBIES!!!
<AIEEE!!!>
CAVE OF EVIL
smash
crash
<SOMEONE CALL THE POLICE!!>
<HELP! HELP!>
<RUN FOR YOUR LIFE!!>

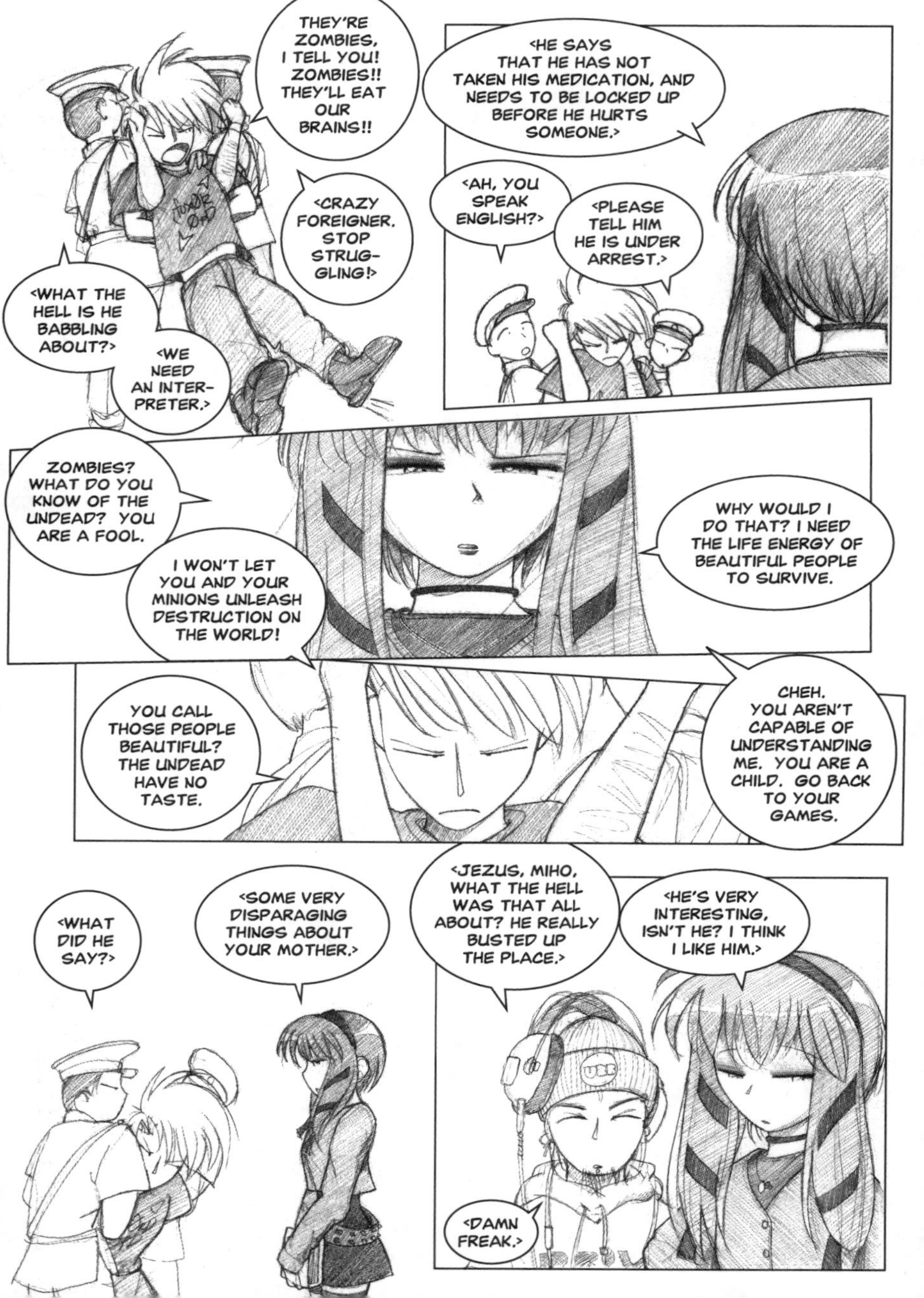
THEY'RE ZOMBIES, I TELL YOU! ZOMBIES!! THEY'LL EAT OUR BRAINS!!
<CRAZY FOREIGNER. STOP STRUG-GLING!>
<WHAT THE HELL IS HE BABBLING ABOUT?>
<WE NEED AN INTER-PRETER.>
<HE SAYS THAT HE HAS NOT TAKEN HIS MEDICATION, AND NEEDS TO BE LOCKED UP BEFORE HE HURTS SOMEONE.>
<AH, YOU SPEAK ENGLISH?>
<PLEASE TELL HIM HE IS UNDER ARREST.>
ZOMBIES? WHAT DO YOU KNOW OF THE UNDEAD? YOU ARE A FOOL.
I WON'T LET YOU AND YOUR MINIONS UNLEASH DESTRUCTION ON THE WORLD!
WHY WOULD I DO THAT? I NEED THE LIFE ENERGY OF BEAUTIFUL PEOPLE TO SURVIVE.
YOU CALL THOSE PEOPLE BEAUTIFUL? THE UNDEAD HAVE NO TASTE.
CHEH. YOU AREN'T CAPABLE OF UNDERSTANDING ME. YOU ARE A CHILD. GO BACK TO YOUR GAMES.
<WHAT DID HE SAY?>
<SOME VERY DISPARAGING THINGS ABOUT YOUR MOTHER.>
<JEZUS, MIHO, WHAT THE HELL WAS THAT ALL ABOUT? HE REALLY BUSTED UP THE PLACE.>
<HE'S VERY INTERESTING, ISN'T HE? I THINK I LIKE HIM.>
<DAMN FREAK.>

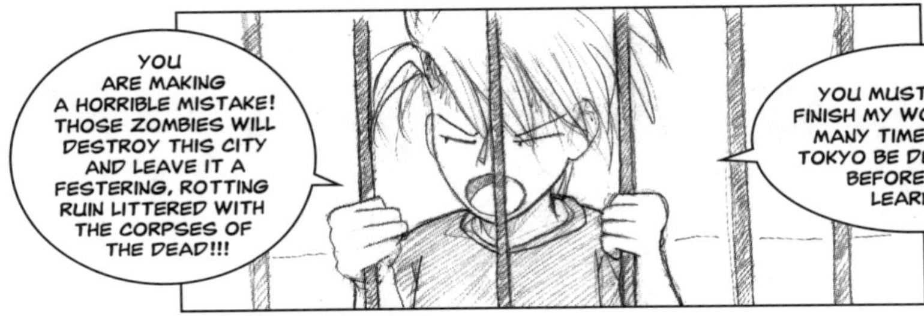
YOU ARE MAKING A HORRIBLE MISTAKE! THOSE ZOMBIES WILL DESTROY THIS CITY AND LEAVE IT A FESTERING, ROTTING RUIN LITTERED WITH THE CORPSES OF THE DEAD!!!
YOU MUST LET ME FINISH MY WORK!! HOW MANY TIMES MUST TOKYO BE DESTROYED BEFORE YOU LEARN??

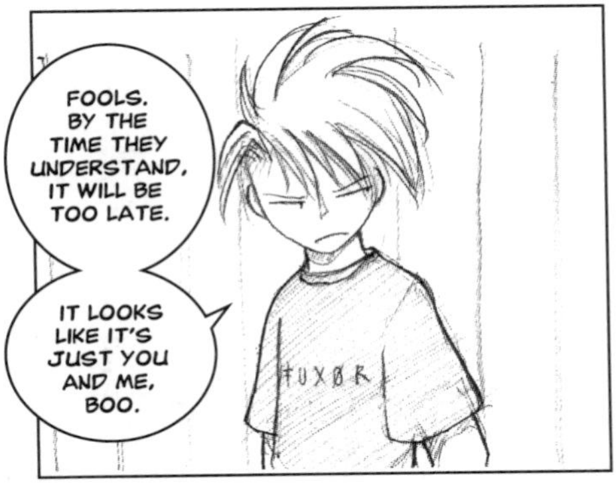
FOOLS. BY THE TIME THEY UNDERSTAND, IT WILL BE TOO LATE.
IT LOOKS LIKE IT'S JUST YOU AND ME, BOO.
FUXØR

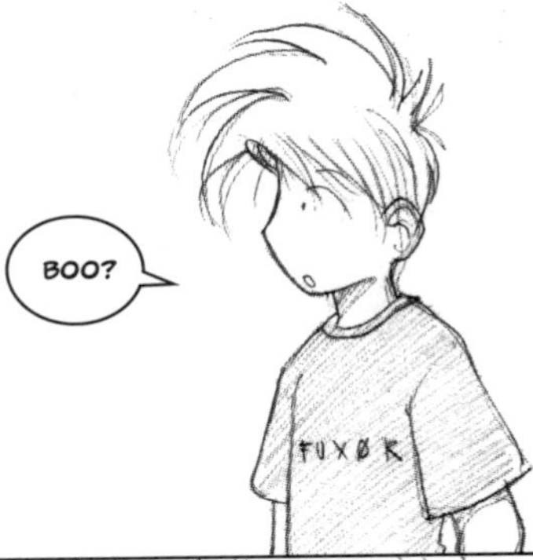
BOO?
FUXØR

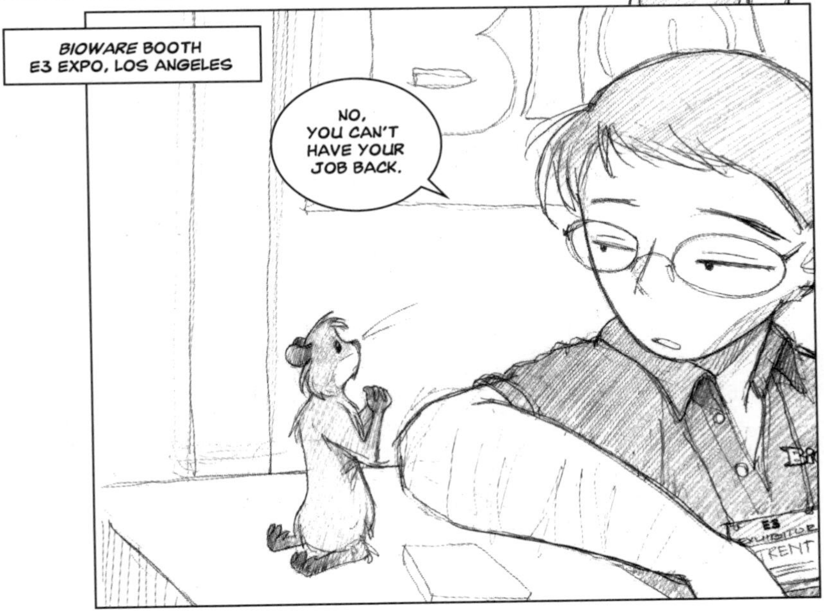
BIOWARE BOOTH
E3 EXPO, LOS ANGELES
NO, YOU CAN'T HAVE YOUR JOB BACK.
TRENT

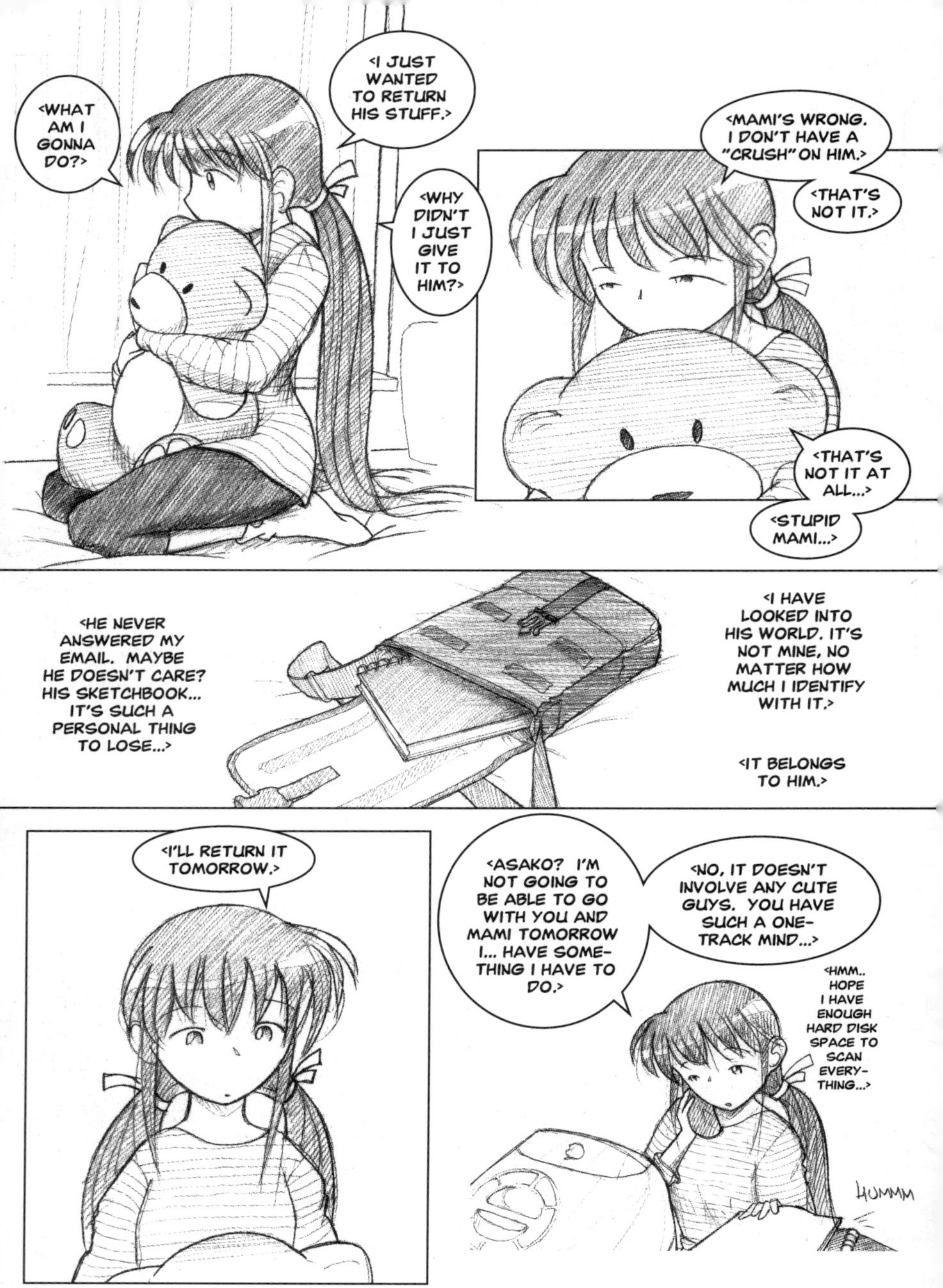
<WHAT AM I GONNA DO?>
<I JUST WANTED TO RETURN HIS STUFF.>
<WHY DIDN'T I JUST GIVE IT TO HIM?>
<MAMI'S WRONG. I DON'T HAVE A "CRUSH" ON HIM.>
<THAT'S NOT IT.>
<THAT'S NOT IT AT ALL...>
<STUPID MAMI...>
<HE NEVER ANSWERED MY EMAIL. MAYBE HE DOESN'T CARE? HIS SKETCHBOOK... IT'S SUCH A PERSONAL THING TO LOSE...>
<I HAVE LOOKED INTO HIS WORLD. IT'S NOT MINE, NO MATTER HOW MUCH I IDENTIFY WITH IT.>
<IT BELONGS TO HIM.>
<I'LL RETURN IT TOMORROW.>
<ASAKO? I'M NOT GOING TO BE ABLE TO GO WITH YOU AND MAMI TOMORROW I... HAVE SOMETHING I HAVE TO DO.>
<NO, IT DOESN'T INVOLVE ANY CUTE GUYS. YOU HAVE SUCH A ONE-TRACK MIND...>
<HMM.. HOPE I HAVE ENOUGH HARD DISK SPACE TO SCAN EVERYTHING...>
HUMMM

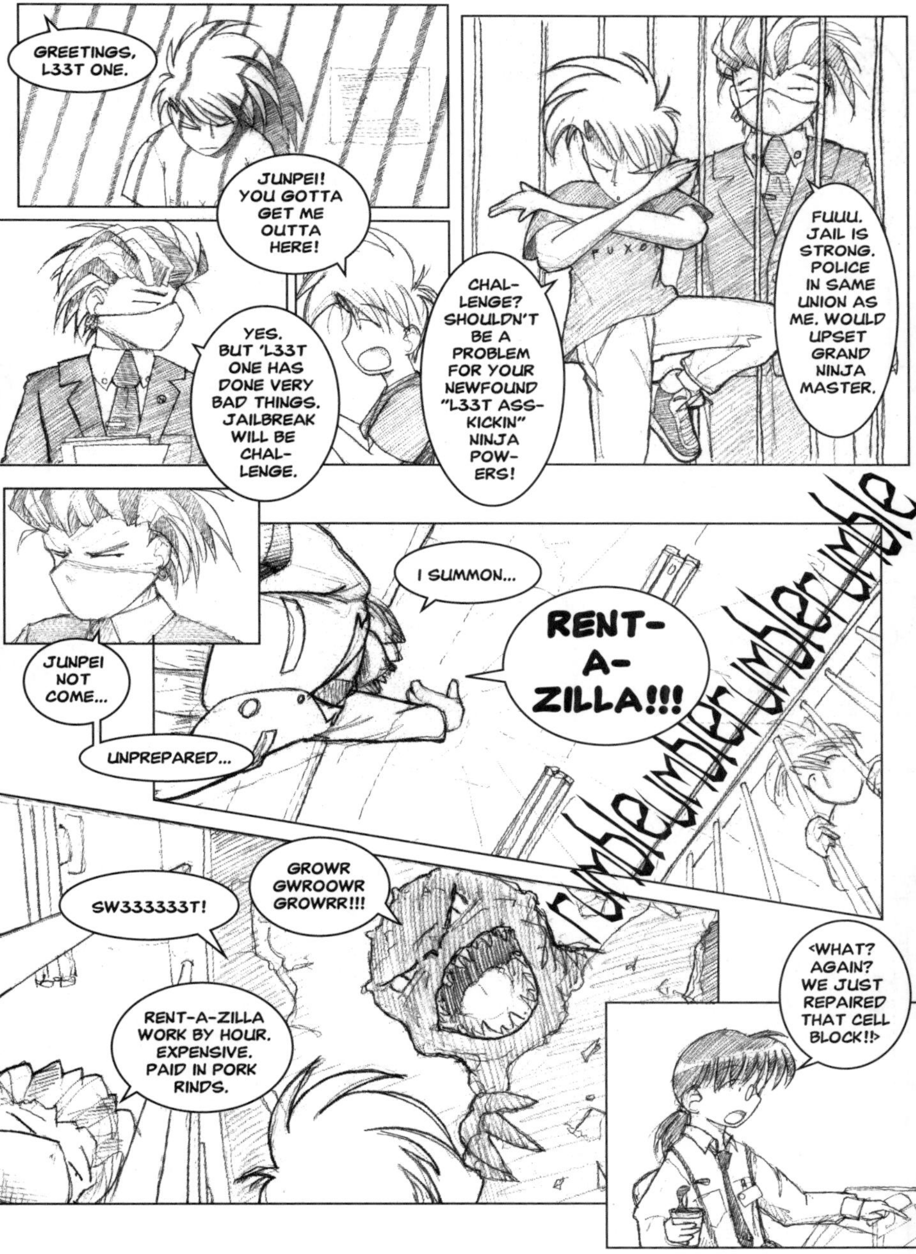

GREETINGS, L33T ONE.
JUNPEI! YOU GOTTA GET ME OUTTA HERE!
YES. BUT 'L33T ONE HAS DONE VERY BAD THINGS. JAILBREAK WILL BE CHAL-LENGE.
CHAL-LENGE? SHOULDN'T BE A PROBLEM FOR YOUR NEWFOUND "L33T ASS-KICKIN" NINJA POW-ERS!
FUUU. JAIL IS STRONG. POLICE IN SAME UNION AS ME. WOULD UPSET GRAND NINJA MASTER.
JUNPEI NOT COME...
UNPREPARED...
I SUMMON...
RENT-A-ZILLA!!!
rumblerumblerumblerumblerumble
SW333333T!
GROWR GWROOWR GROWRR!!!
RENT-A-ZILLA WORK BY HOUR. EXPENSIVE. PAID IN PORK RINDS.
<WHAT? AGAIN? WE JUST REPAIRED THAT CELL BLOCK!!>

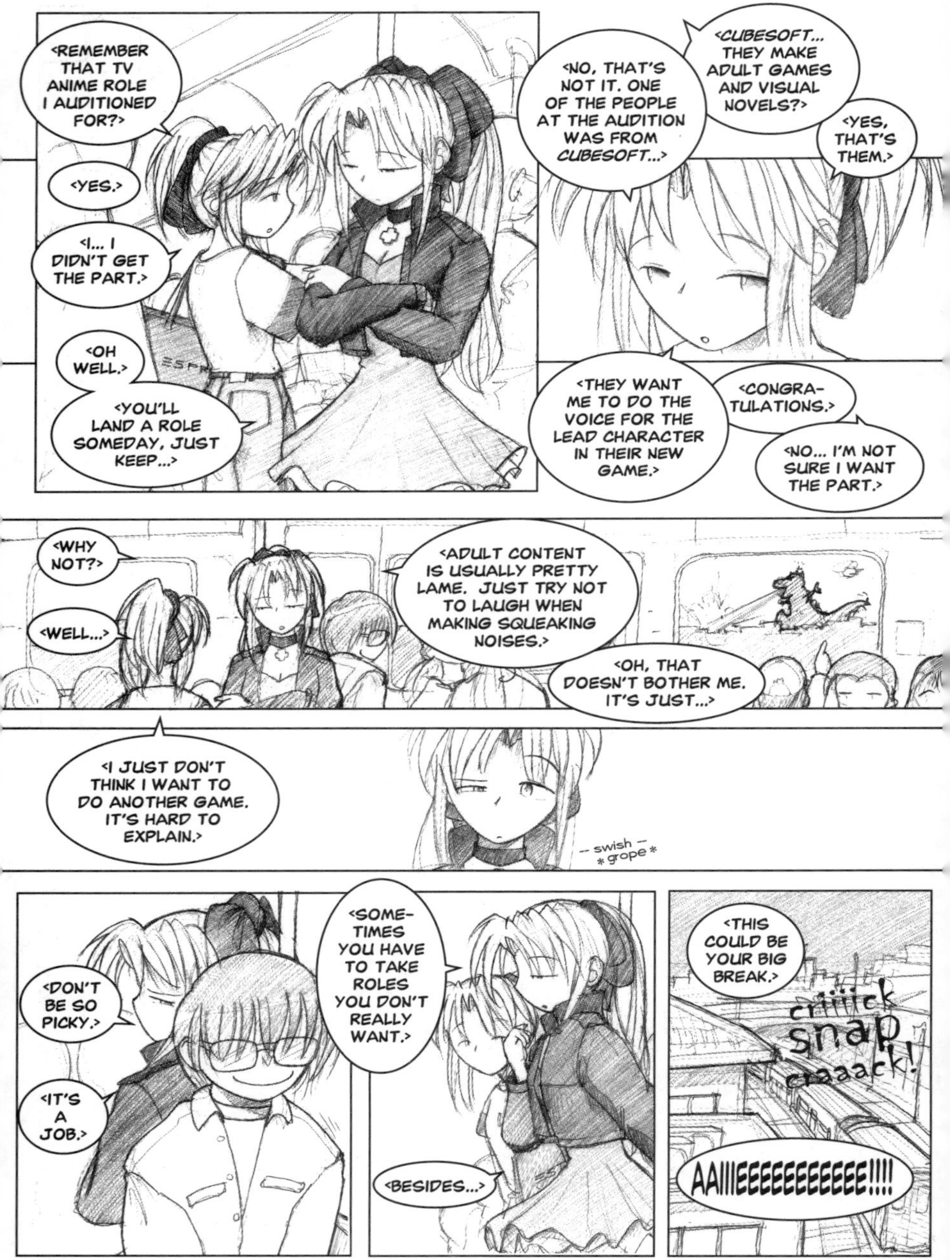

<REMEMBER THAT TV ANIME ROLE I AUDITIONED FOR?>
<YES.>
<I... I DIDN'T GET THE PART.>
<OH WELL.>
<YOU'LL LAND A ROLE SOMEDAY, JUST KEEP...>
<NO, THAT'S NOT IT. ONE OF THE PEOPLE AT THE AUDITION WAS FROM CUBESOFT...>
<CUBESOFT... THEY MAKE ADULT GAMES AND VISUAL NOVELS?>
<YES, THAT'S THEM.>
<THEY WANT ME TO DO THE VOICE FOR THE LEAD CHARACTER IN THEIR NEW GAME.>
<CONGRA-TULATIONS.>
<NO... I'M NOT SURE I WANT THE PART.>
<WHY NOT?>
<WELL...>
<ADULT CONTENT IS USUALLY PRETTY LAME. JUST TRY NOT TO LAUGH WHEN MAKING SQUEAKING NOISES.>
<OH, THAT DOESN'T BOTHER ME. IT'S JUST...>
<I JUST DON'T THINK I WANT TO DO ANOTHER GAME. IT'S HARD TO EXPLAIN.>
-- swish --
* grope *
<DON'T BE SO PICKY.>
<IT'S A JOB.>
<SOME-TIMES YOU HAVE TO TAKE ROLES YOU DON'T REALLY WANT.>
<BESIDES...>
<THIS COULD BE YOUR BIG BREAK.>
criiiick
snap
craaack!
AAIIIEEEEEEEEEEE!!!!

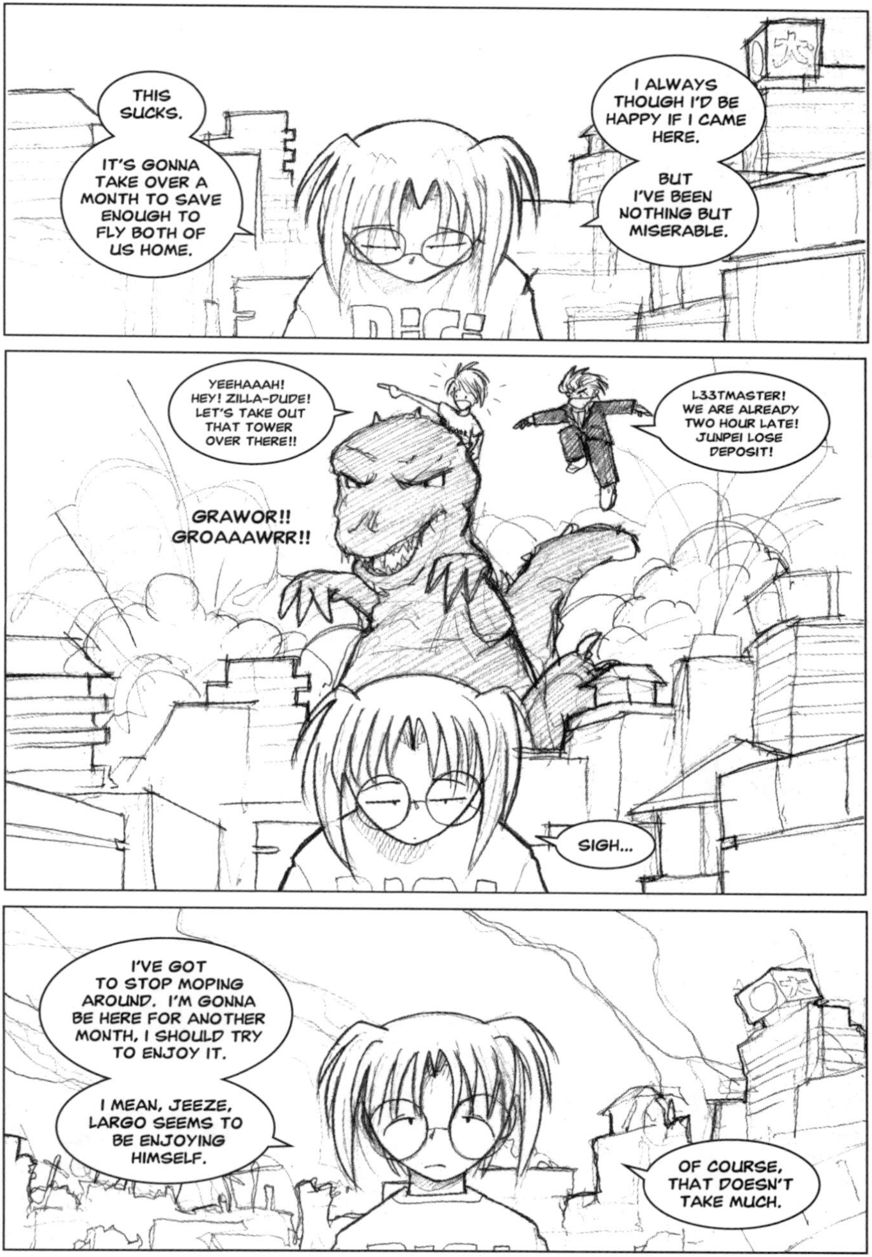
THIS SUCKS.
IT'S GONNA TAKE OVER A MONTH TO SAVE ENOUGH TO FLY BOTH OF US HOME.
I ALWAYS THOUGH I'D BE HAPPY IF I CAME HERE.
BUT I'VE BEEN NOTHING BUT MISERABLE.
YEEHAAAH! HEY! ZILLA-DUDE! LET'S TAKE OUT THAT TOWER OVER THERE!!
L33TMASTER! WE ARE ALREADY TWO HOUR LATE! JUNPEI LOSE DEPOSIT!
GRAWOR!! GROAAAWRR!!
SIGH...
I'VE GOT TO STOP MOPING AROUND. I'M GONNA BE HERE FOR ANOTHER MONTH, I SHOULD TRY TO ENJOY IT.
I MEAN, JEEZE, LARGO SEEMS TO BE ENJOYING HIMSELF.
OF COURSE, THAT DOESN'T TAKE MUCH.

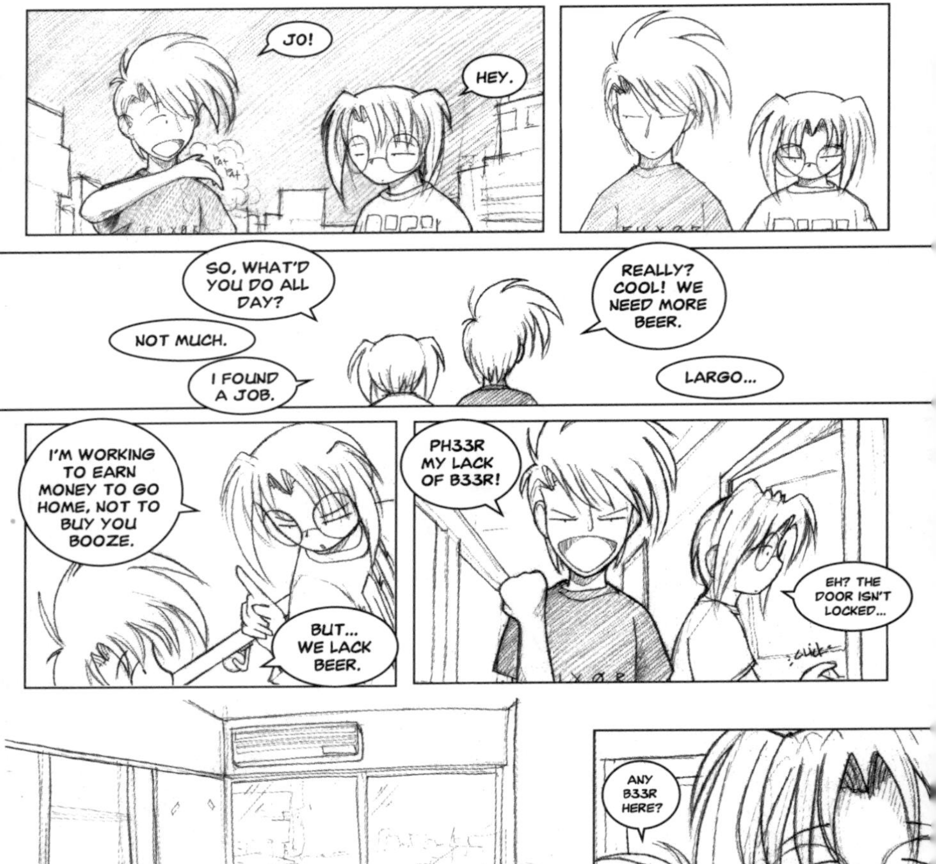
JO!
HEY.
SO, WHAT'D YOU DO ALL DAY?
NOT MUCH.
I FOUND A JOB.
REALLY? COOL! WE NEED MORE BEER.
LARGO...
I'M WORKING TO EARN MONEY TO GO HOME, NOT TO BUY YOU BOOZE.
BUT... WE LACK BEER.
PH33R MY LACK OF B33R!
EH? THE DOOR ISN'T LOCKED...
ANY B33R HERE?
WHAT IN THE WORLD...

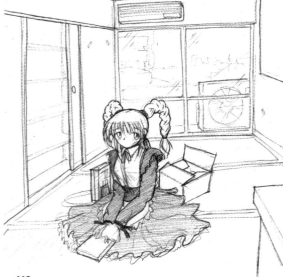

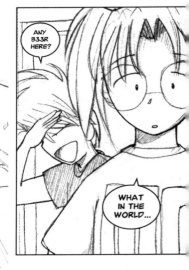

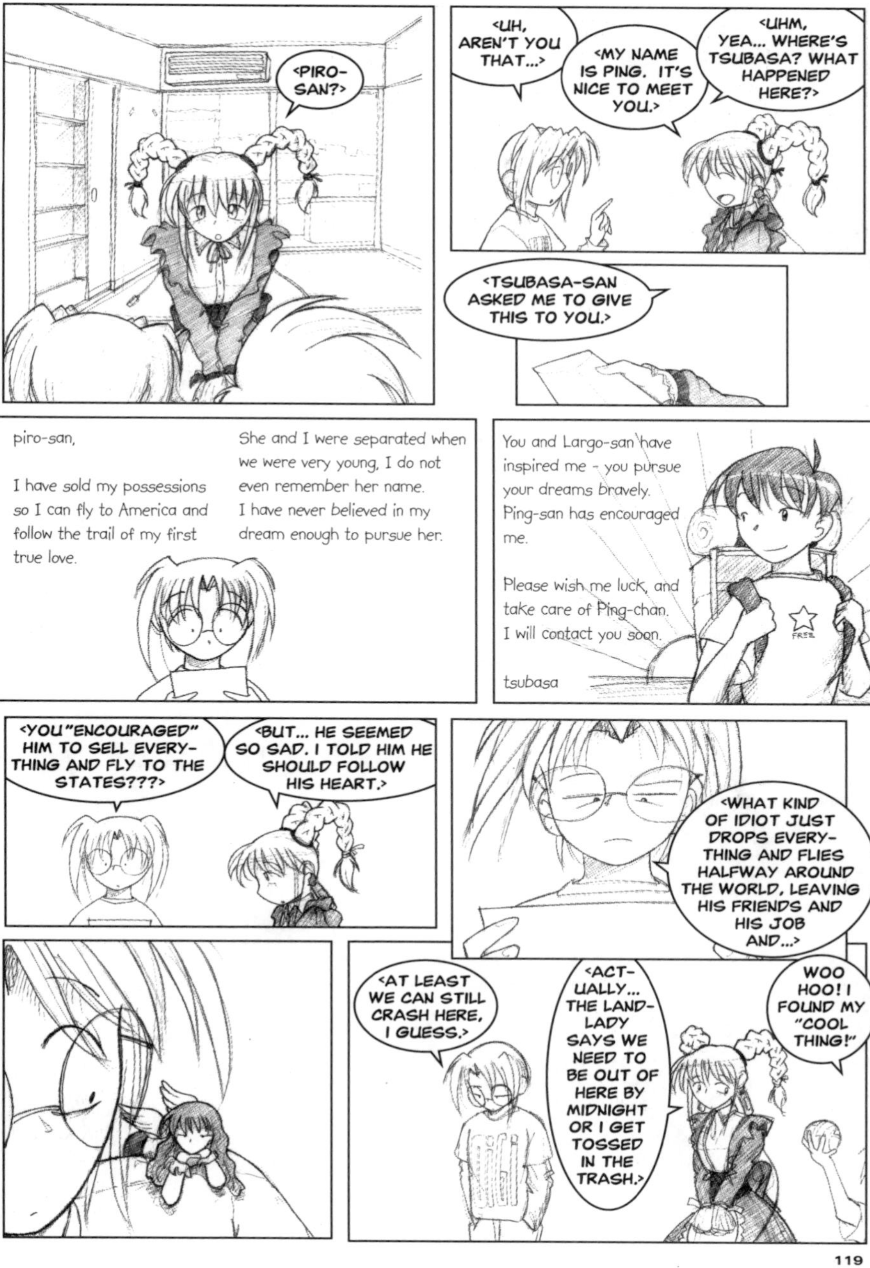

<PIRO-SAN?>
<UH, AREN'T YOU THAT...>
<MY NAME IS PING. IT'S NICE TO MEET YOU.>
<UHM, YEA... WHERE'S TSUBASA? WHAT HAPPENED HERE?>
<TSUBASA-SAN ASKED ME TO GIVE THIS TO YOU.>
piro-san,
I have sold my possessions so I can fly to America and follow the trail of my first true love.
She and I were separated when we were very young, I do not even remember her name.
I have never believed in my dream enough to pursue her.
You and Largo-san have inspired me - you pursue your dreams bravely.
Ping-san has encouraged me.
Please wish me luck, and take care of Ping-chan.
I will contact you soon.
tsubasa
<YOU "ENCOURAGED" HIM TO SELL EVERY-THING AND FLY TO THE STATES???>
<BUT... HE SEEMED SO SAD. I TOLD HIM HE SHOULD FOLLOW HIS HEART.>
<WHAT KIND OF IDIOT JUST DROPS EVERY-THING AND FLIES HALFWAY AROUND THE WORLD, LEAVING HIS FRIENDS AND HIS JOB AND...>
<AT LEAST WE CAN STILL CRASH HERE, I GUESS.>
<ACT-UALLY... THE LAND-LADY SAYS WE NEED TO BE OUT OF HERE BY MIDNIGHT OR I GET TOSSED IN THE TRASH.>
WOO HOO! I FOUND MY "COOL THING!"

<SO, WHERE WE GOIN?>

WOO, SHINY!

Conscience Enforcement Authority (CEA)
Special Counseling Division

FIELD REPORT

client:	Piro
case worker:	Seraphim
case:	CEA-010844FGP21224-4S
status:	level 6, no change

Comments:

While interesting, the Piro case is extremely frustrating. After several months, he remains stranded in Japan and is currently homeless. Surprisingly, he is currently employed. Unfortunately, I believe that most of what he earns will be spent before he leaves the store.

The chances of him saving enough for plane tickets back to the US are slim.

I am concerned that Piro lacks the aggressive-ness and positive attitude he will need to resolve his current situation. He is in way over his head. I am hopeful that additional counseling and 'encouragement' will help him conquer his current set of problems.

footnote:

My 'assistant', Boo, has actually succeeded in making Largo worse than he was before. Due to the lack of professional support from the home office, I reserve the right to implement special tactics where and when i deem fit. Once again, I submit my futile request for additional funds, equipment and resources.

Seraphim - conscience operative, level 9

[send document.... done]

[close window]
[open recent documents]
[open **seraphim-resume.2002**]

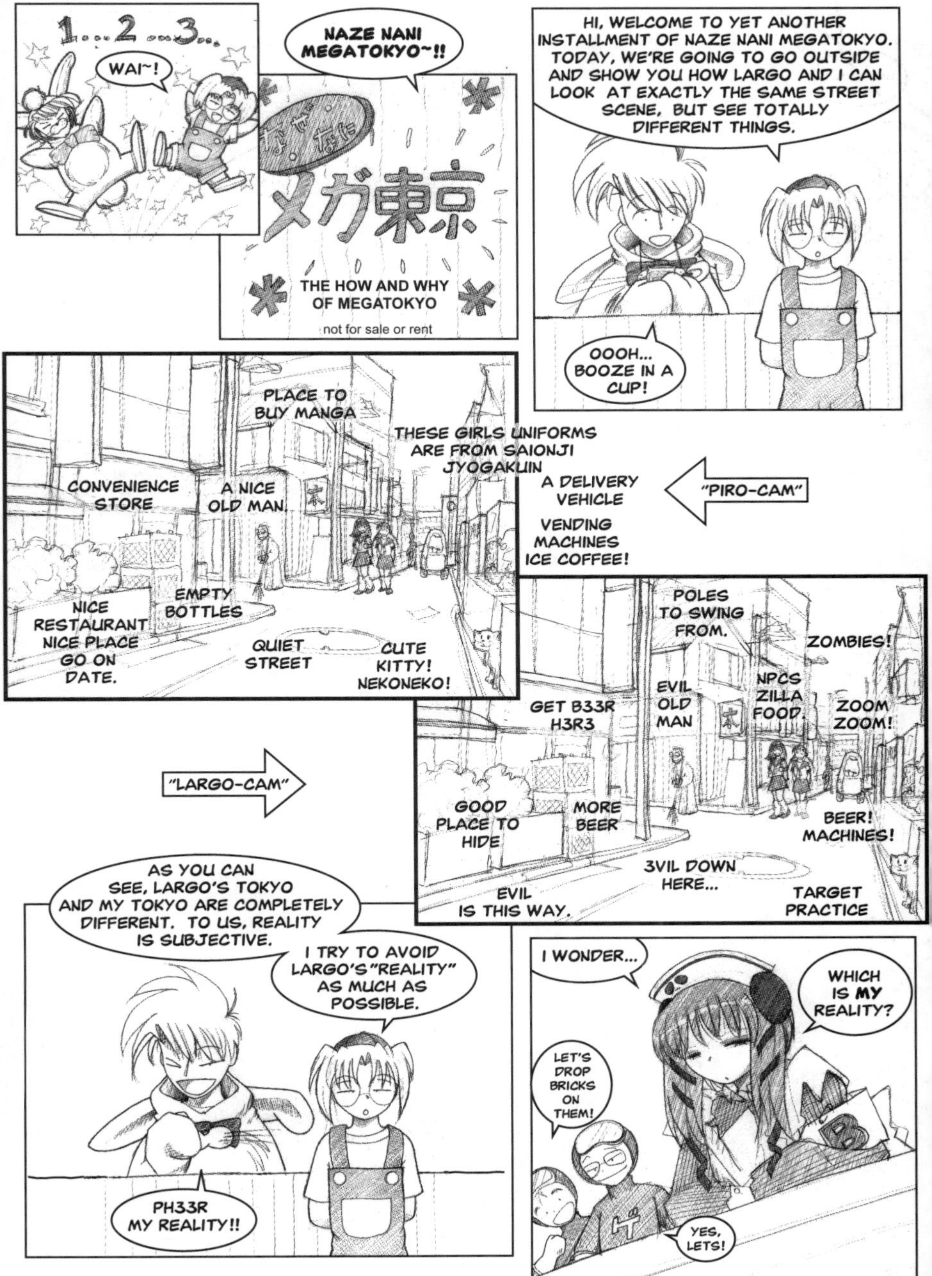

1...2...3...
WAI~!
NAZE NANI MEGATOKYO~!!
なぜなに
メガ東京
THE HOW AND WHY OF MEGATOKYO
not for sale or rent
HI, WELCOME TO YET ANOTHER INSTALLMENT OF NAZE NANI MEGATOKYO. TODAY, WE'RE GOING TO GO OUTSIDE AND SHOW YOU HOW LARGO AND I CAN LOOK AT EXACTLY THE SAME STREET SCENE, BUT SEE TOTALLY DIFFERENT THINGS.
OOOH... BOOZE IN A CUP!
PLACE TO BUY MANGA
THESE GIRLS UNIFORMS ARE FROM SAIONJI JYOGAKUIN
CONVENIENCE STORE
A NICE OLD MAN.
A DELIVERY VEHICLE
"PIRO-CAM"
VENDING MACHINES ICE COFFEE!
EMPTY BOTTLES
NICE RESTAURANT NICE PLACE GO ON DATE.
QUIET STREET
CUTE KITTY! NEKONEKO!
"LARGO-CAM"
POLES TO SWING FROM.
ZOMBIES!
GET B33R H3R3
EVIL OLD MAN
NPCS ZILLA FOOD.
ZOOM ZOOM!
GOOD PLACE TO HIDE
MORE BEER
BEER! MACHINES!
3VIL DOWN HERE...
EVIL IS THIS WAY.
TARGET PRACTICE
AS YOU CAN SEE, LARGO'S TOKYO AND MY TOKYO ARE COMPLETELY DIFFERENT. TO US, REALITY IS SUBJECTIVE.
I TRY TO AVOID LARGO'S "REALITY" AS MUCH AS POSSIBLE.
PH33R MY REALITY!!
I WONDER...
WHICH IS **MY** REALITY?
LET'S DROP BRICKS ON THEM!
YES, LETS!

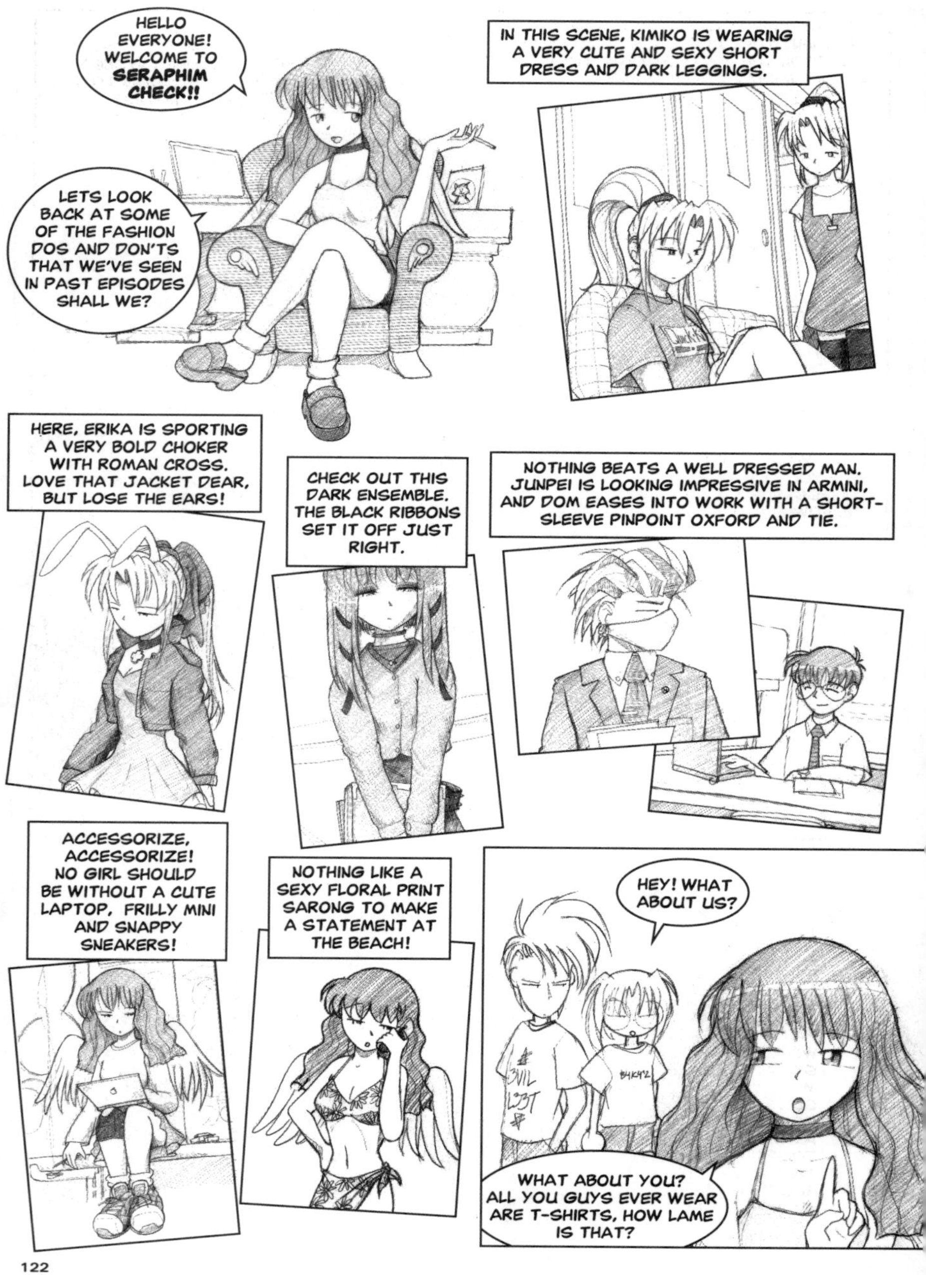
HELLO EVERYONE! WELCOME TO **SERAPHIM CHECK!!**
LETS LOOK BACK AT SOME OF THE FASHION DOS AND DON'TS THAT WE'VE SEEN IN PAST EPISODES SHALL WE?
IN THIS SCENE, KIMIKO IS WEARING A VERY CUTE AND SEXY SHORT DRESS AND DARK LEGGINGS.
HERE, ERIKA IS SPORTING A VERY BOLD CHOKER WITH ROMAN CROSS. LOVE THAT JACKET DEAR, BUT LOSE THE EARS!
CHECK OUT THIS DARK ENSEMBLE. THE BLACK RIBBONS SET IT OFF JUST RIGHT.
NOTHING BEATS A WELL DRESSED MAN. JUNPEI IS LOOKING IMPRESSIVE IN ARMINI, AND DOM EASES INTO WORK WITH A SHORT-SLEEVE PINPOINT OXFORD AND TIE.
ACCESSORIZE, ACCESSORIZE! NO GIRL SHOULD BE WITHOUT A CUTE LAPTOP, FRILLY MINI AND SNAPPY SNEAKERS!
NOTHING LIKE A SEXY FLORAL PRINT SARONG TO MAKE A STATEMENT AT THE BEACH!
HEY! WHAT ABOUT US?
WHAT ABOUT YOU? ALL YOU GUYS EVER WEAR ARE T-SHIRTS, HOW LAME IS THAT?

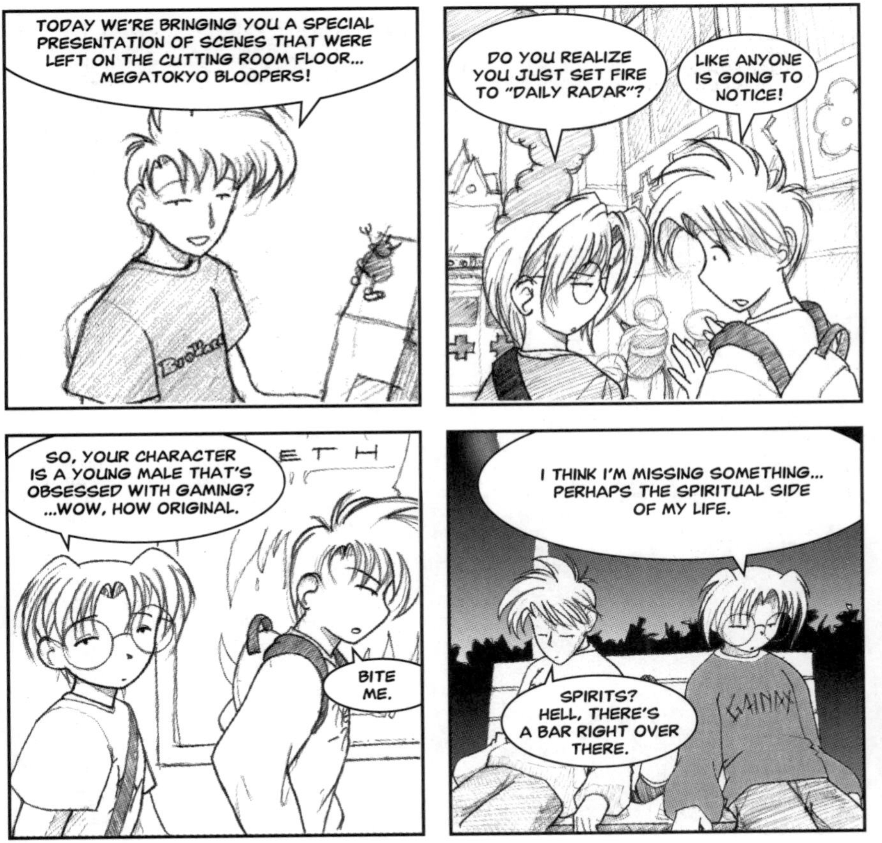
TODAY WE'RE BRINGING YOU A SPECIAL PRESENTATION OF SCENES THAT WERE LEFT ON THE CUTTING ROOM FLOOR... MEGATOKYO BLOOPERS!
DO YOU REALIZE YOU JUST SET FIRE TO "DAILY RADAR"?
LIKE ANYONE IS GOING TO NOTICE!
SO, YOUR CHARACTER IS A YOUNG MALE THAT'S OBSESSED WITH GAMING? ...WOW, HOW ORIGINAL.
BITE ME.
I THINK I'M MISSING SOMETHING... PERHAPS THE SPIRITUAL SIDE OF MY LIFE.
SPIRITS? HELL, THERE'S A BAR RIGHT OVER THERE.

THE LAST COMIC YOU READ WAS TECHNICALLY THE END OF CHAPTER 0.

WE DID A LOT OF COMICS THAT WERE NOT REALLY PART OF THE STORY BUT WERE MORE LIKE 'ONE SHOT' STAND ALONE EPISODES. MANY OF THESE STAND QUITE WELL ON THEIR OWN, SO I'VE PULLED THEM OUT AND GROUPED THEM TOGETHER HERE AT THE END OF THE BOOK TO GIVE THE STORY BETTER FLOW.

LARGO PUT THIS ONE TOGETHER USING FRAMES FROM PREVIOUS COMICS. UNFORTUNATELY, I'VE LOST THE ORIGINAL ART FOR FRAME 1, SO WHAT YOU SEE HERE IS A 'WEB RESOLUTION' VERSION.

OUT OF EVERYTHING IN CHAPTER 0, I LOST ONLY TWO PIECES OF ART. NOT BAD, CONSIDERING.

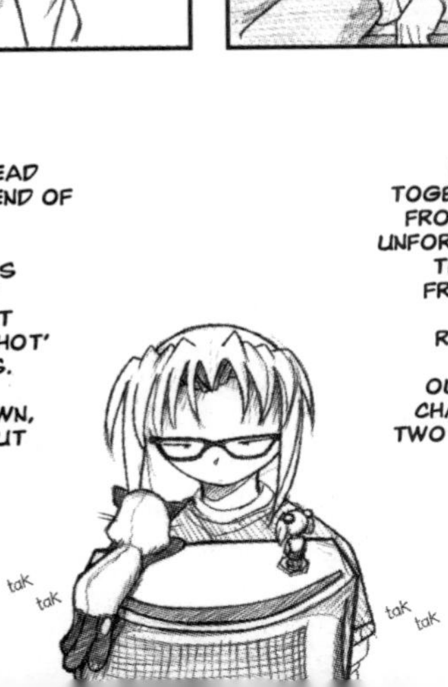
tak
tak
tak
tak

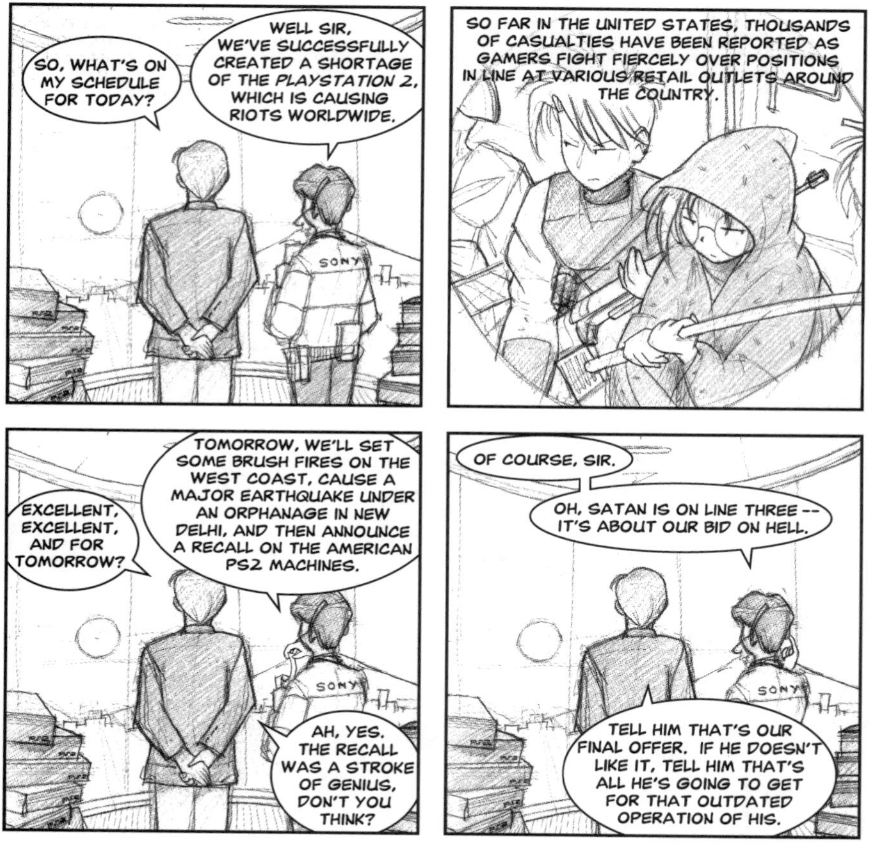
SO, WHAT'S ON MY SCHEDULE FOR TODAY?
WELL SIR, WE'VE SUCCESSFULLY CREATED A SHORTAGE OF THE *PLAYSTATION 2*, WHICH IS CAUSING RIOTS WORLDWIDE.
SONY
SO FAR IN THE UNITED STATES, THOUSANDS OF CASUALTIES HAVE BEEN REPORTED AS GAMERS FIGHT FIERCELY OVER POSITIONS IN LINE AT VARIOUS RETAIL OUTLETS AROUND THE COUNTRY.
EXCELLENT, EXCELLENT, AND FOR TOMORROW?
TOMORROW, WE'LL SET SOME BRUSH FIRES ON THE WEST COAST, CAUSE A MAJOR EARTHQUAKE UNDER AN ORPHANAGE IN NEW DELHI, AND THEN ANNOUNCE A RECALL ON THE AMERICAN PS2 MACHINES.
SONY
AH, YES. THE RECALL WAS A STROKE OF GENIUS, DON'T YOU THINK?
OF COURSE, SIR.
OH, SATAN IS ON LINE THREE -- IT'S ABOUT OUR BID ON HELL.
SONY
TELL HIM THAT'S OUR FINAL OFFER. IF HE DOESN'T LIKE IT, TELL HIM THAT'S ALL HE'S GOING TO GET FOR THAT OUTDATED OPERATION OF HIS.

REMEMBER WHEN THE PLAYSTATION 2 CAME OUT?

THIS IS A "BAD ART DAY SPECIAL" BECAUSE I DIDN'T TRACE AND CLEAN THE IMAGES BEFORE PUTTING THE COMIC TOGETHER. EVEN SO, IT DIDN'T COME OUT TOO BAD.

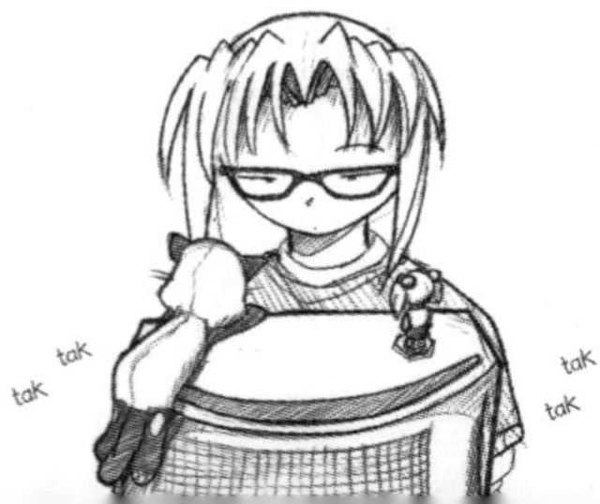
tak
tak
tak
tak

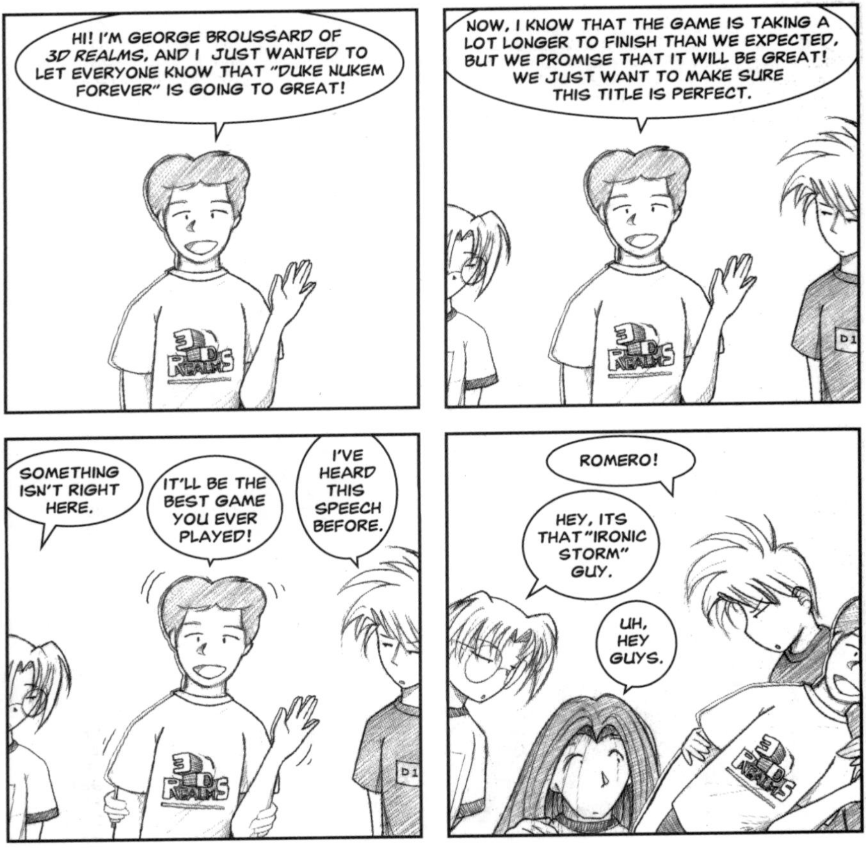
HI! I'M GEORGE BROUSSARD OF 3D REALMS, AND I JUST WANTED TO LET EVERYONE KNOW THAT "DUKE NUKEM FOREVER" IS GOING TO GREAT!
NOW, I KNOW THAT THE GAME IS TAKING A LOT LONGER TO FINISH THAN WE EXPECTED, BUT WE PROMISE THAT IT WILL BE GREAT! WE JUST WANT TO MAKE SURE THIS TITLE IS PERFECT.
SOMETHING ISN'T RIGHT HERE.
IT'LL BE THE BEST GAME YOU EVER PLAYED!
I'VE HEARD THIS SPEECH BEFORE.
ROMERO!
HEY, ITS THAT "IRONIC STORM" GUY.
UH, HEY GUYS.

LARGO LOVES TO POKE FUN AT PEOPLE IN THE GAMING INDUSTRY. HE REALLY WANTED TO GET US INTO TROUBLE, I THINK.

THE IDEA OF WIGGLING AROUND A CARDBOARD CUTOUT REALLY CRACKED ME UP FOR SOME REASON. ROMERO IS SO MUCH FUN TO DRAW.

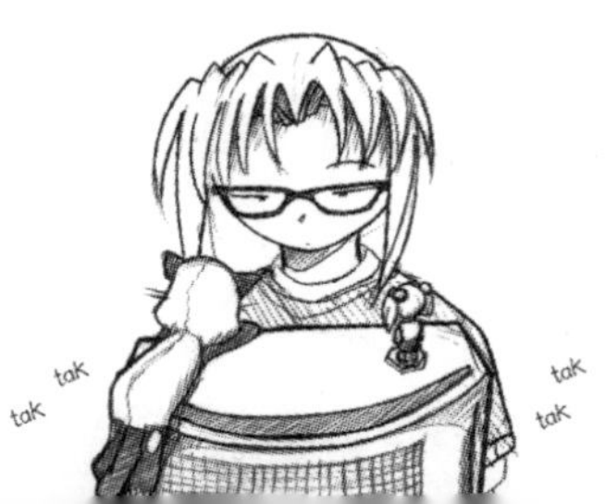
tak
tak
tak
tak

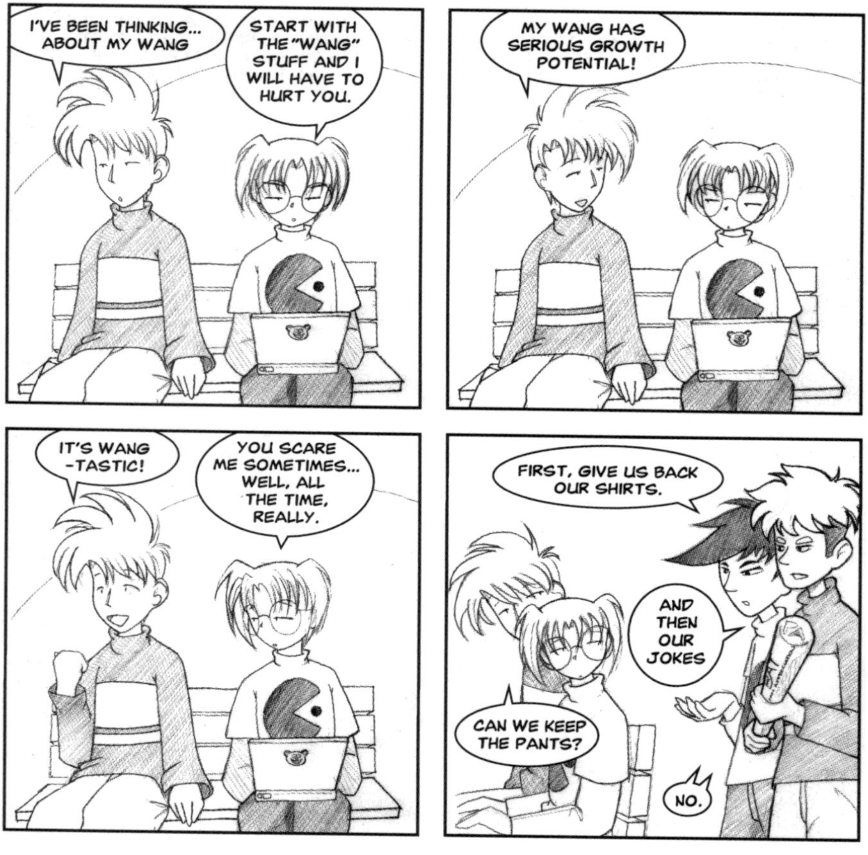
I'VE BEEN THINKING... ABOUT MY WANG
START WITH THE "WANG" STUFF AND I WILL HAVE TO HURT YOU.
MY WANG HAS SERIOUS GROWTH POTENTIAL!
IT'S WANG -TASTIC!
YOU SCARE ME SOMETIMES... WELL, ALL THE TIME, REALLY.
FIRST, GIVE US BACK OUR SHIRTS.
AND THEN OUR JOKES
CAN WE KEEP THE PANTS?
NO.

WE OWE A LOT OF OUR SUCCESS WITH MEGATOKYO TO THE GENEROUS LINKAGE FROM A VERY POPULAR WEBCOMIC CALLED "PENNY ARCADE."

PENNY ARCADE USED TO HAVE A SITE WHERE YOU COULD MAKE YOUR OWN *PENNY ARCADE* COMIC CALLED "THE BENCH." THIS WAS OUR SUBMISSION.

OH, IT SAYS "FAN APPRECIATION BAT," ON THE BAT. I'VE OFTEN FELT THAT I NEED ONE OF THOSE.

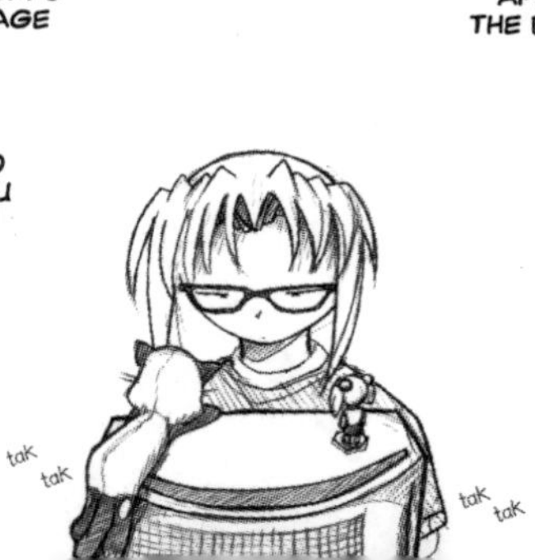
tak
tak
tak
tak

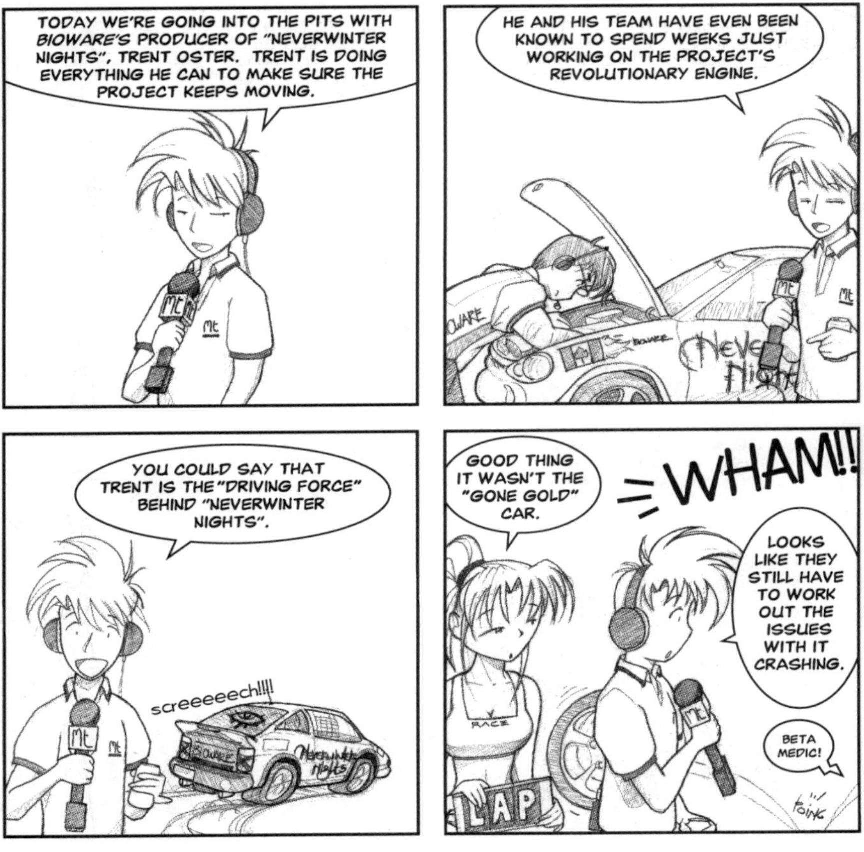
TODAY WE'RE GOING INTO THE PITS WITH *BIOWARE'S* PRODUCER OF "NEVERWINTER NIGHTS", TRENT OSTER. TRENT IS DOING EVERYTHING HE CAN TO MAKE SURE THE PROJECT KEEPS MOVING.
HE AND HIS TEAM HAVE EVEN BEEN KNOWN TO SPEND WEEKS JUST WORKING ON THE PROJECT'S REVOLUTIONARY ENGINE.
YOU COULD SAY THAT TRENT IS THE "DRIVING FORCE" BEHIND "NEVERWINTER NIGHTS".
screeeeeech!!!!
GOOD THING IT WASN'T THE "GONE GOLD" CAR.
WHAM!!
LOOKS LIKE THEY STILL HAVE TO WORK OUT THE ISSUES WITH IT CRASHING.
BETA MEDIC!
LAP
poing

NEEDLESS TO SAY, LARGO'S ANTICIPATION OF THE NEW *BIOWARE* GAME "NEVERWINTER NIGHTS" BORDERED ON THE CLINICALLY OBSESSIVE.

THANK GOD THE GUYS AT BIOWARE HAVE SUCH A GREAT SENSE OF HUMOR. CANADIANS ARE COOL.

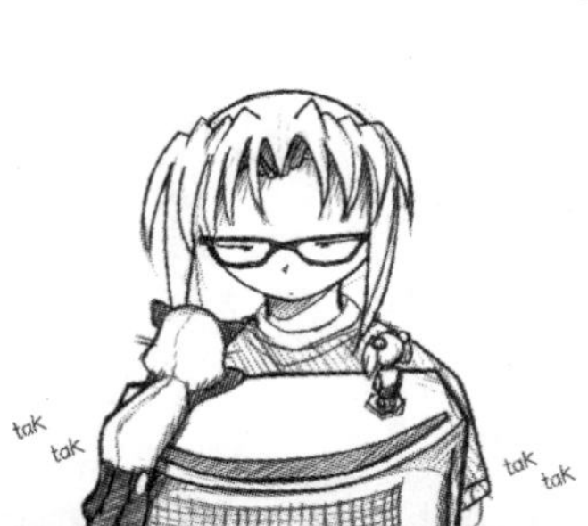
tak
tak
tak
tak

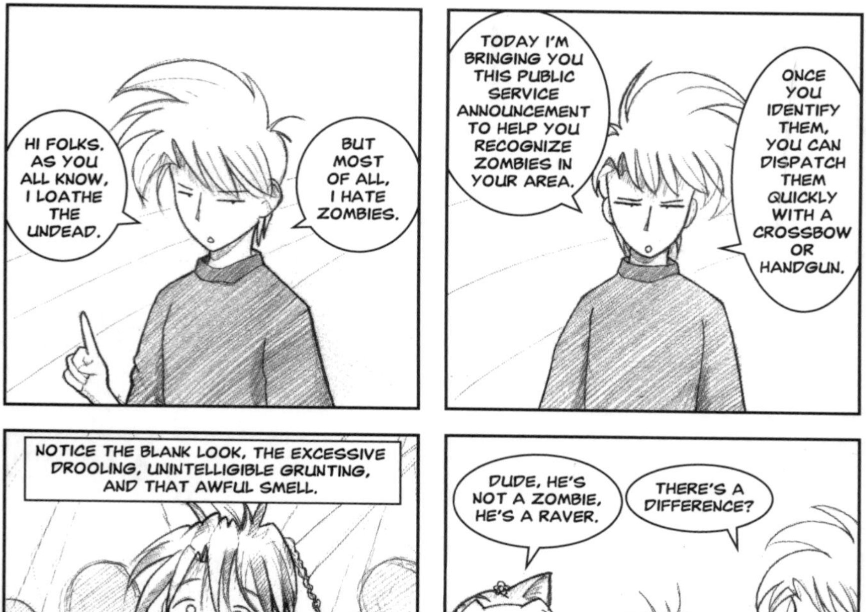
HI FOLKS. AS YOU ALL KNOW, I LOATHE THE UNDEAD.
BUT MOST OF ALL, I HATE ZOMBIES.
TODAY I'M BRINGING YOU THIS PUBLIC SERVICE ANNOUNCEMENT TO HELP YOU RECOGNIZE ZOMBIES IN YOUR AREA.
ONCE YOU IDENTIFY THEM, YOU CAN DISPATCH THEM QUICKLY WITH A CROSSBOW OR HANDGUN.
NOTICE THE BLANK LOOK, THE EXCESSIVE DROOLING, UNINTELLIGIBLE GRUNTING, AND THAT AWFUL SMELL.
BURIED
|-|U|-|?
DUDE, HE'S NOT A ZOMBIE, HE'S A RAVER.
THERE'S A DIFFERENCE?
DID I MISS SOM3T|-|IN?
BURIED

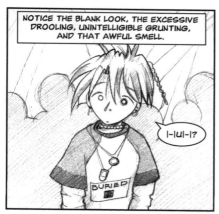

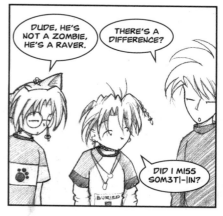

LARGO WANTED TO DO A LOT OF THESE "PSA" OR "PUBLIC SERVICE ANNOUNCEMENT" TYPE STRIPS.

I SWEAR, I'LL NEVER UNDERSTAND THIS WHOLE "ZOMBIE" THING.

WE GOT A LOT OF EMAIL FROM "RAVERS" WHO WERE OFFENDED BY THIS COMIC – AND AT THE SAME TIME GOT EMAIL FROM RAVERS WHO THOUGHT IT WAS A HOOT.

FOR THE RECORD, I LOVE RAVE CULTURE. I'M A BIG MUSIC FAN – I LISTEN TO EVERYTHING FROM TRANCE, TECHNO, EBM, HOUSE AND INDUSTRIAL TO DOWNTEMPO, AMBIENT AND CHILL. INTERNET RADIO ROCKS.

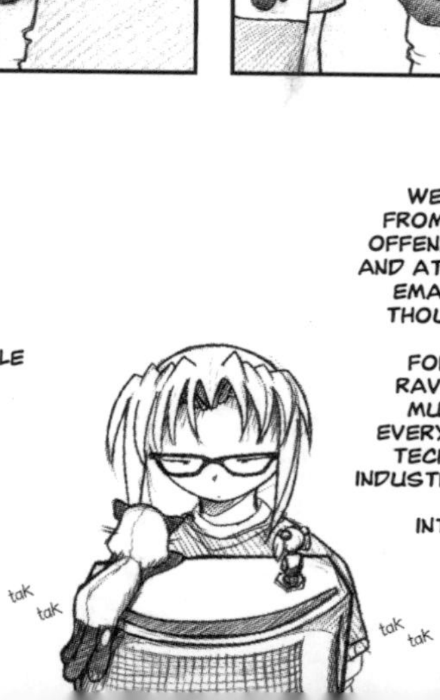
tak
tak
tak
tak

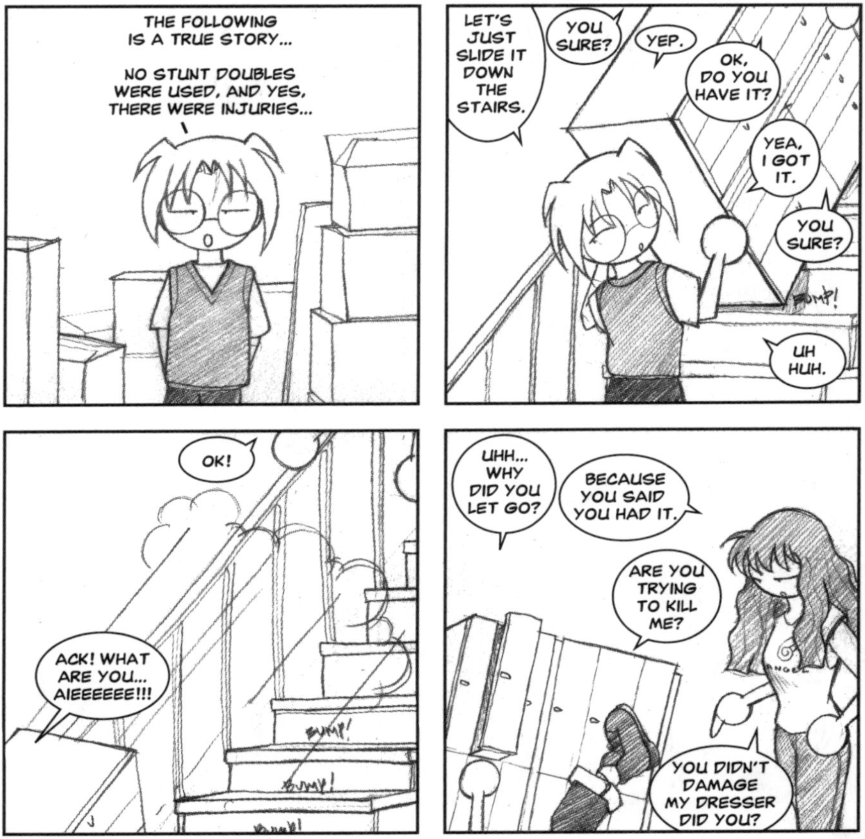
THE FOLLOWING IS A TRUE STORY...
NO STUNT DOUBLES WERE USED, AND YES, THERE WERE INJURIES...
LET'S JUST SLIDE IT DOWN THE STAIRS.
YOU SURE?
YEP.
OK, DO YOU HAVE IT?
YEA, I GOT IT.
YOU SURE?
BUMP!
UH HUH.
OK!
ACK! WHAT ARE YOU... AIEEEEEE!!!
BUMP!
BUMP!
BUMP!
UHH... WHY DID YOU LET GO?
BECAUSE YOU SAID YOU HAD IT.
ARE YOU TRYING TO KILL ME?
YOU DIDN'T DAMAGE MY DRESSER DID YOU?

I'VE MOVED TWICE SINCE I STARTED MEGATOKYO. I HATE MOVING.

YES, THIS REALLY DID HAPPEN. THANK GOD WE EMPTIED THE DRAWERS FIRST.

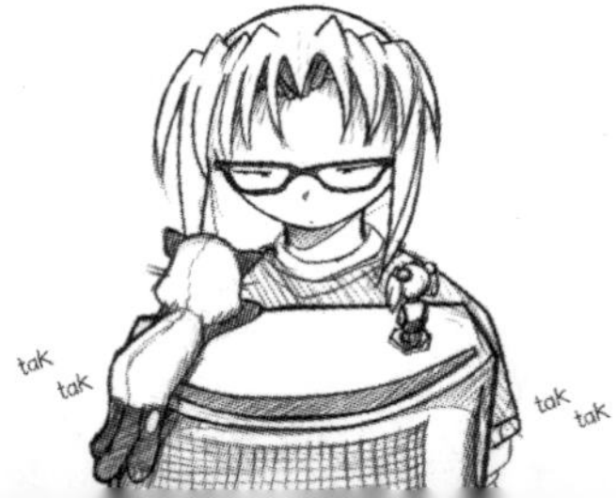
tak
tak
tak
tak

SPECIAL! ANIME CENTRAL 2001 SNAPSHOT

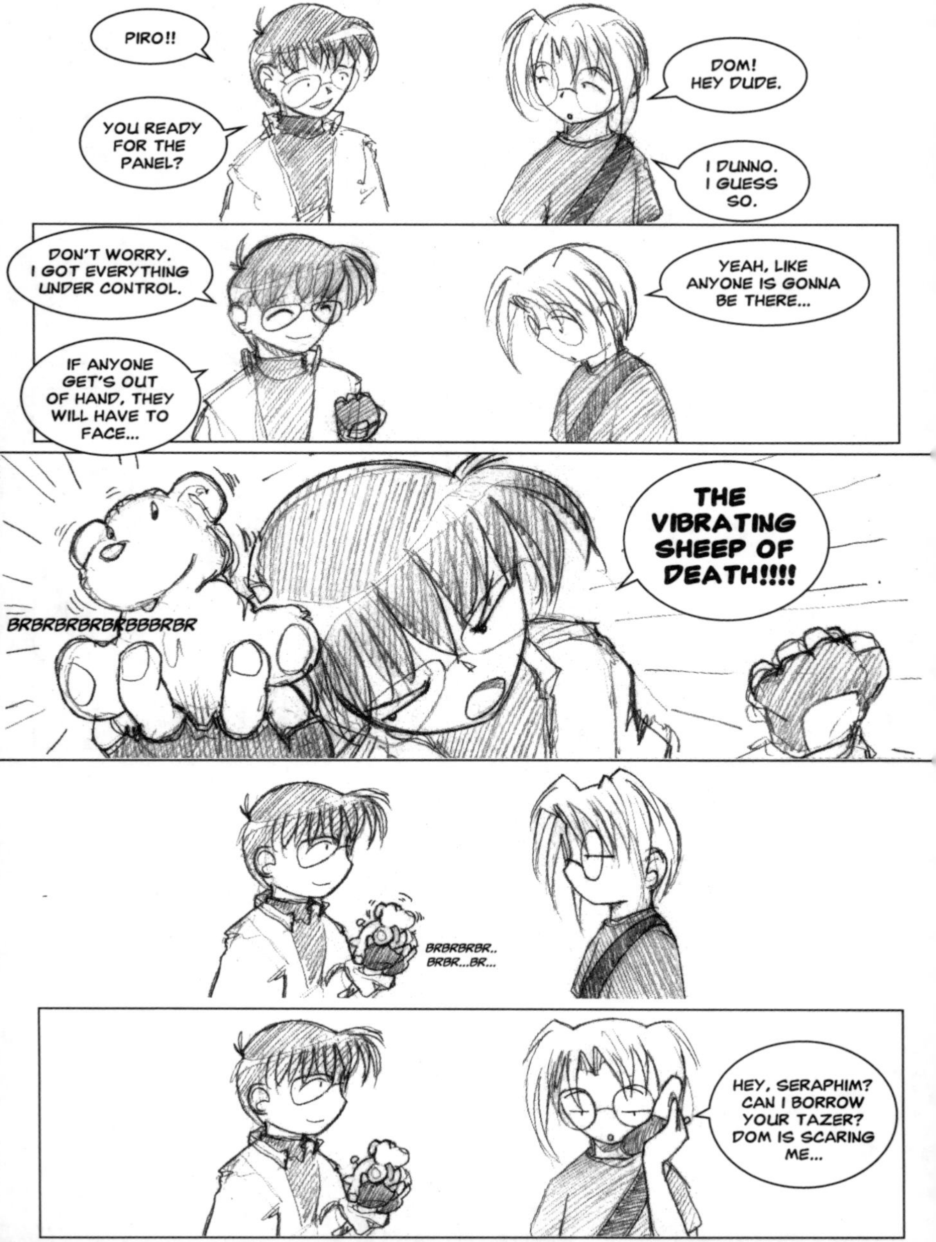
PIRO!!
YOU READY FOR THE PANEL?
DOM! HEY DUDE.
I DUNNO. I GUESS SO.
DON'T WORRY. I GOT EVERYTHING UNDER CONTROL.
IF ANYONE GET'S OUT OF HAND, THEY WILL HAVE TO FACE...
YEAH, LIKE ANYONE IS GONNA BE THERE...
BRBRBRBRBRBRBBBRBR
THE VIBRATING SHEEP OF DEATH!!!!
BRBRBRBR.. BRBR...BR...
HEY, SERAPHIM? CAN I BORROW YOUR TAZER? DOM IS SCARING ME...

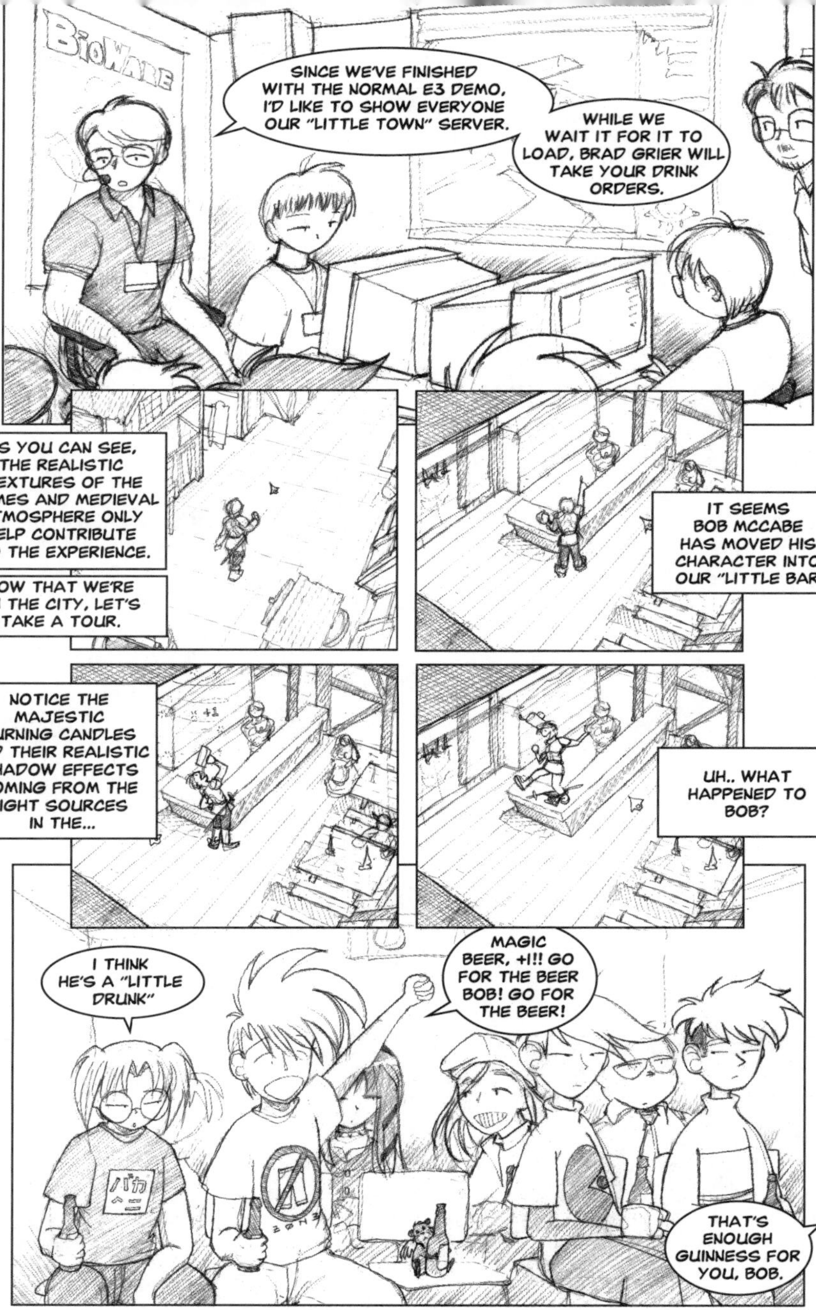
BioWare
SINCE WE'VE FINISHED WITH THE NORMAL E3 DEMO, I'D LIKE TO SHOW EVERYONE OUR "LITTLE TOWN" SERVER.
WHILE WE WAIT IT FOR IT TO LOAD, BRAD GRIER WILL TAKE YOUR DRINK ORDERS.
AS YOU CAN SEE, THE REALISTIC TEXTURES OF THE HOMES AND MEDIEVAL ATMOSPHERE ONLY HELP CONTRIBUTE TO THE EXPERIENCE.
NOW THAT WE'RE IN THE CITY, LET'S TAKE A TOUR.
IT SEEMS BOB MCCABE HAS MOVED HIS CHARACTER INTO OUR "LITTLE BAR"
NOTICE THE MAJESTIC BURNING CANDLES AND THEIR REALISTIC SHADOW EFFECTS COMING FROM THE LIGHT SOURCES IN THE...
UH.. WHAT HAPPENED TO BOB?
I THINK HE'S A "LITTLE DRUNK"
MAGIC BEER, +1!! GO FOR THE BEER BOB! GO FOR THE BEER!
THAT'S ENOUGH GUINNESS FOR YOU, BOB.

SERAPHIM ART-DAY SPECIAL!

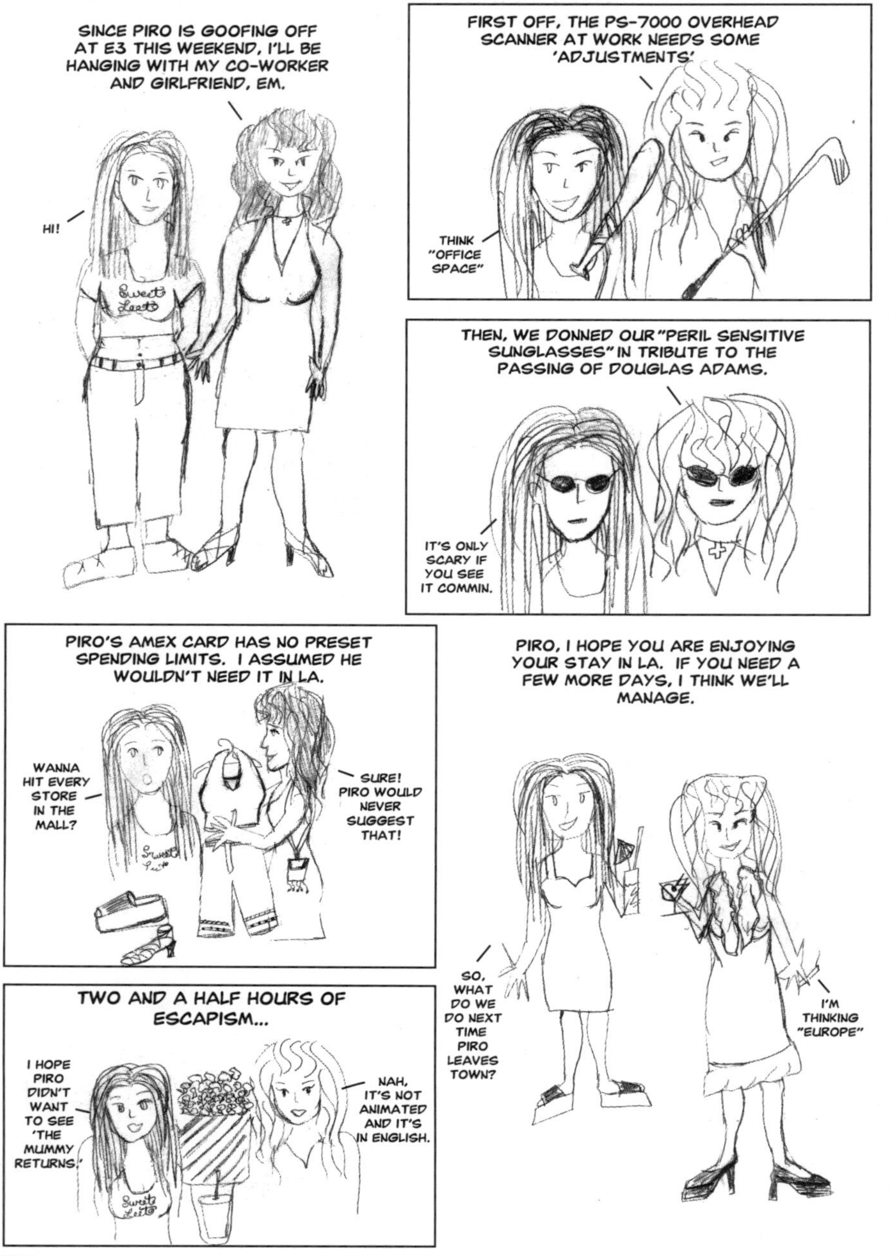

SINCE PIRO IS GOOFING OFF AT E3 THIS WEEKEND, I'LL BE HANGING WITH MY CO-WORKER AND GIRLFRIEND, EM.
HI!
FIRST OFF, THE PS-7000 OVERHEAD SCANNER AT WORK NEEDS SOME 'ADJUSTMENTS'
THINK "OFFICE SPACE"
THEN, WE DONNED OUR "PERIL SENSITIVE SUNGLASSES" IN TRIBUTE TO THE PASSING OF DOUGLAS ADAMS.
IT'S ONLY SCARY IF YOU SEE IT COMMIN.
PIRO'S AMEX CARD HAS NO PRESET SPENDING LIMITS. I ASSUMED HE WOULDN'T NEED IT IN LA.
WANNA HIT EVERY STORE IN THE MALL?
SURE! PIRO WOULD NEVER SUGGEST THAT!
TWO AND A HALF HOURS OF ESCAPISM...
I HOPE PIRO DIDN'T WANT TO SEE 'THE MUMMY RETURNS.'
NAH, IT'S NOT ANIMATED AND IT'S IN ENGLISH.
PIRO, I HOPE YOU ARE ENJOYING YOUR STAY IN LA. IF YOU NEED A FEW MORE DAYS, I THINK WE'LL MANAGE.
SO, WHAT DO WE DO NEXT TIME PIRO LEAVES TOWN?
I'M THINKING "EUROPE"

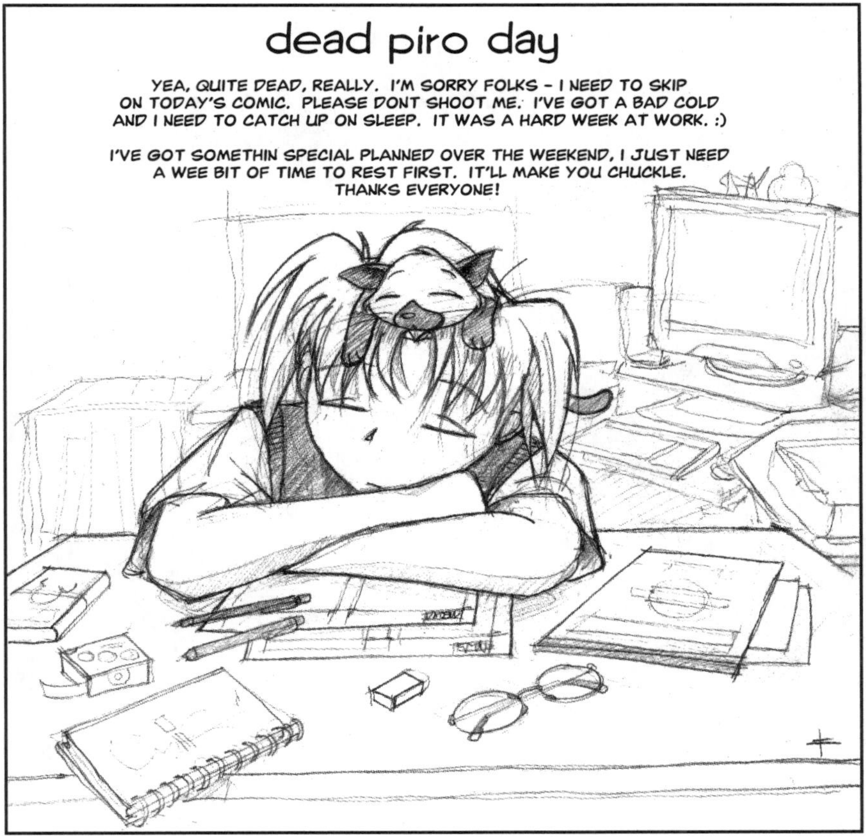
dead piro day
YEA, QUITE DEAD, REALLY. I'M SORRY FOLKS - I NEED TO SKIP ON TODAY'S COMIC. PLEASE DONT SHOOT ME. I'VE GOT A BAD COLD AND I NEED TO CATCH UP ON SLEEP. IT WAS A HARD WEEK AT WORK. :)
I'VE GOT SOMETHIN SPECIAL PLANNED OVER THE WEEKEND, I JUST NEED A WEE BIT OF TIME TO REST FIRST. IT'LL MAKE YOU CHUCKLE. THANKS EVERYONE!

AROUND THE TIME OF THE "ANNA MILLER'S" COMIC I HAD A PRETTY BAD COLD. TIRED, GRUMPY, AND NOT WANTING TO DRAW ANYTHING, I DID THIS "DEAD PIRO DAY" JOKE. FOR SOME REASON, THE TERM "DEAD PIRO DAY" STUCK.

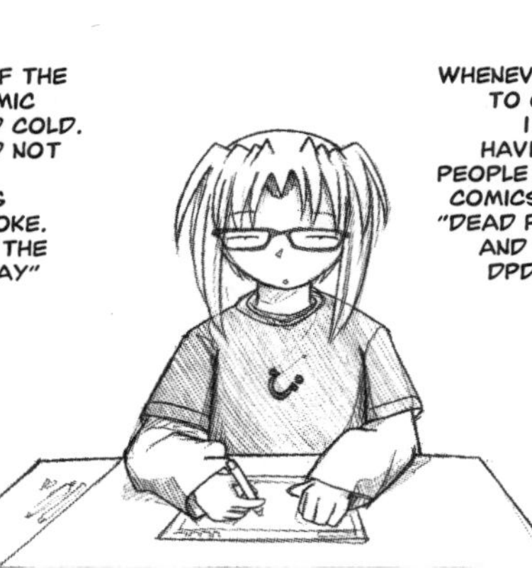

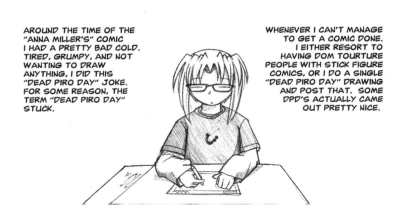

WHENEVER I CAN'T MANAGE TO GET A COMIC DONE. I EITHER RESORT TO HAVING DOM TOURTURE PEOPLE WITH STICK FIGURE COMICS, OR I DO A SINGLE "DEAD PIRO DAY" DRAWING AND POST THAT. SOME DPD'S ACTUALLY CAME OUT PRETTY NICE.

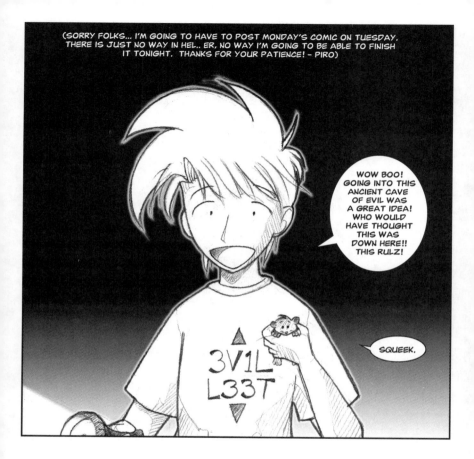

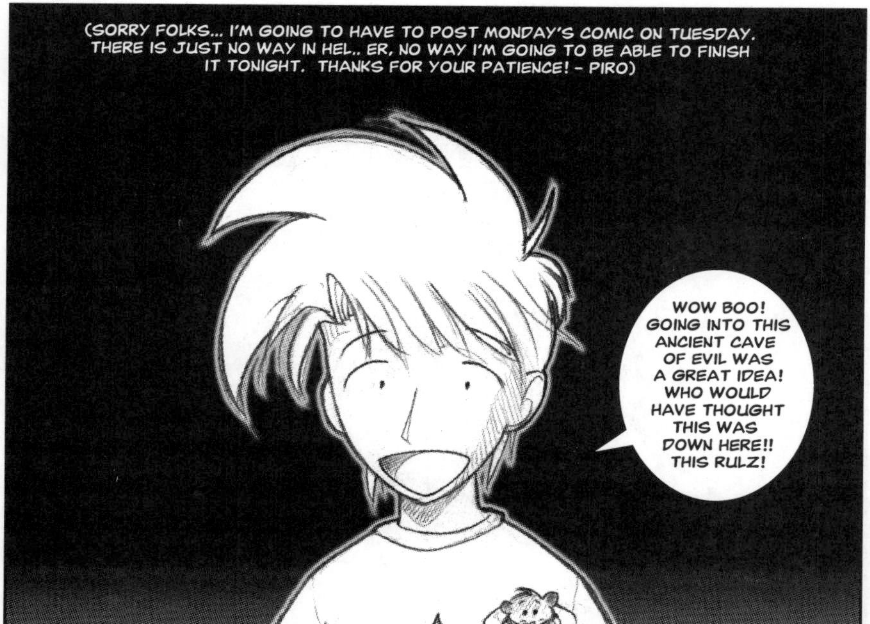
(SORRY FOLKS... I'M GOING TO HAVE TO POST MONDAY'S COMIC ON TUESDAY. THERE IS JUST NO WAY IN HEL.. ER, NO WAY I'M GOING TO BE ABLE TO FINISH IT TONIGHT. THANKS FOR YOUR PATIENCE! - PIRO)
WOW BOO! GOING INTO THIS ANCIENT CAVE OF EVIL WAS A GREAT IDEA! WHO WOULD HAVE THOUGHT THIS WAS DOWN HERE!! THIS RULZ!
SQUEEK.
3V1L L33T

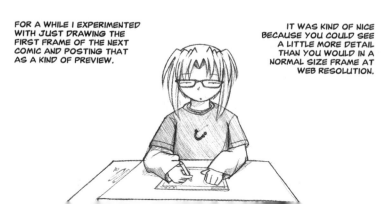

FOR A WHILE I EXPERIMENTED WITH JUST DRAWING THE FIRST FRAME OF THE NEXT COMIC AND POSTING THAT AS A KIND OF PREVIEW.

IT WAS KIND OF NICE BECAUSE YOU COULD SEE A LITTLE MORE DETAIL THAN YOU WOULD IN A NORMAL SIZE FRAME AT WEB RESOLUTION.

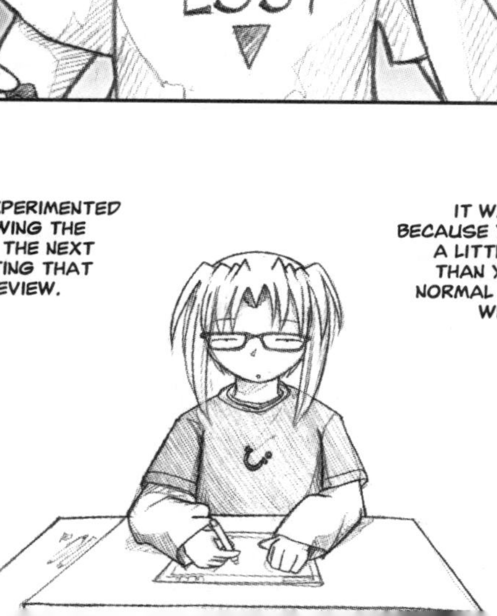

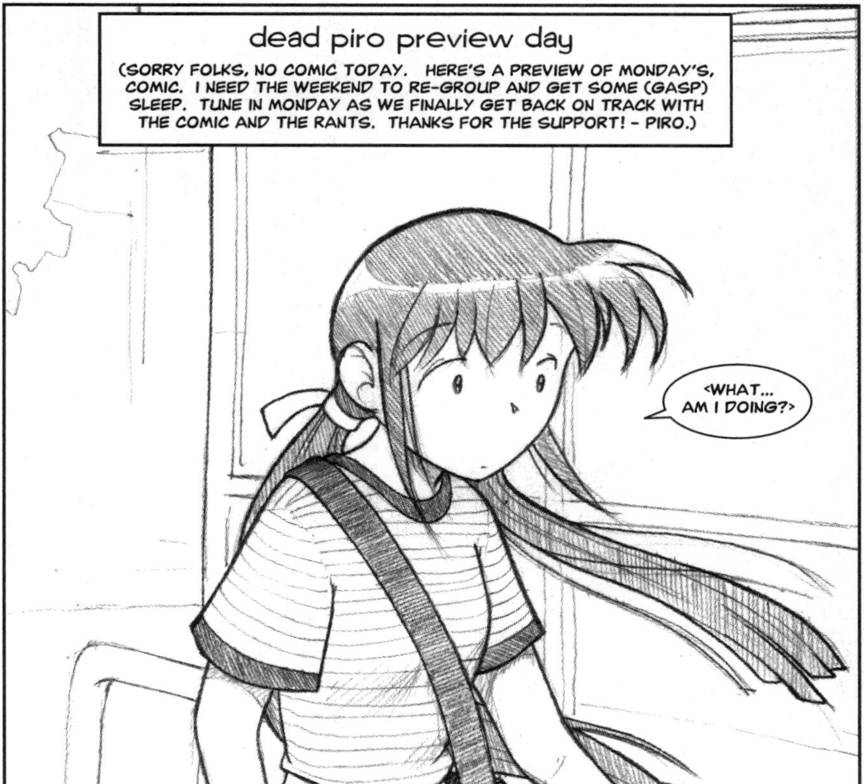
dead piro preview day
(SORRY FOLKS, NO COMIC TODAY. HERE'S A PREVIEW OF MONDAY'S, COMIC. I NEED THE WEEKEND TO RE-GROUP AND GET SOME (GASP) SLEEP. TUNE IN MONDAY AS WE FINALLY GET BACK ON TRACK WITH THE COMIC AND THE RANTS. THANKS FOR THE SUPPORT! - PIRO.)
<WHAT... AM I DOING?>

BUT IN THE END I DECIDED THAT IT WAS MORE OF A COP-OUT THAN SOMETHING THAT WAS REALLY ENTERTAINING.

MT FANS HAVE BEEN VERY PATIENT. THERE HAVE BEEN A LOT OF DELAYS AND MISSED COMICS OVER THE PAST FEW YEARS, AND I'VE FELT BAD ABOUT EVERY SINGLE ONE.

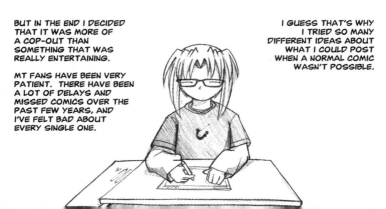

I GUESS THAT'S WHY I TRIED SO MANY DIFFERENT IDEAS ABOUT WHAT I COULD POST WHEN A NORMAL COMIC WASN'T POSSIBLE.

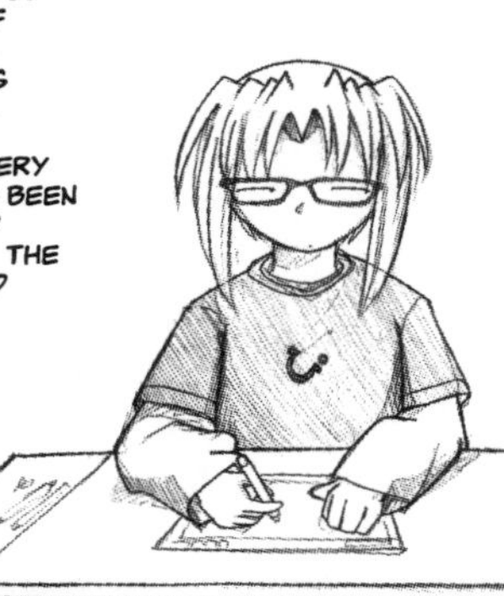

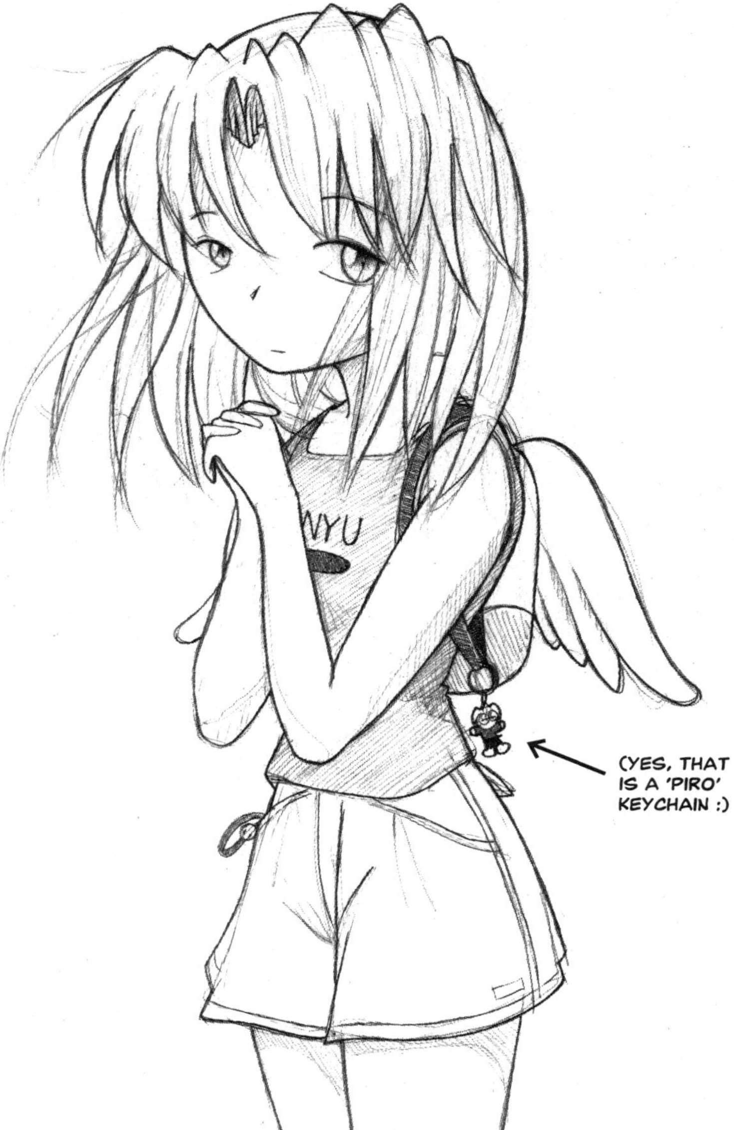
NYU
(YES, THAT
IS A 'PIRO'
KEYCHAIN :)

PIRO ART DAY SPECIAL #001

KIMIKO NANASAWA

MEGATOKYO

F 05 10 01

FRED GALLAGHER

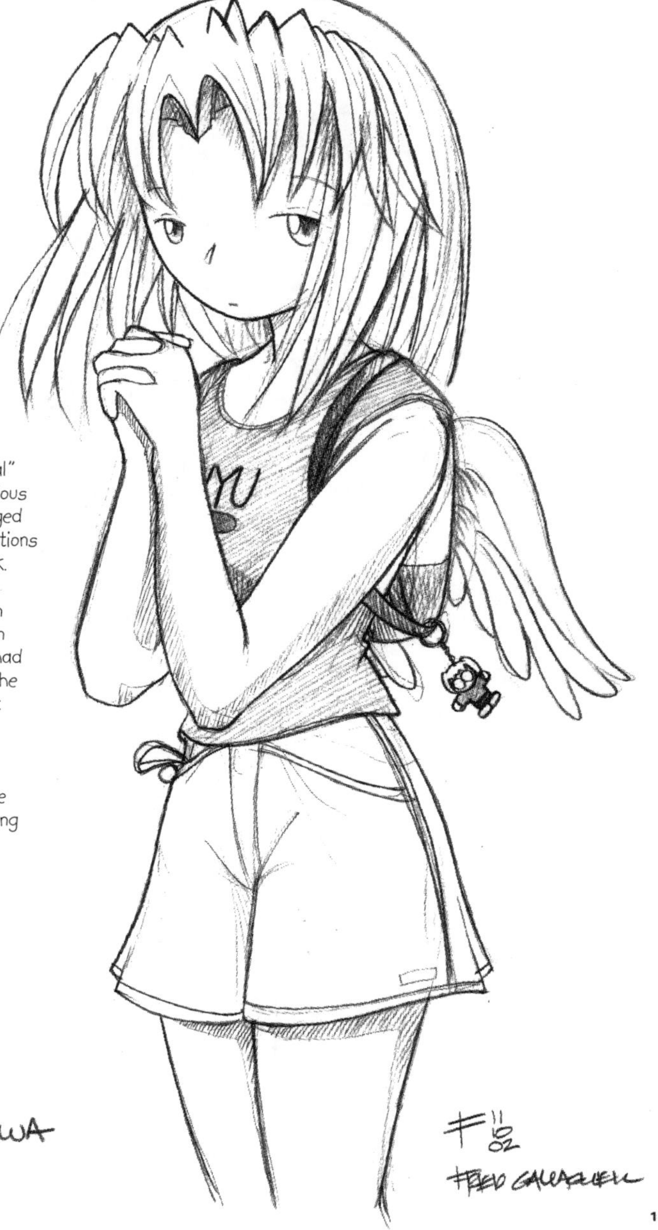
11
10
02
FRED GALLAGHER

The
"Piro Art Day Special"
of Kimiko on the previous
page has always bugged
me because the proportions
are way out of wack.

For the first edition
of this book back in
November of 2002 i had
decided to re-draw the
image to try to get
it right.

I still don't think
I got it right. There
is still something wrong
with her head.

Let me try one
more time...

KIMIKO NANASAWA
MEGATOKYO

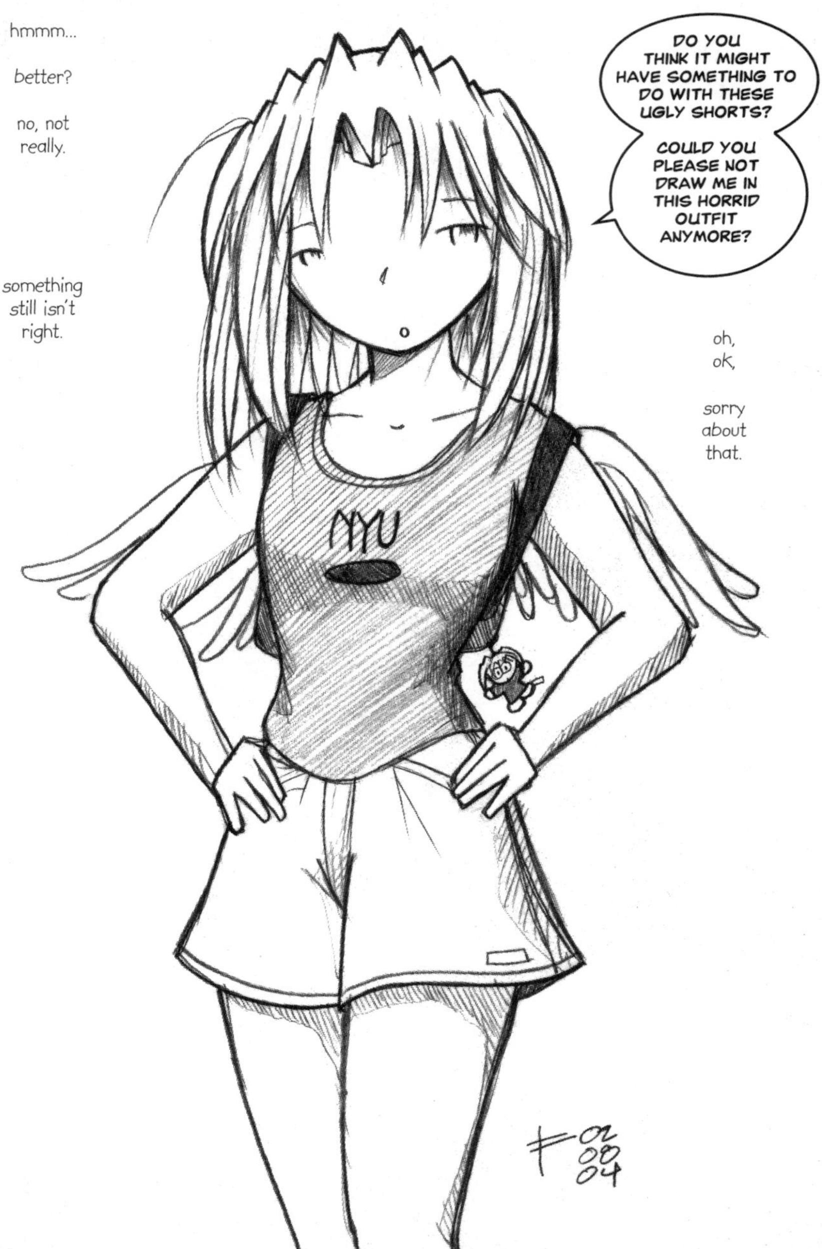
hmmm...
better?
no, not really.
DO YOU THINK IT MIGHT HAVE SOMETHING TO DO WITH THESE UGLY SHORTS?
COULD YOU PLEASE NOT DRAW ME IN THIS HORRID OUTFIT ANYMORE?
something still isn't right.
oh, ok,
sorry about that.
NYU
02 08 04

how about
one more?

HEY.

sorry. ^^;;

actually, this isn't
a fourth attempt at
redrawing that original
Dead Piro Day sketch
of Kimiko -- this is
the original sketch
from which the
DPD was traced
back in May 2001.

i found this while i was
gathering material
together for this section
of the book...

piro's
sketchbook:
the early years.

often i've found that drawings lose something
when you ink or trace them. much of that has
to do with the fact that a heavily medicated
monkey can ink better than i can, but some of
it is because the first lines you put on paper
are often the most potent, and it's a shame to
loose them. that's why most of my drawings
start and finish on the same piece of paper.

the following pages are filled with sketches and
drawings from the early, developmental years of
megatokyo. most are embarrassingly bad, but you
might find some of them interesting.

the trouble with sketchbooks is that you really CAN go back too far, prompting the desire to stab one's eyes out with a dull pencil, so we won't go too far back.

before megatokyo, i'd never really done any "comics" or "sequential art". i've always wanted to, and i've always loved to write stories, but doing actual comics seemed beyond my abilities.

it was rare, however, that a drawing i did didn't have some little story associated with it. i found that drawing really helped bring my story ideas to life.

these drawings i did back in October 1994 are for some vague story idea i had called "Art Police." I've never been good at naming things.

note the influence of the works of Kosuke Fujishima (Ah My Goddess!) i'm sure he'd stab his eyes out if he ever knew his stuff inspired these.

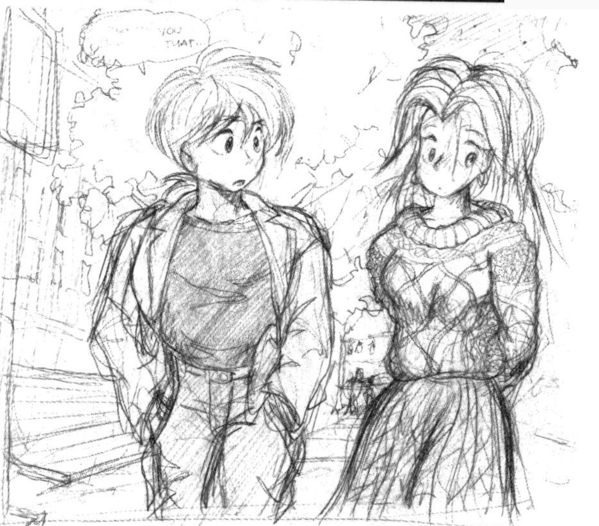
ART
police

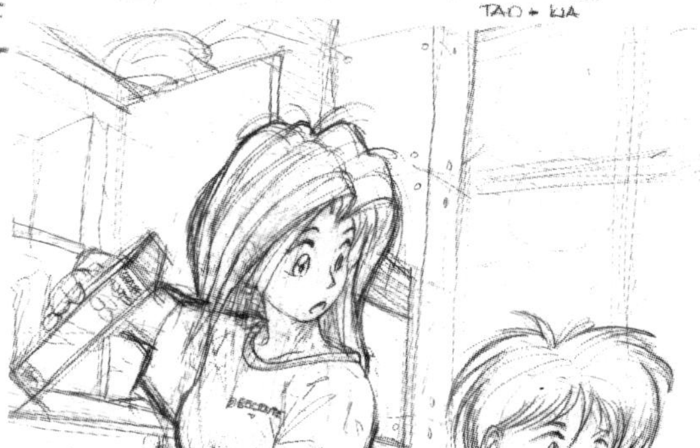

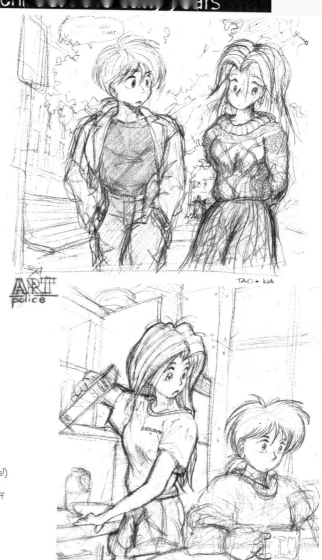

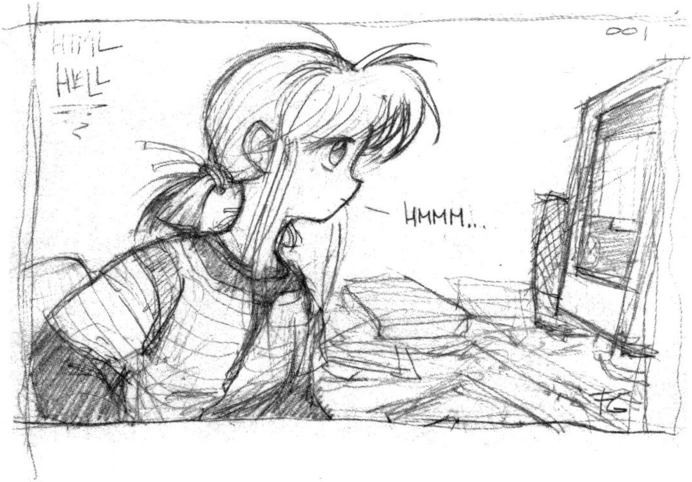
HTML
HELL
001
HMMM...

"megatokyo" wasn't really my first lame attempt at a webcomic.

at one time i planned on doing one-panel-at-a-time comics for my art website, fredart.com.

there were several ideas i knocked around, including "HTML Hell" (above left) and "Daily Scratch" (below left).

i never did that many of them.

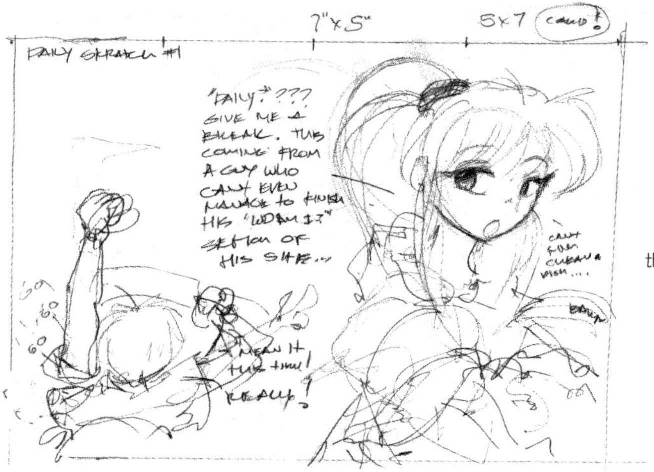
7"x5"
5x7

"daily?? give me a break. this coming from a guy who can't even manage to finish the 'who am I?' section of his website."

almost prophetic, this one.

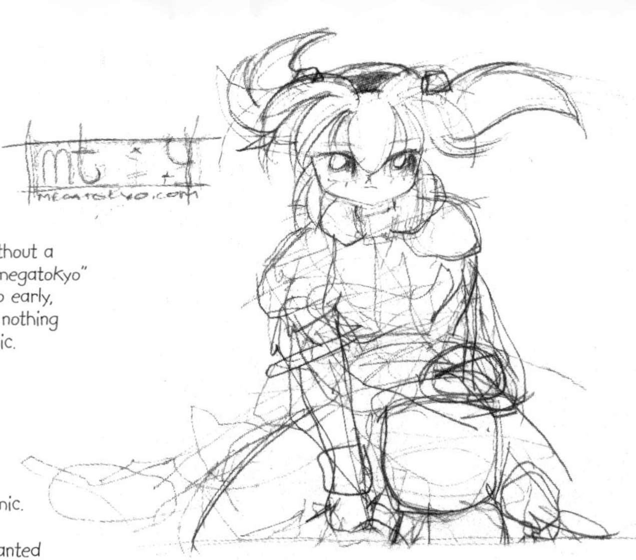

these are probably, without a doubt, the very first "megatokyo" drawings i ever did. so early, in fact, that they have nothing to do with the webcomic.

Largo had owned the "megatokyo.com" domain name for years before we turned it into a webcomic. during those years he wasn't sure what he wanted to do with it. we named the webcomic "megatokyo" simply because he owned the domain name.

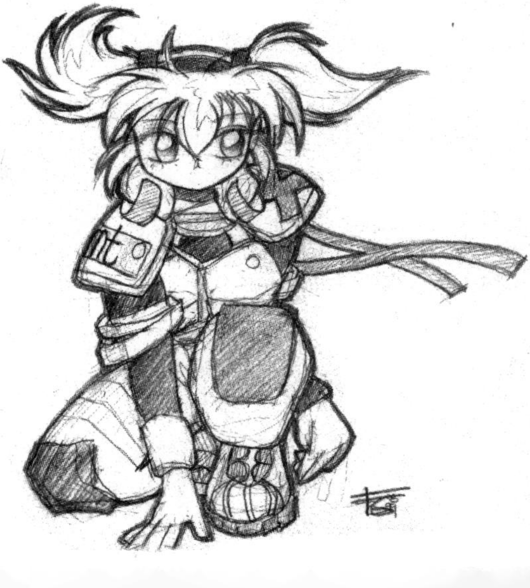

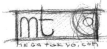

Largo had asked me to draw something for him to use on the website (thinking that he was going to start an anime / japanese pop culture news site or something like that) and this is what i drew for him.

megatokyo-chan
August, 1999.

here is a slightly more detailed drawing of MT-chan. i think that these are all the drawings i ever did of her.

you can almost see a little bit of Piroko in her.

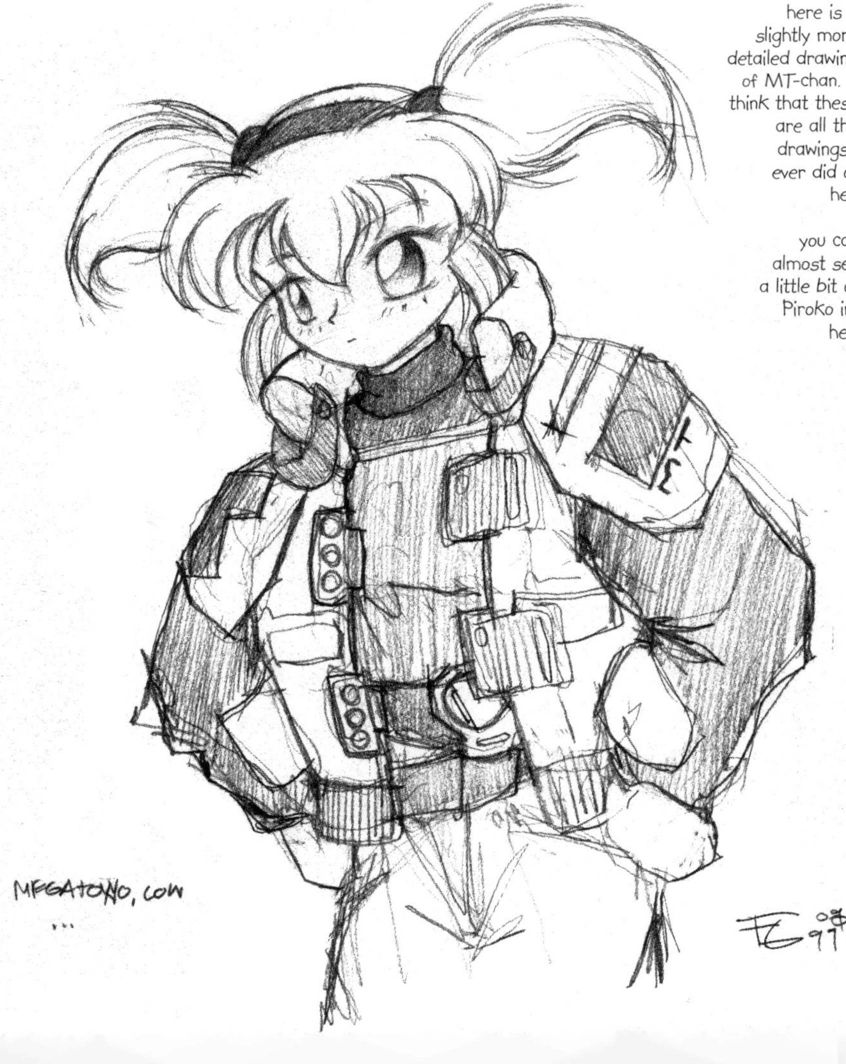
MEGATOKYO, COM
...

well, these are the first sketches
of Piro and Largo i ever did.

one of the sad things about
megatokyo is that we didn't
spend a lot of time developing things.
we just sort of... started.

the basic concepts for Piro
and Largo came together
pretty quickly -- they were
loosely based on us. Largo's
design is based on a college
photo of Rodney. Piro's design is...
well... me in college? sort of, but
not really, i guess.

the basic designs haven't
really changed much, just
the hair. Largo's hair
keeps getting bigger, and
Piro's bangs keep getting
longer.

a whole
page of mt
scribbles...

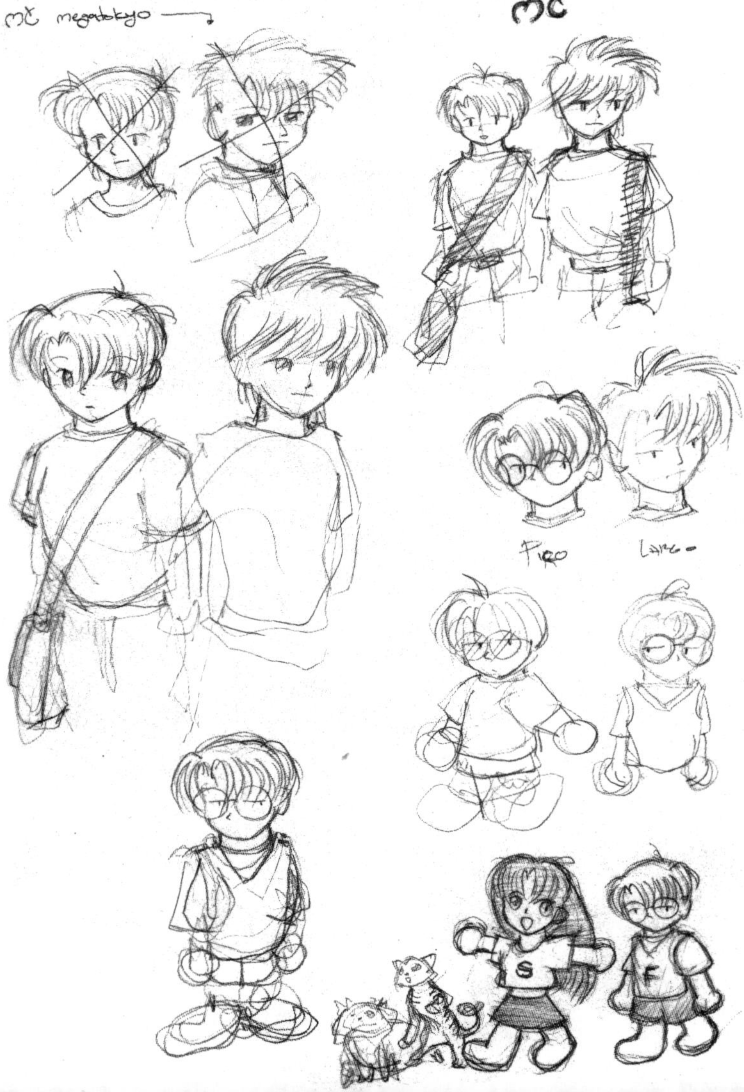
mt megatokyo
mt
Piro
Largo

piro's sketchbook: the early years

writing scripts is really the hardest part of doing MT. at the bottom is a sample of the original script Largo sent me. to the right is the finished script for the "Sp33K l33t" comic.

i also usually make quick sketches to lay out the comic, like the one below.

Flight Attendant: Sir are you alright? Do you need a docto

[Panel 3]

Man in pain: j00 3Y3 |\|33d j0 t0 g4t 4 d0c70r. I g07z b4d chest, | n33d m4 p|11z!

[Panel 4]

(show largo and piro raising there hands to answer this)

Flight Attendant: Does anyone here speak l33t?

Largo: j0

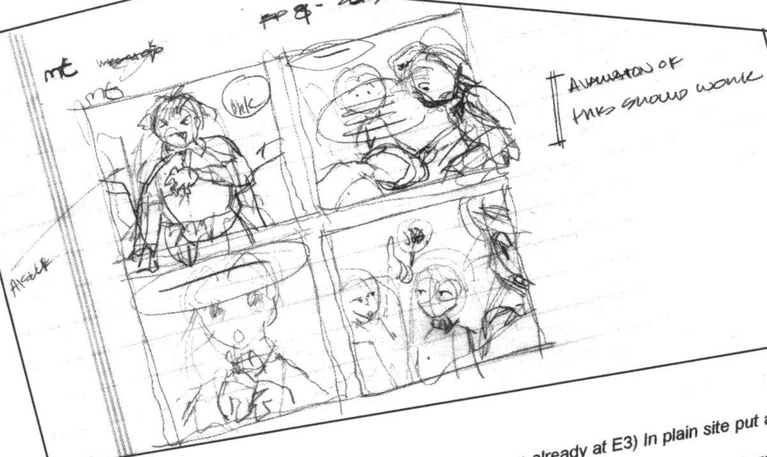

Episode 1: E3 Nightmare
[Pane l]
(Open to Registration at E3 (we'll start it off with a kick, have them already at E3) In plain site put a sign that reads, "Electronic Entertainment Expo" (draw E3 logo)
Largo: The heart of the gaming world beats here! We few that enter will peer into the future of the gaming industry and be blessed with it's vision!
Piro: The only vision you want is of that model that's dressed as Lara Croft.
[Panel 2]
(Still standing in line, largo and Piro are now at the reg desk; have largo have this pale/sick/stoned/dazed/stunned look.)
E3 Registration Guy: I'm sorry but you can't enter, to register for E3 you must be a game developer or a member of the press.
[Panel 3]
(Largo is unchanged from last frame, Piro will be poking or prodding largo)
E3 Registration Guy: Is your friend alright?
E3 Registration ... think he's gone into shock! Quick, get him a booth-babe(c)!
... shirts that say "Ionstorm")
... Now where are our badges?

random embarrassing stuff from piro's early sketchbooks

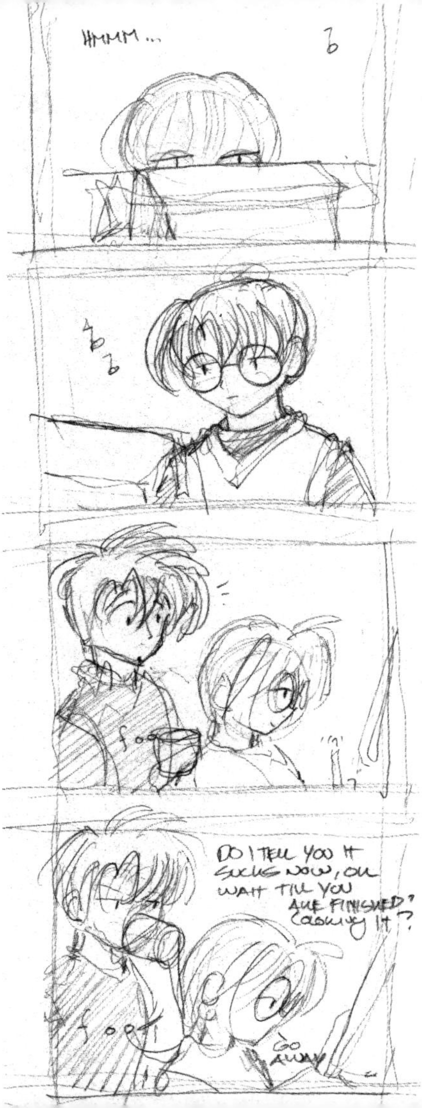
HMMM...
DO I TELL YOU IT SUCKS NOW, OR WAIT TILL YOU ARE FINISHED COLORING IT?
GO AWAY

here's a pre-MT comic i did while messing around with format.

originally, i wanted to do things in a Japanese style "4-Koma" format like this (4 panels vertically).

Largo wanted to do things in an American style newspaper comic format (4 panels horizontally).

we ended up comprimising on the four square layout used for the first hundred or so comics.

it's odd, but Piro and Largo, who's personalities are very dependent on computers, don't really have much access to them for most of the comic.

piro's sketchbook: the early years

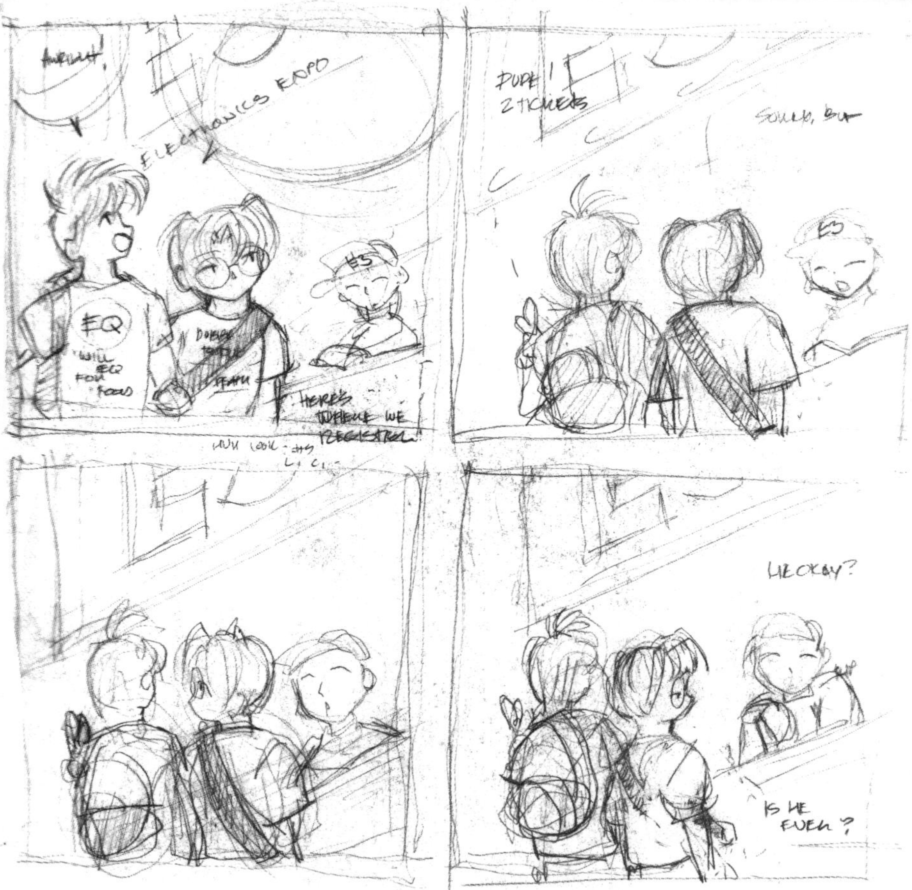
ELECTRONICS EXPO
EQ
WILL EQ FOR FOOD
DUDE! 2 TICKETS
IS HE EVEN?

when i first started doing MT, i would sketch out all the frames on one big sheet of paper. this is the rough for the first MT comic. Once the rough sketch was done, i would place a sheet of marker paper over it and hardline trace it all in pencil. These were then cleaned up in Photoshop, and the comic itself finished in Illustrator.

after a few months, i started using templates printed out on 8 x 11 sheets of inkjet paper (like the drawings for "Sp33K L33t" shown on the next page). I started doing the roughs two panels at a time. after a few months of practice, I was getting clean enough with my drawings that I was able to eliminate having to trace them to create a final image.

megatokyo layout sheet - date: ____ episode: __________ title: ______________________________

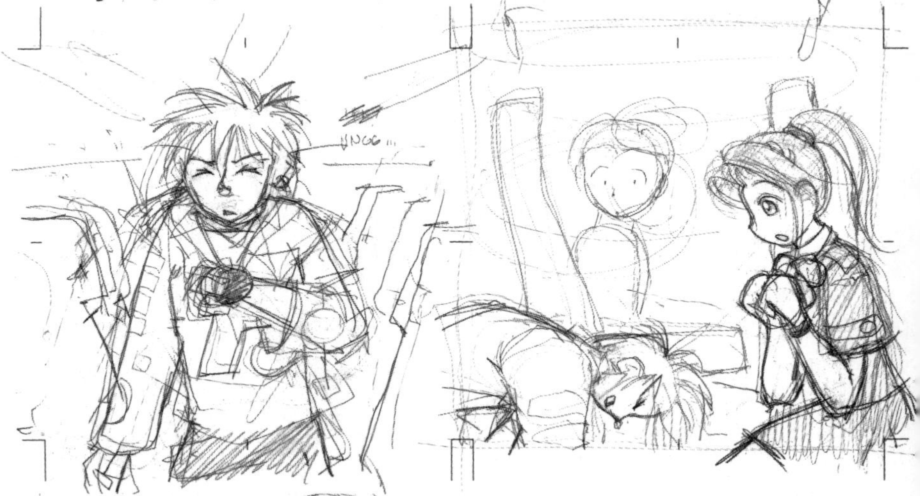
UNGG...

megatokyo layout sheet - date: ____ episode: __________ title: ______________________________

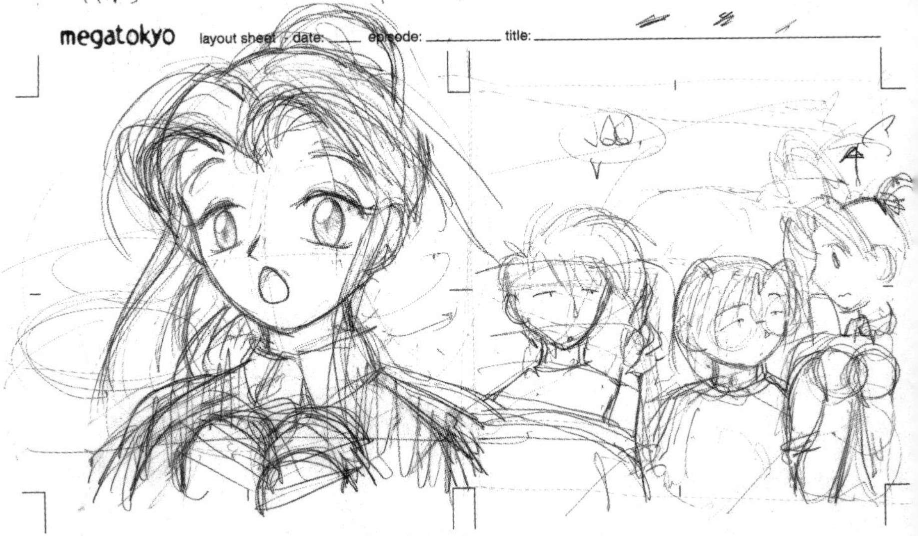

notes:

ok, so we've covered the rather lame development of the guys. once i scribbled them out, they didn't change al that much.

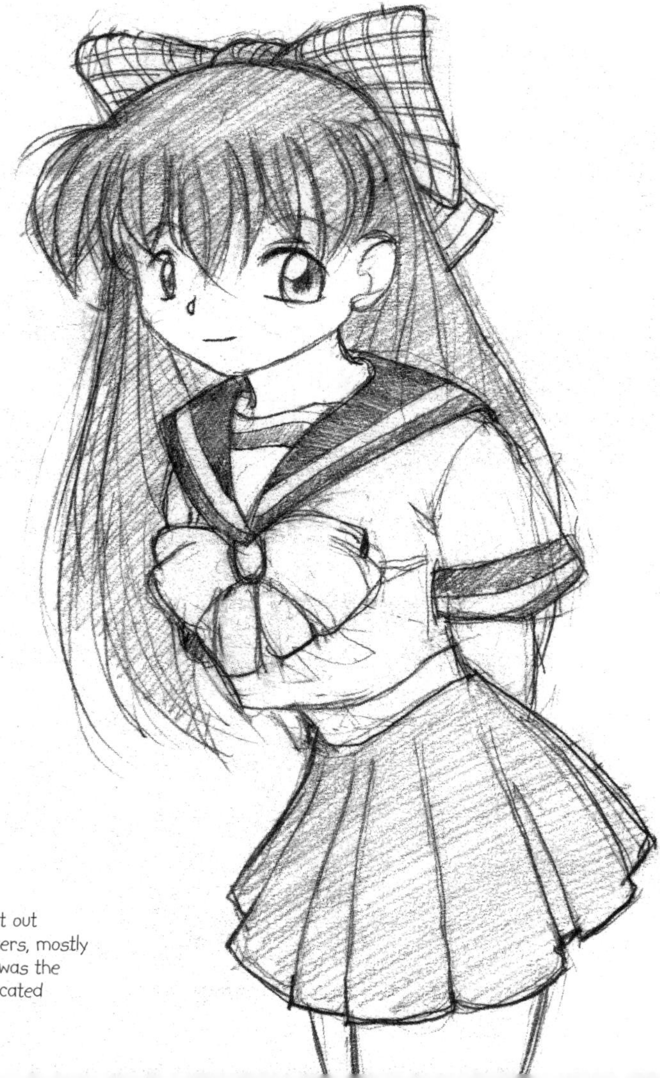

so what about the girls?

who the hell is this girl?

believe it or not, this is Kimiko -- as she originally was designed.

Kimiko changed the most out of all the female characters, mostly because her personality was the most difficult and complicated to nail down.

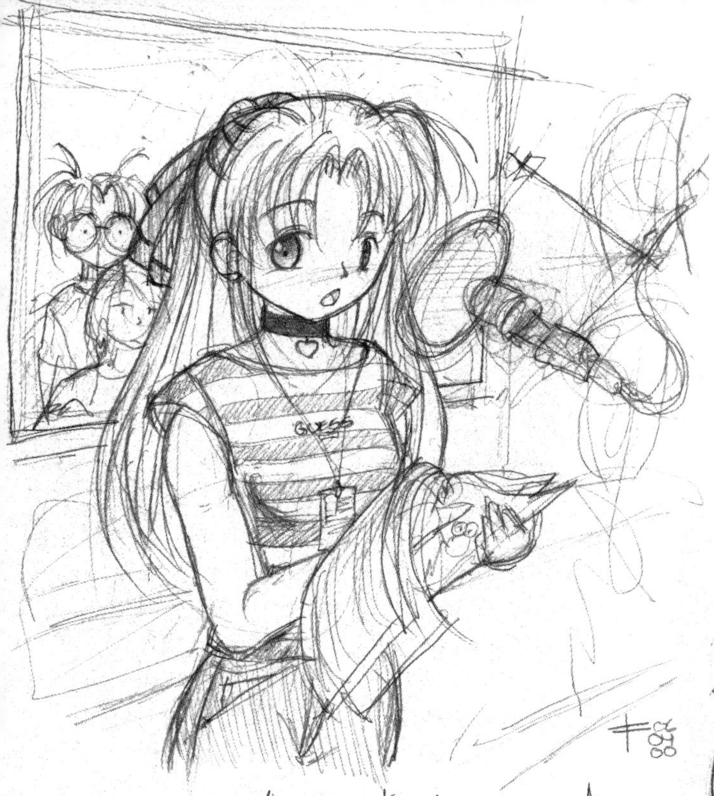
GUESS

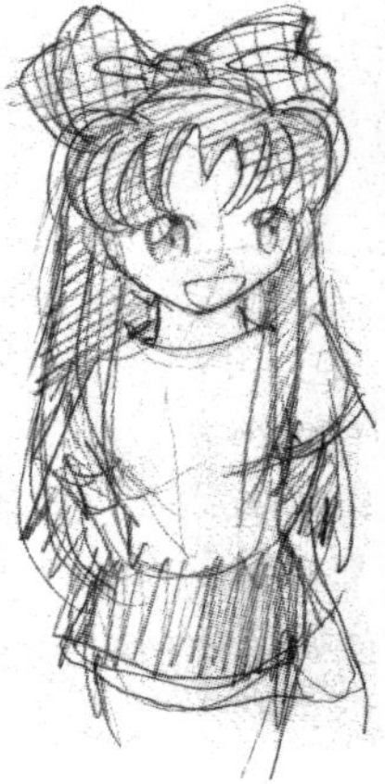

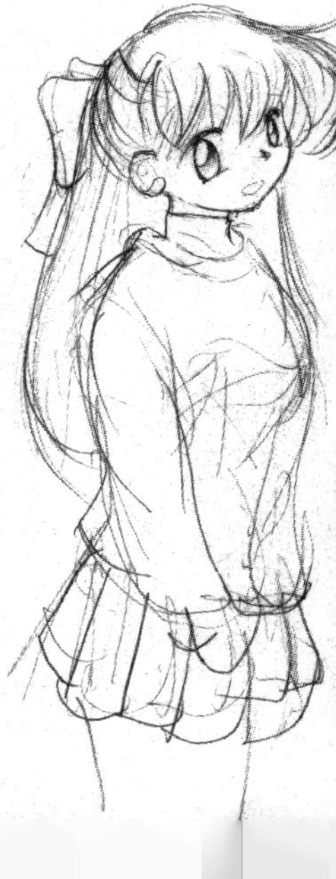

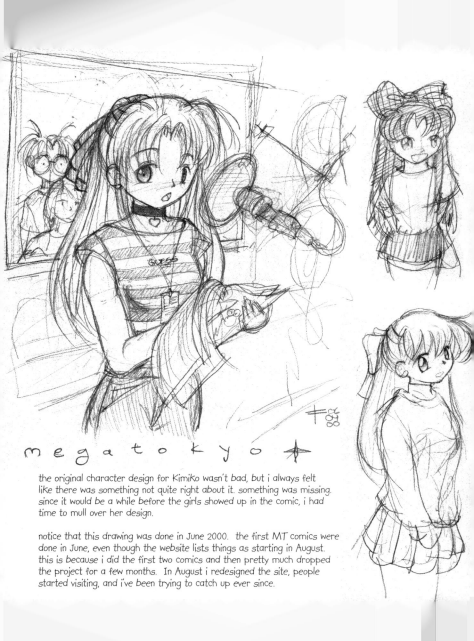

megatokyo

the original character design for Kimiko wasn't *bad*, but i always felt like there was something not quite right about it. something was missing. since it would be a while before the girls showed up in the comic, i had time to mull over her design.

notice that this drawing was done in June 2000. the first MT comics were done in June, even though the website lists things as starting in August. this is *because* i did the first two comics and then pretty much dropped the project for a few months. In August i redesigned the site, people started visiting, and i've been trying to catch up ever since.

one day, while sitting on the couch watching TV, i drew this drawing, and it clicked. finally, Kimiko was looking back up at me from the page.

all the "cute" things about her previous design -- the long hair, the bow, the big happy eyes -- they all seemed to get in the way of what made her who she was.

character designing is harder than most people realize.

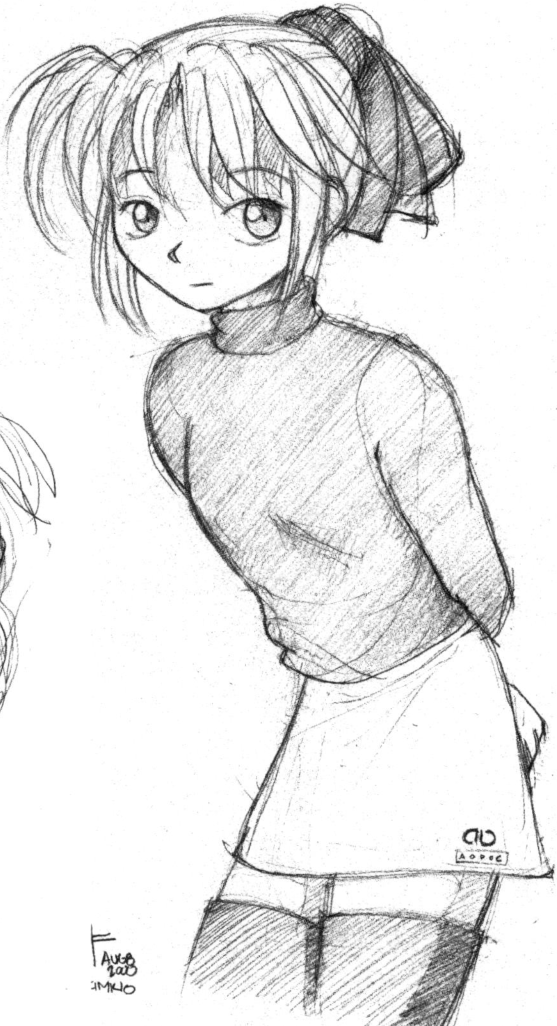

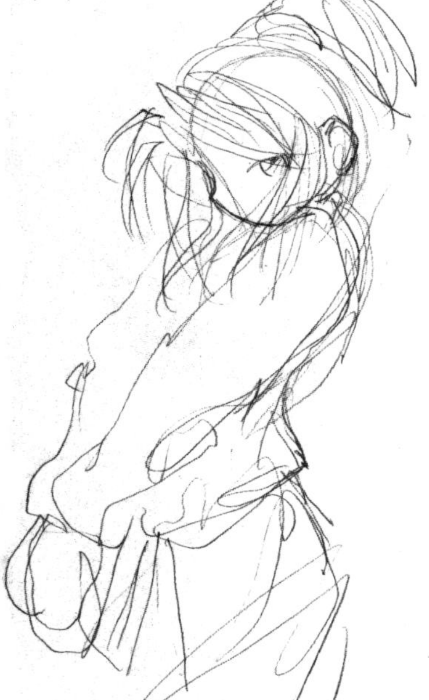

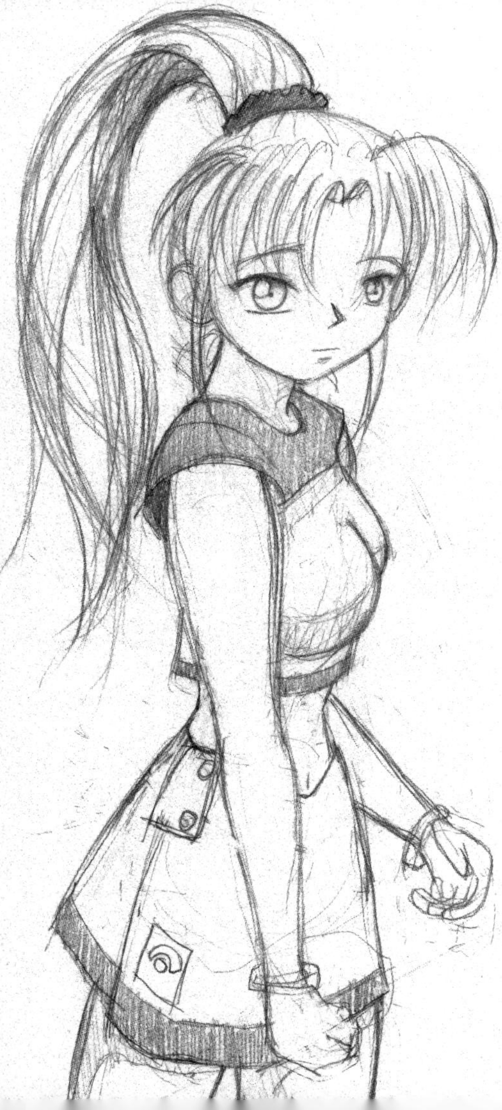

Erika's design
hasn't really changed much
(except for the fact that i no
longer draw her with those freaky
i-am-a-serial-killer-who-just-ate-a-busload-of-children eyes).

honestly, i had a lot
of trouble drawing Erika
because she's supposed to
have this to-die-for body,
and with my rather primitive
understanding of how the
human body goes together
this was difficult for me
to draw convincingly.

unlike her design,
Erika's personality has
changed and developed
in unexpected ways.
she has really taken
on a life of her own and
continues to surprise
me when i write
for her.

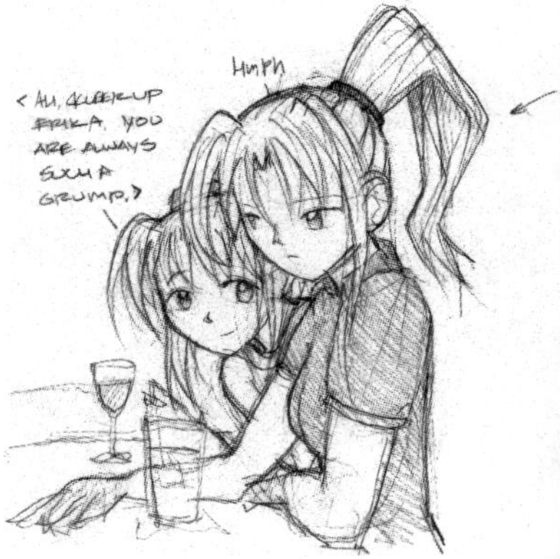
Hmph
<AW, CHEER UP ERIKA. YOU ARE ALWAYS SUCH A GRUMP.>

most of the development of Miho took place in this little black notebook.

no, i'm not going to show you any more :)

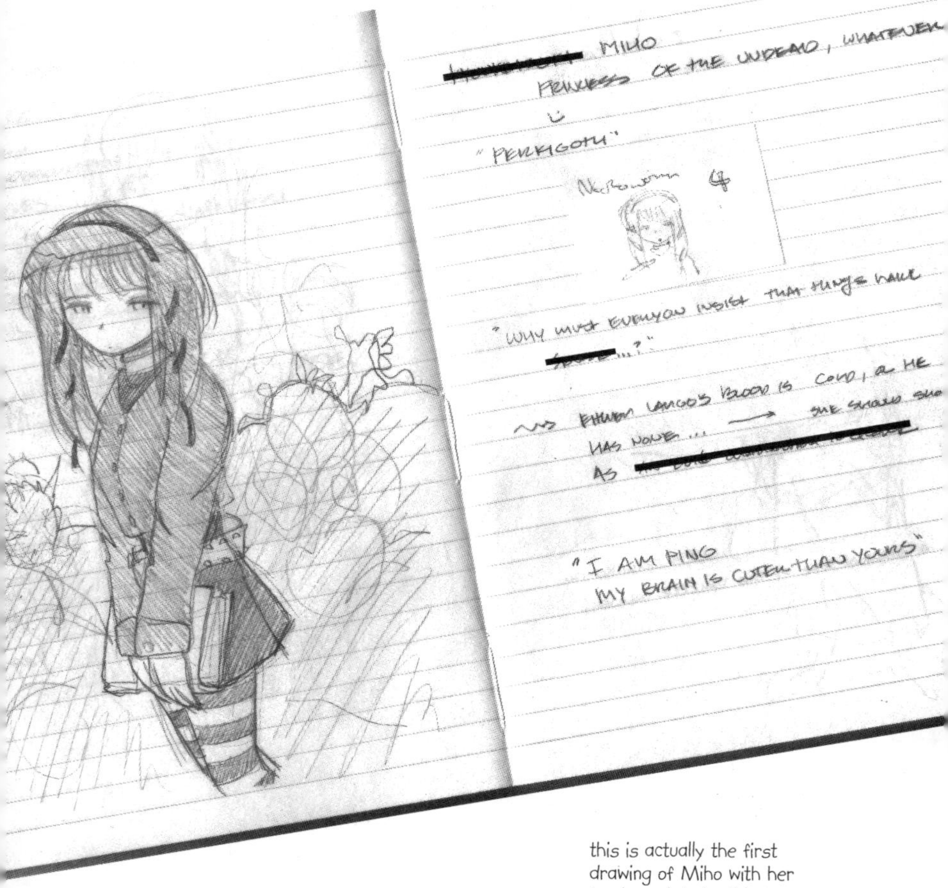
[redacted] MIHO
PRINCESS OF THE UNDEAD, WHATEVER
"WHY MUST EVERYONE INSIST THAT THINGS HAVE [redacted]...?"
ETHAN LANGO'S BLOOD IS COLD, & HE HAS NONE ...
AS [redacted]
"I AM PING
MY BRAIN IS CUTER THAN YOURS"

this is actually the first drawing of Miho with her trademark hair ribbons.

the emergence
of Yuki is actually
the result of this
sketch.

this drawing somehow
inspired the idea of including
a plucky japanese school
girl in the story.

SONADA - YUKI

YUKI- ALT HAIR
STYLE (UNDONE)
CARDIGAN IN
SNOW
PIC

WHAT ARE
THE
FACIAL FEATURES
THAT ARE
UNIQUE?

LARGER
BOOKBAG

F OCT 15
2000

i think a good
character design
doesn't require the
character to always
wear his/her hair
the same way.

After all, people
change sometimes,
characters should be
able to too.

i wanted ping to be a physical manifestation of the games that Piro plays -- the influence on Largo's world wasn't something i planned.

Robot girls are quite common in ren'ai games and anime, and Ping was influenced by the genre, not any one specific character.

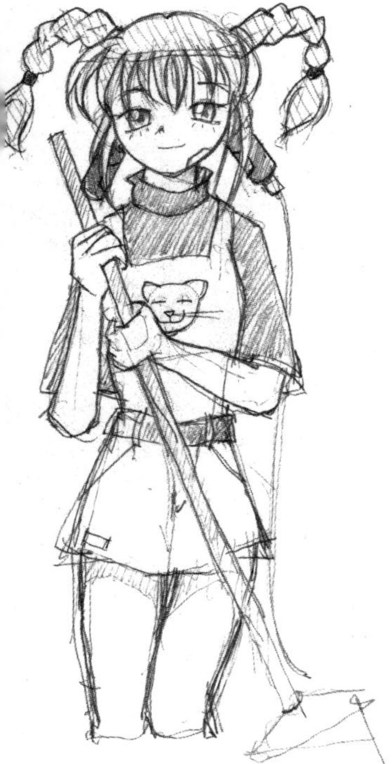

well, that's that. i wish i had more room - this has been just a sampling of some of the stuff i dug out of my sketchbooks. i hope you found it interesting :)

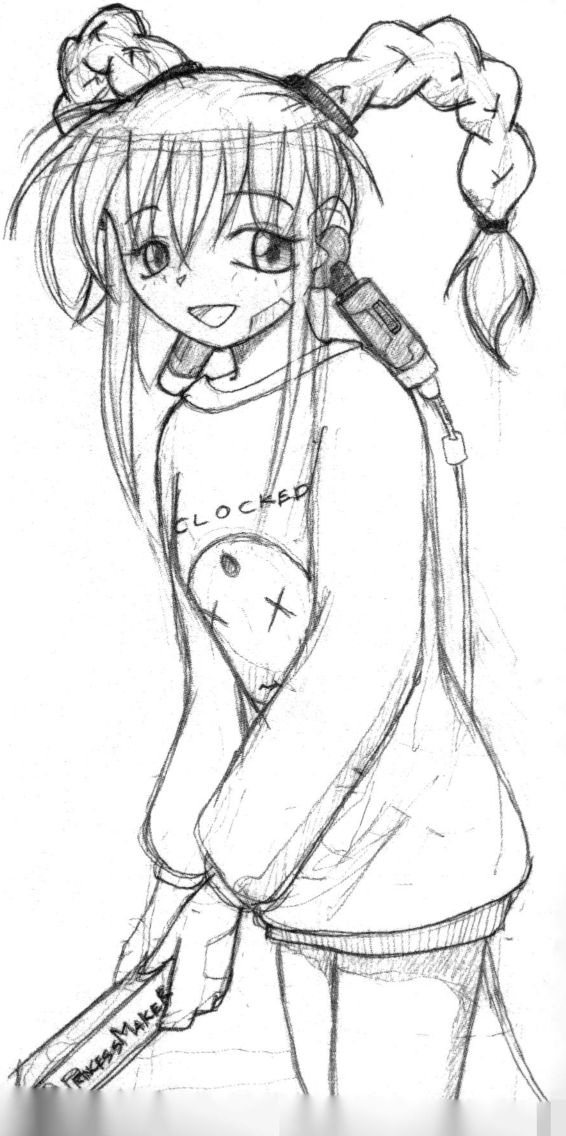
CLOCKED
PRINCESS MAKER

Megatokyo - Volume 1 Index

This book contains all the strips from Chapter 0 and includes extra material produced between August 2000 and June 2001. For more information and more comics, visit www.megatokyo.com

Page No.	Strip Title	Date	Online Strip ID
74	Mr. Piro-san	2001-02-02	075
75	Close Call	2001-02-07	077
76	Boo!	2001-02-12	079
77	Stupid Bag	2001-02-14	080
78	What I don't like about you	2001-02-23	084
79	it's so sad	2001-02-28	087
80	what the...?	2001-03-02	088
81	that was close, nyu!	2001-03-05	089
82	go for the beer, boo!	2001-03-07	090
83	watch the store	2001-03-09	091
84	a-way with the ladies	2001-03-12	092
85	the little dramas	2001-03-16	094
86	The Necrowombicon	2001-03-21	096
87	did you steal something?	2001-03-26	098
88	something darkly cute...	2001-03-28	099
89	do what the lady says	2001-03-30	100
90	guns, boo, lots of guns.	2001-04-02	101
91	kimiko in-between	2001-04-04	102
92	bathroom cleaning chemicals	2001-04-06	103
93	Zombie Ping	2001-04-11	105
94	Ping the PS2 Accessory	2001-04-13	106
95	don't look into her eyes!	2001-04-16	107
96	Tail Chase	2001-04-18	108
97	Naze Nani: 4 panel format	2001-04-20	109
106	the tail looses its death grip	2001-04-23	110
107	what's with the knee brace?	2001-04-25	111
108	Army of Largo	2001-04-27	112
109	New Blood	2001-04-30	113
110	things noticed...	2001-05-02	114
111	club crashing	2001-05-04	115
112	you're a fool	2001-05-07	116
113	E3 Special: how many times...	2001-05-18	121
114	sad girl with bear	2001-05-23	123
115	rent-a-zilla	2001-05-25	124
116	a big break	2001-05-28	125
117	it doesn't take much	2001-05-30	126
118	no b33r h3r3	2001-06-01	127
119	osana najimi	2001-06-04	128
120	field report	2001-06-06	129
121	NNM: reality-pyo	2001-06-13	132
122	Seraphim Check	2001-06-15	133

Shirt Guy Dom strips

99	Never Again	2000-10-23	031
100	SGD: Dom Day 3	2001-01-10	065
101	SGD: Ed does a bad thing	2001-02-19	082
102	SGD: Dance Dance Violation	2001-02-27	086
103	SGD: Dom gets Dom'd	2001-03-14	093
104	SGD: the acen that wasn't	2001-06-08	130

One-Shot (non-story) Episodes

123	Bloopers	2000-10-20	030
124	Sony Buys Hell	2000-10-27	033
125	I've heard that before	2000-12-06	050
126	The Bench	2000-12-22	057
127	In the pits with Bioware	2001-02-12	066
128	Public Service Annoucement: Zombies	2001-02-16	081
129	Bad Art Day: Move Violation	2001-02-26	085
130	Vibrating Sheep of Death	2001-05-14	119
131	E3 Special: Neverwinter Beer	2001-06-11	131
132	Seraphim Amex Fun	2001-05-21	122

Dead Piro Art Days

133	Dead Piro Day	2000-10-13	027
134	dead piro preview #1	2001-03-19	095
135	dead piro preview #2	2001-03-23	097
136	Art Day 001 - Kimiko	2001-05-11	118

USAGI YOJIMBO™

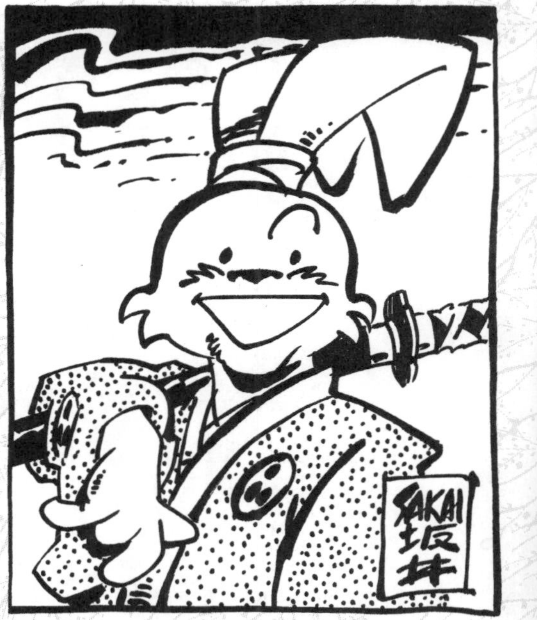
SAKAI
坂井

Celebrate 20 years of Stan Sakai's award-winning adventure stories and Usagi's three YALSA Popular Paperbacks for Young Adults Awards!

"Like the best animated characters, Usagi and the rest of the cast is capable of a broad range of emotions. Blending classic storytelling, flawlessly designed art, and lovingly researched period touches, *Usagi Yojimbo* is a true all-ages comic treat." —***Publishers Weekly***

Share the humor and adventures of Usagi with your friends, family, and librarians! Winner of the Parents' Choice award for children (ages 7 and up), *Usagi Yojimbo* has also received Eisner, Harvey, National Cartoonists Society, and Spanish Haxtur awards.

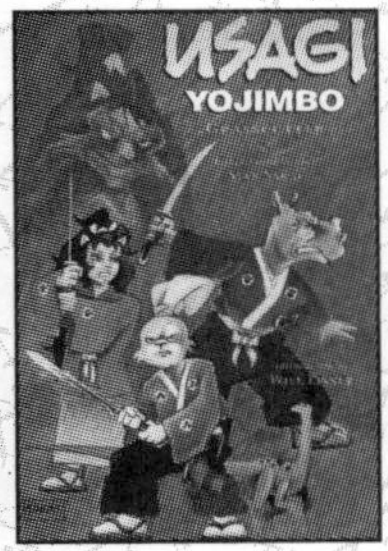
USAGI
YOJIMBO

Book 12
Grasscutter
1-56971-413-4
Softcover • 256 pages
Ages 7+ • $16.95

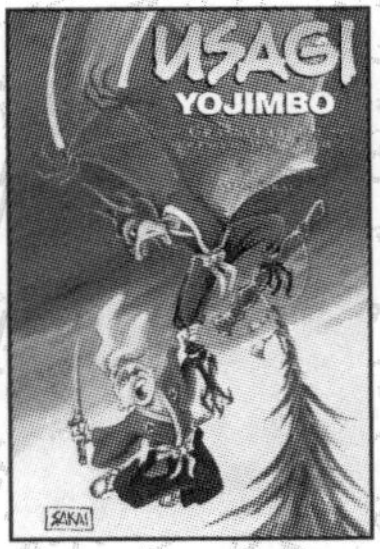
USAGI
YOJIMBO

Book 15
Grasscutter II: Journey to Atsuta Shrine
1-56971-660-9
Softcover • 184 pages
Ages 7+ • $15.95

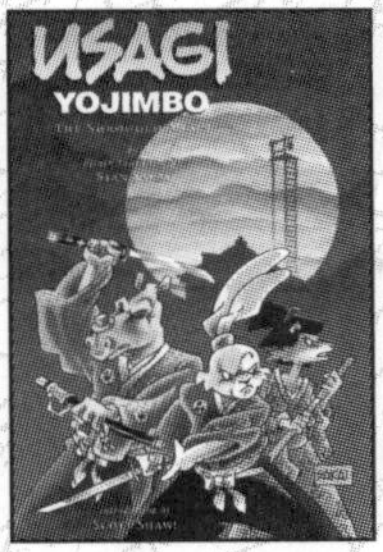
USAGI
YOJIMBO

Book 16
The Shrouded Moon
1-56971-883-0
Softcover • 184 pages
Ages 7+ • $15.95

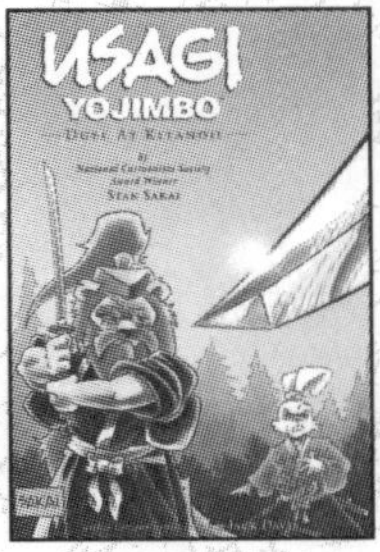
USAGI
YOJIMBO

Book 17
Duel at Kitanoji
1-56971-973-X
Softcover • 224 pages
Ages 7+ • $16.95

DARK HORSE BOOKS

Volumes 1-7 available through Fantagraphics Books;
all additional volumes available through Dark Horse Comics.

AVAILABLE AT YOUR LOCAL COMICS SHOP OR BOOKSTORE
To find a comics shop in your area, call 1-888-266-4226 For more information or to order direct: •On the web: www.darkhorse.com •E-mail: mailorder@darkhorse.com •Phone: 1-800-862-0052 or (503) 652-9701 Mon.-Sat. 9 A.M. to 5 P.M. Pacific Time

TWENTIETH ANNIVERSARY

⚠️STOP

This is the back of the book!

Now, now, people. *Megatokyo* was originally done in English, so it naturally reads from left to right. Be a good little reader, turn the book over and start from the other side.